Arthur Penrhyn Stanley

# Christian Institutions

Essays on ecclesiastical subjects. Second Edition

Arthur Penrhyn Stanley

**Christian Institutions**
*Essays on ecclesiastical subjects. Second Edition*

ISBN/EAN: 9783337164539

Printed in Europe, USA, Canada, Australia, Japan

Cover: Foto ©Lupo / pixelio.de

More available books at **www.hansebooks.com**

# CHRISTIAN INSTITUTIONS

*ESSAYS*

ON

*ECCLESIASTICAL SUBJECTS*

By ARTHUR PENRHYN STANLEY, D.D.

DEAN OF WESTMINSTER

CORRESPONDING MEMBER OF THE INSTITUTE OF FRANCE

*SECOND EDITION*

LONDON

JOHN MURRAY, ALBEMARLE STREET

1881

LONDON : PRINTED BY
SPOTTISWOODE AND CO., NEW-STREET SQUARE
AND PARLIAMENT STREET

LONDON : PRINTED BY
SPOTTISWOODE AND CO., NEW-STREET SQUARE
AND PARLIAMENT STREET

# PREFACE.

THIS VOLUME, though not pretending to completeness, forms a connected whole. The Essays touch on a variety of topics, and were written at long intervals of time, but they are united by the common bond which connects the institutions to which they relate. It may be well to state here some of the general conclusions which they suggest.

1. Underneath the sentiments and usages which have accumulated round the forms of Christianity, it is believed that there is a class of principles—a Religion as it were behind the religion—which, however dimly expressed, has given them whatever vitality they possess. It is not intended to assert that these principles were continuously present to the minds of the early Christians, or that they were not combined with much heterogeneous matter which interfered with their development. But it is maintained that there is enough in them of valuable truth to give to these ancient institutions a use in times and circumstances most different from those in which they originated. If this be shown to be the case the main purpose of these Essays will have been accomplished. The Sacraments—the Clergy —the Pope—the Creed—will take a long time in dying, if die they must. It is not useless to indicate a rational point of view, from which they may be approached, and to

show the germs which, without a violent dislocation, may be developed into higher truth.

2. The entire unlikeness of the early days of Christianity (or, if we prefer so to put it, of the times of the Roman Empire) to our own is a point which such a study will bring out. It has been truly said to be a great misfortune to have the power of seeing likenesses without the power of seeing differences. In practical matters the power of seeing likenesses is certainly a rare and valuable gift. The divergences and disputes of theologians or theological parties have been in great measure occasioned by the want of it. But in historical matters the power of seeing differences cannot be too highly prized. The tendency of ordinary men is to invest every age with the attributes of their own time. This is specially the case in religious history. The Puritan idea that there was a Biblical counterpart to every—the most trivial—incident or institution of modern ecclesiastical life, and that all ecclesiastical statesmanship consisted in reducing the varieties of civilisation to the crudity of the times when Christianity was as yet in its infancy, has met with an unsparing criticism from the hand of Hooker. The same fancy has been exhibited on a larger scale by the endeavour of Roman Catholic and High Church divines to discover their own theories of the Papacy, the Hierarchy, the administration of the Sacraments, in the early Church. Such a passion for going back to an imaginary past, or transferring to the past the peculiarities of later times, may be best corrected by keeping in view the total unlikeness of the first, second, or third centuries to anything which now exists in any part of the world.

3. This reluctance to look the facts of history in the face has favoured the growth of a vast superstructure of fable. It used to be said in the early days of the revival of mystical and ecclesiastical Christianity at Oxford that it was impossible

to conceive that the medieval system could ever have been developed out of a state of things quite dissimilar. 'That is the fundamental fallacy of the ecclesiastical theory,' it was remarked in answer by a distinguished statesman. 'It is forgotten how very soon out of a state of things entirely opposite may be born a religious system which claims to be the genuine successor. Witness the growth of "the Catholic and Apostolic Church," with its hierarchy and liturgy, out of the bald Presbyterianism and excited utterances of Edward Irving and his companions.' A like example might be pointed out in the formation of the Society of Friends, as founded by William Penn and his associates, with the sober self-control which has ever since characterised them, out of the enthusiastic, strange, indecorous acts of George Fox. Another might be found in the succession which, though with some exaggeration, has been traced, of the Oxford movement to the Wesleyan or so-called Evangelical movement of the last generation.

Such a transformation may have occurred with regard to Christianity. If its earlier forms were quite unlike to those which have sprung out of them, it may be instructive to see in various instances the process by which the change took place. It does not follow that the earlier form was more correct than the later; but it is necessary to a candid view of the subject to know that it existed.

4. Another point which is disclosed in any attempt to go below the surface of ecclesiastical history is the strong contrast between the under current of popular feeling and the manifestations of opinion in the published literature of the time. Especially is this brought to light in the representations of the Roman catacombs—hardly to be recognised in any work of any Christian writer of the time, and yet unquestionably familiar to the Christians of that age. Forms often retain an impress of the opinions of which they

were the vehicles, long after the opinions themselves have perished.

5. There is an advantage in perceiving clearly the close community of origin which unites secular and sacred usages. It is evident that the greater part of the early Christian institutions sprang from social customs which prevailed at the time. It is satisfactory to see that this community of thought, which it has been the constant effort of later times to tear asunder, was not unknown to the primitive epoch. It has been the tendency of the lower and more vulgar forms of religious life to separate the secular and the sacred. It will always be the tendency of the loftier forms of religious thought to bring them together. Such a union is to a certain extent exhibited in these early centuries.

6. It has been attempted to find on all these points a better and not the darker side of these institutions. This is a principle which may be pushed to excess. But it is believed to be safer and more generous than the reverse policy. No doubt every one of these forms has a magical or superstitious element. But even for the purpose of superseding those barbarous elements, it is wiser to dwell on the noble and spiritual aspect which the same forms may wear; and with the purpose of reconciling the ultimate progress of civilisation with Christianity, it is the only course which can be advantageously pursued.

7. Finally, two conclusions are obvious. First, that which existed in the early ages of the Church cannot be deemed incompatible with its essence in later ages. Secondly, that which did not exist in primitive times cannot be deemed indispensable to the essence of the Church, either late or early.

DEANERY, WESTMINSTER
*December* 1880.

# CONTENTS.

## CHAPTER IV.

### THE EUCHARISTIC SACRIFICE.



## CHAPTER V.

### THE REAL PRESENCE.



## CHAPTER VI.

### THE BODY AND BLOOD OF CHRIST.

# CHAPTER VII.

## ABSOLUTION.



# CHAPTER VIII.

## ECCLESIASTICAL VESTMENTS.



# CHAPTER IX.

## THE BASILICA.



# CHAPTER X.

## THE CLERGY.

# CHAPTER XI.

## THE POPE.



# CHAPTER XII.

## THE LITANY.



# CHAPTER XIII.

## THE ROMAN CATACOMBS.

## CHAPTER XIV.

### THE CREED OF THE EARLY CHRISTIANS.



## CHAPTER XV.

### THE LORD'S PRAYER.



## CHAPTER XVI.

### THE COUNCIL AND CREED OF CONSTANTINOPLE.



## CHAPTER XVII.

### THE TEN COMMANDMENTS.

# CHRISTIAN INSTITUTIONS.

## CHAPTER I.

### BAPTISM.

WHAT was Baptism in the Apostolic age? It coincided with a vast religious change both of individuals and of nations. Multitudes of men and women were seized with one common impulse, and abandoned, by the irresistible conviction of a day, an hour, a moment, their former habits, friends, associates, to be enrolled in a new society under the banner of a new faith. That new society was intended to be a society of 'brothers'; bound by ties closer than any earthly brotherhood—filled with life and energy such as fall to the lot of none but the most ardent enthusiasts, yet tempered by a moderation and a wisdom such as enthusiasts have rarely possessed. It was moreover a society swayed by the presence of men whose words even now cause the heart to burn, and by the recent recollections of One whom 'not seeing they loved with love unspeakable.' Into this society they passed by an act as natural as it was expressive. The plunge into the bath of purification, long known among the Jewish nation as the symbol of a change of life, had been revived with a fresh energy by the Essenes, and it received a definite signification and impulse from the austere Prophet who derived his name

B

from the ordinance.[1] This rite was retained as the pledge of entrance into a new and universal communion. In that early age the scene of the transaction was either some deep wayside spring or well, as for the Ethiopian, or some rushing river, as the Jordan, or some vast reservoir, as at Jericho[2] or Jerusalem, whither, as in the Baths of Caracalla at Rome, the whole population resorted for swimming or washing.

The earliest scene of the immersion was in the Jordan. That rushing river—the one river of Palestine—found at last its fit purpose. Although no details are given of the external parts of the ceremony, a lively notion may be formed of the transaction by the scene which now takes place at the bathing of the pilgrims at Easter.[3] Their approach to the spot is by night. Above is the bright Paschal moon, before them moves a bright flare of torches, on each side huge watchfires break the darkness of the night, and act as beacons for the successive descents of the road. The sun breaks over the eastern hills as the head of the cavalcade reaches the brink of the Jordan. The Sacred River rushes through its thicket of tamarisk, poplar, willow, and agnus-castus, with rapid eddies, and of a turbid yellow colour, like the Tiber at Rome, and about as broad. They dismount, and set to work to perform their bathe; most on the open space, some further up amongst the thickets; some plunging in naked—most, however, with white dresses, which they bring with them, and which, having been so used, are kept for their winding-sheets. Most of the bathers keep within the shelter of the bank, where the water is about four feet in depth, though with a bottom of very deep mud. The Coptic pilgrims are curiously distinguished from the rest by the bold-

---

[1] For John the Baptist, see *Lectures on the Jewish Church*, iii. 399.

[2] Compare the account of the young courtiers of Herod plunging in the tank at Jericho. Joseph. *Ant.* xv. 33. The word βαπτίζω is used for it.

[3] This account is taken from *Sinai and Palestine*, chap. 7. I have hardly altered it, lest the original impression should be lost.

ness with which they dart into the main current, striking the water after their fashion alternately with their two arms, and playing with the eddies, which hurry them down and across as if they were in the cataracts of their own Nile; crashing through the thick boughs of the jungle which, on the eastern bank of the stream, intercepts their progress, and then re-crossing the river higher up, where they can wade, assisted by long poles which they have cut from the opposite thickets. It is remarkable, considering the mixed assemblage of men and women in such a scene, that there is so little appearance of levity or indecorum. A primitive domestic character pervades in a singular form the whole transaction. The families which have come on their single mule or camel now bathe together, with the utmost gravity; the father receiving from the mother the infant, which has been brought to receive the one immersion which will suffice for the rest of its life, and thus, by a curious economy of resources, save it from the expense and danger of a future pilgrimage in after-years. In about two hours the shores are cleared; with the same quiet they remount their camels and horses, and, before the noonday heat has set in, are again encamped on the upper plain of Jericho. Once more they may be seen. At the dead of night, the drum again wakes them for their homeward march. The torches again go before; behind follows the vast multitude, mounted, passing in pro-found silence over that silent plain—so silent that, but for the tinkling of the drum, its departure would hardly be perceptible. The troops stay on the ground to the end, to guard the rear, and when the last roll of the drum announces that the last soldier is gone, the whole plain returns again to its perfect solitude.

Such, on the whole, was the first Baptism. We are able to track its history through the next three centuries. The rite was still in great measure what in its origin it had been almost universally, the change from darkness to light, from evil to good; the 'second birth' of men from the corrupt society of the dying Roman Empire into the purifying and for the most part elevating influence of the living Christian Church. In some respects the moral responsibility of the act must have been impressed upon the converts by the severe, sometimes the life-long, preparation for the final pledge, more deeply than by the sudden and almost instantaneous transition which characterised the Baptism of the Apostolic age. But gradually the consciousness of this 'questioning of the good conscience towards God' was lost in the stress laid with greater and greater emphasis on the 'putting away the filth of the flesh.'

Let us conceive ourselves present at those extraordinary scenes, to which no existing ritual of any European Church Celebration offers any likeness. There was, as a general rule, in the Patristic age. but one baptistery[4] in each city, and such baptisteries were apart from the churches. There was but one time of the year when the rite was administered—namely, between Easter and Pentecost. There was but one personage who could administer it—the presiding officer of the community, the Bishop, as the Chief Presbyter was called after the first century. There was but one hour for the ceremony; it was midnight. The torches flared through the dark hall as the troops of converts flocked in. The baptistery[5] consisted of an inner and an outer chamber. In the outer chamber stood the candidates for baptism, stripped to their shirts; and, turning to the west as the region of sunset, they stretched forth their hands through the dimly lit chamber, as in a defiant attitude towards the Evil Spirit of Darkness, and speaking to him by name, said: 'I renounce thee, Satan, and all thy works, and all thy pomp, and all thy service.' Then they turned, like a regiment, facing right round to the east, and repeated, in a form more or less long, the belief in the Father, the Son, and the Spirit, which has grown up into the

[4] At Rome there was more than one.

[5] In the most beautiful baptistery in the world, at Pisa, baptisms even in the Middle Ages only took place on the two days of the Nativity and the Decollation of John the Baptist, and the nobles stood in the galleries to witness the ceremony. See Dr. Smith's *Dictionary of Christian Antiquities*, i. pp. 160, 161.

so-called Apostles' Creed in the West, and the so-called Nicene
Creed in the East.   They then advanced into the inner chamber.   Before them yawned the deep pool or reservoir, and
standing by the deacon, or deaconess, as the case might be,
to arrange that all should be done with decency.   The whole
troop undressed completely as if for a bath, and stood up,[6]
naked, before the Bishop, who put to each the questions, to
which the answer was returned in a loud and distinct voice,
as of those who knew what they had undertaken.   They then
plunged into the water.   Both before and after the immersion
their bare limbs were rubbed with oil from head to foot;[7]
they were then clothed in white gowns, and received, as
token of the kindly feeling of their new brotherhood, the
kiss of peace, and a taste of honey and milk; and they expressed their new faith by using for the first time the Lord's
Prayer.

These are the outer forms of which, in the Western
Churches, almost every particular is altered even in the
most material points.   Immersion has become the exception
and not the rule.   Adult baptism, as well as immersion,
exists only among the Baptists.   The dramatic action of the
scene is lost.   The anointing, like the bath, is reduced to a
few drops of oil in the Roman Church, and in the Protestant churches has entirely disappeared.   What once could
only be administered by Bishops is now administered by
every clergyman, and throughout the Roman Church by
laymen and even by women.   We propose then to ask what
is the residue of the meaning of Baptism which has survived,
and what we may learn from it, and from the changes through
which it has passed.

I. The ordinance of Baptism was founded on the Jewish —
we may say the Oriental—custom, which, both in ancient and
modern times, regards ablution, cleansing of the hands, the
face, and the person, at once as a means of health and as a

---

[6] Bingham, xi. ii. § 1, 2.
[7] Ibid. xi. 9, § 3, 45; xii. 1, 4.   Possibly after immersion the undressing
and the anointing were partial.

sign of purity. We shall presently see that here as elsewhere the Founder of Christianity chose rather to sanctify and elevate what already existed than to create and invent a new form for Himself. Baptism is the oldest ceremonial ordinance that Christianity possesses; it is the only one which is inherited from Judaism. It is thus interesting as the only ordinance of the Christian Church which equally belonged to the merciful Jesus and the austere John. Out of all the manifold religious practices of the ancient law— sacrifices, offerings, temple, tabernacle, scapegoat, sacred vestments, sacred trumpets—He chose this one alone; the most homely, the most universal, the most innocent of all. He might have chosen the peculiar Nazarite custom of the long tresses and the rigid abstinence by which Samson and Samuel and John had been dedicated to the service of the Lord. He did nothing of the sort. He might have continued the strange and painful right of circumcision. He, or at least His Apostles, rejected it altogether. He might have chosen some elaborate ceremonial like the initiation into the old Egyptian and Grecian mysteries. He chose instead what every one could understand. He took what, at least in Eastern and Southern countries, was the most delightful, the most ordinary, the most salutary, of social observances.

1. By choosing water and the use of the bath, He indicated one chief characteristic of the Christian religion. Whatever else the Christian was to be, Baptism [a]— the use of water—showed that he was to be clean and pure, in body, soul, and spirit; clean even in body. Cleanliness is a duty which some of the monastic communities of Christendom have despised, and some have even

Baptism as a cleansing rite.

---

[a] This is the meaning of the frequent reference to 'water' in St. John's writings. As in John vi. 54, the phrases 'eating' and 'drinking,' 'flesh and blood,' refer to the spiritual nourishment of which the Eucharist, never mentioned in the Fourth Gospel, was the outward expression, so in John iii. 5, the word 'water' refers to the moral purity symbolised by Baptism, which in like manner (as a universal institution) is never mentioned in that Gospel.

treated as a crime.   But such was not the mind of Him who
chose the washing with water for the prime ordinance of His
followers.   ' Wash and be clean ' was the prophet's admonition
of old to the Syrian whom he sent to bathe in the river Jordan.   It was the text of the one only sermon by which a well-
known geologist of this country was known to his generation.
' Cleanliness next to godliness ' was the maxim of the great
religious prophet of England in the last century, John
Wesley.   With the Essenes, amongst whom Baptism originated, we may almost say that it was godliness.[9]   If the early
Christians had, as we shall see, their daily Communion, the
Essenes, for the sake of maintaining their punctilious cleanliness, had even more than daily Baptism.   Every time
that we see the drops of water poured over the face in
Baptism, they are signs to us of the cleanly habits which
our Master prized when He founded the rite of Baptism,
and when, by His own Baptism in the sweet soft stream of
the rapid Jordan, He blessed the element of water for use
as the best and choicest of God's natural gifts to man in his
thirsty, weary, wayworn passage through the dust and heat
of the world.   But the cleanness of the body, in the
adoption of Baptism by Christ and His forerunner, was
meant to indicate the perfect cleanness, the unsullied purity,
of the soul ; or, as the English Baptismal Service quaintly
expresses it, the mystical washing away of sin—that is, the
washing, cleansing process that effaces the dark spots of
selfishness and passion in the human character, in which, by
nature and by habit, they had been so deeply ingrained.   It
was a homely maxim of Keble, ' Associate the idea of sin
with the idea of dirt.'   It indicates also that as the Christian
heart must be bathed in an atmosphere of purity, so the
Christian mind must be bathed in an atmosphere of truth,
of love of truth, of perfect truthfulness, of transparent
veracity and sincerity.   What filthy, indecent talk or action
is to the heart and affections, that a lie however white, a
fraud however pious, is to the mind and conscience.   Sir

[9] *Lectures on the Jewish Church*, iii. 397.

Isaac Newton is said by his friends to have had the whitest soul that they ever knew. That is the likeness of a truly Christian soul as indicated by the old baptismal washing : the whiteness of purity, the clearness and transparency of truth.

There was one form of this idea which continued far down into the Middle Ages, long after it had been dissociated from Baptism, but which may be given as an illustration of the same idea represented by the same form. The order of knighthood in England, of which the banners hang in King Henry the Seventh's Chapel in Westminster Abbey, and which is distinguished from all the other orders as the 'most honourable,' is called the Order of the Bath. This name was given because in the early days of chivalry the knights who were enlisted in defence of right against wrong, truth against falsehood, honour against dishonour, on the evening before they were admitted to the Order, were laid in a bath [1] and thoroughly washed, in order to show how bright and pure ought to be the lives of those who engage in noble enterprises. Sir Galahad, amongst King Arthur's Knights of the Round Table, is the type at once of a true ancient Knight of the Bath and of a true Apostolic Christian.

> My good blade carves the casques of men,
> My tough lance thrusteth sure,
> My strength is as the strength of ten,
> Because my heart is pure.

2. This leads us to the second characteristic of the act of Baptism. ' Baptism ' was not only a bath but a plunge—

Baptism as a plunge. an entire submersion in the deep water, a leap as into the rolling sea or the rushing river, where for the moment the waves close over the bather's head, and he emerges again as from a momentary grave ; or it was the shock of a shower-bath—the rush of water passed over the whole person from capacious vessels, so as to wrap the recipient as within the veil of a splashing cataract. [2] This was the part

---

[1] To 'dub' a knight is said to be taken from 'the dip,' 'doob' in the bath. Evelyn saw the Knights in their baths (*Diary*, April 19, 1661).

[2] See Dr. Smith's *Dictionary of Christian Antiquities*, vol. i. p. 169.

of the ceremony on which the Apostles laid so much stress. It seemed to them like a burial of the old former self and the rising up again of the new self.   So St. Paul compared it to the Israelites passing through the roaring waves of the Red Sea, and St. Peter to the passing through the deep waters of the flood.   'We are buried,' said St. Paul, 'with Christ by baptism at His death ; that, like as Christ was raised, thus we also should walk in the newness of life.'[3]   Baptism, as the entrance into the Christian society, was a complete change from the old superstitions or restrictions of Judaism to the freedom and confidence of the gospel; from the idolatries and profligacies of the old heathen world to the light and purity of Christianity.   It was a change effected only by the same effort and struggle as that with which a strong swimmer or an adventurous diver throws himself into the stream and struggles with the waves, and comes up with increased energy out of the depths of the dark abyss.

This, too, is a lesson taught by Baptism which still lives, although the essence of the material form is gone.   There is now no disappearance as in a watery grave.   There is now no conscious and deliberate choice made by the eager convert at the cost of cruel partings from friends, perhaps of a painful death.   It is but the few drops sprinkled, a ceremony undertaken long before or long after the adoption of Christianity has occurred.   But the thing signified by the ancient form still keeps before us that which Christians were intended to be.   This is why it was connected both in name and in substance with 'Conversion.'   In the early Church the careful distinction which later times have made between Baptism, Regeneration, Conversion, and Repentance did not exist.   They all meant the same thing.   In the Apostolic age they were, as we have seen, absolutely combined with Baptism.   There was then no waiting till Easter or Pentecost for the great reservoir when the catechumens met the Bishop —the river, the wayside well were taken the moment the convert was disposed to turn, as we say, the new leaf in his

[3] Rom. vi. 4; 1 Cor. x. 2; 1 Pet. iii. 20, 21.

life. And even afterwards, in the second century, Regeneration (παλιγγενεσία), which gradually was taken to be the equivalent of Baptism, was, in the first instance, the equivalent of Repentance and Conversion.[4] A long and tedious controversy about thirty years ago took place on the supposed distinction between these words. Such a controversy would have been unintelligible to Justin Martyr or Clement of Alexandria.[5] But the common idea which the words represent is still as necessary, and has played as great a part in the later history of the Church as it did at the beginning.[6]

[4] As a general rule, in the writings of the later Fathers there is no doubt that the word which we translate ‘Regeneration’ is used exclusively for Baptism. But it is equally certain that in the earlier Fathers it is used for *Repentance*, or, as we should now say, *Conversion*. See Clem. Rom. i. 9. Justin. *Dial. in Tryph.* p. 231, B.D. Clemens Alex. (apud Eus. *H. E.* iii. 23), *Strom.* lib. ii. 8, 425, A.

[5] The Gorham litigation of 1850, which turned on the necessity of ‘an unconditional regeneration in Baptism,’ has now drifted into the limbo of extinct controversies. The epigram of Sir George Rose and the judgment of Bishop Thirlwall had indeed sealed its doom at the time. I quote a sentence from each :—

> ‘ Bishop and vicar,
>   Why do you bicker
>     Each with the other,
>   When both are right,
>   Or each is quite
>     As wrong as the other? ’
>
> *The Gorham Judgment Versified.*

‘ In no part of the controversy was it stated in what sense the word “ Regeneration ” was understood by either party. In no other instance has there been so great a disproportion between the intrinsic moment of the fact and the excitement which it has occasioned.’—Thirlwall, *Remains*, i. 153, 158.

But it was not till some years afterwards that the wit of the lawyer and judgment of the Bishop were confirmed from an unexpected quarter. Dr. Mozley, afterwards Regius Professor of Divinity at Oxford, had in his calmer moments reviewed the whole question, and decided that the decision of the Privy Council, so vehemently attacked at the time by his school as subversive of the Christian faith, was right, and that its opponents had wasted their fears and their indignation in behalf of a phantom. See his two works on *The Augustinian Doctrine of Predestination*, 1855, and on *Baptismal Regeneration*, 1856.

[6] It has been often remarked that examples of such total renewal of character are very rare outside of the influence of Christianity. But (not to speak of Mohammedan and Indian instances) a striking instance, corresponding almost entirely to the conversions in Christendom, has been

Conversion is the turning round from a wrong to a right direction; Repentance ($\mu\epsilon\tau\acute{a}\nu o\iota a$) is a change of thoughts and feelings which is always going on in any one who reforms himself at all; Regeneration is the growth of a second character, always recurring, though at times with a more sudden shock. With us these changes are brought about by a thousand different methods; education, affliction, illness, change of position in life, a happy marriage, a new field of usefulness—every one of these gives us some notion of the early Baptism in its better and more permanent side, and in every one of these that better side of the early Baptism may be reproduced. We lie down to sleep, and we wake up and find ourselves new creatures, with new hopes, new affections, new interests, new aspirations. Every such case which we have known, every such experience in ourselves, helps us better to understand what Baptism once was; and the recollection of that original Baptism helps us better to apply to ourselves the language of the Bible concerning it—to that which now most nearly resembles it. We must, if we would act in the spirit of the Apostolic Baptism, be not once only, but ' continually,' ' mortifying,' that is, killing, drowning, burning out our selfish affections and narrow prejudices; and not once only, but ' daily,' proceeding,—daily renewed and born again in all virtue and godliness of living, all strength and uprightness of character.

3. And this brings us to the third characteristic of the early Baptism. 'Baptism,' says the English Baptismal Service, ' doth represent unto us our Christian profession, which is to follow Christ and to be made like unto Him.' This is the element added to the Baptism of John. In the first two characteristics of Baptism which we have mentioned, water as signifying cleanliness of body and mind, and immersion as indicating the plunge into a new life, the Baptism of John and the Baptism of Christ are identical. John's

pointed out—that of Polemo, under the teaching of Xenocrates. See Horace, *Satires*, II. iii. 254, with the annotations from Valerius Maximus and Diogenes Laertius.

Baptism, no less than Christian Baptism, was the Baptism of purity, of regeneration, 'of remission of sins.'[7] But Christ added yet this further; that the new atmosphere into which they rose was to be the atmosphere of the Spirit of Christ. This was expressed to the Christians of the first centuries in two ways: First, when they came up from the waters, naked and shivering, from the cold plunge into the bath or river, they were wrapped round in a white robe, and this suggested the thought that the recipients of baptism put on—that is, were clothed, wrapped, enveloped in—the fine linen, white and clean, which is the goodness and right-eousness of Christ and of His saints, not by any fictitious transfer, but in deed and in truth; His character, His grace, His mercy, His truthfulness were to be the clothing, the uniform, the badge, the armour of those who by this act enrolled themselves in His service. And, secondly, this was what made Baptism especially a 'Sacrament.' It is common now to speak of the Eucharist as '*the* Sacrament.' But in the early ages it was rather Baptism which was *the* special Sacrament (*sacramentum*), the oath, the pledge in which, as the soldiers enlisting in the Roman army swore a great oath on the sacred eagles of allegiance to the Emperor, so con-verts bound themselves by a great oath to follow their Divine Commander wherever He led them. And this was further impressed upon them by the name in which they were baptised. It was, if not always, yet whenever we hear of its use in the Acts of the Apostles, in *the name of the 'Lord Jesus.'*[8] Doubtless the more comprehensive form in which Baptism is now everywhere administered in the threefold name of the Father, the Son, and the Holy Spirit, soon superseded the simpler form of that in the name of the Lord Jesus only. But the earlier use points out clearly how,

---

[7] Luke iii. 3.

[8] Acts ii. 38, viii. 16. x. 48. The form of the name of the Father, Son, and Holy Ghost, though found in early times, was not universal. Cyprian first and Pope Nicholas I. afterwards acknowledged the validity of Baptism 'In the name of the Lord Jesus.' See Dr. Smith's *Dictionary of Christian Antiquities*, vol. i. p. 162.

along with the all-embracing love of the Universal Father, and the all-penetrating presence of the Eternal Spirit, the historical, personal, gracious, endearing form of the Founder of the Faith was the first and leading thought that was planted in the mind of the early Christians as they rose out of the font of their first immersion to enter on their new and difficult course.

It has thus far been intended to show what is the essential meaning of the early Baptism which has endured through all its changes. And it is in full accordance with the primitive records of Christianity to dwell on these essentials as distinct from its forms. It is not by the water, much or little, but by the Spirit (as it is expressed in the Fourth Gospel),[9] that the second birth of man is wrought in the heart. It is not by the putting away the natural filth of the outward flesh,[1] but (as it is expressed in the First Epistle of St. Peter) by the inward questioning of a good conscience towards God, that Baptism can ever save any one. It was not by the act of baptising, but by proclaiming the glad tidings of the kingdom of God, that the world was converted. Jesus,[2] we are told, never baptised, and Paul thanked God that, with a few insignificant exceptions, he baptised none of the Corinthians.

II. But there is the further instruction to be derived from a nearer view of the changes through which the forms passed.

1. First there are the curious notions which have congregated round the ceremony, and which have almost entirely passed away. There was the belief in early ages that it was like a magical charm, which acted on the persons who received it, without any consent or intention either of administrator or recipient, as in the case of children or actors performing the rite with no serious intention. There was also the belief that it wiped away all sins,

*Ancient opinion on Baptism.*

---

[9] John iii. 5–8.
[1] See Professor Plumptre's Notes on 1 Peter iii. 21.
[2] John iv. 2 ; 1 Cor. i. 14–16.

however long they had been accumulating, and however late
it was administered. This is illustrated by the striking
instance of the postponement of the baptism of the first
Christian Emperor Constantine, who had presided at the
Council of Nicæa, preached in churches, directed the whole
religion of the empire, and yet was all the while unbaptised
till the moment of his death, when, in the last hours of his
mortal illness, the ceremony was performed by Eusebius of
Nicomedia. There was also the belief, in the third and fourth
centuries almost as firmly fixed as the corresponding belief
in regard to the Eucharist, that the water was changed into
the blood of Christ.

There was the yet more strange persuasion that no one
could be saved unless he had passed through the immersion
of Baptism. It was not the effect of Divine grace upon the
soul, but of the actual water upon the body, on which
those ancient Baptists built their hopes of immortality.
If only the person of a human being be wrapt in the
purifying element, he was thought to be redeemed from the
uncleanness of his birth. The boy Athanasius throwing
water in jest over his playmate on the seashore performed,
as it was believed, a valid baptism ; the Apostles in the spray
of the storm on the sea of Galilee, the penitent thief in the
water that rushed from the wound of the Crucified, were
imagined to have received the baptism which had else been
withheld from them. And this ‘ washing of water ’ was now
deemed absolutely necessary for salvation. No human
being could pass into the presence of God hereafter unless
he had passed through the waters of baptism here. ‘ This,’
says Vossius, ‘ is the judgment of all antiquity, that they
perish everlastingly who will not be baptised, when they
may.’ From this belief followed gradually, but surely, the
conclusion that the natural end not only of all heathens,
but of all the patriarchs and saints of the Old Testament,
was in the realms of perdition. And, further, the Pelagian
controversy drew out the mournful doctrine, that infants
dying before baptism were excluded from the Divine

presence—the doctrine, when expressed in its darkest form, that they were consigned to everlasting fire. At the close of the fifth century this belief had become universal, chiefly through the means of Augustine. It was the turning-point of his contest with Pelagius. It was the dogma from which nothing could induce him to part. It was this which he meant by insisting on 'the remission of original sin in infant baptism.' In his earlier years he had doubted whether, possibly, he might not leave it an open question ; but in his full age, 'God forbid,' said he, 'that I should leave the matter so.' The extremest case of a child dying beyond the reach of baptism is put to him, and he decides against it. In the Fifth Council of Carthage, the milder view is mentioned of those who, reposing on the gracious promise, 'In my Father's house are many mansions,' trusted that among those many mansions, there might still be found, even for those infants who, by want of baptism, were shut out from the Divine presence, some place of shelter. That milder view, doubtless under Augustine's influence, was anathematised. Happily, this dark doctrine was never sanctioned by the formal Creeds of the Church. On this, as on every other point connected with the doctrine of Baptism, they preserved a silence, whether by design, indifference, or accident, we know not. But among the individual Fathers from the time of Augustine it seems impossible to dispute the judgment of the great English authority on Baptism : 'How hard soever this opinion may seem, it is the constant opinion of the ancients.'[3] 'I am sorry,' says Bishop Hall, and we share his sorrow, 'that so harsh an opinion should be graced with the name of a father so reverend, so divine—whose sentence yet let no man plead by halves.' All who profess to go by the opinion of the ancients and the teaching of Augustine must be prepared to believe that immersion is essential to the

---

[3] Wall's *History of Infant Baptism*, vol. i. p. 200. In this work, and in Bingham's *Antiquities*, will be found most of the authorities for the statements in the text.

efficacy of baptism, that unbaptised infants must be lost
for ever, that baptised infants must receive the Eucharist,
or be lost in like manner. For this, too, strange as it
may seem, was yet a necessary consequence of the same
materialising system. 'He who held it impossible' (we
again use the words of Bishop Hall) ' for a child to be saved
unless the baptismal water were poured on his face, held it
also as impossible for the same infant unless the sacramental
bread were received in his mouth. And, lest any should
plead different interpretations, the same St. Augustine avers
this later opinion also, touching the necessary communicating
of children, to have been once the common judgment of the
Church of Rome.' [4]

Such were the doctrines of the Fathers on Infant Baptism ;
—doctrines so deeply affecting our whole conceptions of God
and of man, that, in comparison, the gravest questions of late
times shrink into insignificance ;—doctrines so different from
those professed by any English, we may almost add any European, clergyman, of the present day, that had the Pope himself appeared before the Bishop of Hippo, he would have
been rejected at once as an unbaptised heretic.

It is a more pleasing task to trace the struggle of
Christian goodness and wisdom by which the Church was
gradually delivered from this iron yoke. No doctrine has
ever arisen in the Church more entirely contrary to the
plainest teaching of its original documents. In the Old
Testament, especially in the Psalms,[5]—where the requisites
of moral life are enumerated as alone necessary to propitiate
the Divine favour,—it is needless to say that Baptism is never
mentioned. In the New Testament the highest blessings
are pronounced on those who, whether children or adults,[6]
had never been baptised. Even in the Patristic age itself
(in its earlier stage) the recollection of the original freedom

<hr>

[4] Bishop Hall's *Letter to the Lady Honoria Hay.*

[5] See Psalms xv. xix. xxiv. cxix.

[6] Matt. v. 1–11, vii. 24, 25, viii. 10, 11, xii. 50, xviii. 3–5, xxv. 34–39 ;
Mark x. 14 ; Luke xv. 32 ; John xiv. 23 ; Acts x. 4, 44.

of Christianity had not quite died out.   Tertullian must
have accepted with hesitation, if he accepted at all, the
universal condemnation of unbaptised children.   Salvian,
who acknowledged freely the virtues of the Vandal heretics, must have scrupled to repudiate the virtues of the
unbaptised heathens.   No General or Provincial Council,
except the Fifth of Carthage, ventured to affirm any doctrine on the subject.   The exception in behalf of martyrs
left an opening, at least in principle, which would by logical consequence admit other exceptions.   The saints of the
Old Testament were believed to have been rescued from
their long prison-house by the hypothesis of a liberation
effected for them through the Descent into Hell.   But
these were contradictions and exceptions to the prevailing
doctrine; and the gloomy period which immediately followed
the death of Augustine, fraught as it was with every imagin-
able horror of a falling empire, was not likely to soften
the harsh creed which he had bequeathed to it; and
the chains which the 'durus pater infantum' had thrown
round the souls of children were riveted by Gregory the
Great.   At last, however, with the new birth of the
European nations, the humanity of Christendom revived.
One by one the chief strongholds of the ancient belief
yielded to the purer and loftier instincts (to use no higher
name) which guided the Christian Church in its onward
progress, dawning more and more unto the perfect day.
First disappeared the necessity of immersion.   Then, to
the Master of the Sentences we owe the decisive change
of doctrine which delivered the souls of infants from the
everlasting fire to which they had been handed over by
Augustine and Fulgentius, and placed them, with the heroes
of the heathen world, in that mild Limbo or Elysium which is
so vividly described in the pages of Dante.   Next fell the
practice of administering to them the Eucharistic elements.
Last of all, in the fourteenth century, the strong though
silent protest against the magical theory of Baptism itself
was effected in the postponement of the rite of Confirmation,

which, down to that time, had been regarded as an essential part of Baptism, and, as such, was administered simultaneously with it. An ineffectual stand was made in behalf of the receding doctrine of Augustine by Gregory of Rimini, known amongst his ‘seraphic’ and ‘angelic’ colleagues by the unenviable title of ‘Tormentor Infantum’; and some of the severer Reformers, both in England and Germany, for a few years clung to the sterner view. But the victory was really won; and the Council of Trent, no less than the Confession of Augsburg and the Thirty-nine Articles, has virtually abandoned the position, by which Popes and Fathers once maintained the absolute, unconditional, mystical efficacy of sacramental elements on the body and soul of the unconscious infant. The Eastern Church, indeed, with its usual tenacity of ancient forms, still immerses, still communicates, and still confirms its infant members. But in the Western Church the Christian religion has taken its more natural course; and in the boldness which substituted a few drops of water for the ancient bath, which pronounced a charitable judgment on the innocent babes who die without the sacraments, which restored to the Eucharist something of its original intention, and gave to Confirmation a meaning of its own, by deferring both these solemn rites to years of discretion, we have at once the best proof of the total and necessary divergence of modern from ancient doctrine, and the best guarantee that surely, though slowly, the true wisdom of Christianity will be justified of all her children.

‘The constant opinion of the ancients’ in favour of the unconditional efficacy and necessity of Baptism has been happily exchanged for a constant opinion of the moderns, which has almost, if not entirely, spread through Christendom. No doubt traces of the old opinion may occasionally be found. It is said that a Roman peasant, on receiving a remonstrance for spinning a cockchafer, replied, with a complete assurance of conviction, ‘There is no harm in doing it. Non è roba battezzata.’—‘It is not baptised stuff.’ ‘They are not baptised things’ is the reply which many a scholastic divine would have made to the complaint

that Socrates and Marcus Aurelius were excluded from
Paradise. The French peasants, we are told, regard their
children before baptism simply as animals.[9] The unbaptised children are often considered of no sex.[1] In the
Tyrol some mothers will not suckle unbaptised children,
because it is nourishing a heathen.[2] Even in the English
Church we sometimes hear a horror expressed by some
excellent clergymen at using any religious words over the
graves of unbaptised persons. The rubric which, in the
disastrous epoch of 1662, was for the first time introduced
into the English Prayer Book, forbidding the performance of
its burial service over the unbaptised, which till then had
been permitted, still, through the influence of the Southern
Convocation, maintains its place. But these are like the
ghosts of former beliefs—lingering in dens and caves of the
Church, visiting here and there their ancient haunts, but
almost everywhere receding, if slowly yet inevitably, from
the light of day.

Such changes on such a momentous subject are amongst
the most encouraging lessons of ecclesiastical history. They
show how variable and contradictory, and therefore how
capable of improvement, has been the theology of the Catholic
as well as of the Protestant Churches, and how pregnant,
therefore, are the hopes for the future of both.

2. We now pass to the changes in the form itself. For
the first thirteen centuries the almost universal practice of
Baptism was that of which we read in the New
Testament, and which is the very meaning of the
word 'baptise'[3]—that those who were baptised

*Immersion exchanged for sprinkling.*

were plunged, submerged, immersed into the water. That
practice is still, as we have seen, continued in Eastern
Churches. In the Western Church it still lingers amongst
Roman Catholics in the solitary instance of the cathedral of
Milan, amongst Protestants in the numerous sect of the Bap-

---

[9] *Round my House,* by P. G. Hamerton, pp. 254, 263.
[1] Thiers, *Traité des Superstitions.*
[2] Goodman's *Gaddings in the Tyrol.*
[3] It is the meaning of the word *taufen* ('dip').

tists.  It lasted long into the Middle Ages.  Even the Icelanders, who at first shrank from the water of their freezing lakes, were reconciled when they found that they could use the warm water of the Geysers.  And the cold climate of Russia has not been found an obstacle to its continuance throughout that vast empire.  Even in the Church of England it is still observed in theory.  The rubric in the Public Baptism for Infants enjoins that, unless for special cases, they are to be dipped, not sprinkled.  Edward the Sixth and Elizabeth were both immersed.  But since the beginning of the seventeenth century, the practice has become exceedingly rare.  With the few exceptions just mentioned, the whole of the Western Churches have now substituted for the ancient bath the ceremony of letting fall a few drops of water on the face.  The reason of the change is obvious.  The practice of immersion, though peculiarly suitable to the Southern and Eastern countries for which it was designed, was not found seasonable in the countries of the North and West.  Not by any decree of Council or Parliament, but by the general sentiment of Christian liberty, this remarkable change was effected.  Beginning in the thirteenth century, it has gradually driven the ancient Catholic usage out of the whole of Europe.  There is no one who would now wish to go back to the old practice.  It followed no doubt the example of the Apostles and of their Master.  It had the sanction of the venerable Churches of the early ages, and of the sacred countries of the East.  Baptism by sprinkling was rejected by the whole ancient Church (except in the rare case of deathbeds or extreme necessity) as no baptism at all.  Almost the first exception was the heretic Novatian.  It still has the sanction of the powerful religious community which numbers amongst its members such noble characters as John Bunyan, Robert Hall, and Havelock.  In a version of the Bible which the Baptist Church has compiled for its own use in America, where it excels in numbers all but the Methodists, it is thought necessary, and on philological grounds it is quite correct, to translate 'John the Baptist' by 'John the Immerser.'  It has even been defended on sanitary grounds. Sir John Floyer dated the prevalence of consumption to the discontinuance of baptism by immersion.[4] But, speaking generally, the Christian civilised world has decided against it. It is a striking example of the triumph of common sense and convenience over the bondage of form and custom. Perhaps no greater change has ever taken place in the outward form of Christian ceremony with such general agreement. It is a larger change even than that which the Roman Catholic Church has made in administering the sacrament of the Lord's Supper in the bread without the wine. For whilst that was a change which did not affect the thing that was signified, the change from immersion to sprinkling has set aside most of the Apostolic expressions regarding Baptism, and has altered the very meaning of the word. But whereas the withholding of the cup produced the long and sanguinary war of Bohemia, and has been one of the standing grievances of Protestants against the Roman Catholic Church, the withdrawal of the ancient rite of immersion, decided by the usage of the whole ancient Church to be essential to the sacrament of Baptism, has been, with the exception of the insurrection of the Anabaptists of Münster, conceded almost without a struggle. The whole transaction shows the wisdom of refraining from the enforcement of the customs of other regions and other climates on unwilling recipients. It shows how the spirit which lives and moves in human society can override even the most sacred ordinances. It remains an instructive example of the facility and silence with which, in matters of form, even the widest changes can be effected without any serious loss to Christian truth, and with great advantage to Christian solemnity and edification. The substitution of sprinkling for immersion must to many at the time, as to the Baptists[5] now, have seemed the greatest and most dangerous innovation. Now, by most Catholics and by most Protestants, it is regarded almost as a second nature.

[4] *Archæological Journal,* No. 113, p. 77.

[5] How dangerous this change is regarded by the excellent community of Baptists has been strongly brought out by the horror which this Essay has occasioned amongst them since it was originally published.

3. Another change is not so complete, but is perhaps more important. In the Apostolic age, and in the three centuries which followed, it is evident that, as a general rule, those who came to baptism came in full age, of their own deliberate choice. We find a few cases of the baptism of children; in the third century we find one case of the baptism of infants. Even amongst Christian households the instances of Chrysostom, Gregory Nazianzen, Basil, Ephrem of Edessa, Augustine, Ambrose, are decisive proofs that it was not only not obligatory but not usual. All these distinguished personages had Christian parents, and yet were not baptised till they reached maturity. The old liturgical service of Baptism was framed for full-grown converts, and is only by considerable adaptation applied to the case of infants. Gradually the practice of baptising infants spread, and after the fifth century the whole Christian world, East and West, Catholic and Protestant, Episcopal and Presbyterian (with the single exception of the sect of the Baptists before mentioned), have adopted it. Whereas, in the early ages, adult baptism was the rule, and infant baptism the exception, in later times infant baptism [6] is the rule, and adult baptism the exception.

What is the justification of this almost universal departure from the primitive usage? There may have been many reasons, some bad, some good. One, no doubt, was the superstitious feeling already mentioned, which regarded Baptism as a charm, indispensable to salvation, and which insisted on imparting it to every human being who could be touched with water, however unconscious. Hence the eagerness with which Roman Catholic missionaries, like St. Francis Xavier, have made it the chief glory of their mission to baptise heathen populations wholesale, in utter disregard of the primitive or Protestant practice of long previous preparation.[7] Hence the capture of children for baptism

---

[6] In the Church of England there was no office for adult baptism in the Prayer Book before 1662, and that which was then added is evidently intended for the baptism of heathen tribes collectively.

[7] See a powerful description of this mode of baptism in Lord Elgin's *Life and Letters*, ed. by Theodore Walrond, p. 338.

without the consent of their parents, as in the celebrated case of the Jewish boy Mortara.   Hence the curious decision of the Sorbonne quoted in 'Tristram Shandy.'   Hence in the early centuries, and still in the Eastern Churches, coextensive with Infant Baptism, the practice of Infant Communion, both justified on the same grounds, and both based on the mechanical application of Biblical texts to cases which by their very nature were not contemplated in the Apostolic age.

But there is a better side to the growth of this practice which, even if it did not mingle in its origin, is at least the cause of its continuance.   It lay deep in early Christian feeling that the fact of belonging to a Christian household consecrated every member of it.   Whether baptised or not, the Apostle[8] urged that, because the parents were holy, therefore the children were holy.   They were not to be treated as outcasts; they were not to be treated as heathens; they were to be recognised as part of the chosen people. This passage, whilst it is conclusive against the practice of Infant Baptism in the Apostolic age, is a recognition of the legitimate reason and permanent principle on which it is founded.   It is the acknowledgment of the Christian saintliness and union of family life.   The goodness, the holiness, the purity of a Christian fireside, of a Christian marriage, of a good deathbed, extends to all those who come within its reach.   As we are all drawn nearer to each other by the natural bonds of affection, so we are drawn still nearer when these bonds of affection are cemented by Christianity. Every gathering, therefore, for the christening of a little child is truly a family gathering.   It teaches us how closely we are members one of another.   It teaches parents how deeply responsible they are for the growth of that little creature throughout its future education.   It teaches brothers and sisters how by them is formed the atmosphere, good  or bad, in which the soul of their little new-born brother or sister is trained to good or to evil.   It teaches us the value of the purity of those domestic relations in

which from childhood to old age all our best thoughts are
fostered and encouraged.  It also surmounts and avoids the
difficulty which encompasses Adult Baptism in any country
or society already impregnated with Christian influences.
If the New Testament has no example of Infant Baptism,
neither has it any example of adult Christian Baptism ; that
is, of the baptism of those who had been already born and
bred Christians.  The artificial formality of a Baptismal
Service for those who in our time have grown up as Christians is happily precluded by the administration of the rite
at the commencement of the natural life.

But there is a further reason to be found in the character
of children.  This is contained in the Gospel which is read
in the Baptismal Service for infants throughout the Western
Church.[9]  In the early ages there probably were those who
doubted whether children could be regarded worthy to be
dedicated to God or to Christ.  The answer is very simple.
If our Divine Master did not think them unfit to be taken
in His arms and receive His own gracious blessing when He
was actually on earth in bodily presence, we need not fear to
ask His blessing upon them now.

Infant baptism is thus a recognition of the good which
there is in every human soul.  It declares that in every
child of Adam, whilst there is much evil, there is more
good ; whilst there is much which needs to be purified and
elevated, there is much also which in itself shows a capacity
for purity and virtue.  In those little children of Galilee,
all unbaptised as they were, not yet even within the reach
of a Christian family, Jesus Christ saw the likeness of the
Kingdom of Heaven ; merely because they were little
children, merely because they were innocent human beings,
He saw in them the objects, not of Divine malediction, but
of Divine benediction.  Lord Palmerston was once severely
attacked for having said ' Children are born good.'  But he,
in fact, only said what Chrysostom had said before him, and

---

[9] In the English Church it is Mark x. 13-16 ; in the Roman Church it is
Matt. xix. 13-15.  But in the Eastern Church the passages are still those
that apply to adult baptism, Rom. vi. 3-12 ; Matt. xxviii. 16-20.

Chrysostom said only what in the Gospels had been already said of the natural state of the unbaptised Galilean children, 'Of such is the Kingdom of Heaven.' The substitution of infant baptism for adult baptism, like the change from immersion to sprinkling, is thus a triumph of Christian charity. It exemplifies at the first beginning of life that Divine Grace which hopes all things, believes all things, endures all things. In each such little child our Saviour saw, and we may see, the promise of a glorious future. In those little hands folded in unconscious repose, in those bright eyes first awakening to the outer world, in that soft forehead unfurrowed by the ruffle of care or sin, He saw, and we may see, the undeveloped rudimental instruments of the labour, and intelligence, and energy of a whole life. And not only so—not only in hope, but in actual reality, does the blessing on little children, whether as expressed in the Gospel story, or as implied in Infant Baptism, acknowledge the excellency and the value of the childlike soul. Not once only in His life, but again and again, He held them up to His disciples, as the best corrective of the ambitions and passions of mankind. He exhorted all men to follow their innocency, their unconsciousness, their guilelessness, their truthfulness, their purity. He saw in them the regenerating, sanctifying element of every family, of every household, of every nation. He saw, and we may see, in their natural, unaffected, simple, unconstrained acts and words the best antidote to the artificial, fantastic, exclusive spirit which beset the Pharisees of His own time, and must beset the Pharisees, whether of the religious or of the irreligious world, in all times. Infant Baptism thus is the standing testimony to the truth, the value, the eternal significance of what is called 'natural religion,' of what Butler calls the constitution of human nature. It is also in a more special sense still the glorification of children. It is the outward expression of their proper place in the Christian Church, and in the instincts of the civilised world. It teaches us how much we all have to learn from children, how much to enjoy, how much to imitate. It is the response to all that

poetry of children which in our days has been specially consecrated by Wordsworth and by Keble.[1]

When we see what a child is—how helpless, how
trusting, how hopeful—the most hardened of men must be
softened by its presence, and feel the reverence due to its
tender conscience as to its tender limbs.  When we remember that before their innocent faces the demons of selfishness,
and impurity, and worldliness, and uncharitableness are put
to flight; when we hope that for their innocent souls there
is a place in a better world, though they are ignorant of
those theological problems which rend their elders asunder,
this may possibly teach us that it is not 'before all
things necessary' to know the differences which divide
the Churches of the East or West, or the Churches of
the North or South.  When we think of the sweet repose
of a child as it lies in the arms of its nurse, or its pastor at
the font, it may recall to us the true attitude of humble
trust and confidence which most befits the human soul,
whether of saint or philosopher.  'Like as a weaned child
on its mother's breast, my soul is even as a weaned child.'
When we meditate on the imperfect knowledge of a child,
it is the best picture to us of our imperfect knowledge in
this mortal state.  'I am but as a little child,' said Sir
Isaac Newton, ' picking up pebbles on the shore of the vast
ocean of truth.'  'When I was a child—when I was an infant,'
said St. Paul, ' I spake as an "infant," I thought as an "infant"; but when I became a man, the thoughts and the spirit
of an "infant" were done away.'  This thought is the pledge
of a perpetual progress.  The baptism of an infant, as the
birth of an infant, would be nothing were it not that it
includes within it the hope and the assurance of all that is

---

[1] It is instructive to observe that whilst the sentiments of the two
poets on the natural attractiveness of children are identical, Keble often
endeavours to force it into a connection with Baptism which to Wordsworth is almost unknown.  It is said that Wordsworth, once reading with
admiration a well-known poem in the *Christian Year*, stumbled at the
opening lines 'Where is it mothers learn their love?' (to which the
answer is 'the Font').  'No, no,' said the old poet: 'it is from their own
maternal hearts.

to follow after.  In those feeble cries, in those unconscious movements, there is the first stirring of the giant within ;—the first dawn of that reasonable soul which will never die ; the first budding of

> The seminal form which in the deeps
> Of that little chaos sleeps.

The investment of this first beginning with a religious and solemn character teaches us that, as we must grow from infancy to manhood, so also we must grow from the infancy, the limited perceptions, the narrow faith, the stunted hope, the imperfect knowledge, the straitened affections of the infancy of this mortal state to the full-grown manhood of our immortal life.  It suggests that we have to pass from the momentary baptism of unconscious infants through the transforming baptism of Fire and the Spirit—that is, of Experience and of Character—which is wrought out through the many vicissitudes of life and the great change of death.

4. There are many other changes consequent on the substitution of Infant for Adult Baptism.  The whole institution of sponsors is of a later date.  In the early centuries the answers as a general rule were made for the child by the parents.  In later times the practice of transferring to a child the dramatic form which had been originally used for grown-up converts led to the system of sponsors.  And the pursuance of the allegory of a second birth was pushed into the further detail of placing the sponsors in the place of parents, and thus creating a new series of affinities.  In the Roman and the Eastern Church, the ‘gossips’[2] cannot intermarry with each other; and in the Middle Ages even the touch of the baptised infant was believed to unite in this spiritual kindred.  The modern system of sponsors, whether with or without these elaborate inquiries, doubtless has some social and moral advantages; but it is impossible to

---

[2] This word, as is well known, expresses ‘the God sib ’—the religious relationship—of the several parties, and has acquired its secondary sense from the tittle-tattle of christenings.

overlook the difficulties which so complex an arrangement awakens in the minds of the uneducated, and it was with the view of surmounting these entanglements of the conscience and understanding that the late Royal Commissioners on the Rubrics on one occasion recommended the permission to hold the whole of that part of the Baptismal Service as optional.

The connection of the Christian name with Baptism is also a result of the change. Properly speaking, the name is not given in Baptism, but, having been already given, it is announced in Baptism as the name by which the individuality and personality of the baptised person is for the first time publicly recognised in the Christian assembly. In the case of the adult baptism of the early ages this was obvious. Flavius Constantinus had always been Flavius Constantinus, and Aurelius Augustinus always Aurelius Augustinus. It was only when the time of the name-giving and of the baptism, as in the case of infants, so nearly coincided, that the two came to be confounded.

Confirmation, which once formed a part of Baptism, has been separated from it, and turned into a new ordinance, which in the Roman Catholic Church has been made into another sacrament. Along with this disruption between Confirmation and Baptism has taken place another change—the absolute prohibition throughout the Western Church of Infant Communion, which in the early Church was, as it still is in the East, the inseparable accompaniment of Infant Baptism. In early ages, as in the Eastern Church, Confirmation was the title given to the unction which accompanied Baptism; in the later Roman Church,[3] and in most Protestant Churches, it is the title given to the open adoption of the Christian faith and life in mature years.

Another curious series of changes has taken place in regard to the persons who administered Baptism. In the

---

[3] In the Roman Catholic Church, as well as in the Church of Scotland, including the Episcopal Church in Charles the Second's time (see the proceedings of the Synod of Dunblane), the preparation for confirmation is virtually superseded by the preparation for the first communion, which in the Roman Church precedes confirmation, and in the Scottish Church has taken its place.

early centuries it was only the Bishop, and hence probably
has originated the retention by the Episcopal order of that
part of the old Baptism which, as we have just said, is now
known by the name of Confirmation.  As the Episcopate
became more separate from the Presbyterate, as the belief in
the paramount necessity of Baptism became stronger, as the
population of Christendom increased, the right was extended
to Presbyters, then to Deacons, and at last to laymen, and,
in defiance of all early usage, to women.  And thus it has
happened by one of those curious introversions of sentiment
which are so instructive in ecclesiastical history, that whilst
in Protestant Churches which lay least stress on the outward
rite, the administration is virtually confined to the clergy, in
the Roman Catholic Church, which lays most stress on the
rite, the administration is extended to the laity and to the
female sex.[4]  This is a formidable breach in the usual theories
concerning the indispensable necessity of the clerical order
for the administration of the sacramental rites, and it is
difficult to justify the difference in principle which in the
Roman Church has rendered the practice with regard to the
sacrament of Baptism so exceedingly lax, with regard to the
sacrament of the Eucharist so exceedingly rigid.

Such are some of the general reflections suggested by
the revolutions through which the oldest ordinance of the
Church has come down to our day.  They may possibly make
that ordinance more intelligible both to those who adopt and
to those who have not adopted it.  They may also serve to
illustrate the transformation both of letter and spirit through
which all sacred ordinances which retain any portion of their
original vitality must pass.

---

[4] There were exceptions to this laxity.  In 1375 the attack of St.
Vitus's Dance was believed to be, in the Netherlands, the result of baptism
by immoral priests (Hecker's *Epidemics of Middle Ages*, pp. 91, 143); and
somnambulism was supposed to be occasioned from baptism by a drunken
priest.  In some English parish registers some children are called
'creatures of Christ,' perhaps as being baptised by laymen, or perhaps
rather as unbaptised children, without names (*Church Quarterly*, January
1877, p. 390).

# CHAPTER II.

### THE EUCHARIST.

IT is proposed to give an account of the primitive institution of the Sacrament of the Lord's Supper—unquestionably the greatest religious ordinance of the world, whether as regards its almost universal adoption in the civilised world, or the passions which it has enkindled, or the opposition which it has evoked.

Unlike many of the records of the Gospel story, which from the variety and contradiction of the narratives, and from the question as to the date and authorship of the Gospels, are involved in difficulty, the narrative of the Institution of the Lord's Supper is preserved to us on the whole with singular uniformity in the first three Gospels; and more than this, it is preserved to us almost in the same form in St. Paul's First Epistle to the Corinthians, and in that case in one of the few writings of the New Testament of which the authority has never been questioned at all, and which belongs to a date long anterior to any of the Gospels, and which is therefore at once the earliest and the most authentic of any part of the Gospel History. What St. Paul tells us about the Last Supper is a fragment of the Gospel History which all critics and scholars will at once admit. ' The Supper was universally instituted or founded by Jesus.' [2] There is nothing startling, nothing difficult to accept in the account, no miraculous portents, no doctrine difficult of apprehension ; but it contains many of the best character-

---

[2] Strauss's *Life of Jesus.*

istics of Our Lord's discourses—His deep affection to His disciples—His parabolical mode of expression—His desire to be remembered after He was gone—His mixture of joyous festivity with serious earnestness. It contains also by implication the story of His arrival in Jerusalem, of His betrayal, and of His death. We have enough in this to build upon. No one doubts it. Every one may construct from it a Christianity sufficient for his belief and for his conduct.

By dwelling on the original form we pass out of the mist of modern controversy to a better, simpler, higher atmosphere. It is said that a great genius in France,[3] when on the point of receiving a first communion in the years which followed the first Revolution, was overwhelmed by the distracting and perplexing thoughts suggested by all the doubts which raged on the subject, but was restored to calm by fixing the mind on the one original scene from which the Christian Eucharist has sprung. Let us do the same. Let us go back to that one occasion, out of which, all are agreed, both its unity and its differences arose.

It was not, as with us, in the early morning or at noon-day, but in the evening, shortly after sunset— not on the first day of the week, nor the seventh, but on the fifth, or Thursday, that the Master and His disciples *The time.* met together. The remembrance of the day of the week has now entirely perished except in Passion Week. It was revived in the time of Calvin, who proposed in recollection of it to have the chief Christian festival and day of rest transferred on this account from Sunday to Thursday. But this was never carried out, and the day now remains unremembered. The remembrance of the hour still lingers in the name when we call it a *supper*—the Lord's *Supper*—and still more in Germany, the Holy *Evening Meal*. For such it was. It was the evening feast, of which every Jewish household partook on the night, as it might be, before or after the Passover. They were collected together, the Master and His twelve disciples, in one of the large upper rooms above the open

---

[3] *Memoirs of George Sand.*

court of the inn or caravanserai to which they had been guided. The couches or mats were spread round the room, as in all Eastern houses, and on those the guests lay reclined, three on each couch, according to the custom derived from the universal usage of the Greek or Roman world. The ancient Jewish usage of eating the Passover standing had given way, and a symbolical meaning was given to what was in fact a mere social fashion, that they might lie then like kings, with the ease becoming free men.[4]

There they lay, the Lord in the midst, next to the beloved disciple, and next to him the eldest, Peter. Of the position of the others we know nothing. There was placed on the table in front of the guests, one, two, perhaps four cups or rather bowls. There is at Genoa a bowl which professes to be the original chalice—a mere fancy, no doubt—but probably representing the original shape. This bowl was filled with wine mixed up with water. The wine of old times was always mixed with water. No one ever thought of taking it without, just as now no one would think of taking syrup or lemon-juice without water. Beside the cup was one or more of the large thin Passover cakes of unleavened bread, such as may still at the Paschal season be seen in all Jewish houses. It is this of which the outward form has been preserved in the thin round wafer which is used in the Roman Catholic and Lutheran Churches. It was the recollection of the unleavened bread of the Israelites when they left Egypt. As the wine was mixed with water, so the bread was probably served up with fish. The two always went together. We see examples of this in the earlier meals in the Gospel, and so doubtless it was in this last. Close beside this cake was another recollection of the Passover—a thick sop, which was supposed to be like the Egyptian clay, and in which the fragments of the Paschal cake were dipped. Round this table, leaning on each other's breasts, reclining on those couches, were the twelve disciples and their Master. From

The elements.

---

[4] Maimonides, *Posach*, 10, 1 ; Farrar, *Life of Christ*, ii. 278.

mouth to mouth passed to and fro the eager inquiry, and the startled look when they heard that one of them should betray Him.[5]   Across the table and from side to side were shot the earnest questions from Peter, from Jude, from Thomas, from Philip.   In each face might have been traced the character of each—receiving a different impression from what he saw and heard—and in the midst of all this the majestic sorrowful countenance of the Master of the Feast, as He drew towards Him the several cups and the thin transparent cake, and pronounced over each the Jewish blessing with those few words which have become immortal.

Let us see what may be deduced from the first institution of the ordinance.

1. It was the ancient Jewish paschal meal.   The Founder showed by thus using it that He did not mean to part the new from the old.   He intended that there should be this connection, however slight, with the ancient Israelite nation.   *Its connection with Judaism.*   The blessing which He pronounced on the cup and the bread was taken from the blessing which the Jewish householder pronounced on them.   The ' hymn ' which they sang was the long chant from the 113th to the 118th Psalm celebrating the Exodus.   The moon which shone into that upper room, and which shines over our Easter night, is the successor of the moon which lighted up the night to be ever remembered when Israel came out of Egypt.[6]   The most Christian of all Christian ordinances is thus the most Jewish. Whitsunday has hardly any Jewish recollections, Christmas and Good Friday none.   But Easter and the Lord's Supper are the Passover in another form, and the link which binds the old and the new together is the same sense of deliver-

---

[5] In this respect the picture of the Last Supper by Leonardo da Vinci gives a true impression.   The moment represented is that in which, as a bombshell, the declaration that one of them should betray Him has fallen among the Apostles.   It is not a picture of the Last Supper, so much as the expression of the various emotions called forth by that announcement.

[6] The hymn which Sir Walter Scott has put into the mouth of a Jewess, ' When Israel, of the Lord beloved, Out of the land of bondage came,' is also one of the very best hymns of Christians.

ance.  The birthday of the Jewish Religion was the day
of the birth of a free people.  The birthday of the Christian Religion was no less the day of the birth of the freedom of the human race, of the human conscience, of the
human soul.  ' This year,' so says the Jewish service, ' we are
servants here; next year we hope to be freemen in the land
of Israel.'  This year Christendom may be a slave to its
prejudices and its passions; next year it may hope to be free
in the land of goodness.

2. But out of this supper He chose those elements which
were most simple and most enduring.  He left altogether out
Selection of the most universal elements.  of notice the paschal lamb and the bitter herbs.  He
did not think it necessary to accept all or reject all of
what He found.  Here as elsewhere He used the best of what
came before Him.  He exercised His free right of choice.  When
He took into His hands—' His holy and venerable hands,' as
the old Liturgies express it—the paschal bread and the paschal wine, it was the selection of them from the rest of the
Jewish ceremony, as He selected His doctrine from the rest
of the Jewish books and Jewish teaching.  He said nothing
of the water which was mixed with the wine.  That was a
mere passing custom which would change with time and
fashion.  He said nothing of the form or materials of the
bread.  It was unleavened, it was round, it was thin, it
was a cake rather than a loaf.  But He said nothing of
all these things, nothing of the accompanying fish.  All
those questions which have arisen as to the proportions in
which the materials should be mixed were far, very far,
behind Him, or far, very far, beyond Him.  He took the
bread and wine as He found them; He fixed on the bread
and wine as representing those two sustaining elements
which are found almost everywhere—bread that strengtheneth man's heart, wine that maketh glad the heart of
man.  These were the fruits of the earth which He blessed,
for which He gave thanks, to indicate the gratitude of
man for these simple gifts.  As in His teaching He had
chosen the most homely images of the shepherd, the sower,

the guest, the traveller, so in His worship He chose the most homely elements of food. How great is the contrast with the sacred emblems of other religions—the bulls, the goats, the white horses, the jewels, the robes! It is the servants, the inferiors, the precursors, who need these appendages to mark them. The True Master is known by the simplicity of His appearance, the plainness of His manners and His dress.[7]

3. He chose also this particular occasion, His parting supper, His farewell meal, as the foundation of His most sacred ordinance, to show us that here, as elsewhere, His religion was to be part of our common life, not sepa- *Parting meal.* rated from it—that the human affections of friend for friend, the sorrow of parting, the joy of meeting again, are the very bonds by which union and sympathy are formed. The very name of *supper* reminds us that our holiest religious ordinance sprung from a festive meal, amidst eating and drinking, amidst weeping and rejoicing, amidst question and answer. It proves that amongst the means of Christian edification, not the least are those interchanges of hospitality where man talks freely with man, friend with friend, guest with guest. Many such a meal has ere this worked the blessed work of even a Christian sacrament. How wise is that advice given by a great humourist of our age,[8] not less wise than he was witty, that bishops should compose the differences of their clergy not by rebukes, but by meeting at the same social table! How many a quarrel, how many a heart-burning, how many a false estrangement, might in like manner be reconciled and done away with by the Sacred Supper, which is the prototype and ideal of all suppers, of every chief meal of the day everywhere! 'The supper,' says Luther, 'which Christ held with His disciples when He gave them His farewell, must have been full of friendly heart-intercourse; for Christ spoke just as tenderly and cordially to them as a father to his dear little children when he is

---

[7] See *Essays on Church and State.*
[8] Sydney Smith.

obliged to part from them. He made the best of their infirmities and had patience with them, although all the while they were so slow to understand, and still lisped like babes. Yet that must indeed have been choice friendly and delightful converse when Philip said, " Show us the way," and Thomas said, " We know not the way," and Peter, " I will go with thee to prison and to death." It was simple, quiet table-talk; every one opening his heart, and showing his thoughts freely and frankly, and without restraint. Never since the world began was there a more delightful meal than that.' It is the likeness, the model, of all serious conversation, of all family intercourse, of all social reciprocity.

4. And lastly, He gave all these things a new meaning. Here, as elsewhere, what He touched He vivified, what *Its future meaning.* He used He transformed and transfigured. It might have been otherwise. We might have inherited only the Paschal feast—the blessing of the natural gifts—the social meal. But He makes it more than this. He tells them that it is Himself who is to live over again in their thoughts every time they break that bread and drink that wine. What those common earthly sustenances are to their bodies, that His Spirit must be to their souls. This was what the Apostles needed at that moment of depression. They felt that He was going to leave them; He made them feel that He would still be with them. It was to be a memorial of His death, but it was also to be a pledge of His life. Five versions have been handed down to us of the words which He used —one by St. Matthew, one by St. Mark, one by St. Luke, one by St. Paul; a fifth found in the oldest Liturgical forms of the early Church, differing from the others. In the Fourth Gospel, whilst the words are not given at all, their substance extends through the whole of that parting discourse which is in this account a substitute for them. This variety of narratives, whilst it shows the slight value which those early times attached to the letter, shows also the essential spirit of the whole transaction. ' This is my Body.' ' This is my Blood.' ' This is the New Testament.'

'I am the vine.' 'I am the way, the truth, and the life.
'It is expedient for you that I go away, for if I go not
away the Comforter will not come to you.' What the
Apostles are imagined to have felt as they heard those
words is represented by their questions and answers.
In various forms they longed to know whither He was
going—they asked Him to show them the Father—they
asked that He would manifest Himself to them and not
to the world. But, one and all, amidst all their failings,
they were cheered and strengthened. They felt that they
had not parted with Him for ever. The very manner
in which He broke the bread was enough to bring Him
back to their recollections. They recognised Him by it
at Emmaus and on the shores of Gennesaret. It was
not only as they had seen Him at the last supper, but at
those earlier feasts where He had blessed and broken the
bread and distributed the fishes on the hills of Galilee. The
Last Supper was in fact a continuation of those meals.[9] It
belonged to the future side of His existence; that is, as He
Himself had explained to them, not the flesh, which profited
nothing, but the words which were His spirit and His life.
Not only these expressions, but many others yet stronger,
repeat over and over the truth which that last supper taught.
Christ's own inmost self would remain always the life and
soul of the Church and of the world. 'Wherever two or
three are gathered in my name, there am I in the midst
of them.' 'Inasmuch as you did it to the least of these
my brethren you did it to me.' 'Lo, I am with you always,
even to the end of the world.'

It is also the glorification of the power of Memory.
Each one may think of those who are gone, and whose
bequests we still desire to carry on. Each one, as at the
Lord's Table we think of the departed, and think also of any
friendless one to be comforted, of any institution needing
help, of any suffering one to be cheered, may hear the voice,
whatsoever it may be, nearest and dearest, or highest and

<hr>

[9] Renan, *Vie de Jésus*, 302, 303.

holiest, in the other world, saying, ' *This do, in remembrance of Me.*' Remembrance—recalling of the past—is the moral, mental, spiritual means by which ' the Last Supper ' becomes ' the Lord's Supper.'

They who believe in the singular mercy and compassion shown in the Parable of the Prodigal Son, or in the toleration and justice due to those who are of another religion, as in the Parable of the Good Samaritan, they, whether they be Christian in name or not, whether they have or have not partaken of the sacrament, have thus received Christ, because they have received that which was the essence of Christ, His spirit of mercy and toleration.

It is the simple fact, which no one of whatever creed disputes, that Christ has been, and is still, the Soul of Christendom, and that to His life we go back to recover our ideal of what Christianity is—that wherever we meet any good thought or deed, any suffering or want to be relieved in any part of the world, there we touch a hand that is vanished ; there we hear a voice that is still. It is the hand, it is the voice, of our Redeemer. Other teachers, other founders of religions, have cared that their names should be honoured and remembered. He cared not for this, if only Himself, His spirit, His works, survived—if to the poor, the suffering, the good everywhere, were paid the tenderness, the honour due to Him. In their happiness He is blessed, in their honour He is honoured, and in their reception He is received. It is the last triumph of Divine unselfishness, and it is its last and greatest reward. For thus He lives again in His members and they live in Him. Even those who have most questioned and most doubted acknowledge that ' He is a thousand times more living, a thousand times more loved, than He was in His short passage through life,' that ' He presides still day by day over the destiny of the world. He started us on a new direction, and in that direction we still move.'[1]

It used to be said in the wars between the Moors and the Spaniards that a perfect character would be the man who had

---

[1] Renan, *Vie de Jésus*, p. 421.

the virtues of the Mussulman and the creed of the Christian.
But this is exactly reversing our Lord's doctrine.  If the
virtues of the Arabs were greater than the virtues of the
Spaniards, then, whether they accepted Christ in word or not,
it was they who were the true believers, and it was the
Christians who were the infidels.

When the Norman bishops asked Anselm whether Alfege,
who was killed by the Danes at Greenwich, could be called
a martyr, having died not on behalf of the faith of Christ,
but only to prevent the levying of an unjust tax, Anselm
answered—'He was a martyr, because he died for justice ;
justice is the essence of Christ, even although His name is
not mentioned.'  The Norman prelates, so far as their complaint went, were unbelievers in the true nature of Christ.
Anselm was a profound believer, just as Alfege was an illustrious martyr.  When Bishop Pearson in his work on the
Creed vindicates the Divinity of Christ without the slightest
mention of any of those moral qualities by which He has
bowed down the world before Him, his grasp on the doctrine
is far feebler than that of Rousseau or Mill, who have seized
the very attributes which constitute the marrow and essence
of His nature.  When Commander Goodenough, on one of
the most edifying, the most inspiring, deathbeds which can
be imagined, spoke in the most heroic and saintly accents
to his sailors and friends, there were pious souls who were
deeply perplexed because he had not mentioned the name
of Jesus.  It was they who for the moment were faithless,
as it was he who was the true believer, although, except
in a language they did not understand, he had not spoken
expressly of the Saviour with whose Spirit he was so deeply
penetrated.

Such are some of the ways in which the life of Christ is
still lived on the earth.

# CHAPTER III.

## THE EUCHARIST IN THE EARLY CHURCH.

WE now pass from the original institution of the Eucharist to its continuance in the Apostolic age and in the two centuries that followed.

The change had already begun. The Paschal elements had dropped out. The lamb, the bitter herbs, the sop, the hymn had all disappeared; the idea of the last parting of friends had also vanished. Three—possibly four—examples of it are given in the first century. In the Acts the believers at Jerusalem are described as partaking of a daily meal, in their private houses, as part of their religious devotions.[1] At Corinth the same custom can still be traced as part of a meal.[2] At Troas, on the Apostle's last journey, it is again indicated in connection with the first distinct notice of the religious observance of the first day of the week.[3] On the voyage to Rome it can be discerned, though more doubtfully, in the midst of a common meal.[4] One characteristic these accounts possess in common. The earthly and the heavenly, the social and the religious, aspect of life were not yet divided asunder. The meal and the sacrament blended thus together were the complete realisation in outward form of the Apostle's words— perhaps, in fact, suggested by it—'Whether ye eat or drink, or whatsoever ye do, do all to the glory of God;' 'Whatsoever ye do, in word or deed, do all in the name of the Lord Jesus, giving thanks to God and the Father by Him.'

---

[1] Acts. ii. 42.　　[2] 1 Cor. xi. 20.　　[3] Acts xx. 7.　　[4] Acts xxvii. 35.

Perhaps the nearest likeness now existing to the union of social intercourse with religious worship is to be found in the services of the Church which of all others has been least changed in form, however much it may have altered in spirit, from ancient times—the services of the Coptic or Egyptian Church of Alexandria. There is, indeed, even less of a supper in the Coptic Eucharist than there is in that of the Western Churches; but there is more of primitive freedom and of innocent enjoyment—the worshippers coming to meet each other and talk to each other as at a family gathering—than is ever seen in any European Church.

But even in early times, even in the Apostolic age, the difficulties of bringing an ideal and an actual life together made themselves felt. As the faults of Ananias and Sapphira profaned and made impossible a community of property in Jerusalem, so the excesses and disorders of the Corinthian Christians profaned and made impossible a continuance of the primitive celebration of the Eucharist. The community of property had vanished, and so had the community of the sacrament. The time was coming when the secular and the spiritual were disentangled one from the other; the simplicity and the gladness of the primitive communion could no longer be continued, and therefore the form is altered to ease the spirit. This we shall endeavour to unravel in detail.

I. The festive character of the meal, which was its predominant character, in the first age, lasted for some time after the change of its outward detail began to take effect. In some respects it had been enhanced and emphasised by its combination with Gentile usages. It was like the dinner of a club, or, as the Greeks termed it, an *eranus*—a fraternity.

Its festive character.

This was one of the peculiar experiments of Greek social life. The clubs—sometimes called *erani*, sometimes *thiasi*—of Athens, of Rhodes, and of the Ægean isles were savings banks, insurance offices, mutual help societies. They had their devices engraven on tablets. They had their common festive meals—usually in gardens, round an altar with sacrifices. They were the centres of whatever sentiments of piety, charity, and religious morality lingered in Greek society.[5] 'A common meal is the most natural and universal way of expressing, maintaining, and as it were notifying relations of kinship. The spirit of antiquity regarded the meals of human beings as having the nature of sacred things. If, therefore, it sounds degrading to compare or connect the Christian Communion to a club dinner, it is owing to the fact that the moderns connect less dignified associations with meals than the ancients did, and that most clubs have a far less obvious dignity than the first Christian society. . . . When men of different degrees or nations received together as from the hand of God this simple repast, they were reminded in the most forcible manner of their common human wants and their common character of pensioners on the bounty of the Universal Father.'[6]

In the Communion of the first and second centuries this character of the Grecian club was evident in its very outset, for each brought, as to the common meal, his own contribution in his basket, each helped himself from the common table.[7] So we see them in the catacombs, and in a basrelief in S. Ambrogio at Milan, sitting round a semicircular table, men and women together, which so far was an infringement on the Greek custom, where the sexes were kept apart. More than once a woman presides. Two maidens appear; we can hardly tell whether they are real or allegorical, but if allegorical they would not have been introduced unless they might have been real. 'Irene, da calidam—Agape, misce mi'[8] (Peace, give me the hot water—Love, mix it for me). It was also, in connection with the dead, a likeness of the funeral feast, such as existed in pagan households, the family

---

[5] See the authorities quoted in Renan, *Les Apôtres*, pp. 352, 353.
[6] *Ecce Homo*, pp. 173, 174.
[7] This was changed before Tertullian's time (*De Corona*, 2, 3).
[8] Renan, *St. Paul*, 266.

meeting annually to a repast, in the *cellæ memoriæ*, with couches, coverlets, and dresses provided.[9]

This combination of a repast and a religious rite is already familiar by the practice of the religious world amongst the Jews. There were the meals of the priests, who, coming up from their homes in the country for the Temple service, lived together like fellows of a college, and dined at a common table, with the strictness of etiquette which became their position, always washing before sitting down, blessing the bread and wine, and uttering thanks after the close. These common meals were usually on festivals or Sabbaths.[1] The schools of the Pharisees carried out the imitation of this in their ordinary life, adding every care to preserve the likeness of a meal in the Temple. In order to avoid breaking the Sabbath by going or carrying provisions more than 2,000 cubits, they invented a plan of depositing their provisions at intervals of 2,000 cubits so as to create imaginary houses, from each of which they could lawfully go to the next. The Essenes always took their meals in common with the same object.[2]

Gradually the repast was parted from the religious act. The repast became more and more secular, the religious act more and more sacred. Already in the Apostolic age the Apostle's stern rebuke had commenced the separation. From century to century the breach widened. The two remained for a time together, but distinct, the meal immediately preceding or succeeding the sacrament. Then the ministers alone, instead of the congregation, took the charge of distributing the elements. Then by the second century the daily administration ceased, and was confined to Sundays and festivals. Then the meal came to be known by the distinct name of *agape*. Even the Apostolical description of ' the Lord's Supper ' was regarded as belonging to a

---

[9] Smith's *Dictionary of Christian Antiquities*, ' Cellæ Memoriæ,' p. 387.
[1] Derenbourg, *Palestine*, 142–401 ; Geiger, *Urschrift*, 123.
[2] Ibid. 142.

meal, altogether distinct from the sacrament. Finally the meal itself fell under suspicion. Augustine and Ambrose condemned the thing itself, as the Apostle had condemned its excesses, and in the fifth century [3] that which had been the original form of the Eucharist was forbidden as profane by the councils of Carthage and Laodicea. It was the parallel to the gradual extinction of the bath in baptism.[4]

But of this social, festive characteristic of the Eucharistic meal many vestiges long continued, and some continue still.

1. The name of the Lord's *Supper* was too closely connected with the original institution to be allowed altogether to perish. To this we will return for another reason presently. But even the other names of the ordinance have reference to the social gatherings. The word in the Eastern Church is either σύναξις (synaxis), a *coming together*, or (as in Russian) *obednia*, a feast. *Collecta* is in the Latin Church a translation of *synaxis*, and 'collect' for the prayer used in the Communion Service is probably derived from the whole service. It was 'oratio ad collectum'; then by way of abbreviation the prayer itself came to be called '*collect*.' *Communion* is a word which conveys the same import. It is *joint participation*. The word *mass* or *missa* is often derived from the accidental phrase at the end of the service. '*Ite missa* [5] *est*,' as if the heathen sacrifices had been called '*Ilicet*.' But it is at least an ingenious explanation that it is a phrase taken from the food placed on the table— *missus* [6]—or possibly from the table itself—*mensa*—and thence perpetuating itself in the old English word—'*mess*

---

[3] Renan's *St. Paul*, 262; Bingham's *Antiquities*, xv. 7.

[4] An exactly analogous process may be seen in the usage of the Church of Scotland. Originally there was no religious service at a Scottish funeral, only a meal with a grace at the dead man's house. The meal has gradually dwindled away to a glass of wine and a few morsels of biscuit ; the grace has swelled into a chapter, a prayer, a blessing, and contains the germ of the whole funeral service of the Church of England.

[5] The first certain use of the word is in Ambrose (Sermon 34).

[6] *Missus* is a 'course' (Capitolinus *in Pertinax*, c. 12 ; Lampridius *in Elagabalus*, c. 30), as in the French *mets*, *entremets*.

of pottage,' ' soldier's *mess* '[7]—and in the solemn words for feasts, as Christ*mas* for the Feast of the Nativity, Michael*mas* for the Feast of St. Michael, and the like. In that case ' the mass ' would be an example of a word which has come to convey an absolutely different, if not an exactly opposite, impression from that which it originally expressed.

2. Besides the name there are fragments of the ancient usage preserved in various Churches.

At Milan an old man and an old woman [8] bring up to the altar the pitcher and the loaves, as representing the ancient gifts of the Church.

In England the sacred elements are provided not by the minister, but by the parish.

In the East always, and in the West occasionally, there is the distribution amongst the congregation of the bread, from which the consecrated food is taken under the name of ' eulogia '—' blessed bread.' Eulogia is in fact another name for Eucharistia.

There lingered in the fifth century the practice of invoking the name of Christ whenever they drank,[9] and Gregory of Tours describes the act of eating and drinking together as a kind of sacred pledge or benediction.[1]

The order in the Church of England and in the Roman basilicas is that the priest is not to communicate alone.

The practice in the Eastern and Roman Catholic Church of the priest communicating daily is a relic of the time when it was a daily event. It had been gradually restricted to the first day of the week, but traces of its continuance on other days are never altogether absent. It is now continued partly as a form, partly perhaps from a sense of its necessity. But the practice has its root in the original intention of its being the daily meal.[2]

---

[7] Crabbe Robinson, in *Archæologia*, xxvi. 242-53.

[8] Bona, *Rer. Lit.* i. 10.

[9] Greg. Naz. *Hist.* iv. 84 ; Sozomen, *Hist.* i. 17.

[1] *Hist.* vi. 5, viii. 2.

[2] This is proved from the passages cited in Freeman's *Principles of Divine Service*, i. 180-90, of which the object is to show the reverse.

II. Another part of the original idea, both as derived *Its evening character.* from the first institution and also from this festive social character, was that it was an *evening* meal. Such was evidently the case at Corinth and at Troas.

This also is still preserved in its name, 'Supper,' δεῖπνον Cœna, la *Sainte Cène, Abendmahl.* The δεῖπνον (supper) of the Greeks was especially contrasted with the ἄριστον (dinner, lunch), or midday meal, as being in the evening, usually after sunset, corresponding to the Homeric δόρπνον. The *cœna* of the Romans was not quite so late, but was certainly in the afternoon. The word 'supper' in English has never had any other meaning. Of this usage, one trace is the use of candles, lighted or unlighted. Partly it may have originated in the necessity of illuminating the darkness of the catacombs, but probably its chief origin is their introduction at the evening Eucharist. The practice of the nightly Communion lingered till the fifth century in the neighbourhood of Alexandria,[3] and in the Thebaid, and in North Africa on Maundy Thursday; but as a general rule it was changed in the second century to an early hour in the morning,[4] perhaps to avoid possible scandals— and thus what had been an accidental deviation from the original intention has become a sacred regulation, which by some Christians is regarded as absolutely inviolable.[5]

III. The posture of the guests at the sacred meal must have been kneeling, standing, sitting, or recumbent. Of *The posture.* these four positions no single Church practises that which certainly was the original one. It is quite certain that at the original institution, the couches or divans were spread round the upper chamber, as in all Eastern—it may

[3] Cyprian, *Ep.* 63; Socrates, v. 22; Sozomen, iv. 22; Augustine, *Ep.* 118.
[4] Plin. *Ep.* x. 97; *Const. Apost.* ii. 39; Tertullian, *De Fugâ in Pers.* 14; *De Cor.* 3; *Minutius Felix*, 8. There were still nocturnal masses till the time of Pius V. (Bona, i. 211).
[5] It is a curious fact that the practice of 'evening communions' in the Church of England is said to have been originated by the High Church party, to whom it has now become the most offensive of all deviations from the ordinary usage. (*Evangelicals and Evening Communion. An Address to the Inhabitants of Dover* p. 3.)

be said, in all Roman houses; and on these the guests lay reclined, three on each couch. This posture, which probably
continued throughout the Apostolic age, is now observed nowhere.[6] Even the famous pictures which bring it before us
have almost all shrunk from the ancient reality. They dare
not be so bold as the truth. One painter only—Poussin—
has ventured to delineate the event as it actually occurred.[7]

The next posture is sitting, and is the nearest approach
in spirit, though not in form, to the original practice
of reclining. It has since disappeared everywhere with
two exceptions. The Presbyterian Churches receive the
Communion sitting, by way of return to the old practice.
The Pope for many centuries also received it sitting, probably
by way of direct continuation from ancient times. It is disputed whether he does so now. It would seem that about
the fifteenth century he exchanged the posture for one half
sitting, half standing, just as in the procession of Corpus
Christi he adopts a posture in which he seems to kneel but
really sits.[8]

The next posture is that which indicates the transition
from the social meal to the religious ordinance. It is the
attitude of standing, which throughout the East, as in the
Apostolic and Jewish Church, is the usual posture of prayer.
This is preserved in the Western Church only in the attitude
of the celebrating priest, who in the Roman Catholic Church
remains standing. Whether in the English Church the
rubric enjoins the clergyman to stand or to kneel while receiving has been much disputed. If the former, it is then in
conformity with the ancient usage of the Roman Church; if
the latter, it is in conformity with modern usage.

The fourth is the posture of kneeling. This, which prevails amongst all members of the English Church, and
amongst lay members of the Roman Catholic Church, is the

---

[6] The words ἀνεκεῖτο—ἀνακειμένων—ἀνέπεσε (Matt. xxvi. 4; Mark xiv.
13; Luke xxii. 14; John xiii. 23, 28) are decisive.

[7] There is also a quite modern representation of the same kind in the
altarpiece of a church in Darlington.

[8] The question is discussed at length in the chapter on *the Pope*.

most modern of all. It expresses reverence, in the most suitable way for Western Christians; but all trace of the original, festive, Oriental character of the ordinance is altogether superseded by it.

We now come to the sacred elements.

IV. The lamb, the bitter herbs of the first Paschal feast, if they were retained at all in the Apostolic times, soon disappeared. It was not on these, but on the homely, universal elements of the bread and wine that the First Founder of the ordinance laid the whole stress.

The original bread of the original institution was not a loaf, but the Paschal cake—a large round thin biscuit, such as may be seen every Easter in Jewish houses. 'He *broke* the bread,' 'the *breaking* of bread,' is far more suitable to this than to a loaf. Of this form the trace remains reduced to the smallest particle, in the wafer [9] as used in the Roman and Lutheran Churches. It may be doubted, however, whether they took it direct from the Paschal cake—first, because the Greek Churches, which are more tenacious of ancient usages than the Latin, have not done so ; secondly, because the round form is sufficiently accounted for by the fact that the bread as used by the ancient world (as seen in the bakers' shops at Pompeii and also in the paintings of the catacombs) was in the shape of round flat cakes. It is also alleged (though this is doubtful) that the common bread of the poor in early times was in the West unleavened, whereas

The bread.

---

[9] A long argument was maintained in an English newspaper to repudiate the validity of the Roman Sacrament, on the ground that its wafers were made not of bread, but of paste  A curious example of an adventitious sacredness attaching itself to a particular form of Sacramental bread is to be found in the use of 'shortbread,' instead of the ordinary leavened or unleavened bread, amongst the 'hill men' of Scotland. 'I myself,' writes a well-informed minister of the Church of Scotland, 'thirty years ago assisted at an open air Communion in the parish of Dalry, in Galloway, where this had been the custom from time immemorial. The minister's wife sent so many pounds of fresh butter to a distant baker, and received back, preparatory to the Communion, so many cakes of "shortbread," *i.e.* brittle bread, which was kept nearly as carefully as a Roman Catholic would keep his wafer.'

in the East it was leavened.  There are some parts of the
Greek Church where the use of leavened bread is justified
by the assertion that they have an actual piece of the very
loaf used at the Last Supper, and that it is leavened.[1]

This peculiarity of form is an illustration of two general
principles.  First, it is evident that the Roman and Lutheran
Churches, by adhering to the literal form of the old institution, have lost its meaning; and the Reformed Churches,
whilst certainly departing from the original form, have preserved the meaning.  The bread of common life, which was
in the first three centuries represented by the thin unleavened
cake, is now represented by the ordinary loaf.  The mystical
fancy of the Middle Ages which attached to the wafer is in
fact founded on that which was once the most ordinary form
of food.  Secondly, the fierce controversy which broke out
afterwards between the Greek and Latin Churches, on the
question whether the bread should be leavened or unleavened,
arose, in the first instance, out of the most trivial divergence
of an usage of ordinary life.

The *wine* in the original institution was (as we know from
the Paschal Supper) arranged in two, three, or sometimes
four cups, or rather bowls.  In the bowl was the
wine of Palestine mixed with water.  The water is    The wine.
not expressly mentioned either in the account of the original
institution or in the earliest accounts of the primitive Communion; but it was beyond question there, in accordance with
the universal practice of the ancient world.  To drink wine[2]
without water was like drinking pure brandy now.  The
name for a drinking goblet was κρατήρ, which means a
'mixing' vessel.  To this day wine in modern Greek is
called κρασί, 'the mixed.'

The deviations from the original use of the cup are
instructive from their variety.  Not a single Church now

---

[1] Pashley's *Crete*, i, 316.

[2] Thus in the Syro-Jacobitic liturgy (see Neale's *Translations of Primitive
Liturgies*, pp. 202, 223) it is said He 'temperately and moderately' mingled
the wine and water.  It is also mentioned in Justin Martyr, *Apol.* c. 67.

communicates in the form in which it was originally given. The Reformed Churches, on the same principle as that on which they have adopted a common loaf instead of a thin wafer, have dropped the water. The Greek Churches have mixed the bread with the wine. The Roman Churches have dropped the use of the cup altogether except for the officiating priest. It was an innovation which spread slowly, and which but for the Reformation would have become universal, except in a few curious instances in which the original practice continued. The King of France always took the cup. The Bohemians[3] extorted the use of it from the Pope. The laity in England were long conciliated by having unconsecrated wine. The Abbot of Westminster always administered it to the King and Queen at the coronation. And in the three northern churches[4] of Jarrow, Monkwearmouth, and Norham it was given till 1515.[5]

There remains one other usage, more doubtful perhaps but exceedingly interesting, and from which the variation has been of the same kind as those we have noticed.

The fish.

In ancient times a meal, even of bread, was not thought complete without fish ($ὄψον$) whenever it could be had. ' Bread and fish ' went together like ' bread and cheese ' or ' bread and butter ' in England, or (as we have just observed) like ' wine and water ' in the old classical world. Meat was the exception and fish[6] the rule. And accordingly, if not in the original institution of the Last Supper, yet in those indications of the first continuation of it which are contained in the last chapters of St. Luke and St. John, fish is always mentioned with bread as part of the sacred meal. In the local traditions of the Roman peasants—many of them no doubt mere plays of fancy, yet some probably imbued with the continuous traditions of antiquity—it is said that when Jesus Christ

---

[3] Two chalices remain in one of the Bohemian churches, which were carried at the head of the Hussite armies.

[4] Blunt's *Reformation*, p. 34.

[5] The Wesleyans in the Sandwich Islands celebrated the Eucharist with treacle instead of wine—there being no vines—and were opposed by the Quakers on principle. I owe this to the late Count Strelecski.

[6] Becker's *Charicles*, 323, 324.

came to the house of an old woman and asked for food, she answered, 'There is a little fish' (it was a little fish, 'that is not so long as my hand,' said the peasant) 'and some crusts of bread which they gave me at the eating-house for charity, and this flask of wine and water which they gave me there.' [7] Further, the early representations of the Sacred Supper (whether we call it Eucharist or Agape) which appear in the catacombs, almost always include *fishes*—sometimes placed on the cakes of bread, sometimes on a platter by themselves. It is almost impossible to resist the inference which has been drawn, that this too was part of the primitive celebration. It was a part which would be doubly cherished—a recollection not only of the upper chamber of Jerusalem, but of the still more sacred shores of the Lake of Gennesareth. [8] There was in the Middle Ages a fish called 'the Paschal pickerel,' from the tradition that the Lord had in the Last Supper substituted a fish for the Paschal lamb. [9] In the Cathedral of Salerno there is a picture of the Last Supper (in the sacristy) with a fish. It disappeared from the Christian monuments altogether at the end of the fifth century, and is common only in the second and third. It has now entirely vanished, and the recollection of it has been obliterated by the symbolism to which it has given birth. Just as the ordinary form of the cake furnished occasion for the fanciful interpretation that it was the likeness of the thirty pieces for which the Betrayal was made, and the water and wine (the ordinary mode of drinking wine) were made to symbolise the water and the blood, or the double nature, or the two Testaments, so the fish was in the fourth century interpreted by a curious acrostic to be our Lord Himself—Ἰησοῦς Χριστὸς Θεοῦ Υἱὸς Σωτήρ. [1] This interpretation, which first appears [2]

---

[7] Busk's *Folk Lore of Rome*, 174.

[8] Renan, *Vie de Jésus*, 303.

[9] Gunton's *History of Peterborough*, p. 337.

[1] Northcote, 210–15.

[2] Wharton Marriott's *Essay on the Fish of Autun.* (*Inscriptions of the Catacombs*, pp. 120–126.) It was used as a symbol for Christ, as the sacred food by Mellito and Tertullian, but not in the acrostic form.

in Optatus of Milevis (A.D. 384), was not known in earlier times, and was very imperfectly recognised even by Augustine. The fish itself, if as we may suppose it formed part of the original and primitive ordinance, is one of those particulars of sacred antiquity which are gone beyond recall. Not a trace of it exists in the New Testament. It is gone from all celebrations of the Eucharist, as the water from the wine in Protestant celebrations, as the wine from the bread in Roman administrations.

V. One more trace of the social festive character of the original ordinance was the *table*. To the question whether it was ever called an altar in those ages we will return presently. But there is no doubt that it was always of wood, and that the *mensa* or *τράπεζα* was its ordinary name. In the representations in the catacombs, it is as if a circular table.[3] In the earliest forms of churches, whether as in the small chapels in the catacombs, or as in the great basilicas of Rome, or in the Eastern churches, it stood and stands in front of the apse. This in Western churches was superseded in later times by stone structures fastened to the east end of the church. But in the Protestant churches, both Reformed and Lutheran, the wooden structure and the detached position were retained, and in the English and Scottish Churches, both Episcopal and Presbyterian, wooden tables were brought at the time of the Holy Communion into the middle of the church. There was only this difference in their position from that in the primitive Church, that in the English Church they were placed lengthwise, the officiating minister standing in the middle of the side facing the people. On this arrangement all the rubrics are founded, and, curiously enough, were not altered, when after Laud's time the position of the table was again brought back to what it had been before the Reformation. Deerhurst Church in Gloucestershire alone retains for it the position which was given in the time of Edward VI.[4]

The table.

---

[3] See the various authorities quoted in Renan's *St. Paul*, 266.

[4] The table generally was placed in the centre of the apse in 1603, and it continued east and west till 1846. Its orientation was then changed,

Thus while the position of the Holy Table in England is now conformable to the mediæval practice of the Latin Church, the rubric which speaks of 'the north side,' which is no longer capable of being observed, remains the sole relic in the English service of the conformity with which it was intended to be brought with the primitive usage.

VI. We have now reached the last trace of the social, and, as it may be called, secular character of the primitive Eucharist. We pass to the forms by which, no doubt from the first, but increasingly as time rolled on, the religious or sacred character with which it had been invested was brought out into words; and in doing so we are at once brought into the presence of all that we know of the early Christian worship. The Liturgy, properly speaking, was the celebration of the Holy Communion. The worship of the early Christians gathered round this as the nucleus. We must picture to ourselves the scene according to the arrangement which has been clearly described. The Bishop, or Presiding Minister, as he is called by Justin Martyr, is on his lofty seat behind the table, overlooking it, facing the congregation who stand on the other side of it in front of him. The other ministers, if there were any—probably Deacons—sat or stood in a semicircle immediately beneath and around him. This position is now almost entirely lost. The Pope to a certain degree keeps it up, as he always, in celebrating mass, stands behind the altar, facing the people. The arrangements of ancient churches, like that of Torcello at Venice, though long disused, are proofs of the ancient custom. The nearest likeness is to be seen in the Scottish Presbyterian Church, where the minister, from his lofty pulpit behind the table, addresses the congregation, with his elders beneath him on the pulpit stairs, or round its base. It also appears in the original position of the episcopal throne at Norwich. The dress of the bishop and clergy who are to officiate, except by mere accident, in no way distinguishes them from the congregation in front of them.[5]

but its general position remains. The same was the case in Taynton Church till 1826.

[5] See the case, as discussed by Cardinal Bona, and the futility of the

The prayers are uttered throughout standing, and with outstretched hands. The posture of devotion was standing, as is the universal practice in the East. The outstretched hands are open in Mussulman devotions, as also in the catacombs. They express the hope of receiving into them the blessings from above. Of the outstretched hands a reminiscence was very long present in the benediction—*manibus extensis* [6]—of the priest. As in other cases, so here, when the original meaning was lost, this simple posture was mystically explained as the extension of the hands of Christ on the cross.[7]

Of this standing posture of the congregation which still prevails throughout the East, all traces have disappeared in the Western Church, except in the attitude of the officiating minister at the Eucharist, and always in the worship of the Presbyterian Churches till recently. Its extinction is the more remarkable because it was enjoined by the only canon of the Council of Nicæa, which related to public worship, and which ordered that on every Sunday (whatever licence might be permitted on other days) and on every day between Easter and Pentecost, kneeling should be forbidden and standing enjoined. In the controversy between the Church and the Puritans in the seventeenth century, there was a vehement contention whether kneeling at the Sacrament should be permitted. It was the point on which the Church most passionately insisted, and which the Puritans most passionately resisted. The Church party in this were resisting the usage of ancient Catholic Christendom, and disobeying the Canon of the First Œcumenical Council, to which they professed the most complete adhesion. The Puritans, who rejected the authority of either, were in the most entire conformity with both.

VII. Another element of the worship was the reading of the Scriptures. This has continued in most Christian Churches, but in none can it be said to occupy the same solemn promi-

arguments by which he endeavours to refute the mass of authority on the other side. See Chapter VIII.

[6] Maskell, p. 79. The last trace of it in England is in the Life of St. Dunstan.

[7] Ibid.

nence as in early times, when it was a continuation of the tradition of reading the Law and the Prophets in the Jewish synagogues.    A trace of this is visible in the *ambones*— the magnificent reading-desks of the early Roman churches, from which the Gospel and Epistle were read.    Long were these preserved in Italian churches after the use of them had been discontinued.    Nothing can be more splendid than the ambones in the church at Ravello near Amalfi, which though long deserted remain a witness to the predominant importance attributed in ancient times to the reading of the Bible in the public service.    In the French Church the very name of the lofty screens which parted the nave from the choir bears testimony to the same principle.    They were called *Jubé*, from the opening words of the introduction of the Gospel, *Jube, Domine*.    Those that still exist, like that at Troyes, and also in the King's College Chapel at Aberdeen,[1] by their stately height and broad platforms, show how imposing must have been this part of the service, now so humiliated and neglected.    Few such now remain.    The passion for revolutionary equality on one side and ecclesiastical uniformity on the other have done their worst.    They have either disappeared altogether, or are never used for their original purpose.

In England the huge reading-desk or ' pew ' long supplied the place of the old ambo, but that is now being gradually swept away, and there only remains the lectern, in modern times reduced to so small a dimension as to be almost invisible.

The Prophets of the Old Testament, the Epistles of the New—chiefly St. Paul's—were read from the lower step of the staircase leading up to the ambo.    In some churches the Gospel of Thomas and the first Epistle of Clement were added.    The Gospel was from one of the four Gospels, and was read from the upper step, or sometimes from a separate ambo.    Selections from the Scriptures were not fixed; each reader chose them at his discretion.    There is an instance in France as late as the fifth century of their being chosen

<hr>

[1] At Rheims, the Kings of France were crowned upon the screen, so as to be visible at once to those in the choir and those in the nave.

by opening the book at hazard. The reader was usually the deacon or subdeacon; not, as with us, the chief clergyman present. Of this a trace remains in the English Church, especially in the Channel Islands, where laymen may read the lessons. The reader of the Gospel if possible faced, not as with us to the west, but to the south, because the men sate [9] on the south, and it was a fine idea that in a manly religion like Christianity the Gospel belonged especially to them.

VIII. Then came the address, sometimes preached from one of the ambones, but more usually from the Bishop's seat behind the table. It was called a ' Homily ' or ' Ser-

The Homily.

mon '—that is, a conversation; not a speech or set discourse, but a talk, a homely colloquial instruction. The idea is still kept up in the French word *conference*. It is not possible that the sermon or homily should ever return to its original meaning. But it is well for us to remember what that meaning was. It was the talking, the conversation, of one Christian man with another: the practical address, as Justin Martyr says, exhorting the people to the imitation of the good things that they have just had read to them from the Bible; the mutual instruction which is implied in animated discussion. It is, in short, the very reverse of what is usually meant by a ' homily.'

Thus far any one might attend at the worship. In the Christian Church of the early times, before infant baptism had become common, a large part of the congregation consisted of unbaptised persons, and when the time for the more sacred part of the service came, they were warned off. There is a part of the service of the Eastern Church when the deacon comes forward and says, ' The doors, the doors!' meaning that all who are not Christians are to go away and the doors are to be shut. But now they do not go away, and the doors—at least, the doors of the church—are not shut.

IX. The more solemn service opened with a practice which belongs to the childlike joyous innocence of the early ages,

The kiss.

and which as such was upheld as absolutely essential to the Christian worship, but which now has, with one

* *Ordo Rom.* ii. 8 (see *Dictionary of Antiquities*).

exception, disappeared from the West, and with two exceptions
from the East.  It was the *kiss of peace*.  Justin mentions it as
the universal mode of opening the service.  It came down direct
from the Apostolic time.[1]  Sometimes the men kissed the
men, the women the women; sometimes it was without
distinction.  But it was thought so essential that to
abstain from it was a mark of mourning or excessive
austerity.  In the West this primitive practice now exists
only in the small Scottish sect of the Glassites or Sande-
manians.  In the Latin Church, it was continued till the end
of the thirteenth century, and was then transferred to the close
of the service.  In its place was then substituted a piece of
the altar furniture called a *Pax*, and this was given to the
deacon with the words, ' *Pax tibi*[2] *et ecclesiæ*.'  This is a singular instance of the introduction of a purely mechanical and
mediæval contrivance instead of a living social observance.[3]
The only trace of it remaining in the English service is the
final benediction, which begins with the words ' The peace of
God.'  In the Eastern Church it still remains to some extent.
In the Russian Church, perhaps in other Eastern churches,
the clergy kiss each other during the recital of the Nicene
Creed, to show that charity and orthodoxy should always go
together, not, as is too often the case, parted asunder.  In
the Coptic Church, the most primitive and conservative of all
Christian Churches, it still continues in full force.  Travellers
now living have had their faces stroked, and been kissed by
the Coptic priest, in the cathedral at Cairo, whilst at the same
moment everybody else was kissing everybody throughout the
church.  Had any primitive Christians been told that the time
would come when this, the very sign of Christian brotherhood
and sisterhood, would be absolutely proscribed in the Christian
Church, they would have thought that this must be the result of unprecedented persecution or unprecedented unbelief.

[1] 1 Thess. v. 26; 1 Cor. xvi. 20; 2 Cor. xiii. 12; Rom. xvi. 16; 1 Pet.
v. 14.

[2] See Renan's *St. Paul*, 262.

[3] Maskell, 116.  The importance of the 'kiss' as a token of reconcilia-
tion is illustrated by the importance attached in the contention between
Henry II. and Becket to the question whether ' the kiss ' had fairly been given.

It is impossible to imagine the omission of any act more sacred, more significant, more necessary (according to the view which then prevailed) to the edification of the service.

X. Then came the offering of the bread and wine by the people. It was, as we have seen, the memorial of the ancient practice of the contribution of the Christian com- munity towards a common meal. The prayer in which this was offered was in fact the centre of the whole service. This is a point at which we first come into contact with the germ of a fixed Liturgy.[4] It has been often main- tained that there are still existing forms which have come down to us from the first century, and even that the Liturgies which go under the names of St. James, St. Clement, and St. Mark were written by them. There are two fatal objections to this hypothesis. The first is the positive statement[5] of St. Basil that there was no written authority for any of the Liturgical forms of the Church in his time. The second is the fact that whilst there is a general resemblance in the ancient Liturgies to the forms known to exist in early times, there are such material variations from those forms as to render it impossible to suppose that the exact representatives of them anywhere exist. This will appear as we proceed, and therefore we shall only notice the details of the Liturgies so far as they contain the relics of the earlier state of things, or illustrate the changes which have brought us to the present state of Liturgical observances.

*The Liturgy.*

[4] An argument often used to account for the absence of written litur- gies is the doctrine of 'reserve,' an argument which has been even pushed to the extent of thus accounting for the absence of any detailed account of the Sacrament in the New Testament or in the early Creeds. (Maskell, Preface to the *Ancient Liturgy*, pp. xxviii.-xxxi.) It is evident that the same feeling, if it operated at all, would have prevented such descrip- tions as are given by Justin, in a work avowedly intended for the outside world.

[5] *De Spiritu Sancto*, c. 27. The passage is quoted at length in Maskell (Pref. p. xxvi.) with the opinions strongly expressed to the same effect, of Renaudot and Lebrun, and the confirmatory argument that had written liturgies existed they would have been discoverable in the time of the Diocletian persecution. 'There are no Liturgies,' says Lebrun, 'earlier than the fifth century' (iii. 1-17),

The Prayer was said by the Bishop or Chief Presbyter, as best he could—that is, as it would seem, not read, but spoken.[6]  It is thus the first sanction of extempore prayer in the public service of the Church.  But extempore prayer always tends to become fixed or liturgical.  If we hear the usual Prayers in the Church of Scotland, they are sure to retain on the whole the same ideas, and often the very same words.  Thus it was in the early Church, and thus a Liturgy arose.

There was one long prayer, of which the likenesses are preserved in the long prayers before or after the sermon in Presbyterian or Nonconformist churches, the Bidding Prayer and the Prayer of Consecration in the Church of England.  The main difference is that in the early Church this prayer was all on one occasion, namely, at the time of the consecration of the elements; in the Roman and in the English Prayer Book it is, as it were, scattered through the service.

In this prayer there are two peculiarities which belong to the ancient Church, and have since not been brought forward prominently in any Church.  It is best seen in the Roman Missal, which incorporates here, as elsewhere, passages quite inconsistent with the later forms with which it has been incrusted.

It is clear, from the Missal, that the priest officiates as one of the people, and as the representative of the people, seeing that throughout the Office of the Mass he associates the people with himself as concerned equally with himself in every prayer that he offers and every act that he performs.  Just as he unites the people's prayers with his own by the use of the plural forms, ' *We* pray,' ' *We* beseech Thee,' instead of the singular, so in the most solemn acts of the Eucharist, after the consecration of the elements as well as before, he uses the plural form, ' *We* offer,' that is, we, priest and people, offer ; thereby including the people with himself in the act of sacrificing.  And this is made still more clear

<hr>

[6] Justin, *Apol.* c. 67.

when he is told to say, 'We beseech Thee that Thou wouldest graciously accept this offering of Thy whole family, and also we Thy servants and also Thy holy people offer to Thy glorious Majesty a pure sacrifice.' And not only so, but the attention of the people is called to it as a fact which it is desirable they should not be allowed to forget. Addressing the people the priest says, 'All you, both brethren and sisters, pray that my sacrifice and your sacrifice, which is equally yours as well as mine, may be meet for the Lord.' And so in the intercessory prayer of oblation for the living the language which the priest uses carefully shows that the sacrificial act is not his but theirs. 'Remember,' he says, ' Thy servants and Thy handmaids, and all who stand around, and who offer to Thee this sacrifice of praise for themselves and for all their relations.'

But there is the further question of what is the chief offering which is presented. The offering which is presented is, throughout, one of two things ; first the sacrifice of praise and thanksgiving, as in the words which we have already quoted, or secondly, the gifts of the fruits of the earth, especially the bread and wine, which are brought in, and which are expressly called ' a holy sacrifice,' and ' the immaculate host.' Every term which is applied to the elements after consecration is distinctly and freely applied to them before. What is done by the consecration in the Missal is the prayer that these natural elements of the earth may be transformed to our spiritual use by the blessing of God upon them. It is necessary to observe that the sacrifice offered, whether in the early Church or in the original Roman Missal, was either of praise and thanksgiving, which we in modern times still offer, both clergy and people, or else of the natural fruits of the earth, which we do still indeed offer in name, but of which the full idea and meaning has so much passed out of the minds of all Christians in modern days, that we seldom think of it. It is one of the differences between the early Church and our own, which it is impossible to recover, but which it is necessary to bear in mind, both because the idea was in itself exceedingly beautiful, and because it does not connect itself in the least degree with any of our modern controversies.[7]

The ancient form expresses in the strongest manner the goodness of God in Nature. It is we might almost say a worship—or more properly, an actual enjoyment and thankful recognition— of the gifts of Creation. So completely was this felt in the early times, that a custom prevailed, which as time went on was checked by the increasing rigidity of ecclesiastical rules, that not only bread and wine,[8] but honey, milk, strong drink, and birds were offered on the altar; and even after these were forbidden, ears of corn and grapes were allowed, and other fruits, though not offered on the altars, were given to the Bishops and presbyters.

All this appears in unmistakable force both in the heathen and the Jewish worship, and from them it overflowed into the Christian, and received there an additional life, from the tendency which, as we have seen, runs through the whole of these early forms to identify the sacred and profane, to elevate the profane by making it sacred, and to realise the sacred by making it common. It lingers in a few words in the English Prayer for the Church Militant, 'the oblations which we offer,' and in the expression 'It is very meet and right to give thanks.' It included the recollection of, and the prayers for, the main objects of human interest—the Emperor, the army, their friends dead and living, the rain, the springs and wells so dear in Eastern countries, the rising of the Nile so dear in Egypt, the floods to be deprecated at Constantinople. The whole of their common life was made to pass before them. Nothing was ' common or unclean ' to them at that moment. They gave thanks for it, they hoped that it might be blessed and continued to them.[9]

There is a representation in the catacombs of a man and

---

[7] *The Mass disowned by the Missal.* A very able and exhaustive paper in the *Madras Times* by Bishop Caldwell, Oct. 1867.

[8] *Apostolical Canons*, 2.

[9] See Bunsen, *Christianity and Mankind*, vii. 24.

a woman joining in the offering of bread.  The woman, it is sometimes said, is the Church; but if so this confirms the same idea.  The bread and wine are still in, England, as above noticed, the gifts not of the minister, but of the parish, and this offering by the congregation, which prevailed in the Catholic countries of Europe generally till the tenth century, lingered on in some French abbeys till the eighteenth.  It is this offering of the fruits of the earth to which Cyprian [1] and Irenæus [2] give the name of 'sacrifice.'  It is probable that the tenacity with which this word clung to these outward elements in the early ages was occasioned by the eagerness to claim for Christian worship something which resembled the old animal and vegetable sacrifices of Judaism and heathenism, and that its comparative disappearance from all Christian worship in later times in like manner was coincident with the disappearance of the temples and altars alike of Palestine and of Italy.

This offering formed the main bulk of the prayer.  Then followed what in modern times would be called 'the consecration.'  The earlier accounts of the Liturgy, The Lord's Prayer. whether in Justin or Irenæus, agree in the statement that after the completion of the offering followed an invocation to the Spirit of God 'to make the bread and wine the body and blood of Christ.'  But in what did it consist?  Here again seems to be disclosed a divergence of which very slight traces remain in any celebrations of the Eucharist, whether Protestant or Catholic.  It is at least probable that it consisted of nothing else than the Lord's Prayer.  This was the immense importance of the Lord's Prayer; not as with us, repeated many times over, but reserved for this one prominent place.  The first Eucharistic prayer was amplified more or less according to the capacities of the minister.

---

[1] Cyprian, *De Op.* p. 203, ed. Tell. (Palmer's *Antiquities*, ii. 86).

[2] See the Pfaffian fragment of Irenæus quoted in Arnold's *Fragments on the Church*, p. 129; and this, with all the other passages from Irenæus bearing on the question in Bunsen's *Christianity and Mankind*, ii. 424-29.

The Lord's Prayer was the one fixed formula. It was in fact
the whole 'liturgy' properly so called. 'The change'—
whatever it were that he meant by it—'the change of the
bread and wine into the body and blood of Christ,' says
Justin, 'is by the Word of Prayer which comes from Him.'[3]
'It was the custom,' says Gregory the First, 'of the Apostles
to consecrate the oblation only by the Lord's Prayer.' There
is a trace of its accommodation to this purpose of giving a
moral and spiritual purport to the natural gifts in the variation recorded by Tertullian, where,[4] instead of 'Thy kingdom
come,' it is 'May Thy Holy Spirit come upon us and purify
us.' It is also obvious that 'Give us this day our daily
bread' would thus contain a peculiar significance. 'Lead us
not into temptation, but deliver us from evil,' had also a
peculiar stress laid upon it.[5] It also lingers in the Consecration Prayer of the Eastern Church, where the petition
for the coming of the Spirit is amplified, and made the chief
point in the consecration. In the East the whole congregation joined in the Lord's Prayer,[6] and thus participated
in the consecration. In the Coptic Church, accordingly, the
Lord's Prayer is the only part of the service which is recited
in Arabic—the vulgar tongue.[7] In the Russian Church it is
sung by the choir, and of all the impressive effects produced
by the magnificent swell of human voices in the Imperial
Chapel of the Winter Palace at St. Petersburg, none is
greater than that of the recitation of the Lord's Prayer by the
choir without, while the consecration goes forward within. In

[3] Compare Justin, *Apol.* 66; Jerome, *Adv. Pelag.* 3: 'Apostolos quotidie
Orationem Domini solitos dicere.' (Maskell, Pref. p. xxxviii.) See also
Ambrosiaster, *De Sacramentis,* iv. 4: 'consecrated by the words of Christ.'
Bunsen vii. 15, 55; ii. 177. See Chapter XIV.

[4] *Adv. Marcion,* iv. 21.

[5] Cardinal Bona (*Rer. Lit.* i. 5) and Mr. Maskell (Preface, pp. xx.-xxii.)
endeavour to attenuate the force of this passage by quoting passages from
Walafridus Strabo and later writers, and by their own conjectures, that 'at
least the words of the institution were also recited.' But of this there is
not a trace, either in Gregory or Justin. Bunsen, vii. 121.

[6] Bunsen, vii. 280.

[7] Renaudot, *Lit. Or.* i. 262.

the Mozarabic Liturgy the people said Amen to every clause except the fourth, where they said, *Quia es Deus*.[8] In the West the priest alone recited it. But both in the East and the West the consecration was not complete till it had been ratified in the most solemn way by the congregation. For it was at this point that there came, like the peal of thunder, the one word which has lasted through all changes and all Liturgies—the word which was intended to express the entire, truthful assent of the people to what was done and said—Amen.

Then came forward the deacons and gave the bread, the water, and the wine to all who were present, and then to those who were absent. The latter half of the practice has perished everywhere. For what is called the ' reservation,' or even taking the sacramental elements to the occasional sick, is evidently a totally different practice from that of enabling the absent members of the community to join in the ordinance itself.

These are the original elements of the Christian Liturgy. The Lord's Prayer, which was thus once conspicuous, has lost its place. In the Roman Church, as well as the Eastern, in spite of the efforts of Gregory the Great, it now follows the Prayer of Consecration.[9] In the Clementine Liturgy it is omitted altogether.[1] In the first English Liturgy of Edward VI., as in that introduced by Laud into Scotland, it occurs after the Prayer of Consecration, but still before the administration. In the present Liturgy it is separated from the Consecration Prayer altogether; though on the other hand, as if to give it more dignity, it is twice repeated.

The sacramental words have passed through three stages —first, the Lord's Prayer; then in the East, the Prayer of Invocation; then in the West, the words of institution.[2]

---

[8] *Les Anciennes Liturgies*, p. 671.

[9] Neale, *Introd.* 570, 622.

[1] See the long and strange arguments to account for this in Palmer, i. 40, and Maskell, Pref. xxxviii.

[2] The Western Church has not used a Prayer of Invocation for a thousand years. How exclusively Western is the notion that the words of

There is a spiritual meaning in each of these three forms. The original form of the Lord's Prayer was the most spiritual of all. The Western form, though excellent as bringing out the commemorative character of the Sacrament, is perhaps the most liable to fall into a mechanical observance. This has been reached in the fullest degree, in the opinion which has been entertained in the Roman Church that the words must be recited by the priest secretly, lest laymen overhearing them should indiscreetly repeat them over ordinary bread and wine, and thus inadvertently transform them into celestial substances. Such an incident, it was believed, had actually taken place in the case of some shepherds who thus changed their bread and wine in a field into flesh and blood, and were struck dead by a divine judgment.[3]

This is the summary of the celebration of the early Sacrament, so far as we can attach it to the framework furnished by Justin. But there are a few fragments of ancient worship, which, though we cannot exactly adjust their place, partly belong to the second century. Some have perished, and some continue. In the morning was an antistrophic hymn (perhaps the germ of the 'Te Deum') to Christ[4] as God, and also the sixty-third Psalm. In the evening there was the hundred and forty-first Psalm.[5] The evening hymn on bringing in the candles, as now in Mussulman countries, is a touching reminiscence of the custom in the Eastern Church. The 'Sursum corda' ('Lift up your hearts') and the 'Holy, holy, holy,' were parts of the hymns of which we find traces in the accounts of all the old Liturgies. The 'Gloria in excelsis' was sung at the beginning of the service. Down to the beginning of the eleventh century, it was (except on Easter Day) only said by Bishops.[6]

This survey brings before us the wide diversity and

institution have the effect of consecration is clear from the authorities quoted in Maskell, pp. cv, cvi, xcv.

[3] See the authorities quoted in Maskell, Preface, p. ciii.

[4] Pliny, *Ep.* x. 97.

[5] Bunsen, ii. 50.                [6] Maskell, p. 25.

yet unity of Christian worship. That so fragile an ordinance should have survived so many shocks, so many superstitions, so many centuries, is in itself a proof of the immense vitality of the religion which it represents—of the prophetic insight of its Founder.

# CHAPTER IV.

## THE EUCHARISTIC SACRIFICE.

IT is proposed to bring out in more detail what is meant by Sacrifice in the Christian Church. In order to do this, we must first understand what is meant by it, first in the Jewish and Pagan dispensations, and secondly in the Christian dispensation.

I. We hardly think sufficiently what was the nature of an ancient sacrifice. Let us conceive the changes which would be necessary in any modern church in order to make it fit for such a ceremony. In the midst of an open court, so that the smoke of the fire and the odours of the slain animals might go up into the air, as from the hearths of our ancient baronial or collegiate halls, stood the Altar—a huge platform —detached from all around, and with steps approaching it from behind and from before, from the right and from the left. Around this structure, as in the shambles of a great city, were collected, bleating, lowing, bellowing, the oxen, sheep, and goats, in herds and flocks, which one by one were led up to the altar, where with the rapid stroke of the sacrificer's knife, directed either by the king or priest, they received their death-wounds. Their dead carcases lay throughout the court, the pavement streaming with their blood, their quivering flesh placed on the altar to be burnt, the black columns of smoke going up to the sky, the remains afterwards consumed by the priests or worshippers who were gathered for the occasion as to an immense banquet.[1]

See an exhaustive account in Ewald's *Alterthümer*, pp. 29-84.

This was a Jewish sacrifice. This, with slight variation, was the form of heathen sacrifice also. This is still the form of sacrifice in the great Mahometan Sanctuary[2] at Mecca. This—except that the victims were not irrational animals, but human beings—was the dreadful spectacle presented in the sacred inclosure at Coomassie, in Ashantee, as it was in the Carthaginian and Phœnician temples of old time.

II. All these sacrifices, in every shape or form, have long disappeared from the religions of the civilised world. Already, under the ancient dispensation, the voices of Psalm-ist and Prophet had been lifted up against them 'Sacrifice and meat-offering Thou wouldest not;' 'Thinkest thou that I will eat bull's flesh or drink the blood of goats:' 'I delight not in the blood of bullocks, or of lambs, or of he-goats;' 'I will not accept your burnt-offerings or your meat-offerings, neither will I regard the peace-offerings of your fat beasts.'

*Substitution of new ideas.*

Has sacrifice then entirely ceased out of religious worship? And had those old sacrifices no spiritual meaning hid under their mechanical, their strange, must we not even say their revolting, forms?

In themselves they have entirely ceased. Of all the forms of ancient worship they are the most repugnant to our feelings of humane and of Divine religion. But there was in these, as in most of the ceremonies of the old world, a higher element which it has been the purpose of Christianity to bring out. In point of fact, the name of 'Sacrifice' has survived, after the form has perished.

Let us for a moment go back to the ancient sacrifices, and ask what was their object. It was, in one word, an endeavour, whether from remorse, or thankfulness, or fear, to approach the Unseen Divinity. It was an attempt to propitiate, to gratify, the Supreme Power, by giving up something dear to ourselves which was also dear to Him,—to feed, to nourish, as it were, the great God above by the same food by which we also are fed,—to send messages to Him by the smoke, the sweet-

[2] Burton's *Pilgrimage to Mecca.*

smelling odour which went up from the animals which the sacrificer had slain or caused to be slain.   The one purpose which is given after every sacrifice in the first chapters of Leviticus[3] is that it 'shall make a sweet savour unto the Lord.'

Now, in the place of this gross, earthly conception of the approach of man to God, arose gradually three totally different ideas of approaching God, which have entirely superseded the old notion of priest and altar and victim and hecatomb and holocaust and incense, and to which, because of their taking the place of those ancient ceremonies, the name of sacrifice has in some degree been always applied.

(1) The first is the elevation of the heart towards God in prayer and thanksgiving.   In the ancient Jewish and Pagan public worship, there was, properly speaking, no prayer and no praise. Whatever devotion the people expressed was only through the dumb show of roasted flesh and ascending smoke and fragrance of incense.   But the Psalmist and Prophets introduced the lofty spiritual thought, that there was something much more acceptable to the Divine nature, much more capable of penetrating the Sanctuary of the Unseen, than these outward things,—namely, the words and thoughts of the divine speech and intellect of man. To these reasonable utterances, accordingly, by a bold metaphor, the Prophets transferred the phrase which had hitherto been used for the slaughter of beasts at the altar. In the 141st Psalm, the Psalmist says, 'Let the lifting up of my hands in prayer be to Thee as the evening sacrifice ;' that is, let the simple peaceful act of prayer take the place of the blood-stained animal, struggling in the hands of a butcher.   In the 50th Psalm, after repudiating altogether the value of dead bulls and goats, the Psalmist says, ' Whosoever offereth,—whosoever brings up as a victim to God,— thankful hymns of praise, *he* it is that honoureth Me.'   In the 51st Psalm, after rejecting altogether burnt-offerings and sacrifices for sin, the Psalmist says, ' the true sacrifice of God,' far more than this, ' is a broken and contrite heart.'

Prayer and thanks-giving.

---

[3] Lev. i. 13, 27, ii. 2, 12, iii. 8, 26.

This was a mighty change, and it has gone on growing ever since. The psalms of the Psalmists, the prayers of the Prophets, took the place of the dead animals which the priests had slain. The worship of the Synagogue, which consisted only of prayer and praise, superseded the worship of the Temple, which consisted almost entirely of slaughtering and burning; and the worship of the Christian Church, which consisted also only of prayer and praise, superseded both Temple and Synagogue. As it has sometimes been said that the invention of printing inflicted a deathblow on mediæval architecture, so much more did the discovery, the revelation, of prayer and praise, kill the old institution of sacrifice.

It would have seemed strange to an old Jewish or Pagan worshipper to be told that the Deity would be more intimately approached by a word or a series of words, invisible to sense or touch, than by the tangible, material shapes of fat oxen or carefully reared sheep. Yet so it is; and however much modern thought may disparage the use of articulate prayer, yet there is no one who will not say that the marvellous faculty of expressing the various shades of mental feeling in the grandest forms of human speech is an immense advance on the irrational, inarticulate, mechanical work which made the place of worship a vast slaughter-house.

(2) Secondly, in the place of the early sacrifices, which were of no use to any one, or which were only of use as the Charitable efforts. great banquets of a civic feast, was revealed the truth that the offerings acceptable to God were those which contributed to the good of mankind. Thus the Prophet Hosea tells us that 'God will have mercy instead of sacrifice.' The Proverbs and the Book of Tobit tell us that sins are purged away, not by the blood of senseless animals, but by kindness to the poor. Beneficent, useful, generous schemes for the good of mankind are the substitutes for those useless offerings of the ancient world. And because such beneficent acts can rarely be rendered except at some cost and pain and loss to ourselves, the word 'sacrifice' has gradually been appropriated in modern language to such cost and pain and loss. 'Such

an one did such an act,' we say, 'but it was a great *sacrifice* for him.'

(3) And this leads to the third or chief truth which has sprung up in place of the ancient doctrine of sacrifices. It is that the sacrifice which God values more than any- thing else is the willing obedience of the heart to the eternal law of truth and goodness—the willing obedience, even though it cost life, and limb, and blood, and suffering, and death. The Psalmist, after saying that ' Sacrifice and offering for sin were not required,' declared that in the place thereof, ' Lo, I come to do Thy will, O my God.' The Prophets declared that to obey was better than sacrifice, and to ' hearken ' to God's laws was better than the fattest portions of rams or of oxen ; that 'to do justly and walk humbly was more than rivers of oil or ten thousands of burnt-offerings.' The sacrifice, the surrender of self, the fragrance of a holy and upright life, was the innermost access to the Divine nature, of which every outward sacrifice, however costly, was but a poor and imperfect shadow. This is the true food fit for the Holy Spirit of God, because it is the only sustaining food of the best spirit of man.

These three things then—the lifting up of the heart in words of devotion to God, the performance of kindly and useful deeds to men, and the dedication of self—are the three things by which the Supreme Goodness and Truth, according to true Religion, is pleased, propitiated, satisfied.

III. In the great exemplar and essence of Christianity, these three things are seen in perfection.

In Jesus Christ there was the complete lifting up of the soul to God in prayer, of which He was Himself the most perfect example, and of which He has given us the most perfect pattern. The Lord's Prayer is the sweet-smelling incense of all Churches and of all nations.

In Jesus Christ, who went about doing good, who lived and died for the sake of man, there was the most complete beneficence, compassion, and love.

In Jesus Christ, who lived not for Himself, but for others,

who shed His blood that man might come to God; whose meat, whose food, whose daily bread it was 'to do His Father's will,' and whose whole life and death was summed up in the words, 'Not My will, but Thine be done,' was the most complete instance of that self-denial and self-dedication, which from Him has come to be called 'self-sacrifice'; and thus in Him all those anticipations and aspirations of the Psalmists and Prophets were amply and largely fulfilled. Thus by this true sacrifice of Himself, He abolished for ever those false sacrifices.

IV. But here arises the question, How far can any sacrifice be continued in the Christian Church now? This has been in part answered by showing what were the universal spiritual truths which the Prophets put in the place of the ancient sacrifices, and how these spiritual truths were fulfilled in the Founder of our religion. But it may make the whole subject more clear if we show how these same truths are carried on almost in the same words by the Apostles. The word 'sacrifice' is not applied in any sense in the Gospels, unless, in the seventeenth chapter of St. John, the word 'Consecrate' may be so read. But there are several cases in the other books of the New Testament in which it is employed in this sense. All Christians are 'kings and priests.'[4] All Christians can at all times offer those real spiritual sacrifices of which those old heathen and Jewish sacrifices were only the shadows and figures, and which could only be offered at stated occasions by a particular order of men. When the word is used, it is used solely in those three senses of which we have been speaking.

'Let us offer,' says the Epistle to the Hebrews, 'the *sacrifice* of praise always to God, that is, the fruit of lips giving thanks to His name.'[5] This, the continual duty of thankfulness, is the first sacrifice of the Christian Church. 'To do good and to distribute forget not' (says the same Epistle), 'for it is with *such sacrifices*[6] that God is well pleased;' and again, St. Paul in the Epistle to the Philip-

*The sacrifices in the Christian Church.*

---

[4] Rev. i. 6.   [5] Heb. xiii. 15.   [6] Heb. xiii. 16.

pians says of the contributions which his friends at Philippi had sent to him to assist him in his sickness and distress, that it was 'the odour of a sweet smell, a *sacrifice* acceptable, well-pleasing to God.'  This, the duty of Christian usefulness and beneficence, is the second sacrifice of the Christian Church.  'I beseech you to present your bodies reasonable, holy and living *sacrifices* unto God.'[7]  This perpetual self-dedication of ourselves to the Supreme Good is the third and chief sacrifice of the Christian Church always and everywhere, and it is also the sense in which, in the Epistle to the Ephesians,[8] Christ is said to have 'given Himself for us an offering and a sacrifice to God for a sweet-smelling savour.'

In these three senses the Christian Religion, whilst destroying utterly and for ever all outward sacrifices, whether animal sacrifice or vegetable sacrifice or human sacrifice, is yet, in a moral and spiritual sense, sacrificial from beginning to end.  Every position, every aspect of every true Christian, east or west, or north or south, in church or out of church, is a sacrificial position.  Every Christian is, in the only sense in which the word is used in the New Testament, 'a priest of good things to come,' to offer up 'spiritual sacrifices acceptable to God through Jesus Christ.'  Every domestic hearth, every holy and peaceful deathbed, every battlefield of duty, every arena of public or private life, is the altar from which the thoughts and energies of human souls and spirits ought to be for ever ascending to the Father of all goodness.  We are not to say that the use of the word 'sacrifice' in this moral and spiritual sense is a metaphor or figure of speech, and that the use of the word in its gross and carnal sense is the substance.  So far as there can be any sacrifice in the Christian Religion, it is the moral and spiritual sense which is the enduring substance ; the material and carnal sacrifice was but the passing shadow.

V. But there may still arise an intermediate question, and that is—In what sense, over and above this complete

---

[7] Rom. xii. 1 ; comp. 1 Pet. ii. 5.
[8] Eph. v. 2 ; compare Heb. ix. 14, x. 5-12.

and ideal sacrifice of our great Example,—over and above this essential sacrifice of our own daily lives,—in what sense is there any sacrifice in our outward worship, especially in the Holy Communion?

It is clear from what has been said, that in order to claim any share in the true Christian sacrifice, whether that rendered once for all by Jesus Christ, or that offered by all good Christians in every hour of their lives, any sacrifice in our outward worship must exhibit one or other of these three essential characteristics which we have mentioned: 1. Prayer and praise; 2. Beneficence; 3. Self-devotion and self-dedication.

(1) The Sacrament of the Lord's Supper is certainly, as its name of 'Eucharist' implies, as it is called in the English Communion Service, 'a sacrifice of praise and thanks-giving.' It is this which makes us say in a part of the service, which belongs to its most ancient fragments, 'It is very meet, right, and our bounden duty, that we should at all times and in all places, but chiefly now, give thanks to Thee.' And in the ancient services of the Church, of which only a very slight trace remains in our own, or in any Church now, this thanksgiving was yet further expressed by the Christian people bringing to the table the loaves of bread and the cups of wine, as samples of the fruits of the earth, for which every day and hour of their lives they wish to express their gratitude. In the English Church this is indicated only by the few words where in the Prayer for the Church Militant we say, 'We (i.e. not the clergyman, but the people) offer unto Thee our oblations.' In the Roman Church, this and this only was what was originally meant by the sacrifice, the host or offering; not a dead corpse, but the daily bread and wine of our earthly sustenance, offered not by the priest, but by the whole Christian congregation, as an expression of their thankfulness for the gracious kindness of God our Father in His beautiful and bountiful creation.

It is true that in a later part of the service, the bread and wine are made to represent, as in the Last Supper, the Body and Blood, that is, the inmost spirit of the dying

Redeemer. But at the time of the service when in the Ancient Liturgies they were offered by the congregation and by the minister, and when they were called by the name of 'sacrifice,' or 'victim,' they represented only the natural products of the earth. It was as if the early Church had meant to say—'In Pagan and Jewish times there were human sacrifices, animal sacrifices. In Christian times this has ceased; we wish to express to God our thankfulness for the daily bread that strengthens man's heart, and the wine that makes glad our hearts, and we express our gratitude by bringing our bread and wine for the common enjoyment and joint participation of the whole Christian community.'

(2) This brings us to the second idea of sacrifice, that is, the rendering of acts of kindness to our brethren. The offering, the contribution of bread and wine which formed the original sacrifice or offering of the Eucharist, es- sentially partook of this idea, because the Eucharist in those early times was the common festive gathering of rich and poor in the same social meal, to which, as St. Paul enjoined, every one was to bring his portion. And further, with this practice, of which almost all traces have disappeared from all modern modes of administering the Lord's Supper, there was united from the earliest times the practice of collecting alms and contributions for the poor, at the time when our Christian communion and fellowship with each other is most impressed upon us. This is the practice which is called, in the English Church and others, the *offertory*, that is, the offerings, and which is urged upon us in the most moving passages that can be drawn from the Scriptures to stir up our Christian compassion. Here again, it is clear that the sacrifice, the offering, is made not by the priest, not by the minister, but by the congregation. It is not the clergy who give alms or offerings for the people, it is the people who bring alms or offerings for one another or for the clergy. They make these sacrifices from their own substance, and with such sacrifices, so far as they come from a willing and bountiful heart, God is well pleased.

(3) The service of the Sacrament, in whatever form, expresses the sacrifice, the dedication of ourselves. Even if there were not words to set this forth, it could not be otherwise. Every serious communicant does at least for the moment intend to declare his resolution to lead a new life, and abandon his evil self. But in the English Reformed Church, this, the highest form of sacrifice, is, and was formerly much more than in the present form, brought out much more strongly than either in the Roman Church or in most other Protestant Churches. There is a solemn Prayer at the close of the service, in which it is said, ' Here we offer and present unto Thee ourselves, our souls and bodies, to be a reasonable, holy, and lively sacrifice unto Thee.' But in the first Reformed Prayer Book of Edward VI., this true spiritual Protestant sacrifice was even still more forcibly expressed, for this dedication of ourselves was not, as now, at the close of the service, but was introduced into the very heart of the Consecration Prayer, and made the chief and turning point of the whole Liturgy. It was this on which so much stress was always laid by one of the profoundest scholars and the most devout men of our time, of whom one of his friends used to say that he was essentially a Liturgical Christian—the late Chevalier Bunsen. It is this which is present in the Scottish and the American Prayer Books, and, contrary to the usual opinion entertained of them, places them in the foremost rank of Protestant forms of devotion. In this Prayer it is evident that this the most important of the sacrifices of Christian Religion is not-offered by the clergy for the people, but is the offering of the people by themselves; that when the clergyman says, ' we offer,' he speaks not of himself alone, but of himself only as one of them, with them, acting and speaking as their mouthpiece and representative, and they speaking and acting with him and for him.

These are the three ideas, the three meanings, of the sacrifice of the Eucharist. There is no other sense of sacrifice in the Eucharist than these three, and these three meanings absorb all others.[9]   No doubt the realities of sacrifice which they are intended to express are not there or in any outward sign, but in actual life, as when we speak of 'a heavy sacrifice,' of 'a self-sacrifice,' and the like.   But the outward sign reminds us of the spiritual reality, and often in the Lord's Supper the two are brought together.[1]

When we see the bread and wine, the gifts of the parish or people, placed on the Table, this should remind us of the deep and constant thankfulness that we ought to feel from morning till evening for the blessings of our daily bread, of our happy lives,—perhaps even of our daily sorrows and sicknesses and trials.

When we drop into the plate our piece of gold or silver or copper, as the case may be, this prelude of the Lord's Supper, slight though it be, should remind us that the true Christian Communion requires as its indispensable condition true Christian beneficence ; beneficence exercised not it may be at that moment, but always, and wherever we are, in the wisest, most effectual mode which Christian prudence and generosity can suggest.

When we dedicate ourselves at the Table in remembrance of Him who dedicated Himself for us—when we come to Him in order to be made strong with His strength—the act, the words, the remembrance should remind us that not then only, but at all times and in all places ought the sweet-

---

[9] By a strange solecism the Eucharist is sometimes called 'a commemorative sacrifice.'   This is as if the Waterloo banquet were called 'a commemorative battle.'   Still the sacrifice of Christ which it commemorates is of the same kind as the sacrifice of the worshippers, viz. the sacrifice of a spotless life for the good of others.

[1] 'The requirement of the Sacrament has, fortunately, never been to any great extent one of the requirements of the social code, and a rite which of all Christian institutes is the most admirable in its touching solemnity has for the most part been left to sincere and earnest believers. Something of the fervour, something of the deep sincerity, of the early Christians, may even now be seen around the sacred table, and prayers instinct with the deepest and most solemn emotion may be employed without appearing almost blasphemous by their contrast with the tone and the demeanour of the worshippers.'—(From some admirable remarks of Mr. Lecky on the Test Act. *History of the Eighteenth Century*, vol. i. p. 255.)

smelling savour of our lives to be ascending towards Him who delights above all things in a pure, holy, self-sacrificing heart and will.

Other ideas no doubt there are besides in the Eucharist. But so far as there is any idea of sacrifice, or thanksgiving, or offering to God, whether we take the English Prayer Book, or the older Liturgies out of which the Prayer Book is formed, it is the threefold idea which has been described, and not any of those imaginary sacrifices which, whether in the English or the Roman Church or in other Churches, have been in modern days engrafted upon it. And this threefold sacrifice of prayer and praise, of generosity, and of self-dedication, are in the Eucharist, because they pervade all Christian worship and life, of which the Eucharist is or ought to be the crowning representation and exemplification.

Such are the ideas which, imperfectly and disproportionately, but yet sufficiently, pervade the early service of the Eucharist.

# CHAPTER V

### THE REAL PRESENCE.

IT might have been thought that in a religion like Christianity, which is distinguished from Judaism and from Paganism by its essentially moral and spiritual character, no doubt could have arisen on the material presence of its Founder. In other religions, the continuance of such a presence of the Founder is a sufficiently familiar idea. In Buddhism, the Lama is supposed still to be an incarnation of the historical Buddha. In Hinduism, Vishnu was supposed to be from time to time incarnate in particular persons. In the Greek and Roman worship, though doubtless with more confusion of thought, the Divinities were believed to reside in the particular statues erected to their honour; and the cells or shrines of the temples in which such statues were erected were regarded as 'the habitations of the God.' In Judaism, although here again with many protestations and qualifications, the 'Shechineh' or glory of Jehovah was believed to have resided, at any rate till the destruction of the ark, within the innermost sanctuary of the Temple. But in Christianity the reverse of this was involved in the very essence of the religion. Not only was the withdrawal of the Founder from earth recognised as an incontestable fact and recorded as such in the ancient creeds, but it is put forth in the original documents as a necessary condition for the propagation of His religion. 'It is expedient for you that I go away.' 'If I go not away the Comforter will not come unto you.' Whenever the phraseology of the older religions is for a moment employed in the Christian Scriptures, it is at once lifted into a higher sphere. 'The Temple' of the primitive Christian's object of worship, 'the Altar' on which his praises were offered, was not in any outward building, but either in the ideal invisible world, or in the living frames and hearts of men. There are, indeed, numerous passages in the New Testament which speak of the continued presence of the Redeemer amongst His people. But these all are so evidently intended in a moral and spiritual sense that they have in fact hardly ever been interpreted in any other way. They all either relate to the communion which through His Spirit is maintained with the spirits of men—as in the well-known texts, 'I am with you always;' 'Where two or three are gathered together in my name, there am I in the midst of them;' 'I will come to you;' 'Come unto Me, all ye that are weary and heavy laden'—or else they express that remarkable doctrine of Christianity, that the invisible God, the invisible Redeemer, can be best served and honoured by the service and honour of those amongst men who most need it, whether by their characters or their suffering condition. 'He that receiveth you receiveth Me.' 'Inasmuch as ye have done it unto them, ye have done it unto Me.' 'Ye visited Me.' The Church—the Christian community—is 'His body.' None of these expressions have been permanently divorced from their high moral signification. No controversy concerning the mode of His presence in holy thoughts, or heroic lives, or afflicted sufferers, has rent the Church asunder. Stories more or less authentic, legends more or less touching, have represented these spiritual manifestations of the departed Founder in vivid forms to men. We have the well-known incident of the apparition of the Crucified to St. Francis on the heights of Laverna, which issued in the belief of the sacred wounds as received in his own person. We have the story of Benvenuto Cellini, who, meditating suicide in his dungeon, was deterred by a vision of the like appearance, from which he is said on waking to have carved the exqui-

site ivory crucifix subsequently transported on the shoulders
of men from Barcelona to the Escurial, where it is now
exposed to view in the great ceremonials of the Spanish Court.
We have the conversion of the gay Presbyterian soldier,
Colonel Gardiner, from a life of sin to a life of unblemished
piety by the midnight apparition of the Cross and the gracious
words, ' I have done so much for thee, and wilt thou do nothing
for Me?'  Or again, in connection with the other train of
passages above cited, there is the beggar who received the
divided cloak from St. Martin, and whom the saint saw in
the visions of the night as the Redeemer showing it with
gratitude to the angelic hosts.  There is the leper who, when
tended by St. Elizabeth of Hungary, and placed in her bed, appeared to be the Man of Sorrows, represented in the Vulgate
rendering of the 53rd chapter of Isaiah as a leper, ' smitten
of God and afflicted.'  There is the general Protestant sentiment as expressed in the beautiful poem of the Moravian
Montgomery :—

> A poor wayfaring man of grief
> Hath often passed me on my way :
> I did not pause to ask His name—
> Whither He went, or whence He came—
> Yet there was something in His eye
> That won my love, I know not why.

But these stories, these legends, one and all, either confessedly exhibit the effect produced on the inward, not
the outward, sense; or, even if some should contend for
their actual external reality, they are acknowledged to be
rare, exceptional, transitory phenomena, arising out of and
representing the inner spiritual truth which is above and
beyond them.

How is it then, we may ask, that the Presence in the
Sacrament of the Lord's Supper has ever been regarded in
any other light ?  How is it that the expressions in the New
Testament which bear on this subject have been interpreted
in a different manner from the precisely similar expressions
of which we have just spoken ?

These expressions, one would suppose, had been sufficiently guarded in the original context. In the very discourse in which Jesus Christ is represented as first using the terms which He afterwards represented in the outward forms of the parting meal—speaking of moral converse with Himself under the strong figure of 'eating His flesh and drinking His blood,'—it is not only obvious to every reader that the literal sense was absolutely impossible, but He Himself concluded the whole argument by the words which ought to have precluded for ever all question on the subject: ' It is the spirit that quickeneth, the flesh profiteth nothing.'

This assertion of the moral and spiritual character of the Presence of Christ in the Sacrament, as everywhere else, has, as we shall see, never been wholly obliterated. The words of Ignatius, ' Faith is the body of Christ,' and ' Charity is the blood of Christ ; ' the words of Augustine, ' Crede et manducasti,' have ever found an echo in the higher and deeper intelligence of Christendom. But not the less, almost from the earliest times, and in almost every Church, a counter-current of thought has prevailed, which has endeavoured to confine the Redeemer's Presence to the material elements of the sacred ordinance. We discover the first traces of it, although vaguely and indefinitely, in the prayer mentioned by Justin Martyr, and more or less transmitted through the ancient liturgies, that the bread and wine ' may become the Body and Blood.' We trace it in the peculiar ceremonial sanctity with which not only the ordinance but the elements came to be invested, during the first five centuries. We see it in the scruple which has descended even to our own time, which insists on fasting as a necessary condition of the reception [1] of the Communion, in flagrant defiance of the well-

---

[1] Perhaps, as this scruple in early times extended to *both* sacraments it had not then, in regard to the Eucharist, assumed the gross corporeal form which it represents in later times. But it may be worth while to give as an instance, both of the force with which it was held, and the utter recklessness of the example and teaching of Christ Himself with which it was accompanied, the following passage from even so eminent a man as Chrysostom : ' They say I have given the Communion to some after they

known circumstances not only of its original institution, but of all the details of its celebration during the whole of the Apostolic age. We see it again in the practice (which began at least as early as Infant Baptism, and which is still continued in the Eastern Church) of giving the Communion to unconscious infants. We see it finally in the innumerable regulations with which the rite is fenced about in the Roman Catholic, the Greek, and some of the Presbyterian Churches, as well as in the theories which have been drawn up to explain or to enforce the doctrine, and of which we will presently speak more at length.

But in order to do this effectually, we must recur to the question suggested above : ' Why is it that the spiritual and obvious explanation, accepted almost without murmur or exception for all other passages where the Divine Presence is indicated, should have ever been rejected in the case of the Eucharist, which, in its first institution, had for its evident object the expression of that identical thought ? '

It was a wise saying of Coleridge, ' Presume yourself ignorant of a writer's understanding, until you understand his ignorance ; ' and so in regard to doctrines or ceremonies, however extravagant they may seem to us, it is almost useless to discuss them unless we endeavour to see how they have originated.

I. First, then, it may be said that the material interpretation of this ordinance arose from a defect in the intellectual condition of the early recipients of Christianity, Misuse of parabolical language. reaching back to its very beginning. The parabolical and figurative language of the Gospel teaching was chosen designedly. There were many reasons for its adoption, some accidental, some permanent. It was the language of the East, and therefore the almost necessary vehicle

had eaten ; but if I did this let my name be *blotted out of the book of Bishops*, and not written in the book of orthodox faith. Lo ! if I did anything of the sort, *Christ will cast me out of His kingdom* ; but *if they persist* in urging this, and are contentious, let them also *pass sentence against the Lord Himself, who gave the Communion to the Apostles after supper.*' (*Ep.* 128.)—*The Life and Times of St. Chrysostom*, by the Rev. W. Stephens.

of thought for One who spoke as an Oriental to Orientals.  It was the language best suited, then as always, to the rude, child-like minds to which the Gospel discourses were addressed. It was the language in which profound doctrines were most likely to be preserved for future ages, distinct from the dog-matic or philosophical turns of speech, which, whilst aiming at forms which shall endure for eternity, are often the most transitory of all, often far more transitory than the humblest tale or the simplest figure of speech.  It was the sanction, for all time, of the use of fiction and poetry as a means of convey-ing moral and religious truth.  In the Parables of the Prodigal Son and of the Rich Man and Lazarus, are wrapt up by an-ticipation the drama and romance of modern Europe.  But with these immense and preponderating advantages of the parabolic style of instruction was combined one inevitable danger and drawback.  Great, exalted, general as is the poetic instinct of mankind, it yet is not universal or in all cases supreme.  There is a prosaic element in the human mind which turns into matter of fact even the highest flights of genius and the purest aspirations of devotion.  And, strange to say, this prosaic turn is sometimes found side by side with the development of the parabolic tendency of which we have been speaking ; sometimes even in the same mind. Nothing can be more figurative and poetic than Bunyan's ‘ Pilgrim ’; nothing more homely and pedantic than his ‘ Grace Abounding.’  This union of the two tendencies is nowhere more striking than in the East, and in the first age of Chris-tianity.  It appeared in the Gospel narrative itself.  Appro-priate, elevating, unmistakable as were our Lord's figures, they were again and again brought down by His hearers to the most vulgar and commonplace meaning.  The reply of the Samaritan woman at the well—the comment of the Apos-tles on the leaven of the Pharisees—the gross materialism of the people of Capernaum in regard to the very expressions which have in part been pressed into modern Eucharistic controversies, are well known cases in point.  The Talmud is one vast system of turning figures into facts.  The passionate exclamation of the Psalmist, 'Thou hast saved me from among the horns of the unicorns,' has been turned by the Rabbis into an elaborate chronicle of adventures. 'Imagination and defect of imagination have each contributed to the result.'[2] The whole history of early Millenarianism implies the same incapacity for distinguishing between poetry and prose. The strange tradition of our Lord's words which Irenæus quoted from Papias, and which Papias quoted from the Apostles, in the full belief that they were genuine, is a sample of some such misunderstood metaphor:[3] 'The days shall come when each vine will grow with ten thousand boughs, each bough with ten thousand branches, each branch with ten thousand twigs, each twig with ten thousand bunches, each bunch with ten thousand grapes, each grape shall yield twenty-five measures of wine.' A statement like this provokes only a smile, because it never struck root in the Church; but it is not in itself more extravagant than the Sacramental theories built on figures not less evidently poetic.

II. A second cause of the persistency of this physical limitation of the Sacramental doctrine lay in the fascination exercised over the early centuries of our era by the belief in amulets and charms which the Christians inherited, and could not but inherit, from the decaying Roman Empire. In an eloquent passage in Cardinal Newman's 'Essay on Development,' written with the view of identifying the modern Church of Rome with the Church of the early ages, he shows, with all the power of his eloquence, and with a remarkable display of historical ingenuity, the apparent affinity between the magical rites which flooded Roman society during the first three centuries, and what seemed to be their counterparts in the contemporary Christian Church. Doubtless much of this similarity was accidental; much also was due to the vague terror inspired by a new and powerful religion. But much also was well grounded in the likeness which the aspect of early Christianity inevit-

*Prevalence of magic.*

---

[2] Gould's *Legends of the Old Testament*, p. vi.
[3] A striking explanation is given of this in *Philochristus*.

ably bore to the influences by which it was surrounded. It was not mere hostility, nor mere ignorance, which saw in the exorcisms, the purifications, the mysteries of the Church of the first ages, the effects of the same vast wave of superstition which elsewhere produced the witches and soothsayers of Italy, the Mithraic rites of Persia, the strange charms and invocations of the Gnostics. In these likenesses it is a strange inversion, instead of recognising the influence of the perishing Empire on the rising Church, not only to insist on binding down the Church to the effete superstitions of the Empire, but to regard those superstitions as themselves the marks of a divine Catholicity.

Another theologian, with a far truer historical insight, in noticing the like correspondence of the anarchical tendencies of that period with the regenerating elements of Christianity, has taken a juster view of their relation to each other. Whilst fully acknowledging that the Christian movement to the external observer appeared to embrace them both, he has endeavoured not to confound the lower human accretions with Christianity itself, but to distinguish between them. ‘Christianity,’ says Dr. Arnold, ‘shared the common lot of all great moral changes; perfect as it was in itself, its nominal adherents were often neither wise nor good. The seemingly incongruous evils of the thoroughly corrupt society of the Roman Empire, superstition and scepticism, ferocity and sensual profligacy, often sheltered themselves under the name of Christianity; and hence the heresies of the first age of the Christian Church.’[4]

The ‘sensual profligacy’ and the ‘scepticism’ no doubt remained amongst ‘the heresies’; but the ‘ferocity’ and the ‘superstition’ unfortunately lingered in the Church itself. The ‘ferocity’ developed itself somewhat later in hordes of monks that turned the council-hall at Ephesus into a den of thieves, and stained the streets of Alexandria with the blood of Hypatia. The ‘superstition’ clove to the Sacramental ordinances, and too often converted the emblems

[4] *Fragment on the Church*, pp. 85, 86.

of life and light into signs of what most Christians now would regard as mere remnants of sortilege and sorcery. The stories of Sacramental bread carried about as a protection against sickness and storm can deserve no other name; and it was not without reason that in later times the sacred words of consecration, which often degenerated into a mere incantation, became the equivalent for a conjuror's trick. And to this was added a peculiar growth of the third and fourth centuries of the Christian era, which was gradually consolidated amidst the lengthening shadows of the falling Empire,—the sacerdotal claims of the Christian clergy. In themselves these clerical pretensions had no necessary connection with the material view of the Sacramental rites. The administration of Baptism is not regarded even by Roman Catholics as an exclusive privilege of the clergy. In early times, indeed, it was practically confined to the bishops, but this was soon broken through, and in later ages it has in the Roman Church been viewed as the right, and even in some cases as the duty, of the humblest layman or laywoman. But the celebration of the Eucharist, although there is nothing in the terms of its original institution to distinguish it in this respect from the other sacrament, has yet been regarded as a peculiar function of the priesthood. In the second century, like that other sacrament, its administration depended on the permission of the bishops, yet when emancipated from their control, unlike Baptism, it did not descend beyond the order of presbyters, and has ever since been bound up with their dignity and power. Even so there can be found in the Roman Catholic Church those who maintain that there is no essential and necessary connection between their office and the validity of the Sacrament. But this has not been the general view; and it is impossible not to suppose that the belief in the preternatural powers of the priesthood, and the belief in the material efficacy of the Sacramental elements, have acted and reacted upon each other, culminating in the extraordinary hyperbole which regards the priest as the maker of his Creator, and varying

with the importance which has been ascribed to the second
order of the Christian clergy, and through it to the hierarchy
generally.

III. These two tendencies—the early tendency to mistake
parable for prose, and the early superstitious regard for external objects—are sufficient to account for the lower
forms of the irrational theories respecting the Sacrament of the Eucharist. But there is a third cause of a nobler
kind which will lead us gradually and naturally to the consideration of the other side of the question. It is one of the
peculiarities of this Sacrament that partly through its long
history, partly from the original grandeur of its first conception, it suggests a great variety of thoughts which cling
to it with such tenacity as almost to become part of itself.
To disentangle these from the actual forms which they
encompass—to draw precisely the limits where the outward
ends and the inward begins, where the transitory melts into
the eternal and the earthly into the heavenly—is beyond
the power of many, beside the wish of most. An example
may be taken from another great ordinance which belongs
to the world no less than to the Church, and which by more
than half Christendom is regarded as a sacrament—Marriage.
How difficult it would be to analyse the ordinary mode of
feeling regarding the ceremony which unites two human
beings in the most sacred relation of life; how many trains
of association from Jewish patriarchal traditions, from the
usages of Imperial Rome, from the metaphors of Apostolic
teaching, from the purity of Teutonic and of English homes,
have gone to make up the joint sanctity of that solemn
moment, in which the reality and the form are by the
laws of God and man blended in indissoluble union! If
there are mingled with it customs which had once a baser
significance, yet still even these are invested by the feeling
of the moment with a meaning above themselves, which
envelops the whole ceremonial with an atmosphere of grandeur
that no inferior associations can dispel or degrade. Something analogous is the mixture of ideas which has sprung up

The spiritual view.

round the Eucharist.    It has, by the very nature of the case, two sides: its visible material aspect, of a ceremony, of a test, of a mystic chain by which the priest brings the Creator down to earth, and attaches his followers to himself and his order; and its noble spiritual aspect of a sacred memory, of a joyous thanksgiving, of a solemn self-dedication, of an upward aspiration towards the Divine and the Unseen.

We have already spoken of the legends which have represented in an outward form the spiritual presence of the Founder in the world at large.  We have also spoken of those which have represented the same idea in connection with the sufferers or the heroes of humanity.  There are also legends on which we may for a moment dwell as representing in a vivid form both the baser and the loftier view of the same idea in the Eucharist.  The lowest and most material conception of this Presence is brought before us in the legend of the miracle of Bolsena, immortalised by the fresco of Raphael, in which the incredulous priest was persuaded by the falling of drops of blood from the consecrated wafer at the altar of that ancient Etruscan city.  Such stories of bleeding wafers were not unfrequent in the Middle Ages, and it is not impossible that they originated in the curious natural phenomenon, which was described in connection with the appearance of the cholera in Berlin—the discoloration produced by certain small scarlet insects, leaving on the bread which they touched the appearance of drops of blood.  Some such appearance, real or supposed, suggested, probably, the material transformation of the elements into the flesh and blood of the outward frame of the Founder.  This is the foundation of the great festival of Corpus Christi, which from the thirteenth century has in the Latin Church commemorated the miracle of Bolsena, and with it the doctrine supposed to be indicated therein. Another class of legend rises somewhat higher.  It is that of a radiant child appearing on the altar, such as is described in the lives of Edward the Confessor, and engraved on the screen which incloses his shrine in Westminster Abbey.

Leofric, Earl of Mercia, with his famous Countess Godiva, was believed to have been present with the King, and to have seen it also. This apparition, 'pure and bright as a spirit,' is evidently something more refined than the identification of the wafer and wine with the mere flesh and blood of the human body of a full-grown man, and, if both stories were taken literally, each would be inconsistent with the other. A third incident of the kind leads us higher yet, and is the more remarkable from its indicating the doctrine of a Eucharistic Presence in a Church which most English High Churchmen despise as altogether outside the pale of Sacramental graces. It has been told in various places; amongst others, in the twenty-second edition [5] of the interesting reminiscences of Scottish Character, by Dean Ramsay, how a half-witted boy in Forfarshire after long entreaties persuaded the minister to give him what he called his Father's bread, and returned home, exclaiming, 'Oh, I have seen the pretty man!' and died that night in excess of rapture. No savour or tradition of Transubstantiation had invaded the brain of this poor child. No Presbyterian would admit the external reality of the vision. No Catholic or High Episcopalian would acknowledge the reality of that Presbyterian Sacrament. But nevertheless, the purely Protestant idea of a spiritual communion had such an effect as to produce an impression analogous, however superior, to the visions of the Priest of Bolsena or the Saxon King. No serious confusion can arise so long as we hold to the obvious truth that outward appearances can never be more than signs of spiritual and moral excellence; and that even were the Saviour Himself present in visible form before us, that visible presence would be useless to us, except as a token of the Divine Spirit within, and would have no effect on the human soul unless the soul consciously received a moral impulse from it.

Such are the various elements which have gone to make up the sentiment of Christendom on a subject in itself so

<hr>

[5] i. 238.

simple, but complicated by the confluence of the heterogeneous streams of irrelevant argument, misapplied metaphor, and genuine devotion.   How its more material aspect
deepened as time rolled on, we have already indicated.   The
long mediæval controversy was at last closed by the definition
of Transubstantiation in the fourth Council of Lateran, and
this was followed by the stories already cited of the miracle
at Bolsena, and other like incidents, which finally produced
what may be called the popular belief of the Roman Church,
that the bread and wine are, after consecration, neither more
nor less than the body and blood that was crucified on Calvary.

But it is interesting, and for our present purpose instructive, to observe how behind this popular belief, and
even in some of the forms which most directly arose out of
it, there was a constant turning to the higher and more
spiritual view.   Not only had Berengar and Abelard pro-
tested against the grosser conceptions, not only had the
mighty Hildebrand vacillated in his orthodoxy, but the very
statement of 'Transubstantiation,' properly understood, contained a safety-valve, through which the more earthly and
dogmatic expressions of the doctrine evaporate and melt
into something not very unlike the purest Protestantism.
The word is based, as its component parts sufficiently indicate, on the scholastic distinction between ' Substance ' and
' Accidents,' a distinction which has long since vanished out
of every sound system either of physics or metaphysics,[6] but
which at the time must have been like a *Deus ex machinâ*
to relieve the difficulties of theologians struggling to maintain their conscience and sense of truth against the prevailing
superstitions of the age.   Every external object was then believed to consist of two parts—the *accidents*, which represented

* The connection of these materialist views of the Sacrament with the
scholastic distinction between ' substance ' and ' accidents ' has been well
pointed out by two distinguished scholars who, whenever they apply themselves to theological subjects, speak with a lucidity and an authority which
need no addition—Bishop Thirlwall in his Charge of 1854 (*Remains*, i. 238–
46, 249–51), and Dean Liddell in his sermon entitled ' There am I in the
midst.'

the solid visible framework, alone cognisable by the senses, and the *substance*, which was the inward essence or Platonic idea, invisible to mortal eye, incommunicable to mortal touch. The popular notion of the Roman Catholic doctrine is, no doubt, that the change believed to be effected in the Eucharist is not of the 'substance,' but of the 'accidents.' This would seem (on the whole) the view of Aquinas, who maintains, not, indeed, that the *accidents* of the bread and wine are changed, but that the *substance* is changed, not merely into the *substance*, but into the *accidents* of the body and blood.[7] This is clear not only from the legends of the bleeding wafers and the like, but from the common language used as to the portentous miracle by which the visible earthly elements are supposed to be transformed into something invisible and celestial. But the true scholastic doctrine is wholly inconsistent with any such supposition. The 'substance' spoken of is not the material substance, but the impalpable idea. The miracle, if it can be so called in any sense of that much-vexed word, consists in the transformation of one invisible object into another invisible object. The senses have no part or lot in the transaction, on one side or the other. Even the 'substance'[8] into which the ideal essence of the bread and wine is transformed is not the gross corporeal matter of the bones and sinews and fluid of the human frame, but the ideal essence of that frame. It is, probably, not without design that Cardinal Newman, in speaking of the word 'substance,' lays down so anxiously and precisely that 'the greatest philosophers know nothing at all about it.' The doctrine, thus conceived and thus stated in one of the decrees of Trent, is, as Bishop Thirlwall[9] well

---

[7] Lib. iv. Sent. Dist. viii. qu. 2 : quoted in Bishop Thirlwall's Charge of 1854. (*Remains*, i. 250.)

[8] The ambiguity which in the Roman statement attaches to the word 'substance,' in the Anglican statement attaches no less to the word 'real.' ' Nothing in this question can depend on the expression *Real Presence* · everything on the sense which is attached to it.'—Bishop Thirlwall's Charge, 1854. (*Remains*, i. 240.)

[9] Charge, 1854. (*Remains*, i. 250.)

expresses it, the assertion that 'one metaphysical entity is substituted for another, equally beyond the grasp of the human mind, and equally incapable of any predicate by which it may become the subject of an intelligible proposition.' It is evident that under cover of a word which either means nothing or something which no one can understand, the whole idealistic philosophy, the whole rationalistic theology, the whole Biblical and spiritual conceptions of the Eucharist might steal in.

It is difficult, but it is instructive, to track out the course of this Protean logomachy. The confusion pervades not only the words of the doctrine, but the forms which have gathered round it. Whilst some of these forms have intensified the gross popular belief, and are only explicable on the supposition of its truth—such as the minute precautions concerning the mode of disposing of the sacred elements, or of guarding them against the trivial incidents of everyday occurrence—on the other hand, some of them are only defensible on the hypothesis of the more spiritual view to which we have just adverted. This is even more apparent in the Mediæval and Western than in the Patristic and Oriental Church. We have seen that in the earlier ages it was the custom, as it still is in Eastern worship, to give the Communion to infants. This custom since the thirteenth century has in the Latin Church been entirely proscribed. Partly, no doubt, this may have arisen from the fear—increasing with the increase of the superstitious veneration for the actual elements—lest the wine, or, as it was deemed, the sacred blood, should be spilt in the process; but partly also it arose from the repugnance which the more restless, rational, and reforming West felt against an infant's unconscious participation in a rite which, according to any reasonable explanation of its import, could not be considered as useful to any except conscious and intelligent agents. In many of its aspects, no doubt, the same might be said of Baptism. But there it was at least possible to regard the rite in relation to children as equivalent to an enrolment in a new society—a dedication to a merciful Saviour—a hope that they would lead the rest of their lives according to this beginning. Not so the Eucharist. The Eucharist is either a purely moral act, or else it is entirely mechanical. If viewed as a charm, as a medicine, it would be equally applicable to conscious or unconscious persons, to children or to full-grown men. But if viewed as an act of the will, Infant Communion became an obvious incongruity, and accordingly, in spite of the long and venerable traditions which sustained the usage, it was deliberately abandoned by the Latin Church; and we may be sure that the enlightened sense of Christian Europe will for ever prevent its rehabilitation. The rejection of Infant Communion is intelligible on the principle that the efficacy of the Eucharist is a moral influence—it is totally indefensible on the principle whether of Roman or Anglican divines, who maintain its efficacy, irrespectively of any spiritual thought or reflection in the recipient. Another change of the same kind in Western Christendom is equally open to this construction. One of the most common charges of Protestants against the Church of Rome is its withholding of the cup from the laity. The expression is not quite accurate. The cup is not absolutely withheld from laymen, inasmuch as it was the privilege of the Kings of France, and also is still given in cases of illness; and its retention is not from the laity as such, but from all, whether priests or laymen, that are not actually officiating. This, properly understood, places the custom on what is no doubt its true basis. It began probably, like the denial of the Communion to infants, from an apprehension lest the chalice should be spilt in going to and fro, or lest the sacred liquid should adhere to the beards or moustaches of the bristling warriors of the Middle Ages. But it was justified on a ground which is fatal to the localisation of the Divine Presence in the earthly elements. It was maintained that the communicant received the benefits of the Sacrament as completely if he partook of one of the two species as if he partook of both. This was at once to assert that the efficacy of the Sacrament did not depend on the material elements. It was the same revolution with respect to the Eucharist that the almost contemporary substitution of sprinkling for immersion was in Baptism. Such a change in the matter of either sacrament can only be justified on the principle that the matter is but of small importance—that the main stress must be on the spirit. And when to this alteration of form was yet further added, in explanation of it, a distinct scholastic theory that each of the two species contained the substance of both, the doctrine of the supreme indifference of form was consolidated, so far as the metaphysical subtleties and barbarous philosophy of that age would allow, into a separate dogma.

If the fine lines of Thomas Aquinas in his famous hymn, ‘Lauda Sion Salvatorem,’ have any sense at all, they mean that the body of Christ is not contained in the bread, nor the blood in the wine, but that something different from each is contained in both; and what that something is must either be a purely spiritual Presence in the hearts of the faithful or else the presence of two physical bodies existing on every altar at the same moment, which is maintained by no one.

When the Bohemian Utraquists fought with desperate energy to recover the use of the cup, they were in one sense doubtless fighting the cause of the laity against the clergy, of old Catholic latitude against modern Roman restrictions. But with that obliquity of purpose which sometimes characterises the fiercest ecclesiastical struggles, the Roman Church, on the other hand, was fighting the battle of an enlarged and liberal view of the Sacraments against a fanatical insistance on the necessity of a detailed conformity to ancient usage.

Of a piece with these indications of a more reasonable view is the constant under-song of better spirits from the earliest times, which maintains, with regard to both Sacraments, not only that, in extreme cases, they may be dispensed with, but that their essence is to be had without the form at all. The bold doctrine of Wall—the great Anglican

authority on Infant Baptism [1]—that Quakers may be regarded
as baptised, because they have the substance of that of which
baptism is the sign, is justified by the maxim of the early
Church that the martyrdom of the unbaptised is itself a
baptism.  And in like manner, the most Protestant of all
the statements on this subject in the English Prayer Book is
itself taken from an earlier rubric to the same effect in the
mediæval Church : ' If a man . . . by any just impediment
do not receive the Sacrament of Christ's body and blood, the
Church shall instruct him that ' [if he fulfil the moral conditions of Communion,] ' *he doth eat and drink the Body
and Blood* of our Saviour Christ to his soul's health, *although
he do not receive the Sacrament with his mouth.*' This
principle is asserted in the Sarum Manual, which less distinctly, but not less positively, allowed of the possibility of
spiritual communion when actual reception of the elements
was impossible.[2]

Such a concession is in fact the concession of the whole
principle.  In the more stringent view, the outward reception of the two Sacraments was regarded as so absolutely
necessary to salvation, that not even the innocence of the
new-born babe nor the blameless life of Marcus Aurelius was
allowed to plead against the lack of the outward form in
one or the other.  But the moment that the door is opened
for the moral consideration of what is due to mercy and
humanity, the whole fabric of the strict Sacramental system
vanishes, and reason, justice, and charity step in to take their
rightful places.

IV. We have thus far endeavoured to show how in the
vitals of the most mechanical theory of the Sacraments there
was wrapt up a protest in favour of the most spiritual view.
Let us for a moment take the reverse side of the picture,
and show how, in the heart of the Protestant Church, there
has always been wrapt up a lurking tenderness for the purely
outward and material view.

When the shock of the Reformation came, next after the

_______________
[1] See Chapter I.            [2] Blunt's *Annotated Prayer Book*, p. 291.

Pope's Supremacy and the doctrine of Justification by Faith —and in a certain sense more fiercely even than either of these, because it concerned a tangible and visible object—the battle of the Churches was fought over the Sacrament of the Altar.

Each of the Reformers on the Continent made some formidable inroad into the usages or the theories which the Roman Church had built up on the primitive ordinance. Yet they all retained something of the old scholastic theory or the old material sentiment, on the external surroundings of the grand spiritual conception of the Sacrament. The scholastic confusion between substance and accident continued in full force. Luther, in most points the boldest, the most spiritual of all, on this point was the most hesitating and the most superstitious. Under the new name of 'Consubstantiation,' the ancient dogma of 'Transubstantiation' received a fresh lease of life. The unchanged form of the Lutheran altar, with crucifix, candles, and wafer, testified to the comparatively unchanged doctrine of the Lutheran sacrament. Melanchthon, Bucer, Calvin, all trembled on the same inclined slope; all laboured to retain some mixture of the physical with the purer idea of the metaphysical, moral efficacy of the Eucharistic rite. One only, the Reformer of Zurich, 'the clear-headed and intrepid Zwingli,'[3] in treating of this subject, anticipated the necessary conclusion of the whole matter. But his doctrine prevailed in England and on the Continent wherever his influence extended, and in the Roman Church has not been altogether inoperative. In language, perhaps too austerely exact, but transparently clear, he recognised the full Biblical truth, that the operations of the Divine Spirit on the soul can only be through moral means; and that the moral influence of the Sacrament is chiefly or solely through the potency of its unique commemoration of the most touching and transcendent event in history. This is the view, sometimes in contempt called

_Luther._

_Zwingli._

---

[3] See the excellent account of Zwingli, _Bampton Lectures on the Communion of Saints_, by the Rev. H. B. Wilson, p. 135.

Zwinglian, which in substance became the doctrine of all the 'Reformed Churches'[4] properly so called, and in a more or less degree of all Protestant Churches. It is well known how vehemently Luther struggled against it. In the princely hall of the old castle which crowns the romantic town of Marburg took place the stormy discussion in which Luther and Zwingli, in the presence of the Landgrave of Hesse, for two long days met face to face, in the vain hope of convincing one another, with the hope, not equally vain, of at least parting in friendship. Everything which could be said on behalf of the dogmatic, coarse, literal interpretation of the institution was urged with the utmost vigour of word and gesture by the stubborn Saxon. Everything which could be said on behalf of the rational, refined, spiritual construction was urged with a union of the utmost acuteness and gentleness by the sober-minded Swiss. Never before or since have the two views been brought into such close collision.

V. We now turn to the relation of the two conflicting tendencies in England. It will not be surprising to any one who has followed the essentially mixed aspect of the English character and of English institutions, the gradual development of our religious, side by side with the equally gradual development of our political, ordinances and ideas—that the conflict of thought, visible as we have seen even in the compact fabric both of the Roman and the Presbyterian Churches, should have left yet deeper traces in the Church of England. During the reign of Henry VIII. this hesitation was almost a necessary consequence of the laborious efforts by which King and people rose out of their own natural prepossessions into a higher region :—

> Now half appeared
> The tawny lion, pawing to get free
> His hinder parts, then springs as broke from bonds,
> And rampant shakes his brinded mane.

No doubt the ancient doctrine maintained its place during

---

[4] *I.e.* the Swiss, South German, French, and English Churches.

those eventful years. But Tyndale had not spoken and written in vain; and already by the Royal theologian himself was issued one of those statesmanlike documents in which the true doctrine of the relation of form to spirit is set forth with a clearness of exposition and of thought that has never been surpassed.[5] The contradictions and vacillations in the growth of Cranmer's opinions on this point are well known. Nothing can be more natural—nothing, we may add, more creditable to his honesty and discrimination —than that he should have felt his way gradually and carefully through the labyrinth from which he had been slowly emerging. In Edward VI.'s reign, the influence of the Reformer of Zurich at last made itself felt in every corner of the ecclesiastical movement of England;[6] 'De cœnâ omnes Angli rectè sentiunt,' writes Hooper to his Swiss friends in 1549; 'Satisfecit piis Eduardi reformatio,' writes Bullinger. At length Cranmer's agreement with the Helvetic Confession of 1536 was complete. 'Canterbury,' writes a friend to Bullinger in 1548, 'contrary to expectation, maintained your opinion. It is all over with the Lutherans.' Ridley's last sentiments, though guardedly expressed, were at the core the same as Cranmer's. It was its persistent adhesion to the Swiss doctrine on the whole which made the Anglican Church, in spite of its episcopal government and liturgical worship, to be classed not amongst the Lutheran but amongst the Reformed Churches.

Yet still the mediæval, or, if we will, the Lutheran element remained too strongly fixed to be altogether dislodged. At the distance of two centuries, Swift could regard his own Church as represented by Martin rather than by Jack. Lutheranism was, in fact, the exact shade which coloured the mind of Elizabeth, and of the divines who held to her. Her altar was precisely the Lutheran altar with crucifix and lights. Her opinions were represented in almost a continuous line by one divine after another down to our own

---

[5] Froude's *History*, iii. 367.

[6] See Cardwell's *Two Liturgies*, Pref. pp. 26–28.

time. But they were always kept in check by the strong Zwinglian atmosphere which pervaded the original theology of the English Church, and which has been its prevailing hue ever since. Into this more reasonable theology almost every expression that has been since used (till quite our modern times) might be resolved. But in the earlier years of the reign of Elizabeth, not only the Queen herself, but a very large portion of the English clergy, who had been brought up in the Roman doctrine, still held opinions scarcely distinguishable from it. Thus it came to pass that, in the spirit of compromise and conciliation which pervaded all their work, the framers of the formularies, though determined to keep the Zwinglian doctrine intact, yet often so expressed it as to make it look as much like Lutheranism as possible. Elizabeth herself, when cross-questioned in her sister's time, evaded the doctrine rather than stated it distinctly. There are still to be seen rudely carved on a stone under the pulpit of the Church of Walton on Thames the lines in which she gave the answer that to many a devout spirit in the English Church has seemed a sufficient reply to all questionings on the subject:—

> Christ was the Word and spake it,
> He took the bread and brake it;
> And what the Word doth make it
> That I believe and take it.

The Articles as finally drawn up in her reign exhibit this same reluctance to exclude positively one or other of the two views. The 28th Article, as originally written in Edward VI.'s time, had expressed the exact Helvetic doctrine. A sentence was added in which, amidst a crowd of Zwinglian expressions, one word—'given'—was inserted which, though not necessarily Lutheran or Roman, certainly lent itself to that meaning. The 29th Article, on 'the wicked which eat not the Body of Christ in the use of the Lord's Supper,' which was added in Elizabeth's time, was obviously meant to condemn the doctrine that there is any reception possible but a moral reception. But—not to speak of the slight wavering, at its close, of the positiveness of its opening—this very Article, though authorised by the canons of 1603, and by implication in the Caroline Act of Uniformity in 1662, does not occur in the edition of the Articles (which are here only 38 in number), authorised by the 13th of Elizabeth. That is to say, this most Protestant of all the Articles is confirmed by what many regard as the authority of the Church in Convocation, and by the legislature of Charles II.'s time, but it was not confirmed by the Act which first imposed the Articles, and which had for its object the admission of Presbyterian orders.

The Catechism, which originally contained no exposition of the sacraments at all, in the time of James I. received a supplement, in which for one moment the highly rhetorical language of the Fathers and Schoolmen is strongly pressed: 'The Body and Blood of Christ are verily and indeed taken and received in the Lord's Supper.' But then the qualifying clause comes in, 'by the faithful'; and these very words are further restricted as describing, not the bread and wine, but the 'thing signified thereby.' The strong denial of 'the Real and bodily, the Real and essential Presence,' which was in Edward VI.'s time incorporated in the 28th Article, and afterwards appended to the Prayer Book in his Declaration of Kneeling, was in Elizabeth's omitted altogether, and when revived in Charles II.'s time was altered to meet the views of the then predominant High Church divines; though the Declaration itself was restored at the request of the Puritan party. But the words '*real and essential Presence there being*' were omitted, and the words '*corporal presence*' substituted for them. The consequence is, that while the adoration of the elements or of 'any corporal presence of Christ's natural flesh and blood' is strictly forbidden as idolatrous, the worship of 'any real and essential presence there being of Christ's natural flesh and blood' is by implication not condemned by this Declaration of the Rubric.

Most characteristic of all is the combination of the two tendencies in the words of the administration of the Eucha-

rist.  In the first Prayer Book of Edward VI., which retained
as much as possible of the ancient forms both in belief and
usage, the words were almost the same as now in the Roman
Church, and as formerly in the Sarum Missal: 'The Body of
our Lord Jesus Christ which was given for thee, preserve thy
body and soul unto everlasting life.'  In the second Prayer
Book of Edward VI., when the Swiss influence had taken
complete possession of the English Reformers, this clause was
dropped, and in its place were substituted the words, 'Take
and eat this in remembrance that Christ died for thee, and
feed on Him in thy heart by faith with thanksgiving.' In the
Prayer Book of Elizabeth, and no doubt by her desire, the
two clauses were united, and so have remained ever since.
' Excellently well done was it,' says an old Anglican divine,[7]
' of Queen Elizabeth and her Reformers, to link both together:
for between the Body and Blood of Christ in the Eucharist,
and the Sacramental Commemoration of His Passion, there is
so inseparable a league as *subsist* they cannot, except they
*consist.*'  'Excellently well done was it,' we may add, to
leave this standing proof, in the very heart of our most
solemn service, that the two views which have long divided
the Christian Church are compatible with joint Christian
communion—so that here at least Luther and Zwingli might
feel themselves at one; that the Puritan Edward and the
Roman Mary might, had they lived under the Latitudina-
rian though Lutheran Elizabeth, have thus far worshipped
together.

What has occurred in the Church of England is an example of what might occur and has occurred in other
Churches, not so pointedly perhaps, but not less really.

[7] L'Estrange, *Alliance of Divine Offices*, p. 219.

# CHAPTER VI.

### THE BODY AND BLOOD OF CHRIST.

IT may be necessary, in order to justify and explain the preceding chapter, to inquire into the Biblical meaning of the expressions 'the body,' and 'the blood of Christ,' both as they occur in St. John's Gospel, without express reference to the Eucharist, and as they occur in connection with the Eucharist in the three Gospels and the Epistles.

I. The words in St. John's Gospel (vi. 53–56) are as follows— 'Except ye eat the flesh of the Son of man, and drink His blood, ye have no life in you. Whoso eateth My flesh, and drinketh My blood hath eternal life; and I will raise him up at the last day. For My flesh is meat indeed, and My blood is drink indeed. He that eateth My flesh, and drinketh My blood, dwelleth in Me, and I in him.'

It is said that a great orator once gave this advice to a younger speaker who asked his counsel: 'You are more anxious about words than about ideas. Remember that if you are thinking of words you will have no ideas; but if you have ideas, words will come of themselves.'[1] That is true as regards ordinary eloquence. It is no less true in considering the eloquence of religion. In theology, in religious conversation, in religious ordinances, we ought as much as possible to try to get beneath the phrases we use, and never to rest satisfied with the words, however excellent, until we have ascertained what we mean by them. Thus alone can we fathom the depth

---

[1] Mr. Pitt to Lord Wellesley. *Reminiscences of Archdeacon Sinclair,* p. 273.

of such phrases; thus alone can we protect ourselves against the superstition of forms and the 'idols of the market-place'; thus alone can we grasp the realities of which words and forms are the shadow.

The passage under consideration in St. John's Gospel at once contains this principle, and also is one of the most striking examples of it. It is one of those startling expressions used by Christ to show us that He intends to drive us from the letter to the spirit, by which He shatters the crust and shell in order to force us to the kernel. It is as if He said: 'It is not enough for you to see the outward face of the Son of man, or hear His outward words, or touch His outward vesture. That is not Himself. It is not enough that you walk by His side, or hear others talk of Him or use terms of affection and endearment towards Him. You must go deeper than this: you must go to His very inmost heart, to the very core and marrow of His being. You must not only read and understand, but you must mark, learn, and inwardly digest, and make part of yourselves, that which can alone be part of the human spirit and conscience.'[2] It expresses, with regard to the life and death of Jesus Christ, the same general truth as is expressed when St. Paul says: 'Put ye on the Lord Jesus Christ'—that is, clothe yourselves with His spirit as with a garment. Or again: 'Let this mind be in you which was also in Christ Jesus.' It is the general truth which our Lord Himself expressed: 'I am the Vine; ye are the branches.' In all the meaning is the same; but, inasmuch as the figure of speech of which we are now speaking is stronger, it also expresses more fully and forcibly what the others express generally. It is the figure, not altogether strange to Western ears, but more familiar to the Eastern mind, in which intellectual and moral instruction is represented under the image of eating and drinking, feasting and carousing, digesting and nourishing. 'I,' says Wisdom in the book of Ecclesiasticus, 'am the mother of fair

[2] This is well put in an early sermon of Arnold on this passage, vol. i. Sermon XXIV.

love, and fear, and knowledge, and holy hope : I therefore, being eternal, am given to all my children. Come unto me, all ye that be desirous of me, and fill yourselves with my fruits. For my memorial is sweeter than honey, and mine inheritance than the honeycomb. They that eat me shall still hunger for more; they that drink me shall still thirst for more.'[3] It is no doubt to modern culture a repulsive[4] metaphor, but it is the same which has entered into all European languages in speaking of the most refined form of mental appreciation—*taste*. If we ask how this word has thus come to be used, it is difficult to say. ' All that we know about the matter is this. Man has chosen to take a metaphor from the body and apply it to the mind. " Tact " from touch is an analogous instance.'[5] This general usage is sufficient to justify the expression without going back to the more barbarous and literal practices in which, in savage tribes, the conquerors devour the flesh of a hostile chief in order to absorb his courage into themselves, or the parents feed their children with the flesh of strong or spirited children in order to give them energy.[6]

II. We pass to the kindred but yet more famous words of the Synoptic Gospels in the account of the Last Supper (Matt. xxvi. 26, 28 ; Mark xiv. 22, 24 ; Luke xxii. 19, and, with a slight variation, 22). And these *The Synoptic Gospels.* same words, long before the composition of the earliest of the present Gospels, were recorded by St. Paul in his narrative of the same event (1 Cor. xi. 24 and, with the same variation as in St. Luke, 25), and thus form the most incontestable and the most authentic speech of the Founder of our religion : ' *This is My body ; This is My blood.*'

Two circumstances guide us to their historical meaning before we enter on them in detail. The first is that, on their very face, they appear before us as the crowning

---

[3] Ecclesiasticus xxiv. 18-21. Cf. Prov. ix. 5. See also *Sayings of Jewish Fathers*, by C. Taylor, quoted in *Philochristus*, p. 438.

[4] See Foster's *Essays*, p. 279.

[5] Sydney Smith, *Lectures on Moral Philosophy*, pp. 153, 154.

[6] Herbert Spencer, *Sociology*, vol. i. pp. 259, 299, 300.

example of the style of Him whose main characteristic it was that He spoke and acted in parable, or proverb, or figure of speech. The second is that, though the words of the passage, as recorded in St. John's Gospel, could by no possibility have a direct reference to the Last Supper, which, at the time of the discourse at Capernaum was still far in the distance, and to which, even when recording the sacred meal, the author of that Gospel makes no allusion, the probability is that they both contain the moral principle that is indicated in the outward act of the Eucharistic ordinance. What this general truth must be we have already indicated ; namely, that, however material the expressions, the idea wrapped up in them is, as in all the teaching of Christ, not material, but spiritual, and that the conclusion to be drawn from them is not speculative, but moral and practical. All the converging sentiments of reverence for Him who spoke them, all our instinctive feeling of the unity of the Gospel narratives, would lead us in this direction even without any further inquiry into the particular meaning of the separate phrases. In this general sense the meaning of the two words is indivisible, even as in the older Churches of Christendom the outward form of administration confounds the two elements together—in the Roman Church by representing both in the bread, in the Greek Church by mixing both in the same moment. But there is nevertheless a distinction which the original institution expresses, and of which the likeness is preserved in all Protestant Churches by the separate administration of the elements. Following, therefore, this distinction between the two phrases, we will endeavour to ask what is the Biblical meaning, first of ' the body ' and then ' the blood ' of Christ.

1. What are we to suppose that our Lord intended when, holding in His hands the large round Paschal cake, He brake it and said, ' This is My body ' ? And secondly, what are we to suppose that St. Paul meant when he said, speaking of the like action of the Corinthian Christians, ' The bread which we break, is it not the communion of the body of Christ ? '

It is maintained in the Church of Crete that the original
bread is there preserved in fragments, and that this is the literal perpetuation of the first sacramental 'body.' An- *The Body
other like tradition prevails amongst the Nestorians. *the essence
of Christ's
John the Baptist gave to John the Evangelist some *character.*
of the water from the baptism. Jesus gave to John two loaves
at the Last Supper. John mixed his with the water of the
Baptism and with the water and blood which he caught at the
Crucifixion,[7] ground it all into powder and mixed it with flour
and salt into a leaven which is still used. In all other
Churches the bread used can only by a dramatic figure be
supposed to represent the original subject of the words
of institution. The main question is the meaning, in the
Gospels, of the word 'body.' As in other parts of the Bible,
the hand, the heart, the face of God are used for God Himself, so the body, the flesh of Christ are used for Christ Himself, for His whole personality and character. 'The body,'
'the flesh,' 'the bone,' was the Hebrew expression for the
identity of any person or any thing. 'The body of heaven'[8]
meant the very heaven, 'the body of the day' meant the
selfsame day,[9] the body of a man meant his full strength.[1]
Even if we were to suppose that He meant literally His flesh
to be eaten—even if we adopted the belief which the Roman
heathens ascribed to the early Christians, that the sacrament
was a cannibals' feast—even then, unless Christianity had
been the most monstrous of superstitions, this banquet of
human flesh could have been of no use. It would have been
not only revolting, but, by the nature of the case, unprofit-
able. What is external can never, except through the spirit,
touch the spirit. To suppose that the material can of itself
reach the spiritual is not religion, but magic. As in the
communion with our actual friends it is not the countenance
that we value, but the mind which speaks through the
countenance—it is not the sound of the words, but the
meaning of the words, that we delight to hear—so also must

---

[7] Cutts, *Christianity under the Crescent*, p. 24.
[8] Ex. xxiv. 10.        [9] Gen. xvii. 23, 26.        [1] Job xxi. 23.

it be in communion with One who, the more we know and think of Him, can have no other than a moral and spiritual relation to us. 'After the flesh we know Him no more.' It is, as the English Prayer Book expresses it, 'His one oblation of *Himself* once offered.' It is not the mere name of Jesus 'which sounds so sweet to a believer's ear,' but the whole mass of vivifying associations which that name brings with it. The picture of Jesus which we require is not that fabled portrait sent to King Abgarus, or that yet more fabled portrait impressed on the handkerchief of Veronica, but the living image of His sweet reasonableness, His secret of happiness, His method of addressing the human heart. When, some years ago, one of the few learned divines of the Church of France, the Père Gratry, wished to correct some erroneous representations of Christ, he sought for the true picture—*le vrai tableau*—not in the traditions of his own Church, nor in the consecrated wafer, but in the grand and impressive portrait drawn by the profound insight of the foremost of Protestant theologians in the closing volumes of Ewald's ' History of the People of Israel.' The true 'sacred heart' of Jesus is not the physical bleeding anatomical dissection of the Saviour's heart, such as appeared to the sickly visionary of France at Paray-le-Monial in the seventeenth century, but the wide embracing toleration and compassion which even to the holiest sons and daughters of France at that time was as a sealed book. The true cross of Christendom is not one or all of the wooden fragments, be they ever so genuine, found, or imagined to be found, by the Empress Helena, but, in the words of Goethe, ' the depth of divine sorrow ' of which the cross is an emblem. ' It is,' as Luther said, ' that cross of Christ which is divided throughout the whole world not in the particles of broken wood, but that cross which comes to each as his own portion of life. Thou therefore cast not thy portion from thee, but rather take it to thee—thy suffering, whatever it be—as a most sacred relic, and lay it up not in a golden or silver shrine, but in a golden heart, a heart clothed with gentle charity.'

Perhaps the strongest of all these expressions is 'the Spirit' applied to the innermost part alike of God and of man. It is *breath, wind.*[2] On one occasion we are told that our Saviour actually *breathed* on His disciples. But that breath, even though it was the most sacred breath of Christ, was not itself the Spirit—it was, and could be, only its emblem.

And as the cross, the picture, the heart, the breath of Christ must of necessity point to something different from the mere outward form and symbol, so also ' the body,' which is represented in the sacramental bread or spoken of in the sacramental words, must of necessity be not the mere flesh and bones of the Redeemer, but that undying love of truth, that indefatigable beneficence, that absolute resignation to His Father's will, by which alone we recognise His unique personality. The words that He spoke (so He Himself said) were the spirit and the life of His existence—those words of which it was said at the close of a long and venerable career by one[3] who knew well the history of Christianity, that they, and they alone, contain the primal and indefeasible truths of the Christian religion which shall not pass away. That character and those words have been, and are, and will be, the true sustenance of the human spirit, and the heavenly manna of which it may be said, almost without a figure, that ' he who gathers much has nothing over, and even he who gathers little has no lack.' Such, amidst many inconsistencies, was the definition of ' the body of Christ' given by some of the ancient fathers, Origen, Jerome, even Gregory called the Great. Such, amidst many contradictions, was the nobler view maintained at least in one remarkable passage even in the Roman Missal which states that where the sacrament cannot be had ' sufficit vera fides et bona voluntas. Tantum crede et manducasti.' It has been well said by a devout Scottish bishop, in speaking of this subject: ' We should not expect to arrive at the secret of Hamlet by eating a bit

<hr>

[2] Sydney Smith, *Lectures on Moral Philosophy,* p. 12.
[3] Milman's *History of Latin Christianity,* vol. vi. p. 638.

of Shakespeare's body; and so, though we ate ever so much of the material bones or flesh of the Founder of the Eucharist, we should not arrive one whit nearer to "the mind which was in Christ Jesus." ' [4]   It is only by the mind that we can appropriate the mind and heart of Christ—only by the spirit that we can appropriate His spirit.   And therefore (it is an old truth, but one which requires to be again and again repeated) all acts of so-called communion with Christ have no Biblical or spiritual meaning except in proportion as they involve or express a moral fellowship with the Holy, the Just, the Pure, and the Truthful, wherever His likeness can be found—except in proportion as our spirits, minds, and characters move in unison with the parables of the Prodigal Son, and the Good Samaritan, and the Faithful Servant, and the Good Shepherd; with the Beatitudes on the Galilean mountain, with the resignation of Gethsemane, with the courage of Calvary.   In proportion as the ordinance of the Eucharist enables us to do this, it is a true partaking of what the Gospels intended by the body of Christ; in proportion as it fails to do this, it is no partaking of anything.

This is what is adumbrated in the English Communion Office, and by feebler expressions in the Roman Office, when it is said that every communicant pledges himself to walk in the steps of the great Self-sacrificer, and to offer himself a sacrifice of body, soul, and spirit to the Heavenly Father. We must incorporate and incarnate in ourselves—that is, in our moral natures—the substance, the moral substance, of the teaching and character of Jesus Christ.   That is the only true transubstantiation.   We must raise ourselves above the base and mean and commonplace trivialities and follies of the world and of the Church to the lofty ideal of the Gospel story.   That is the only true elevation of the Host.   Nor is there anything fanciful or overstrained in the metaphor, when we grasp the substance of which it is the sign.   The record of the life and death of Jesus Christ, however we in-

' *Memoir of Bishop Ewing.*

terpret it, is, and must be, the body, the substance, the backbone of Christendom.

2. And this leads us to pass from the meaning of the phrase in the Gospels to its meaning in the Epistles. St. Paul distinctly tells us in the same Epistle as that in which he gives the earliest narrative of the Supper (1 Cor. x. 16, 17), 'For we being many are one bread and one body '— *The Body is the Church.* that is, as the bread is one loaf made up of many particles and crumbs, so the Christian society is one body made up of many members, and that body is the body of Christ.   Christ is gone; the body, the outward form and substance that takes His place, is the assembly, the congregation of all His true followers.   In this sense ' the body of Christ ' is (as is expressed in the second prayer of the English Communion Office) ' the blessed company of all faithful people.'   This is the 'body '—the community and fellowship one with another— which the Corinthian Christians were so slow to discern.[5] This is the sense in which the words are used in the vast majority of instances where the expression occurs in St. Paul's Epistles.[6]   It is a use of the word which no doubt varies from that in which it is employed by Christ Himself, and thus shows the extraordinary freedom of the Apostle in dealing even with the most sacred phrases.   But the doctrine is the same as that which in substance pervades the general teaching of our Lord—namely, that the wise, the good, the suffering everywhere are His substitutes.   ' Wheresoever two or three are gathered together, there am I in the midst of them.' ' He that receiveth you receiveth me.'   The whole point of the description of the Last Judgment is, that even the good heathens having never heard His name yet have seen Him and served Him, and when they ask Him ' When saw we

---

[5] 1 Cor xi. 29.   Even if the words were as in the English Authorised Version 'not discerning *the Lord's* body,' the sense would still be governed by the uniform language of the Apostle.   But the meaning is brought out still more strongly in the genuine text, where it is simply 'not discerning *the body*.'

[6] Compare Rom. xii. 4, 5; 1 Cor. xii. 12, 13, 20, 27; Eph. ii. 16, iii. 6, iv. 4, 12, 16; Col. i. 18, ii. 19, iii. 15.

thee?' He answers, without hesitation or reserve: 'Inasmuch as ye did it to the least of these My brethren, ye did it unto Me. It was I who was hungry, and ye gave Me food. It was I who was thirsty, and ye gave Me drink. It was I who was a friendless stranger, and ye took Me in. It was I who was naked, and ye clothed Me. It was I who was on my sick-bed, and ye visited Me. It was I who was shut up in prison, and ye visited Me.' These good deeds, wherever practised, are the true signs that Christ and Christianity have been there. Even if practised without naming His name, they are still the trophies of the victory over evil, for which He lived and died; they are on the desert island of this mortal existence the footmarks which show that something truly human, and therefore truly divine, has passed that way.

If this be so—if every faithful servant of truth and goodness throughout the world is the representative of the Founder of our faith—if every friendless sufferer to whom we can render a service is as if Christ Himself appeared to us—then, not in the scholastic, but certainly in the Biblical sense of the word, there is a Real Presence diffused through our whole daily intercourse. It is the truth which the Swiss Reformer expressed, who, seeing a number of famished people around the church-door, said: 'I will not enter the church over the body of Christ.' And lest this should seem to be a vague or unimpressive or unedifying doctrine, we venture to draw out its consequences more at length.

The whole of Christendom, the whole of humanity, is, in this sense, one body and many members. In the vast variety of human gifts and human characters, it is only by this sympathy, forbearance, appreciation of that which one has and the other lacks, that we reach that ideal of society such as St. Paul imagined, such as Butler in his Sermon on Human Nature so well sets forth. It is the old Roman fable of Menenius Agrippa taken up and sanctified by the Christian apostle. It is the Biblical recognition, as the French would say, of the 'solidarity' of peoples, of churches, and of men. It is the protest against the isolated selfishness in which we often shut ourselves up against wider sympathies. And as a nation we are one body, drawn together by the long tradition and lineage which have made us of one flesh and blood. Blood is thicker than water. Except we acknowledge the unity of our common kindred, we have no true national life abiding in us. We are one 'body politic'—a fine expression which St. Paul has taught us. Our unity as Englishmen is also our unity in Him of whom all the tribes and families in earth are named. We were made one nation and one race by the order of His providence; and they who make more of their party or their sect than of their country are refusing communion with the body of Him 'whose fulness filleth all in all.' And also as a Church, whether the Church Universal or the Church of our country, we are one body; for the likenesses of character and opinion and pursuit which unite us, whether within the pale of the Church or without it, are but as so many bones and sinews, tissues and fibres, whereby 'the whole body, being fitly joined together and compacted by that which every joint supplieth, maketh increase of the body unto the edifying of itself in love.' And there is, also, the one body in which there is the one eternal communion of the living and the dead. Here the partitions of flesh fall away. Here there is but the communion of the spirit. But that communion is the deepest and the most enduring of all, for it is beyond the reach of time or chance. It can never be broken except by our own negligence and selfishness. Whether it be the departure of a soul in the fulness of its glory and its usefulness, or of a soul burdened with the decay and weariness of its long pilgrimage, the union may and shall still subsist. 'We reckon not by months and years where they are gone to dwell;' we know only that they are in Him and with Him in whom we also live and move and have our being. They live because God lives, and we live or may live

I

with them in that unity of soul and spirit which is beyond the grave and gate of death.

3. We now propose to take the expression, the *blood of Christ*, whether as used in the Gospels or in the Epistles.[7]   First, is it the actual physical blood shed on the cross or flowing in the Redeemer's veins ?  In the Middle Ages it was not an uncommon belief that drops of this blood had been preserved in various localities.  There was the legend of the Sangrail or Holy Cup, or, as some used to read it, the Sangreal or the ' real blood,' said to have been brought by Joseph of Arimathea to Glastonbury and sought for by the Knights of King Arthur's Round Table.  There is still shown in the church of the Saint Sang at Bruges a phial containing the blood—' the precious blood,' as it is called—said to have been brought back by the Crusaders.  There was another phial, which the Master of the Temple gave to Henry III., and which he carried in state from St. Paul's to Westminster Abbey, and of which drops were also shown at Ashridge and Hailes Abbey.  The Abbey of Fécamp was also built to receive a casket which brought the like sacred liquid in a miraculous boat to the shores of Normandy.  But even where these relics are not at once condemned as fabulous or spurious, the shrines which contain them are comparatively deserted. The pilgrims to the churches at Fécamp and Brussels cannot be named in comparison with the crowds that flock to the modern centres of French devotion.  And even as far back as the thirteenth century Thomas Aquinas speaks of these literal drops with indifference.

Nor, again, was the actual bloodshed the most conspicuous characteristic of the Crucifixion.  Modes of death there are where the scaffold is deluged with blood—where the spectators, the executioners, the victims, are plunged in the crimson stream.  Not so in the few faint drops

The marginal note reads: The blood of Christ.

<hr>

[7] The phrase 'body of Christ' (with the exception of Heb. x. 5, 10) does not occur in other than St. Paul's Epistles. But the phrase 'the blood of Christ' occurs also in the Epistles of St. Peter and St. John and that to the Hebrews.

which trickled from the hands and feet of the Crucified, or which flowed from His wounded side. There was pallor, and thirst, and anguish, but the physical bloodshed was the last thing that a bystander would have noticed. Nor, again, has it been supposed in the Roman Catholic Church, except by very ignorant persons, that the wine in the Eucharist is the actual physical blood of Christ. There is, indeed, a small chapel on the shores of the Lake of Bolsena in which are pointed out spots of blood as from the sacramental wine, and there was at Wilsnake in the north of Germany a napkin marked with similar stains. But these are now treated either with contempt and incredulity, or at the most as exceptional portents.

It is obvious, then, that, alike in the Catholic and Protestant world, the expression 'blood of Christ' is by all thinking Christians regarded as a figure of speech, sacred and solemn, but still pointing to something beyond itself. What is that something? The wine is confessedly the emblem of the blood of Christ. But the blood of Christ itself, when used as a religious term, must also be the emblem of some spiritual reality. What is that spiritual reality?

What is the moral significance of *blood?* It may be manifold.

There is its peculiar meaning in the crimson colour which overspreads the face in moments of great emotion. It has been well said: 'If God made the blood of man, did he not much more make that feeling which summons the Blush. blood to his face, and makes it the sign of guilt?' [8] and, we must also add, of just indignation, of honest shame, of ingenuous modesty? It would be childish to speak of the mere colour or liquid of the blood in these cases as the thing important. It would be unphilosophical, on the other hand, not to acknowledge the value of the moral quality of which the blood in these cases is the sure sign and sacrament. There is a famous passage in Terence in speaking of the features of a young man: 'He blushes—his face glows with scarlet; he is

---

[8] Sydney Smith, *Lectures on Moral Philosophy*, p. 11.

saved. (*Erubuit; salva res est.*) He was saved by that which the mantling blood in his cheek represented.

There is another idea of which blood is the emblem. It is the idea of suffering. A wound, a blow produces the effusion of blood, and blood therefore suggests the idea of pain. This is no doubt part of the thought in such passages as 'This is He that came by water and by blood,' or 'Without shedding of blood there is no remission,' or again in the magnificent description of the conqueror of Edom (Isa. lxiii. 1–3) advancing knee-deep in the blood, whether of himself or his enemies, there is the lively expression of the truth that without exertion there can be no victory—that ' *via crucis, via lucis.*' It is the thought so well set forth in Keble's hymn on the Circumcision :—

*Suffering.*

> Like sacrificial wine
>    Pour'd on a victim's head
> Are those few precious drops of Thine
>    Now first to offering led.
>
> They are the pledge and seal
>    Of Christ's unswerving faith
> Given to His Sire, our souls to heal,
>    Although it cost His death.[9]

But these and all other moral senses which we can attach to the word *blood* run up into a more general and also a more Biblical significance. 'The blood of a living thing is the life thereof.'[1] This expression of the old Jewish Law, many times repeated, well harmonises with the language of Harvey: ' Blood is the fountain of life, the first to live, and the last to die, and the primary seat of the animal soul.' When anyone was described as shedding his blood for another, or sealing a testament or will or covenant with his blood, it was meant that he sealed or signed it with whatever was most precious, most a part of himself. The

The innermost essence of Christ.

---

* This is well set forth in an interesting volume lately published by Dr. Story, of Roseneath, entitled *Creed and Conduct* (pp. 77-92).

¹ Lev. xvii. 14. See *Speaker's Commentary*, vol. i. part ii. p. 836; Ewald, *Antiquities of the people of Israel,* pp. 35-41, 44-62 (Eng. transl.).

blood is the life-blood—is, as it were, the very soul of those who give it. The spot of blood upon on the altar, whether of human or animal sacrifice, the streak of blood from the Paschal lamb on the forehead of Jew or Samaritan, represented the vital spark of the dead creature which a few moments before had been full of life and vigour.

As, then, the body of Christ, in the language of Scripture means (as we saw) one of two things—either His general character and moral being, or the Christian and human society which now represents Him—so the blood of Christ in like manner means the inmost essence of His character, the self of His self, or else the inmost essence of the Christian society, the life-blood of Christendom and humanity. And therefore we must ask yet another question : What is the most essential characteristic, the most precious part of Christ, the most peculiar and vivifying element of Christendom? This question is not so easy to answer in a single word. Different minds would take a different view of that which to them constitutes the one thing needful, the one indispensable element of the Christian life. To some it would seem to be freedom, to others intellectual progress, to others justice, to others truth, to others purity. But looking at the Bible only, and taking the Bible as a whole —asking what is at once the most comprehensive and the most peculiar characteristic of the life of Jesus Christ and of the best spirits of Christendom—we cannot go far astray in adopting the only definition of the blood of Christ which has come down to us from primitive times. It is contained in one of the three undisputed, or at any rate least disputed, epistles of Ignatius of Antioch. 'The blood of Christ,' he said, 'is love or charity.'[2] With this unquestionably agrees the language of the New Testament as to the essential characteristic of God and of Christ. Love, unselfish love, is there spoken of again and again as the fundamental essence of the highest life of God ; and it is also evident on the face of the Gospels that it is the fundamental motive and

Love.

---

[2] Ignatius, Ad Rom. 7 ; Ad Trall. 8.

characteristic of the life and death of Christ. It is this love stronger than death, this love manifesting itself in death, this love willing to spend itself for others, that is the blood of the life in which God is well pleased. Not the pain or torture of the cross—for that was alike odious to God and useless to man—but the love, the self-devotion, the generosity, the magnanimity, the forgiveness, the toleration, the compassion, of which that blood was the expression, and of which that life and death were the fulfilment. 'Non sanguine sed pietate placatur Deus' is the maxim of more than one of the Fathers. 'What is the blood of Christ?'[3] asked Livingstone of his own solitary soul in the last months of his African wanderings. 'It is Himself. It is the inherent and everlasting mercy of God made apparent to human eyes and ears. The everlasting love was disclosed by our Lord's life and death. It showed that God forgives because He loves to forgive. He rules, if possible, by smiles and not by frowns. Pain is only a means of enforcing love.' The charity of God to men, the charity of men to one another with all its endless consequences—if it be not this, what is it? If there be any other characteristic of Christ more essential to His true nature, any message of the gospel more precious than this, let us know it. But till we are told of any other we may rest contented with believing that it is that which St. John himself describes as the essence of the nature of God ('God is love'), which St. Paul describes as the highest of the virtues of man ('The greatest of these is love'). It is that which Charles Wesley, in one of his most beautiful hymns, describes as the best answer to the soul inquiring after God : not justification or conversion, but—

> Come, O Thou Traveller unknown !
> Whom still I hold, but cannot see—
>
> Speak, or Thou never hence shalt move,
> And tell me if Thy name be Love.
>
> In vain I have not wept and strove :
> Thy nature and Thy name is Love.

---

[3] *Livingstone's Journal*, August 5, 1873. The word used is 'What is the atonement?' But he evidently meant the same thing.

It is that which John Keble, in a poem of which the sentiment might have been from Whichcote or Schleiermacher,
describes as the best answer to the inquiry after the
religious life of man : not the sacraments, not the creeds,
but—

> Would'st thou the life of souls discern ?
>   Nor human wisdom nor divine
> Helps thee by aught beside to learn :
>   *Love* is life's only sign.

It is that which Ken, in a fine passage at the beginning of
his ' Approach to the Altar,' thus states with a bold latitudinarianism, like indeed to the theology of his hymns, but
widely at variance with the dogmatic rigidity of the school
to which he belonged : ' To obtain eternal life, all I am to do
is reduced to one word only, and that is "love."  This is
the first and great command, which comprehends all others—
the proper evangelical grace. . . . The love of God is a grace
rather felt than defined.  It is the general tendency and
inclination of the whole man, of all his heart and soul
and strength, of all his powers and affections, and of the
utmost strength of them all, to God as his chief and only
and perfect and infinite good.'  It is therefore not only from
Calvary, but from Bethlehem and Nazareth and Capernaum—
not only from the Crucifixion, but from all His acts of mercy
and words of wisdom—that ' the blood of Christ' derives its
moral significance.  As so often in ordinary human lives, so
in that Divine life, the death was the crowning consummation ; but as in the best human lives, as in the best deaths
of the best men, so also in that Divine death, the end was of
value only or chiefly because it corresponded so entirely to
the best of lives.  Doubtless love is not the only idea of
perfection—kindness is not the only idea of Heaven.  The
terrible sufferings of this present world are very difficult to
reconcile with the belief that its Maker is all-loving to all his
creatures.  Yet still the Gospel story leaves no doubt that
unselfish kindness and compassion were the leading principles
of the life of Christ ; and the history of Christendom leaves

no doubt that unselfish benevolence and kindness are the most valuable elements of the life of society.

If we now turn to the sacrament of the Lord's Supper, and ask in what special way the fruit of the grape, the chalice of the Communion, represent the love of Christ and the love of His followers, the answer is twofold.

First, as being at a farewell feast, it was the likeness of the blood shed, as we have already noticed, in the signing and seal-ing of treaties or covenants. The earliest account of the institution of the Eucharist (1 Cor. xi. 25) ex-presses this directly. Not 'This is my blood,' but ' *This is the New Covenant in my blood.*' It was the practice of the ancient Arabs to sign their treaties with blood drawn from their own veins. Even in modern times, when the Scottish peasants and nobles desired to express their adhesion to the Solemn League and Covenant, they in some instances wrote their names with their blood. There are also examples of conspi-rators binding themselves together by the practice of drinking a cup filled with human blood, as the most solemn mode of testifying their adhesion to each other. There is again the expression and the image familiar to all of us, of the soldier, the martyr, the patriot shedding his blood for the good of his country, his cause, his religion. From the blood of the righteous Abel to the blood of Zacharias who was slain between the temple and the altar, from the blood of Zacharias to the last soldier who shed his blood on behalf of his country, it is the supreme offering which any human being can make to loyalty, to duty, to faith. And of all these examples of the sacrifice of life, of the shedding of blood, the most sacred, the most efficacious, is that which was offered and shed on Calvary, because it was the offering made not for war or aggression, but for peace and reconcilia-tion ; not in hatred, but in love ; not by a feeble, erring, ordinary mortal, but by Him who is by all of us acknow-ledged to be the Ideal of man and the Likeness of God. It is, therefore, this final and supreme test of our love and loyalty that the cup of the Eucharist suggests—our willingness, if so be, to sacrifice our own selves, to shed our own blood for what we believe to be right and true and for the good of others.

And secondly, the use of wine to represent the blood—that is, the love—of Christ, conveys to us the profound thought that as wine makes glad the heart of man, so the love of God, the love of Christ, the love of man for God and men, makes glad the heart of those who come within its invigorating, enkindling influence. In that fierce war waged in the fifteenth century by the Bohemian nation in order to regain the use of the sacramental wine which the Roman Church had forbidden, when they recovered the use of it, the sacred cup or chalice was henceforth carried as a trophy in front of their armies. With them it was a mere pledge of their ecclesiastical triumph, a token of their national independence. But with us, when we turn from the outward thing to the thing signified, it is only too true that Catholics and Protestants alike have lost the cup from their Communion feasts. If, as we have said, the blood of Christ, of which the sacred wine is the emblem, in itself signifies the self-denying, life-giving love[4] of Christ, have not we often lost from our lives and our ordinances that which is the life of all Christian life, and the wine of all Christian ordinances— namely, the love or charity ' without which whosoever liveth is counted dead before God'? Whosoever regains that chalice, whosoever pours that new wine into our dead hearts, may well bear it as a trophy before the Christian armies. The ground on which the Roman Church withheld the literal wine from all but the officiating priest was the scruple lest the material liquid might possibly be spilled. Our ground for insisting on the cup for the laity ought to be that the Divine charity of which the cup of the Communion is the emblem belongs to the whole Church. To recover that holy cup, that real life-blood of the Redeemer, is a quest worthy of

[4] George Herbert :—

> Love is that liquor sweet and most divine,
> Which my God feels as blood, and I as wine.

A similar striking expression is in a poem in *The Rivulet.*

all the chivalry of our time, worthy of all the courage of Lancelot, worthy of all the purity of Galahad.[5]

This is the wine of that heavenly enthusiasm of which a Persian sage sang of old : ' Bring me a cup of wine, not that wine which drives away wisdom, but that unmixed wine whose hidden force vanquishes fate—that clear wine which sanctifies the garb of the heart—that illuminating wine which shows to lovers of the world the true path—that purifying wine which cleanses the meditative mind from fanciful thoughts.'[6]  This is indeed the likeness of the blood which spoke better things than the blood of Abel, because it was not the mere material blood of an innocent victim, but it was, and is, the aspiring love and life which sank not in the ground, but rose again to be the love and life of a regenerated world.

And this leads us to ask yet one more question.  What is the moral effect of this life-blood on the Christian spirit?  The answer is given by St. John (1 John i. 7, 9): ' It *cleanseth* us from all sin,' or, as is said in the words just following, ' *cleanseth* us from all *unrighteousness*,' from all *injustice, unequal dealing, iniquity*.  This figure of cleansing or washing, which occurs often in the Bible in this connection with blood, seems to be taken not so much from the Hebrew worship as from the Mithraic or Persian sacrifices then so common, in which the worshippers were literally bathed in a stream of blood, not merely sprinkled or touched but plunged from head to foot as in a baptism of blood.  The figure in itself is revolting.  But its very strangeness throws us far away from the sign to the reality. It means that where any soul is imbued with a love, a charity like that of Christ, surrounded, bathed in this as in a holy atmosphere, withdrawn by the contemplation of His death and by the spirit of His life from all the corrupting influences of the world or the Church, there the sin, the hatred, the uncharitableness, the untruthfulness of men are purified and washed away.  So far as the blood—that is, the self-sacrificing love—of Christ effects this, so far it has done its work ; so far as it has

*The cleansing.*

* See C. Stubbs's *Myths of Life*, p. 100.          * *Sacred Anthology*, p. 167.

not done this, it has been shed in vain.  It is said that a young
English soldier of gay and dissolute life was once reading
this chapter of St. John, and when he came to the passage—
'The blood of Jesus Christ. . . . *cleanseth* us from all sin'—
he started up and exclaimed : 'Then henceforth I will live,
by the grace of God, as a man should live who has been
washed in the blood of Jesus Christ.'[7]  That was Hedley
Vicars.  And by this thought he lived thenceforth a pure
and spotless life.  That was indeed to be 'cleansed by the
blood of Christ.'  It was an example the more striking, because
probably unconscious, of the true meaning of the cleansing
effect of 'the blood'—that is, the unselfish life and death—
of Christ.  Cleansing, bathing, washing—these, of course, are
figures of speech when applied to the soul.  But they must
mean for the soul what is meant by cleansing as applied to.
the body.  When, for example, we pray with the Psalmist,
'Make clean our hearts within us,' we pray that our motives
may be made free from all those by-ends and self-regards
that spoil even some of the finest natures.  When the
prophet said that our sins should be made 'as white as wool,'
he meant that so great is the power of the human will, and
of the grace of God, that the human character can be transformed—that the soul which once was stained deep with the
red spots of sin can become white as driven snow.  When we
speak of Christ Himself as the spotless immaculate Lamb, we
mean that He was really without spot of sin.  When we
speak of ourselves as washed in the blood of that Lamb, we
ought to mean not that we continue 'just as we were,' with
a cleanness imputed to us in which our characters have no
share, but that our uncharitableness, our untruthfulness, our
cowardice, our vulgarity, our unfairness, are, so far as human
infirmity will permit, washed out.  When in one part of

---

[7] The belief that a bath of blood has a purifying effect appears from
time to time in the stories of kings, suffering from dreadful maladies, bathing themselves in the blood of children—Pharaoh (Midrash on Ex. ii. 23),
Constantine, Charles IX. of France.  For this reason baptism was often
said to be 'in the blood of Christ.'  See Wilberforce, *Doctrine of the
Eucharist*, p. 228.

the English Communion Service we pray that our souls may be washed in the blood of Christ, it is the same prayer as in substance we pray in that other collect in another part of the same office which John Wesley declared to be[8] the summary of the primitive religion of love, the summary of the religion of the Church of England : ‘ Cleanse the thoughts of our hearts by the inspiration of Thy Holy Spirit, that we may perfectly love Thee and worthily magnify Thy holy name.’  When, in the well-known hymns which are often sung in excited congregations, we speak of ‘the fountain filled with blood drawn from Emmanuel’s veins, where sinners plunged beneath that flood lose all their guilty stains,’ these passages, unless they are only figures without substance, must be the prayer which goes up from every soul which feels the desire to be cleansed from all those defilements of passion or falsehood or self-conceit or hatred which will doubtless cling to us more or less to the end of our mortal life, but disappear in proportion as we are bathed in the Spirit of eternal love and purity.  It is the same prayer as that which is expressed in more refined and chastened language by our own living Laureate in his poem on St. Agnes :—

> Make thou my spirit pure and clear
> As are the frosty skies ;

or in the yet sublimer invocation of Milton to Him who prefers

> Before all temples the upright heart and pure.

But perhaps we ought still to ask—How is it that the love of Christ, which is the love of man and the love of God, and which is the life-blood of the Christian religion—how is it that this love cleanses and purifies the character?  Why is it, more than justice, or truth, or courage, described as the regenerating element of the human heart?  It was long ago described by Sophocles.  In a philosophic sense it is well drawn out in Butler’s Sermon on the Love of God.  With all the energy of an impassioned and devout soul it is

---

[8] Wesley’s *Sermons*, vol. iii. p. 424.

drawn out in the sermons and letters of Charles Kingsley. But still, in order to show that we are not merely dealing in generalities, take some of the special forms in which true affection has this effect in human life. Take gratitude. We have known some one who has done us a lasting service. We wish to repay the kindness. In ninety-nine cases out of a hundred we cannot repay it better than by showing that we are worthy of it. We have, by the exertions of a good friend, been placed in a good situation or set in a good way of life. We keep in mind the effect which our good or evil conduct will have on such friends. It will wound them to the quick if we deceive or disappoint their expectations. It will be as sunshine to their life if we do credit to their recommendation. The boy at school, the public officer ministering for the public good, the private clerk in some responsible situation, the servant in a household great or small, may have always before them the image of their benefactor. The love, the gratitude, which they bear, or ought to bear, towards him, will cleanse and purify their hearts. If he or she is still living, we may think what it would be to meet them with an open or a shame-stricken countenance. The love which they have shown to us, and the gratitude we feel, will drive out the evil spirit.

Or, again, gratitude for some great benefit, say a recovery from illness. It may have been a recovery for which many have anxiously watched—a recovery which has, as it were, given us a new lease of life. He who responds to that experience will have his heart softened, opened, cleansed. That heart which refuses to be softened, opened, and cleansed, after such an experience, must be as hard as the nether mill-stone. Such a one, wherever he may be, if indeed he has so little of the grateful sense of good received, has trodden under foot the love of 'the everlasting covenant' which nature as well as grace has made between man and man, between man and God.

Or, again, the love, the pure affections, of home. We sometimes hear it said that during the last few years the bonds of English society are relaxed, the fountains of English morality poisoned—that things are talked of, and tolerated, and practised, which in the former generation would have been despised, condemned, and put down. Against these defiling, destroying, devastating influences, what is the safeguard? It is surely the maintenance, the encouragement, of that pure domestic love of which we just now spoke. Dr. Chalmers used to preach of the expulsive force of a *new* affection. But it is enough for our purpose to have the expulsive force of an *old* affection—of that old, very old affection which lies in the vitals of human society, which is truly its life-blood—the affection of son for father and mother, of husband for wife and of wife for husband, of brother for sister and of sister for brother. Such an element of affection is the salt of the national existence, is the continuation of the remembrance of that sacred blood of which we are told ' to drink and be thankful.' He who turns his back on these home affections has left himself open to become the prey, whether in the upper or the lower classes, of the basest and vilest of men, of the basest and vilest of women.

Or, again, the love of our country, or, if we prefer so to put it, the love of the public good. It is no fancy to call these feelings by so strong a name. They who have felt it know that it is a passion which cheers us amidst the greatest difficulties, which consoles us even in the deepest private calamities. And it is a passion in the presence of which the meaner trivialities of existence wither and perish. It is a passion in the absence of which there grows up falsehood, and intrigue, and vulgar insolence, and selfish ambition and rancorous faction. It was a passion which animated our great statesmen of times gone by—Chatham, Pitt, Fox, Canning, Wellington, and Peel. It was a passion which once cleansed our Augean stable, which flowed like a generous wine through the veins of the Commonwealth and to the extremities of society. Whether it is now more or less potent than it was then, whether the public service of the State is sought after, or the great questions of the day taken up, more or less than formerly, from the large and sincere conviction of their truth and their goodness, or only, or chiefly, for temporary or personal purposes, let those answer who best know. Only, whenever this lofty passion shall cease in the high places of our land, then the end is not far off; then the blood of patriots will have been wasted, the blood of heroes and of martyrs will have been shed in vain; and with the decay of public spirit and of the affection of our best citizens for our common country, the moral health and strength of State and of Church, of statesmen and of private men, will dwindle, peak, and pine as surely as a sickly frame through which the life-blood has ceased to permeate.

These are some of the examples of the way in which single disinterested affection for what is good makes all duties easy and all vices difficult, and so fulfils the law of God. For the purification thus effected by the love of friends, home, and country is the likeness of what may be effected by that love through which the Supreme Goodness comes down to earth, and through which our imperfect goodness ascends to heaven.

In this brief summary of the Biblical meaning of the words ' Body and Blood of Christ,' it has been intended not so much to run counter to any metaphysical theories on the Eucharist, as to indicate that the only important significance to be attached to the Biblical words belongs to a region which those theories hardly touch, and which, therefore, may be treated beyond and apart from most of the controversies on the subject. In some phrases of the Roman Missal, and perhaps still more in parts of the Roman practice, it is difficult to avoid the impression that a magical process is implied of material particles touching the mind as though it were matter. This accordingly became synonymous with the most vulgar form of sleight of hand. The sacred phrase of ' Hoc est corpus ' by a natural descent was corrupted into 'hocus pocus.' The obligation of fasting before the Communion has been confirmed, if not originated, by the notion that the matter of the sacramental substance might meet the matter of ordinary food in the process of physical digestion. In the Communion Offices of the Reformed Churches, including the English, traces of these material traditions linger, and the higher purpose of moral improvement originally implied in the words has perhaps been also thrown into the background by the prominence of the historical and commemorative element. Still, even in the Roman Office, and much more in the Protestant Offices, the moral element is found, and probably, to the more enlightened members of all Churches, the idea is never altogether absent that the main object of the Eucharist is the moral improvement of the communicants. Nevertheless, it is necessary to bring out as strongly as possible this moral element as the primary, it is hardly too much to say the sole, meaning of the words on which the institution of the Eucharist is founded. It may be that the moral intention of these sacred phrases and acts is, unconsciously if not consciously, so deeply imbedded in their structure as to render any such exposition unnecessary. It may be that the signs, the shadows, the figures have been or shall be so raised above what is local, material, and temporary, that they shall be almost inseparable from the moral improvement which alone is the true food,[9] the true health of the soul. But possibly the materialism of the ecclesiastical sacristy, keeping pace with the materialism of the philosophic school, may so undermine the spiritual element of this almost the only external ordinance of Christianity, as to endanger the ordinance itself. Possibly the carnal and material may so absorb and obliterate the spiritual that it will be necessary in the name of Religion to expect some change in the outward forms of the sacrament, not less incisive than those which in former ages by the general instinct of Christendom swept away those parts which have now perished for ever. Infant Communion, once universal throughout the whole Church, and still retained in the East, has been

---

[9] There is a striking passage in Fénelon to the effect that the true food of the soul is moral goodness. (*Meditations on the Sixteenth Day.*)

forbidden throughout the whole Western Church, Catholic and Protestant alike. Daily Communion, universal in the primitive Church, has for the vast majority of Christians been discontinued both in East and West. Evening Communion, has been forbidden by the Roman Church. Solitary Communion has been forbidden in the English Church. Death-bed Communion has been forbidden in the Scottish Church. It is difficult to imagine changes, short of total abolition, more sweeping than these. But most of them were induced by the repugnance of the higher instinct of Christendom to see its most sacred ceremony degraded into a charm. It is possible that the metaphors of the Bible on this subject shall be felt to have been so misused and distorted that they also shall pass into the same abeyance as has already overtaken some expressions which formerly were no less dear to pious hearts than these. The use of the language of the Canticles, such as was familiar to St. Bernard and Samuel Rutherford, has become impossible, and many terms used in St. Paul's Epistles to the Romans and Galatians on Predestination and Justification are now but very rarely heard in ordinary pulpits. But, whatever betide, it is alike the duty and the hope, whether of those who fondly cling to these forms or words, or of those who think, perhaps too boldly, that they can dispense with them, to keep steadily in view the moral realities, for the sake of which alone (if Christianity be the universal religion) such forms exist, and which will survive the disappearance even of the most venerable ordinances, even of the most sacred phrases.

# CHAPTER VII.

## ABSOLUTION.

IT is well known that in certain parts of Christendom, and in certain sections of the English Church, considerable importance is attached to the words which appear in the Gospels of St. Matthew and St. John, as justifying the paramount duty of all Christians to confess their sins to presbyters who have received episcopal ordination, and the exclusive right of presbyters, so appointed, to absolve them.

It is not here intended to enter on the various objections raised on moral grounds to this theory.   But it may be useful to show the original meaning of the words, and then trace their subsequent history.   It will be then seen that, whatever other grounds there may be for the doctrine or practice in question, these passages have either no relation to it, or whatever relation they have is the exact contradiction of the theory in question.

The texts are (in English) as follows :—

The address to Peter (Matt. xvi. 19) : 'Whatsoever thou shalt bind on earth shall be bound in heaven : and whatsoever thou shalt loose on earth shall be loosed in heaven.'

The address to the disciples (Matt. xviii. 18) : ' Whatsoever ye shall bind on earth shall be bound in heaven : and whatsoever ye shall loose on earth shall be loosed in heaven.'

The address to the disciples (John xx. 23) : ' Whosesoever sins ye remit, they are remitted unto them : and whosesoever sins ye retain, they are retained.'

We will first take the two passages in the Gospel of St.

Matthew. For the purposes of this argument the words addressed to St. Peter need not be distinguished from the words addressed to the disciples, as they are in each case identically the same.[1]

I. The phrase 'binding' and 'loosing' meant, in the language of the Jewish schools, declaring what is right and what is wrong. If any Master, or Rabbi, or Judge declared a thing to be right or true, he was said to have loosed it; if he declared a thing to be wrong or false, he was said to have bound it. That this is the original meaning of the words has been set at rest beyond possibility of question since the decisive quotations given by the most learned Hebrew scholars of the seventeenth century.[2] The meaning, therefore, of the expressions, as addressed to the first disciples, was that, humble as they seemed to be, yet, by virtue of the new spiritual life and new spiritual insight which Christ brought into the world, their decisions in cases of right and wrong would be invested with all and more than all the authority which had belonged before to the Masters of the Jewish Assemblies, to the Rulers and Teachers of the Synagogues. It was the same promise as was expressed in substance in those other well-known passages: 'It is not ye that speak, but the Spirit of my Father which speaketh in you.' 'He that is spiritual judgeth all things.' 'Ye have an unction from the Holy One, and ye know all things, and need not that any one should teach you.' 'The Comforter shall lead you into all truth.'

The sense thus given is as adequate to the occasion as it is certainly true. In the new crisis through which the world was to pass, they—the despised scholars of a despised Master —were to declare what was changeable and what was unchangeable, what was eternal, what was transitory, what

---

[1] For their peculiar meaning as addressed to St. Peter, it may be permitted to refer to a volume published many years ago, entitled *Sermons and Essays on the Apostolic Age*, pp. 127–34.

[2] 'Hebrew and Talmudical Exercitations upon the Evangelist St. Matthew (xvi. 19). By John Lightfoot, D.D.' *Works*, vol. ii. pp. 206–7.

was worthy of approval, and what was worthy of condemnation.    They were to declare the innocence of a thousand
customs of the Gentile world, which their Jewish countrymen
had believed to be sinful; they were to declare the exceeding
sinfulness of a thousand acts which both Jews and Pagans
had believed to be virtuous or indifferent.    They were empowered to announce with unswerving confidence the paramount importance of charity, and the supreme preciousness
of truth.    They were empowered to denounce with unsparing
condemnation the meanness of selfishness, the sacrilege of
impurity, the misery of self-deceit, the impiety of uncharitableness.    And what the first generation of Christians, to
whom these words were addressed, thus decided, has on the
whole been ratified in heaven—has on the whole been ratified
by the voice of Providence in the subsequent history of mankind.    By this discernment of good and evil the Apostolic
writers became the lawgivers of the civilised world.    Eighteen
hundred years have passed, and their judgments in all
essential points have never been reversed.

The authority or the accuracy of portions of the New
Testament on this or that point is often disputed.    The
grammar, the arguments, the history of the authors of the
Gospels and Epistles can often be questioned.    But that
which must govern us all—their declaration of the moral
standard of mankind, the ideal they have placed before us of
that which is to guide our conduct—which is, after all, as has
been said by Matthew Arnold, three fourths of human life—
has hardly been questioned at all by the intelligent and upright part of mankind.    The condemnation of sins, the com-
mendation of graces, in St. Matthew's description of the
Beatitudes, in St. Luke's description of the Prodigal Son, in
St. John's description of the conversation with the woman of
Samaria, in St. Peter's declaration that in every land 'he
that worketh righteousness (of whatever creed or race) is accepted of God,' in St. Paul's description of charity, in St.
James's description of pure religion—have commanded the
entire assent of the world, of Bolingbroke and Voltaire no

less than of Thomas à Kempis and Wesley, because these
moral judgments bear on their face that stamp of the divine,
the superhuman, the truly supernatural, which critical inquiry
cannot touch, which human wisdom and human folly alike,
whilst they may be unwilling or unable to fulfil the precepts,
yet cannot deny.  This is the original meaning in which the
judgments of the first Christians in regard to sin and virtue
were ratified in heaven.  It is necessary to insist on this
point in order to show that an amply sufficient force and
solemnity is inherent in the proper meaning of the words,
without resorting to fictitious modes of aggrandising them in
directions for which they were not intended.

The signification of the phrase in John xx. 23, translated
in the Authorised Version 'remitting and retaining sins,' is
not equally clear.  The words used ($\dot{a}\phi\iota\acute{e}\nu a\iota$, $\ddot{a}\phi\epsilon\sigma\iota s$)   Remitting
do not of necessity mean the declaration of the   and retain-
sins.
innocence or lawfulness of any particular act ; still less does
the corresponding phrase ($\kappa\rho a\tau\epsilon\hat{\iota}\nu$) necessarily mean the
declaration of its unlawfulness.  It may be that the words
rendered 'remit sin' are (as in Mark i. 4, Luke iii. 3) equivalent to the abolition or dismissal of sin ; and it would be
the natural meaning of the word rendered 'retain sin' that
it should signify, as in all the other passages of the New
Testament where it occurs, ' to control,' ' conquer,' 'subdue
sin.'  In that case the words would describe, not the intellectual or didactic side of the Apostolic age, but its moral
and practical side, and would correspond to numerous other
passages, such as, ' Ask and it shall be given unto you ;' ' If
ye will say unto this mountain, Be thou removed and be thou
cast into the sea, it shall be done ;' ' He that humbleth him
self shall be exalted ;' ' Inasmuch as ye have done it unto
the least of these my brethren, ye have done it unto me ;'
' Greater works than these shall ye do ;' ' Be of good cheer,
I have overcome the world ;' ' Sanctify them through Thy
truth ;' 'My grace is sufficient for thee ;' ' I can do all
things through Christ that strengtheneth me ;' ' He that
overcometh and keepeth my words unto the end, to him will

I give power over the nations.' If this assurance of the moral victory of the Apostolic age over sin be the meaning of the phrases, then here also it may be affirmed, without fear of contradiction, that, on the whole, and with the necessary reserves of human imperfection, the moral superiority of the first age of Christendom to those which preceded and those which followed was very remarkable, and that such a fulfilment well corresponded to the significant act of the breathing of the spirit of goodness or holiness upon those to whom the words were addressed. But on this interpretation we need not insist. It is necessary to point it out in order to show that the passage is not clear from ambiguity. But it is enough if, as is commonly supposed, the words, by some peculiar turn of the Fourth Gospel, are identical in meaning with those in St. Matthew. In that case all that we have said of the address to Peter and the address to the disciples in the First Gospel applies equally to this address in the Fourth.

II. Such, then, was the promise as spoken in the first instance. In the literal sense of the words this fulfilment of them can hardly occur again.

No other book of equal authority with the New Testament has ever issued from mortal pen. No epoch has spoken on moral questions with a voice so powerful as the Apostolic age. Shakespeare, Milton, Bacon, and Hegel may be of a wider range. Yet they do not rise to the moral dignity of the best parts of the New Testament. When we leave the purely personal and historical application of these words, then, as in all our Lord's words and precepts, the whole point of the words is, that they are spoken, not to any one person or order of men, or succession of men, but to the whole Christian community of all time—to any in that community that partake of the same spirit, and in proportion as they partake of the same moral qualities as filled the first hearers of the Gospel. When it is sometimes alleged that the promise to Peter was exclusively fulfilled in the Bishops of Rome, who, centuries afterwards, were supposed to have been his successors, it would be just as reasonable, or we may say just as unreasonable, as to say that all the Bishops of Ephesus were specially loved by Jesus because they were supposed to have succeeded St. John at Ephesus.  What the most learned and the most gifted of all the Fathers, Origen,[3] said of the promise to St. Peter in the sixteenth chapter of St. Matthew is at once the best proof of what was believed about it in early times, and also the best explanation of its application to later days: ' He who is gifted with self-control enters the gate of heaven by the key of self-control.  He who is just enters the gate of heaven by the key of justice.  The Saviour gives to those who are not overcome by the gates of hell as many keys as there are virtues.  Against him that judges unjustly, and does not bind on earth according to God's word, the gates of hell prevail; but against whom the gates of hell do not prevail, he judges justly.  If any who is not Peter, and has not the qualities here mentioned, believes that he can bind on earth like Peter, so that what he binds is bound in heaven, such an one is puffed up, not knowing the meaning of the Scriptures.'

That which is clear in the case of the promise to Peter is still more clear in the case of the promise in Matt. xviii. 18 and John xx. 23.  It is obvious from the text in John xx. 23 that there is no special limitation to the Twelve.  For at the meeting spoken of, some of the Twelve were not there; Thomas was absent, Matthias was not yet elected, Paul and Barnabas were not yet called.  And also others were there besides the Eleven, for in the corresponding passage in Luke xxiv. 36–47, it would appear (if we take the narratives in their literal meaning) that the two disciples from Emmaus, who were not apostles, were present, and the evangelist here, as throughout his whole Gospel, never uses any other word than ' disciples.'  What is thus clear from the actual passage

---

[3] Origen *on Matt.* xvi. 19.  Comp. ibid. *De Orat.* c. 28.  An instructive collection of similar expressions from St. Augustine is given in an interesting dissertation on the ancient *Making of Bishops*, by the Rev. Dr. Harrison, vicar of Fenwick.

in John xx. 23 is yet more clear from the context of Matt. xviii. 18. There, in the verses immediately preceding, phrase is heaped on phrase, and argument on argument, to show that the power of binding and loosing was addressed, not to any particular class within the circle of disciples, but to the whole body in its widest sense. Our Lord is there speaking of the forgiveness of offences. He requires the contending parties, if they cannot agree, to hear the CHURCH —that is, the whole congregation or assembly; to appeal, as it were, to the popular instinct of the whole community; and He goes on to say that, if even *two agree* on a matter of this kind, wherever *two or three* are gathered together in His name, there is He in the midst of them. These passages, in fact, form no exception to the universal rule of our Lord's discourses. Here, as elsewhere, as He said Himself, ' What I say unto you, I say unto all.' ' Peter,' as St. Augustine says, ' represents all good men, and the promise in St. John is addressed to all believers everywhere.' ' These words,' says a living divine, ' like the eyes of the Lord, look every way, and may include all forgiveness, whenever or wheresoever any sins are remitted through the agency of men.'[4] They belong to the same class of precepts as ' Let your loins be girded and your lights burning,' ' Ye are the salt of the earth,' ' Ye are the light of the world.' All have a share in their meaning, all have a share in their force, in proportion as we have received from Heaven any portion of that inspiration whereby we seek ' to do and to think the things that be good.'[5]

It was only when the minds of men had become confused by the introduction of limitations and alterations which had no connection with the original words that these promises and precepts began to change their meaning. The ' Church,' which once had meant the people, or the laity, came to mean

---

[4] Pusey *on Absolution*, p. 32.

[5] Even those early Christian writers who restrict these words to a particular act, restrict them to baptism ; and baptism, according to the rules of the ancient Church, can be performed by any one.

the clergy.   The declaration, 'Ye are the light of the world,' was understood to mean only those who were in Holy Orders. The promise to Peter came to be strangely confined to the Italian Prelates who lived on the banks of the Tiber.   The words of St. John's Gospel, which had originally been intended to teach the mutual edification and independent insight into Divine truth of all who were inspired by the Spirit of Christ, became limited to the second of the three orders of the Christian ministry.   But these are merely passing restrictions and mistakes.   The general truth of the words themselves remains unshaken and still applicable to the general growth of Christian truth.

The practical lesson of the passages is that which has been already indicated—namely, that the enlightening, elevating power of the Christian conscience is not confined to any profession or order, however sacred ; is exercised not in virtue of any hereditary or transmitted succession, but in virtue of the spiritual discernment, the insight into truth and character, which has been vouchsafed to all good men, to all Christians, in proportion to their goodness, and wisdom, and discernment. This, as Origen says, is the true power of the keys ; a power which may be exercised, and which is exercised, sometimes by the teaching of a faithful pastor, sometimes by the presence of an innocent child, sometimes by the example of a good mother, sometimes by the warning of a true friend, sometimes by the silent glance of just indignation, sometimes by the reading of a good book—above all, by the straightforward honesty of our own individual consciences, whether in dealing with ourselves or others.

It may be worth while here again to recall the obvious processes by which the amelioration of mankind has taken place.   We see it clearly on the large scale of history.   *Effect of the laity.*  Doubtless there have been long periods when the chief enlightenment of the world has come from the clergy. In most Protestant and in some Catholic and Greek Churches the clergy, as a class, perhaps still do more than any other single class of men to keep alive a sense of goodness and truth.

But there has never been a time when the laity have not had their share in the guidance of the Church; and in proportion as Christian civilisation has increased, in proportion as the clergy have done their duty in enlightening and teaching others, in that proportion the Christian influence, the binding and the loosing power of all good and gifted men, has increased—in that proportion has the principle implied in these passages received a deeper, wider signification.

There have been ages when the clergy were coextensive with the educated class of mankind, and were thus the chief means of stimulating and purifying the moral standard of their age.   But at all times, and specially since other professions have become 'clerks '—that is, scholars and instructors— the advancement of learning, the opening of the gates of heaven, has been as much the work of the Christian Church— that is, of the laity—as of the priesthood.  By the highest rank of the whole profession of the clergy—the Pontificate of Rome— the key of knowledge has been perhaps wielded less than by any other great institution in Christendom.  Of the 256 prelates who have filled the bishopric of Rome, scarcely more than four have done anything by their writings to enlarge the boundaries of knowledge and to raise the moral perceptions of mankind—Leo the Great, Gregory the Great, and (in a higher degree) Benedict XIV. and Clement XIV. Occasional acts of toleration towards the Jews, the rectification of the calendar, and a few like examples of enlightenment may be adduced.   But, as a general rule, whatever else the Popes have done, they have not, in the Biblical sense, bound or loosed the moral duties of mankind.

And, again, as to the clergy generally, the abolition of slavery, though supported by many excellent ecclesiastics, yet had for its chief promoters the laymen Wilberforce and Clarkson.  What these virtuous and gifted men bound on earth was bound in heaven, what they loosed on earth was loosed in heaven, not because they had or had not been set apart for a special office, but because they had received a large measure of the Holy Spirit of God, which enabled them to see the good and refuse the evil of the times in which they lived.

If the aspirations of one half of mediæval Christendom after goodness were guided by the clerical work of Thomas à Kempis, another half must have been no less elevated by the lay work of the divine poem of Dante. If the revelation of God in the universe was partly discovered by Copernicus the ecclesiastic, it was more fully disclosed by the labours of Galileo the layman, which the clergy condemned. If the religion of England has been fed in large part by Hooker, by Butler, by Wesley, and by Arnold, it has also been fed, perhaps in a yet larger part, by Milton, by Bunyan, by Addison, by Cowper, and by Walter Scott.

If we study the process by which false notions of morality and religion have been dispersed, and true notions of morality and religion have been introduced, from Augustus to Charlemagne, from Charlemagne to Luther, from Luther to the present day (as unfolded in Mr. Lecky's four volumes), we shall find that the almost uniform law by which the sins and superstitions of Christendom have been bound or loosed has been, first, that the action of some one conscience or some few consciences—whether of statesmen, students, priests, or soldiers—more enlightened, more Christ-like, than their fellows—has struck a new light, or unwound some old prejudice, or opened some new door into truth ; and then, that this light has been caught up, this opening has been widened by the gradual advance of Christian wisdom and knowledge in the mass.

What is called the public opinion of any age may be in itself as misleading, as corrupt, as the opinion of any individual. It must be touched, corrected, purified by those higher intelligences and nobler hearts, which catch the light as mountain summits before the sunrise has reached the plains. But it is only when the light has reached the plains, only when public opinion has become so elevated by the action of the few, that Providence affixes its seal to the deed —that the binding or loosing is ratified in heaven. It is thus that Christian public opinion is formed; and when it is formed, the sins, which before reigned with a tyrannical sway, fade away and disappear.

Such, for example, was the drunkenness of the upper classes in the last century. It penetrated all the higher society of the land. But when by a few resolute wills, here and there, now and then, there was created a better and purer standard of morals in this respect, it perished as if by an invisible blow. The whole of educated society had placed it under their ban, and that ban was ratified in heaven—was ratified by the course of Providence. It is this same public opinion which, if it can once be created in the humbler classes, will also be as powerful there. They also have, if they will, the same power of retaining, that is, of imprisoning, and condemning, and exterminating this deadly enemy; and by this means alone will it disappear from them as it has disappeared from the society of others who were once as completely slaves to it.

So again, to pass to quite another form of evil, the violent personal scurrility that used once to disgrace our periodical literature. That, as a general rule, has almost entirely disappeared from the leading journals of the day. On the whole they are temperately expressed, and conducted with reasonable fairness. The public has become too highly educated to endure the coarseness of former times. But in the more confined organs of opinion the old Adam still lingers. In some of those newspapers, which are called by a figure of speech our religious journals, the scurrility and personal intolerance which once penetrated the great secular journals still abide. That also, we may trust, will gradually vanish as the religious or ecclesiastical world becomes more penetrated with the true spirit of Christianity which has already taken possession of the lay world.

III. It might be enough, for the purpose of this argument, to have pointed out the original meaning of the sacred words, and their correspondence to the actual facts of history. But the subject could not be completed without touching, however slightly, on the curious limitation and perversion of them which have taken place in later times. This has in great part arisen from their introduction into the liturgical forms by which in some Christian Churches <sup>Ordination.</sup> some of the clergy are appointed to their functions. The words from St. John's Gospel are not, nor ever have been, used to describe the consecration of Bishops or Archbishops.[6] They are not, nor ever have been, used in the ordination of Deacons—an order which, in the fourth century, exercised in some respects a power almost equal to that of the Episcopate, and in our own country has often been entrusted with the most important and exclusively pastoral functions—of instruction, visiting, and preaching. Where used, they are only used in the ordination of Presbyters or (as in the abridged form they are unfortunately called) Priests. And even for this limited object the introduction of the words is comparatively recent, and probably the result of misconception. It is certain that for the first twelve centuries they were never used for the ordination of any Christian minister. It is certain that in the whole Eastern Church they are never used at all for this purpose. It was not till the thirteenth century—the age when the materialistic theories of the Sacraments and the extravagant pretensions of pontifical and sacerdotal power were at their height—that they were first introduced into the Ordinals of the Latin Church. From thence they were, at the Reformation, retained in the Ordination Service of the Episcopal Church of England, and of the Presbyterian Church of Lutheran Germany [7]

---

[6] In the English Office of Consecrating Bishops and Archbishops, the portion of the chapter which contains those words is one of the three alternative Gospels. But the fact that it is an alternative, and one rarely used, shows that it is not regarded as essential. They are also incorporated in a general prayer in the Consecration of Bishops, first found in the Poitiers Ordinal, A.D. 500, reprinted by Baronius and Marteno. It is contained in the Roman Pontifical.

[7] The whole antiquarian and critical side of the introduction of these words into the Latin and English Ordinal has been worked out with the utmost exactness and with the most searching inquiry by Archdeacon Reichel in the *Quarterly Review* of October 1877, ' Ordination and Confession.'

The retention of these words in these two Churches may have been occasioned by various causes. It is clear that they have become a mere stumbling-block and stone of offence, partly as unintelligible, partly as giving rise to the most mistaken conclusions. Their retention is confessedly not in conformity, but in direct antagonism, with ancient and Catholic usages. It is a mere copy of a mediæval interpolation, which has hardly any more claim, on historical or theological grounds, to a place in the English or Lutheran Prayer Book than the admission of the existence of Pope Joan or of the miracle of Bolsena. And, so far from these words being regarded as a necessary part of the validity of Holy Orders, such an assertion, if admitted, would of itself be fatal to the validity of all Holy Orders whatever; for it would prove that every single ordination for the first twelve hundred years of Christianity was invalid, nay, more, that every present ordination in the Roman Church itself was invalid, inasmuch as in the Ordinal itself these words do not occur in the essential parts of the office, but only in an accidental adjunct of it.

IV. But further, the phrase indicates, even in reference to the subject of Confession and Absolution, with which it has no direct connection, the fundamental truth which is incompatible with the exclusive possession of this privilege by the clergy.

Confession and Absolution.

For the principle of the texts, as we have seen, teaches us that we all have to bear each other's burdens. There is no caste or order of men who can relieve us of this dread responsibility, of this noble privilege. The clergyman needs the advice and pardon of the gifted layman quite as much as the layman seeks the advice and pardon of the gifted clergyman. The brother seeks the forgiveness of the brother whom he has offended; the child of the parent; the neighbour of the neighbour. This in the earliest times was the real meaning of *Confession*. 'Confess your faults,' says St. James—to whom? To the elders of the Church whom he had just mentioned? To the Bishop, or the Priest, or the Deacon? No. 'Confess your faults *one to another*.' It is as though he

said, 'Let there be mutual confidence.'   Every one can do his
neighbour some good; every one can protest against some evil ;
and the whole tone of the community shall thus be raised.

The full sympathy which thus prevailed amongst the
members of the infant Church no doubt soon died away.
But its semblance was long continued in the only form of
confession that was known for four centuries, namely, the
acknowledgment of the faults of the penitent, not in private,
but in public to the whole congregation, who then publicly
expressed their forgiveness.   The substitution of a single
priest for a large congregation as the receptacle of confession
arose from the desire of avoiding the scandals occasioned by
the primitive publicity.   It was not till long afterwards that
the notion sprang up of any special virtue attaching to the
forgiveness of a clergyman, or that any private or special confession was made to him.   Even in the very heart of the Roman
Mass is retained a testimony to the independence and equality in this respect of people and minister. There, in the most
solemn ordinance of religion, the priest first turns to the people
and confesses his sins to them, and they publicly absolve him,
in exactly the same form of words as he uses when they in
their turn publicly confess their faults to him.[8]   This striking passage, standing as it does in the forefront of the
Roman Missal, is one of the many variations in the Roman
Church which, if followed out to its logical consequences,
would correct some of the gravest errors which have sprung

[8] The Priest says, 'Confiteor Deo Omnipotenti, Beatæ Mariæ semper
Virgini,' etc., 'et vobis, fratres, quia peccavi nimis cogitatione, verbo,
et opere, meâ culpâ, meâ culpâ, meâ maximâ culpâ.  Ideo precor beatam
Mariam semper Virginem,' etc., 'et vos, fratres, orare pro me ad Dominum
Deum nostrum.'  The attendants reply, 'Misereatur tui Omnipotens Deus,
et, dimissis peccatis tuis, perducat te ad vitam æternam.'  The Priest says
Amen, and stands up.  Then the attendants repeat the confession, only
changing the words 'vobis, fratres' and 'vos, fratres' into 'tibi, pater'
and 'te, pater,' and the Priest replies in like words.  Finally the Priest,
signing himself with the sign of the cross, says, 'Indulgentiam, absolu-
tionem et remissionem peccatorum nostrorum tribuet nobis Omnipotens et
Misericors Dominus;' which is evidently a joint absolution for both himself and the people.  The form 'Ego absolvo te' is, as before observed, of
a much later date.

up within its pale. It has probably escaped attention from the dead language and the inaudible manner in which it is repeated. But it is not the less significant in itself; and had it been transferred to the English Prayer Book, where the vitality of the language and the more audible mode of reading the service would have brought it into prominence, it would have more than counterbalanced those two or three ambiguous passages on the subject which the Reformers left in the Liturgy.

There is a story told of James I., who when, after indulging in a furious passion against a faithful servant,[9] he found that it was under a mistake, sent for him immediately, would neither eat, drink, nor sleep till he saw him, and when the servant entered his chamber the King kneeled down and begged his pardon; nor would he rise from his humble posture till he had compelled the astonished servant to pronounce the words of absolution. That was a grotesque but genuine form of penitence; that was a grotesque but legitimate form of absolution. There was a story told during the Turkish war of 1877, that a Roumanian soldier, after having received the sacraments from a priest on his death-bed, would not be satisfied till he had obtained an interview with the excellent Princess of Roumania. To her he explained that he had tried to escape from the dangers of the battle by mutilating one of his fingers; and against her and her husband, the Prince of Roumania, he felt that this offence had been committed. From the Princess, and not from the priest, must the forgiveness come which alone could bring any comfort to him. That forgiveness was whispered into the dying man's ear by the Princess; with that forgiveness, not sacerdotal, but truly human, and therefore truly divine, the penitent soldier passed in peace to his rest.[1] In fact, the moment that we admit the efficacy of repentance, we deny the necessity of any special absolution. An incantation, of which the virtue rests in the words pronounced, is equally valid whether the

* Aikin, *Life of James I.*, ii. 402.　　¹ *The Times*, Nov. 2, 1877.

person over whom it is pronounced is guilty or innocent, conscious or unconscious. But the moment that the moral condition of the recipient is acknowledged as a necessary element, that of itself becomes the chief part, and the repetition of certain words may be edifying, but is not essential. The welfare of the hearer's soul depends not on any external absolution, but on its own intrinsic state. The value of any absolution or forgiveness depends not on the external condition of the man who pronounces it, but on the intrinsic truth of the forgiveness.

Not long ago, when a French ship foundered in the Atlantic, a brave French priest was overheard repeating the absolution in the last moments of life to a fellow-countryman. All honour to him for the gallant discharge of what he believed to be his duty! But is there a single reflecting man, whether Catholic or Protestant, who would not feel that the intervention of a priest at that moment was in itself absolutely indifferent? The Bible and the enlightened conscience repeatedly assure us that what commends a departing spirit to its Creator and Judge is not the accidental circumstance of his listening to a particular form of words uttered by a particular person, but the sincerity of repentance, the uprightness, the humility, the purity, the faithfulness of the man himself.

It may be a consolation to us to hear from well-known lips which speak to us with tenderness, with knowledge, and with justice, the assurance that we are regarded as innocent: it may be a consolation to hear with our outward ears the solemn declaration that the Supreme Father is always ready to receive the returning penitent; that the soul which returns from evil and does what is lawful and right shall surely live. But this assurance, by the nature of the case, is well known to us already from hundreds of passages in the Bible, and from the knowledge of human nature. And also it can come from any one whom we respect, from any one whom we may have injured, from any one who will give us a true, disinterested verdict on our worse and on our

better qualities. It is finely described in a well-known tale—
' The Heir of Redclyffe '—that when the obstinate Pharisaical
youth, at last, in bitter remorse acknowledges his fault to the
wife of the man whom he has mortally injured, she takes upon
herself to console him and absolve him, and her absolution consists in repeating the words of the Psalmist: ' The sacrifices of
God are a troubled spirit; a broken and a contrite heart, O
God, Thou wilt not despise.' No Pontifical decree could say
more ; no true forgiveness could say less. Whenever any man
is able to see clearly that his fellow-man has truly repented, or
that a course of action is clear and right—then, whoever he
be, he can declare that promise of God's forgiveness. In all
cases each man must strive to act on his own judgment and
on his own conscience. The first duty of the penitent is to
try to minister to his own disease. ' The heart knoweth his
own bitterness, and a stranger doth not intermeddle with
his joy.'

> Why should we faint or fear to live alone,
> Since all alone, so Heav'n has will'd, we die ?

The next duty may be to get sound advice on his future
course. But that advice can be given by any competent
person, and the competency depends not on any ministerial
or sacerdotal character, but on personal insight into character
to be found equally in layman and clergyman.

It is a duty to cultivate the conviction that we all alike
need to be guided and be forgiven, and to have our course
made clear. All alike, according to the several gifts which
God has bestowed on the vast family of mankind, have the
power to forgive, to assist, to enlighten each other. In
the last resort there is no one to be considered or regarded,
but our own immortal struggling souls and the One eternally
Just and Merciful God. Our own responsibility must be
maintained without shifting it to the keeping of any one else.
We, all of us, each with some different gift, are the in-
heritors of the promise to bind and to loose—that is, to warn
and to console our brethren, as we in like manner hope to
be warned and consoled by them.

V. Such is the summary of this question, needlessly complicated by irrelevant discussions.  The texts on which the popular theory and practice of absolution are grounded are, as we have seen, altogether beside the purpose.  They no more relate to it than the promise to Peter *Its true meaning.* relates to the Popes of Rome, or than Isaiah's description of the ruin of the Assyrian King under the figure of Lucifer relates to the Fall of the Angels, or than the two swords at the Last Supper relate to the spiritual and secular jurisdiction, or than the sun and moon in the first chapter of Genesis relate to the Pope and the Emperor.  In all these cases, the misinterpretation has been long and persistent ; in all these, it is acknowledged by all scholars, outside the Roman communion, to be absolutely without foundation.

And, as the misinterpretation of the texts on which the theory of Episcopal or Presbyterian absolution rests will die out before a sound understanding of the Biblical records, so also the theory and practice itself, though with occasional recrudescences, will probably die out with the advance of civilisation.  The true power of the clergy will not be diminished but strengthened by the loss of this fictitious attribute.  Norna of the Fitful Head was a happier and more useful member of society after she abandoned her magical arts than when she practised them.  In proportion as England has become, and in proportion as it will yet more become, a truly free and truly educated people, able of itself to bind what ought to be bound, and to loose what ought to be loosed, in that proportion will the belief in priestly absolution vanish, just as the belief in wizards and necromancers has vanished before the advance of science.  As alchemy has disappeared to give place to chemistry, as astrology has given way to astronomy, as monastic celibacy has given way to domestic purity, as bull-fights and bear-baits have given way to innocent and elevating amusements, as scholastic casuistry has bowed before the philosophy of Bacon and Pascal, so will the belief in the magical offices of a sacerdotal caste vanish before the growth of manly Christian independence and generous Christian sympathy.

# CHAPTER VIII.

## ECCLESIASTICAL VESTMENTS.

At a time when all Churches are or ought to be occupied with so many important questions, when so many interesting inquiries have arisen with regard to the origin and the interpretation of the Sacred Books, when the adjustment of science and theology needs more than ever to be properly balanced, when the framework of the English Prayer Book requires so many changes and expansions in order to meet the wants of the time, when measures for the conciliation of our Nonconformist brethren press so closely on the hearts and consciences of those who care for peace and truth, when so many social and political problems are crying for solution, some apology is due for treating of a subject so apparently trivial as the Vestments of the Clergy. But, inasmuch as it has nevertheless occupied considerable attention in the English Church, its discussion cannot be altogether out of place here.

What has to be said will be divided into two parts: the first, an antiquarian investigation into the origin of ecclesiastical vestments; the second, some practical remarks on the present state of the controversy in England.

I. The antiquarian investigation of this matter is not in itself devoid of interest. It belongs to the general survey of the origin of usages and customs in the early ages of Christianity. The conclusion to which it leads is that the dress of the clergy had no distinct intention—symbolical, sacerdotal, sacrificial, or mystical; but originated simply in fashions common to the whole community of the Roman Empire during the three first centuries.

There is nothing new to be said in favour of this conclusion.

But it has nevertheless been, and is still, persistently denied. In spite of the assertion to the contrary of Cardinal Bona, Père Thomassin, Dr. Rock, and our own lamented Wharton Marriott, it has been asserted, both by the admirers and depreciators of clerical vestments, that they were borrowed in the first instance (to use Milton's phrase in his splendid invective against the English clergy) ' from Aaron's wardrobe or the Flamen's vestry '; that they are intrinsically marks of distinction between the clergy and the laity, between the Eucharist and every other religious service, between a sacerdotal and an anti-sacerdotal view of the Christian Ministry— that if they are abolished, all is lost to the idea of a Christian priesthood ; that if they are retained, all is gained.

In face then of these reiterated statements, it may not be out of place to prove that every one of them is not only not true, but is the reverse of the truth ; that if they symbolise anything, they symbolise ideas the contrary of those now ascribed to them.

II. Let us, in our mind's eye, dress up a lay figure at the time of the Christian era, when the same general costume pervaded all classes of the Roman Empire, from *Dress of the ancient world.* Palestine to Spain, very much as the costume of the nineteenth century pervades at least all the upper classes of Europe now.

The Roman,[1] Greek, or Syrian, whether gentleman or peasant, unless in exceptional cases, had no hat, no coat, no waistcoat, and no trousers. He had shoes or sandals; he wore next his skin a shirt or jacket, double or single ; then a long shawl or plaid ; and again, especially in the later Roman period, a cloak or overcoat.[2]

---

[1] As the vestments in question are chiefly those of the Latin Church, these remarks apply more to the dress of the Western than of the Eastern population of the Empire. But in general (as appears even from the New Testament alone, without referring to secular authorities) the dress even of the Syrian peasants was substantially the same as that of the Greek or the Roman.

[2] For the general dress, see, for the Greek, Becker's *Charicles*, pp. 402–20 ; for the Roman, Becker's *Gallus*, pp. 401–30; for the Syrian, Smith's *Dictionary of the Bible*, under *Dress ;* for the ecclesiastical dresses, Smith's *Dictionary of Christian Antiquities*, under the different words.

1. The first, or inner garb, if we strip the ancient Roman to his shirt, was what is called in classical Greek, *chiton*; in classical Latin, *tunica*; a woollen vest, which sometimes had beneath it another fitting close to the skin, called *subucula*, or *interula*, or, in the case of soldiers, *camisia*.[3] It is this name of *camisia*, which, under the name of *chemise*, has gradually superseded the others, and which has been perpetuated in ecclesiastical phraseology under another synonym derived from its white colour (for shirts, with the ancients as with the moderns, were usually *white*), and hence it came to be called an *alb*.

Inner dress.

This is the dress which became appropriated specially to the Deacon. He, as the working-man of the clergy, officiated, as it were, in his shirt sleeves.

But as the homeliest garments are subject to the varieties of fashion, the *shirt*, the *chemise*, the *camisia*, whether of Pagan or Christian, had two forms.[4] The simpler or more ancient was an under-shirt with short sleeves, or rather with no sleeves at all, called in Greek[5] *exomis*, in Latin *colobium*. The more costly form may be compared to the shirt of Charles II., with fine ruffles. It was called the *Dalmatica*, from its birthplace Dalmatia—in the same way as the cravats of the French in the seventeenth century were called *Steinkerks* from the battle of that name; or the *Ulsters* of the present day from the Northern province of Ireland. The first[6] persons recorded to have worn it are the infamous Emperors Commodus and Heliogabalus. It was thought an outrage on all propriety when Heliogabalus appeared publicly in this dress in the streets after dinner, calling himself a second Fabius or Scipio, because it was the sort of frock which the Cornelii or Fabii were wont to wear in their childhood when they were

---

[3] St. Jerome, *Epist.* 64, *ad Fabiolam.* He apologises for using so vulgar a word as *camisia*.

[4] Bona, 1, 14. Thomassin, *Vetus et Nova Disciplina*, ii. 2, 49. That in Greece there was generally an under-shirt and an outer shirt is proved in *Charicles*, p. 406.

[5] *Charicles*, 415.          [6] Bingham, vi. 4, 19.

naughty boys.   It was as if some English magnate were to walk up St. James's Street in his dressing-gown.   But the fashion spread rapidly, and thirty years afterwards appears as the dress of Cyprian, Bishop of Carthage, when led out to death—not, however, in that instance as his outer garment. It became fixed as the name of the dress of the deacon after the time of Constantine, when it superseded the original *colobium*; and although it quickly spread to the other orders, it is evident that it was, for the reasons above given, particularly suitable to the inferior clergy, who, as having nothing over it, would seem to require a more elaborate shirt.   This was the first element of ecclesiastical vestments, as deacons were the first elements of a Christian ministry.

In later times, after the invasion of the Northern barbarians, this shirt, which must, perhaps, always have been worn over some thicker garment next the skin, was drawn over the fur coat, sheepskin, or otter skin, the *pellisse* of the Northern nations; and hence in the twelfth century arose the barbarous name of *super-pellicium*, or *surplice*—the *over-fur*.   Its name indicates that it is the latest of ecclesiastical vestments, and though, like all the others, generally worn [7] both by clergy and laity, indoors and out of doors, is the most remote in descent from primitive times.   Another form of this dress—also, as its German name implies, dating from the invasion of the barbarians—was the *rochet* or *rocket*, 'the little *rock*' or 'coat' worn by the mediæval bishops out of doors on all occasions, except when they went out hunting; and which now is to them what the surplice is to presbyters. The lawn sleeves [8] are merely an addition to make up for the long-flowing sleeves of the surplice.

But in both cases the fur coat within was the usual dress, of which the overfur was, as it were, merely the mask. Charlemagne in winter wore an otter-skin breast-plate,[9] and hunted in sheepskin.   The butcher of Rouen, who was saved

<hr>

[7] Thomassin, ii. 2, 48.
[8] Hody, *On Convocation.*
[9] Thomassin, ii. 2, c. 48, 69.

alone out of the crew of the *Blanche Nef,* wore a sheepskin.
St. Martin, Apostle of the Gauls, and the first Bishop of
Tours, when he officiated wore also a sheepskin—a fur coat
(as it would seem with no surplice over it, and with no
sleeves), and consecrated the Eucharistic elements with his
bare arms, which came through the sheepskin, like those of
the sturdy deacons who had brandished their sinewy arms
out of the holes of their *colobium.*

2. The second part of the dress was a shawl or blanket,
wrapt round the shoulders over the shirt, in Greek *himation,*

The shawl. in Latin *toga,* or *pallium.* This also was usually
white as the common colour of the ancient dress,
which is still perpetuated in the white flannel robe of the
Pope, but marked with a broad purple stripe. This is what
appears, in the early portion of the fourth century, as the dress
equally of ecclesiastics and laity. After the fourth century the
Christians affected the use of black shawls (like the Geneva
divines of the sixteenth century), in order to imitate the
philosophers and ascetics. Of the general adoption of the
black dress, an interesting illustration is given in the case of
the Bishop Sisinnius, who chose to wear white, and when he
was asked what command in Scripture he found for his white
surplice, replied, 'What command is there for wearing black?'[1]
For reasons which will appear immediately, there are fewer
traces of this part of the ancient dress than of any other in the
vestments of the clergy. The only relic of the Roman *toga*
or *pallium* remains in the *pall* of an Archbishop, which is
only the string which held it together, or the broad stripe
which marked its surface.

3. The third part of the ancient dress, and that from
which the larger part of the ecclesiastical vestments are de-

The over-    rived, was the overcoat, in Latin *lacerna* or *pœnula,*
coat.        in Greek *phæloné.* It ought perhaps to have been
worn over the *toga,* but was sometimes for convenience worn
instead of it, and at last, after the discontinuance of the *toga*[2]

<hr>

[1] Bingham, vi. 4, 19 ; Socrates, vi. 20 ; Thomassin, i. 2-24.
[2] Marriott, *Vestiarium,* p. xii.

—which for practical purposes came to be much like our evening dress coat, and was thus, after the Empire, only worn on official occasions—the overcoat came to be the usual dress, as frock coats, shooting coats, and the like are worn in general morning society in England. What had once been regarded only as a rough soldier's garb, unsuitable within the city, came to be worn everywhere. It was for the most part like a poncho, or cape, or burnous,[3] but it consisted of several varieties.

There was the *birrhus*, or scarlet cloak, worn by Athanasius, as a wealthy person, when he visited the mysterious lady [4] in Alexandria, but not thought by Augustine suitable to his poverty. There was the *caracalla*, a long overall, brought by Antoninus Bassianus from France, whence he derived his name—and it was this which was corrupted into *casacalla, casaca*, and finally *cassock*. It had a hood, and was called in Greek *amphibalus*, and as such appears in the account of the persecution of St. Alban,[5] where, by a strange confusion, the word Amphibalus has been supposed to represent the name of a saint. The reverence for the *cassock*, although highly esteemed, has never reached so high a pitch.

The same form of dress was also called *casula*, a slang name used by the Italian labourers [6] for the *capote*, which they called 'their little house,' as 'tile' is—or was, a short time ago—used for a 'hat,' and as 'coat' is the same word as 'cote,' or 'cottage.' It is this which took the name of *chasuble*, and was afterwards especially known as the outdoor garment of the clergy, as the *sagum* was of the laity, and was not adopted as a vestment for sacred services before the 9th century. Another name by which it was called was *planeta*, 'the wanderer,' because it wandered loosely over the body, as one of these overcoats in our day has been called

---

[3] So it is translated in the Coptic Liturgy.
[4] Marriott, p. lvi. p. 16.
[5] Bede, *H. E.* i. 6.
[6] Columella, Isidore, Augustine; see Marriott, pp. 202, 228.

'zephyr.' This was the common overcoat of the wealthier, as the *casula* of the humbler classes.

Another form of overcoat was the *capa*, or *copa*, 'the hood'—also called the *pluviale*,[7] or 'waterproof,' to be worn in rainy weather out of doors. It was this cape, or cope, that St. Martin divided with the beggar at the gates of Amiens, and hence (according to one derivation of the word) the *capella*, or *chapel*, where the fragment of his *cape* was preserved. It is the vestment of which the secular use has longest retained its hold, having been worn by Bishops in Parliament, by Canons at coronations, and by lay vicars, almsmen and the like, on other similar occasions, till quite recently.

Another form of the same garb, though of a lighter texture, and chiefly used by ladies in riding, was the *cymar*, or *chimere*,[8] of which the trace still lingers in the bishop's satin robe, which so vexed the soul of Bishop Hooper, and which had to be forced on him almost at the point of the sword—but which now apparently is cast [9] aside by advocates of the modern use of clerical vestments.

The *mitre*, as worn in the Eastern Church, may still be seen in the museums of Russia, as the caps or turbans, worn on festive occasions in ancient days by princes and nobles, and even to this day by the peasant women. The division into two points, which appears in Western mitres, is only the mark of the crease which is the consequence of its having been, like an opera hat, folded and carried under the arm.

The *stole* [1] (which, in Greek, is simply another word for the overcoat, or *pænula*) in the ninth century came to be used for the 'orarium.' This was a simple handkerchief for blowing the nose, or wiping off the sweat from the face.

---

[7] Marriott, p. 229.        [8] *Archæologia*, xxx. 27.

[9] See the recent account of the installation of the Bishop of Capetown.

[1] Thomassin, 8, 245. He is perplexed, and justly, by the difficulty of understanding how the '*stola*,' which was the word for the whole dress, should have been appropriated to such a small matter as the handkerchief. An explanation is attempted in Marriott, 75, 84, 90, 112, 115, lxiii.

These handkerchiefs, on State occasions, were used as ribbons, streamers, or scarfs; and hence their adoption by the deacons, who had little else to distinguish them. When Sir James Brooke first returned from Borneo, where the only sign of royalty was to hold a kerchief in the hand, he retained the practice in England.

III. Before we pass to any practical application, it may be remarked that this historical inquiry has a twofold interest. First, the condition of the early Church, which is indicated in this matter of dress, is but one of a hundred similar examples of the secular and social origin of many usages which are now regarded as purely ecclesiastical, and yet more, of the close connection, or rather identity, of common and religious, of lay and clerical life, which it has been the effort of fifteen centuries to rend asunder. Among the treasures[2] which King Edward III. presented to Westminster Abbey, were 'the vestments in which St. Peter was wont to celebrate mass.' What those mediæval relics were we know not, but what the actual vestment of St. Peter was we know perfectly well—it was a 'fisher's coat[3] cast about his naked body.' In like manner, the Church of Rome itself is not so far wrong when it exhibits in St. John Lateran, the altar at which St. Peter fulfilled—if he ever did fulfil—the same functions. It is not a stone or marble monument, but a rough wooden table, such as would have been used at any common meal. And the churches in which, we do not say St. Peter, for there were no churches in his time, but the Bishops of the third and fourth centuries officiated, are not copies of Jewish or Pagan temples, but of town-halls and courts of justice. And the posture in which they officiated was not that of the modern Roman priest, with his back to the people, but that of the ancient Roman prætor,[4] facing



---

[2] Adam de Murimuth, *Harl. MS.* 565, vol. 206.

[3] In like manner the only mention of St. Paul's vestments is the allusion to his cloak—the *phæloné*—described in p. 152. The casual notice of itself precludes the notion of a sacred vestment. 2 Tim. iv. 13.

[4] See the chapters on the Basilica and on the Pope.

the people—for whose sake he was there. And the Latin language, now regarded as consecrated to religious purposes, was but the vulgar dialect of the Italian peasants. And the Eucharist itself was the daily social meal, in which the only sacrifice offered was the natural thanksgiving, offered not by the presiding minister, but by all those who brought their contributions from the kindly fruits of the earth.

We do not deny that in those early ages there were many magical and mystical notions afloat. In a society where the whole atmosphere was still redolent of strange rites, of Pagan witchcraft and demonology, there is quite enough to make us rejoice that even the mediæval Church had, in some respects, made a great advance on the Church of the first ages. What we maintain is, that in the matter of vestments, as in many other respects, the primitive Church was not infected by these superstitions, and is a witness against them. They are incontrovertible proofs that there was a large mass of sentiment and of usage, which was not only not mediæval, not hierarchical, but the very reverse; a mine of Protestantism—of Quakerism if we will—which remained there to explode, when the time came, into the European Reformation. They coincide with the fact which Bishop Lightfoot has proved in his unanswerable Essay,[5] that the idea of a separate clerical priesthood was unknown to the early Church. They remain in the ancient Roman ritual, with other well-known discordant elements, a living protest against the modern theories which have been engrafted upon it.

Secondly, there is the interest of following out the transformation of these names and garments. How early the transition from secular to sacred use took place, it is difficult to determine; but it was gradually and by unequal steps. It is said[6] that even to the ninth century there were Eastern clergy who celebrated the Eucharist in their common costume. In the original Benedictine rule the conventual dress was so well understood to be merely the ordinary dress of

Their transformation.

---

[5] Bishop Lightfoot's *Commentary on the Philippians*, pp. 247-66.
[6] Marriott, p. lvii.

the neighbouring peasants, that in the sketches of early monastic life at Monte Casino the monks are represented in blue,
green, or black, with absolute indifference.   But now the distinction between the lay and clerical dress, which once existed
nowhere, has become universal.   It is not confined to ancient
or to Episcopal Churches.   It is found in the Churches of
Presbyterians and Nonconformists.   The extreme simplicity
of the utmost 'dissidence of Dissent' has, in this respect,
departed further from primitive practice than it has from
any Pontifical or ritual splendour.   A distinguished Baptist
minister, one of the most popular preachers, and one of
the most powerful ecclesiastics in London, was shocked to
find that he could not preach in Calvin's church at Geneva
without adopting the gown, and naturally refused to wear
it except under protest.   But even he, in his London
Tabernacle, had already fallen away from the primitive simplicity which acknowledged no difference of dress between
the clergy and the laity,—for he as well as all other ministers (it is believed) has adopted the black dress which no
layman would think of using except as an evening costume.
The clergy of the Church of England have either adopted the
white surplice, once the common frock, drawn, as it has been
seen, over the fur of our skin-clad ancestors, or else have, in
a few instances, retained or restored shreds and patches of
the clothes worn by Roman nobles and labourers.   The Roman
clergy have done the same, but in a more elaborate form.

In all, the process has been alike.   First the early
Christians, not the clergy only but the laity as well, when
they came to their public assemblies, wore indeed their
ordinary clothes, but took care that they should be clean.
The Pelagians,[7] and the more ascetic clergy, insisted on
coming in rags, but this was contrary to the more moderate
and more general sentiment.

Next, it was natural that the colours and forms chosen
for their Sunday clothes should be of a more grave and sober
tint, as that of the Quakers in Charles the Second's time.

_______
[7] Thomassin, i. 2, 43.

' As there is a garb proper for soldiers, sailors, and magistrates,[8] so,' says Clement of Alexandria, ' there is a garb befitting the sobriety of Christians.'

Then came the process which belongs to all society in every age and which we see actually going on before our eyes —namely, that what in ordinary life is liable to the rapid transitions of fashion, in certain classes becomes fixed at a particular moment; and then—though again in its turn undergoing new changes of fashion—yet retains something of its old form or name; and finally engenders in fanciful minds fanciful reflections as far as possible removed from the original meaning of these garments.[9]

Take for example, the wigs of Bishops. First, there was the long flowing hair of the Cavaliers. Then when this was cut short came the long flowing wigs in their places. Then these were dropped except by the learned professions. Then they were dropped by the lawyers except in court. Then the clergy laid them aside, with the exception of the bishops. Then the bishops laid them aside with the exception of the archbishops. Then the last archbishop laid his wig aside except on official occasions. And now even the archbishop has dropped it. But it is easy to see that, had it been retained, it might have passed like the pall into the mystic symbol of the archiepiscopate, patriarchate, or we know not what. Bands again sprang from the broad [1] white collars, which fell over the shoulders of the higher and middle classes—whether Cavalier or Puritan—Cromwell and Bunyan, no less than Clarendon and Hammond. Then these were

---

[8] Marriott, p. 25.

[9] Extract from *Personal Recollections of Sir Gilbert Scott*, p. 28.—' In the earliest period to which his memory extended, the clergy habitually wore their cassock, gown, and shovel hat, and when this custom went out a sort of interregnum ensued, during which all distinction of dress was abandoned, and clerics followed lay fashions. This is the period which Jane Austen's novels illustrate. Her clergymen are singularly free from any of the ecclesiastical character. Later on the clergy adopted the suit of black, and the white necktie, which had all along been the dress of professional men, lawyers, doctors, architects, and even surveyors : of men in short whose business was to advise.

[1] In the Lutheran Church the same fate has befallen the *ruff*.

confined to the clergy ; then reduced to a single white plait ;
then divided into two parts; then symbolised to mean the
two tables of the law, the two sacraments, or the cloven
tongues; then from a supposed connection with Puritanism,
or from a sense of inconvenience, ceased to be worn, or worn
only by the more old-fashioned of the clergy ; so as to be
regarded by the younger generation as a symbol of Puritan
custom or doctrine.   Just so, and with as much reason did
the surplice in the Middle Ages, from its position as a frock
or pinafore over the fur coat, come to be regarded as an
emblem of imputed righteousness over the skins in which
were clothed our first parents; just so did the turban or *mitra*
when divided by its crease come to be regarded as the cloven
tongue; just so did the handkerchief with which the Roman
gentry wiped their faces come to be regarded in the fifth century as wings of angels, and in the seventh as the yoke of
Christian life.   Just so have the ponchos and waterproofs of
the Roman peasants and labourers come in the nineteenth
century to be regarded as emblems of Sacrifice, Priesthood,
Real Presence, communion with the universal Church,
Christian or ecclesiastical virtues.

It is hardly necessary to answer detailed objections to a
statement of which the general truth is acknowledged by all
the chief authorities on the subject, as well as confirmed by
the general analogy of the origin of the Christian usages.
In fact, the Roman Church has at times even gloried in the
secular origin of its sacred vestments, and based their adoption on the grant by Constantine (in his forged donation) of
his own imperial garments to the Pope, and has then added
that they were occasionally transferred back to the secular
princes,—as when Alexander II. granted to the Duke of
Bohemia the use of the mitre, and Alexander III. to the
Doge of Venice the use of an umbrella like his own,--and
that the Emperor wore the same pall or mantle that was
used by Popes in the most sacred offices.[2]

The only indications adduced to the contrary are :—

1. The golden plate said to have been worn by St. John

2 Thomassin, i. 2, c. 45, s. 52.

and St. James. But even if Bishop Lightfoot had not amply[3] proved that this is a mere metaphor, it would not avail, for a golden plate has never been adopted as part of the ecclesiastical ornaments.

2. The mention in the Clementine Liturgy that the bishop at a certain moment of the service puts on a white[4] garment. But this is an exception which proves the rule. Of all the liturgies, this is the only one which has any indication of dress—and the Clementine Liturgy is so saturated with interpolations of all kinds, some even heretical, that its text cannot be seriously used as an authentic witness.

3. Jerome, in his Commentary on Ezekiel (c. 44), says that ' Divine religion has one habit in service, another in use in common life.' But he is speaking here of the trousers of the Jewish priests; and in all the allegorical interpretations he gives here, or in his letter to Fabiola, of the garments of the Jewish priesthood, there is not one which points to the sacerdotal character of the Christian ministry; and in this very passage, shortly before, he says, ' Thus we learn that we ought not to enter the Holy of Holies with any sort of every-day clothing soiled from the use of life, but handle the Lord's sacraments with a *clean conscience and clean clothes.*' It is evident that, so far as this is not metaphorical, it means only that (according to the description of the first stage of the process of adaptation given above) the clothes of Christians in public worship should not be dirty, but clean.

There may possibly be other apparent exceptions, as, no doubt, in later Roman writers there are contradictory statements. But the general current of practice and opinion during the early ages is that which is well summed up by the Jesuit, Sirmondus,[5] as by our own Bingham—'The colour and form of dress was in the beginning the same for ecclesiastics and laymen.'

[3] *Commentary on the Epistle to the Philippians*, p. 252.

[4] Λαμπρὰν ἐσθῆτα, as in the next quotation from Jerome, probably means ' clean, white gown.'

[5] See Marriott, p. 43; Thomassin, 1. 2, 43.

Should there be any counter statements or counter facts scattered here and there through the ancient customs or literature of the Latin Church, it is no more than is to be expected from the heterogeneous forms which any large historical system embraces within itself.

IV. We now proceed to the practical remarks which this part of our enquiry suggests.

1. First, it is not useless to show that the significance of these dresses as alleged, both in attack, and defence, rests on no historical foundation.  It may be said, perhaps, that the fact of the secular origin of these garments *Their insignificance.* does not exclude their importance when, in after-times, symbolical significations were attached to them; and possibly it may be urged that the most unquestionably sacerdotal symbols were, in the first instance, drawn from homelier objects.  But there is this wide distinction between the origin of the Christian ecclesiastical vestments and of those of other religions.  The Christian dress, as we have indicated, was intended in its origin, not to separate the minister from the people, but to make him, in outward show and appearance, exactly the same.  The Jewish high-priest and the priestly tribe were, on the contrary, as in other matters, so in their dress, from the very first intended to be thereby separated, at least in their public ministrations, as far as possible from the rest of the community.  It would have been perfectly easy, had the Christian Church of the first and second centuries been possessed with the idea of carrying on the Jewish priesthood, to adopt either the very dress worn by the Jewish priests, or some other dress equally distinctive.  The Jewish priest was distinguished from his countrymen by his bare feet, by his trousers, by his white linen robe, by his sash thirty-two yards long,[6] by his fillet, by his tippet or ephod; the high-priest by his breastplate, by his bells, and by his pomegranates; and these vestments were regarded as so indispensable to his office that the high-priesthood was at

---

[6] Bähr's *Symbolik*, p. 68.

last actually conveyed from predecessor to successor by the act of handing them on to each high-priest; the possession of the vestments, in fact, conferred the office itself. Nothing whatever of the kind was done, or, we may add, even in the wildest flights of modern superstition has been done, with the vestments of the Christian clergy. Neither trousers,[7] nor breastplate, nor bells, nor pomegranates, nor long winding sash, nor naked feet, have ever been regarded, and certainly were not in the early ages regarded, as part of the dress or undress of the Christian minister; nor was the act of ordina tion ever performed by the transfer of chasuble, or lawn sleeves, or cassock. The whole stress of the theological argument in favour of the importance of these dresses depends on proving that such as they may by any one now be supposed to be in intention and in significance, such they were in the early ages. It is alleged that, by parting with them, we part with a primitive doctrine of the Church. But, if the facts which we have stated are correct, the connection between these dresses and the sacerdotal theories with which they have been entangled is cut off at the very root. Unless it can be shown that they were sacerdotal in the second or third century, it is wholly irrelevant to allege that they became sacerdotal in the thirteenth or the nineteenth century. Whatever sacerdotal, or symbolical, or sacramental associations have been attached to them may be mediæval, but certainly are not primitive; and those who wish to pre- serve the substance of the primitive usage should officiate, not in the dresses which are at present worn in Roman, Anglican, and Nonconformist Churches, but in the every- day dress of common life—in overcoats, or smock-frocks, or shirt-sleeves, according as they belonged to the higher or inferior grade of the Christian ministry. We are not arguing in favour of such a return to primitive usage. In this, as in a thousand other cases, it is the depth of retrograde absurdity

---

[7] In Jerome's letter to Fabiola (*Ep.* 64), containing an elaborate expo- sition of the dresses of the Jewish priests, there is not a word to indicate that they were adopted by the Christian clergy.

to suppose that we are to throw off the garb, or the institutions, or the language of civilisation in order to accommodate ourselves to the literal platform of the early ages. Matthew Arnold well observes that to declaim against bishops in the House of Lords, or against the Privy Council, because St. Paul knew nothing of them, is just as unreasonable as it would be to declaim against the wearing of braces, because St. Paul wore no braces. And so, on the other hand, to insist on extinguishing the black coat or the black gown of the Nonconformist minister, or the white surplice of the Anglican minister, or the red stockings of the Roman cardinal, because they are not the ordinary everyday dress which is now worn, or would have been worn in early times, would be as superstitious as the vulgar objection to Church establishments. There may be reasons against ecclesiastical vestments of all kinds. But the fact of their being modern is not of itself against them, unless we insist on making them essential as containing ideas which they do not, and never were intended to, symbolise.

2. But secondly, it may be said, partly by the opponents and partly by the advocates of these vestments, that, whatever may be the history of their origin, all that *Their contrasts.* we have practically now to consider is the purpose to which they are at present applied. It was maintained not long ago by a distinguished political leader, that to treat these badges with indifference would be no less absurd than to treat the Red Flag as merely a piece of bunting, whereas it really represents anarchy and revolution and must be dealt with accordingly. We venture to think that this very illustration furnishes an answer to the allegations of importance on the one side or the other brought to bear upon this question. No doubt with the uneducated and ill-educated of all classes a superficial badge or colour often outweighs every other consideration. It is within the memory of living persons in Norfolk, where party feeling ran higher than in the rest of England, that the blue or orange colour of the electioneering flags was the one single notion which the lower classes had of

the great Whig or the great Conservative parties for whom they
were led to vote. An illiterate artisan on his death-bed would
say, as a plea for the condonation of many sins, ' At least I have
been true to my colours.' And on one occasion, when in a
country town, by some accident, the blue and orange colours
were interchanged, the whole mass of the voters followed the
colour to which they were accustomed, although it was attached
to the party which represented the exactly opposite principles.
We cannot deny that in dealing with popular passion and
prejudice on this as on other matters, it may be necessary to
concede far more than either correct history or calm reason will
justify. But it may be worth while in all these cases to show
how insignificant and how valueless is the form. Is it not
our duty, in the first instance, to represent, at least to ourselves and the more educated, the real state of the case—to
be fully persuaded that these things are of themselves, as St.
Paul says, absolutely ' nothing '—even if immediately afterwards, in condescension to weak brethren, we are inclined,
as he was, to go a long way either in avoiding or in adopting
them? Even in that very instance which was just now quoted
of the Red Flag, on an occasion when its adoption might have
led to the most terrible results both in France and in Europe,
when on February 25, 1848, a raging mob, surging round
the steps of the Hôtel de Ville of Paris, demanded that this
crimson banner should be adopted instead of the tricolor,
that calamity, as it certainly would have been, was averted,
even with that savage multitude, by the eloquent appeal of
one man to the indisputable origin of its first appearance in
the history of France. ' The Tricolor,' said Lamartine, ' has
made the tour of the world with our glories and our victories ;
but the Red Flag has only made the tour of the Champ de
Mars, trailed in mire and defiled with blood.' He alluded,
of course, to the fact that the Red Flag was originally the
badge of martial law, and yet more to the first distinct occasion of its adoption, on that dark day—among the most
disgraceful in the annals of the first French Revolution—
which witnessed the execution of one of the noblest of French-

men under the insults of a furious populace who waved the red flag before him, dragged it through the mud, and drew blood with it from his venerable face. By that calm historical allusion, though fully appreciated perhaps only by a few, Lamartine was able to disperse pacifically and reasonably a movement which, had he fired at the flag with shot and shell as a symbol of anarchy, would probably have deluged Paris with blood. If, in like manner, the Comte de Chambord could be convinced that the white flag represented in its origin, not legitimate monarchy, but the white plume of a Huguenot chief, he might be persuaded to abandon that which, as it would seem, no force of arms will ever enable him to relinquish, or the country to adopt.

In all such cases it is our duty, whether as opponents or upholders of these forms, to see things as they really are, and not to adopt the passionate and ill-informed expressions of those whom we ought to guide, and whose guidance we ought to be the last to accept.

3. Thirdly, it may be remarked that in point of fact it is not so much any theory concerning these dresses which arouses popular indignation, as the circumstance that they are unusual, startling, and therefore offensive;  and also that they are regarded as borrowed from the Roman Catholic Church, and therefore viewed with suspicion, not unnaturally, as the outward signs and tokens of a system which is believed to have been the cause of infinite mischief and misery to England three hundred years ago, and to Spain, Italy, and France at this moment. And this ground of indignation, apart from any sacerdotal or sacrificial associations, is further borne out by the fact that it is actually the ground on which these particular vestments are adopted by those who wear them. We are not aware that in any instance there has been an attempt on the part of our English clergy, either to wear what they may imagine to have been actually worn in the second and third centuries, or to wear what is worn in the Greek, the Coptic, or the Armenian Church, or even in the time of Edward VI. in England. They are im-

ported, as we may see by newspaper advertisements, simply from the magazines of France and of Belgium, according to the last fashions of Brussels or Paris.  They represent, therefore, in their actual adoption, merely the usages of these foreign modern Churches, and nothing else.  Indeed, we may say they are copied with almost Chinese exactness of imitation, even to their rents and patches.  An instance may be selected which does not belong at present to the disputed category, but which therefore will the better illustrate the question—the modern practice of cutting off the surplice at the knees.  This, assuredly not copied from either Jewish or primitive ceremonial, is the exact copy of the surplice of the modern Roman Church, but of that garment under peculiar conditions.  It has been said, on good authority, that originally the Roman surplice reached to the feet, but that the lower part was of lace; then that the lace, being too expensive, was cut away, and so left the surplice in that state of economical curtailment which has been adopted as the model of English usage.

We do not say that this peculiarity is calculated to render them less odious to popular feeling; but it at once clears away a mass of useless declamation, either for or against, which we find in speeches, petitions, and pamphlets.  And it is more important to notice this, because the dislike to untimely innovations or foreign costumes rests on a larger basis than concerns the particular clothes which have been introduced during the last ten years.  A surplice adopted suddenly where a gown has hitherto been worn has provoked an opposition quite as violent, and has been defended with a tenacity quite as exaggerated, as has been shown with regard to the more fanciful vestments of latter days.  The cope, which, according to some of the fine-drawn distinctions, both of enemies and of friends, is not supposed to be 'sacrificial,' would produce quite as much consternation in a rustic parish, or even in a country cathedral, as the chasuble, which is alleged to be 'sacrificial.'  It is the foreign, unusual, defiant, and, if so be, illegal introduction of these things which constitutes their offence.

V. Taking these practical principles as our guide, we proceed to ask what, under our actual circumstances, is the best course to pursue with regard to these usages.

1. First, it would seem to be the duty of every one who is a voice and not merely an echo to proclaim their absolute indifference and triviality, when compared with matters of serious religion. It was said by a great divine, some thirty years ago, that it was the peculiar blot of factions or parties in the Church of England to have fought, as for matters of importance, for this or that particular kind of dress. The remark is true. Thrice over has the English Church been distracted by a vestiarian controversy—first, at the Reformation, when Bishop Hooper refused to wear a square cap because God had made heads round ; secondly, in the controversy between Laud and the Puritans ; and, thirdly, in our own time, beginning with the Exeter riots of 1840, and continuing even now. No such controversy has ever distracted either the Church of Rome, or the Church of Luther, or the Church of Calvin. It is high time to see whether we could not now, once and for ever, dispel the idea that the Kingdom of God, or ' the workshop of Satan,' consists in the colour of a coat, or the shape of a cloak, or the use of a handkerchief. Viewed merely in a doctrinal point of view, no more deadly blow could be struck at the ceremonial, and what may be called the Etruscan theory of religion, than to fill the atmosphere with the sense of the entire insignificance of dresses or postures. To speak of them as of no significance is the true translation of the great maxim of the Apostle—' Circumcision availeth nothing, *nor uncircumcision.*'



2. Secondly, if this absolute adiaphorism could be made to take possession of the popular mind, our course would be very much cleared. We might then view more calmly the legal aspect of the question, as depending on the validity and the meaning of the Ornaments' Rubric. This ingenious obscurity is a singular example, either of the disingenuousness or of the negligence with

which the Prayer Book was reconstructed during the passionate period of the Restoration.

But supposing that it should be decided once and again that the rubric forbids the use of these vestments, the fact of their historical insignificance would be a consolation to those who, willing to obey the law, would thus be constrained to give up what the usage of some years has no doubt endeared to them. They would feel then that they were not surrendering any principle, but merely a foreign custom, which having been introduced, let us hope, with the innocent motive of beautifying public worship, they abandoned as good citizens and good Churchmen, when the law declared against it; and that in so doing they were parting with a practice which had no other intrinsic value than what belongs to an antiquarian reminiscence of that early age of the Church when there was no distinction between clergy and laity, between common and ecclesiastical life, and that the only historical association legitimately connected with it was the most anti-sacerdotal—the most Protestant—that Christian antiquity has handed down to us.

And on the other hand, if it should be decided that the rubric requires these vestments to be worn, then again, to those who have hitherto objected to them, it would be no less a consolation to know that such a requirement did not enforce the use of anything which symbolised a doctrine either of the Real Presence or of the priesthood, but was simply the last English, or, if so be, the last Parisian development of the shirts and coats and rugs of the peasants and gentry of the third century. And in this contingency, two considerations occur which might mitigate what, to some persons would appear to be a serious grievance. The first is that if these clothes should be declared legal, the probability is that the interest attaching to them would almost entirely cease. Half of the excitement they now produce, both in those who defend and those who attack them, is from the belief that they are, more or less, contrary to the law. Whatever the Supreme Court of Appeal takes under its patronage, loses, in the eyes of many zealous clergy, its special ecclesiastical value. When, for example, the Credence Table was legalised and shown to be not an appendage to an altar, but a sideboard on which the dishes were placed, in order to be tasted before being set on the table, with the view of seeing whether they contained poison, that part of the church furniture ceased to be a bone of contention. Even the cope has comparatively lost its interest since it was commanded by the Privy Council; just as it may be fairly doubted whether the significance of the eastward position can stand the shock given when it is found that one of the solitary witnesses to it in the past generation was Bishop Maltby, the Whig of Whigs, the Protestant of Protestants, the recipient of the famous Durham letter. There is a story of a distinguished prelate now deceased which may serve to illustrate the probable action of the law. A clergyman, who had contended in his village church for various points of ceremonial, at last ventured to ask, with fear and trembling, whether 'his lordship could allow the choristers to appear in surplices.' 'By all means,' said the bishop, 'let them appear in surplices—it will help to degrade that vestment.' What he meant, of course, was that the surplice would then lose its peculiar sacerdotal significance; and certainly the legalising of any dress by the Protestant Legislature of England would immediately place such dress on a footing and in a light which would admit of no misconception as to what was intended or not intended by it.

And, if the law should be thus pronounced, it would then in all probability become a matter of practical consideration whether an ancient and difficult rubric, thus suddenly revived, could be expected to be universally put in force throughout the country, and would thus open the door to the intervention of that principle which is so well laid down in Canon Robertson's book, 'How shall we Conform to the Liturgy?' and in the succession of admirable articles in the *Quarterly Review* on the same subject—namely, that, in the matter of these ancient rubrical observances, common sense and charity and the discretion of the Ordinary must come in to modify and accommodate rigid rules which otherwise would produce a dead-lock in every office of the Church.

In point of fact, the cope, even since the recent decision in its favour, has, except in a few special cases, been hardly worn at all. There have not been throughout the whole Church more than three or four instances of deference to this reanimated ghost. And with regard to a much larger assortment of clerical vestments, but resting on the same authority as the cope—namely, the Canons of 1604—it may be safely asserted that not one clergyman in ten thousand ever wears or thinks of wearing any of them. Those canons command every clergyman, in walking or travelling, to appear in 'a gown with a standing collar,' or in 'a tippet of silk or sarcenet,' and on no account to wear a cloak with long sleeves, and especially 'not to wear light-coloured stockings.' This 74th Canon is everywhere disregarded, and though it contains the sensible remark that 'its meaning is not to attribute any holiness or special worthiness to the said garments' (the very principle for which we have been contending), 'but for decency, gravity, and order;' yet it is not less precise in its enactments than the 58th and 24th Canons, and must stand or fall with them. It may be quoted on this occasion to show how completely and irrevocably custom has been allowed to override a rule, which is not, indeed, properly speaking, the law of the Church (being only a canon and not a statute), but by which, nevertheless, it has been often attempted in these matters to provide that the laws of the Church shall be regulated.

And this perhaps is the place for considering the question whether, supposing that the existing law fail either from obscurity or obsoleteness to control our present usage, it is desirable to pass a new legislative enactment which shall lay down precisely what clothes are or are not to be worn by the clergy, inside or outside their official ministrations. The same principle of the intrinsic indifference of these things which we have laid down will help us here to

*Uncleanness of rubrics.*

a right solution.   If we can once resolve that the question of clerical, as of all dress, is simply a matter of custom and fashion, or, as the 74th Canon says, of 'decency, gravity, and order,' then we may safely venture to say that to enumerate any catalogue or wardrobe of such clothes either in an Act of Parliament, or even in a canon, would be entirely unworthy of the dignity of an Act of the Legislature or even of the Convocations.   It would be unworthy, and (unless it entered into details which would be absolutely ridiculous) it would soon be utterly useless.   For who can now say exactly what it is which constitutes a legal cope or chasuble, or the legal length of a surplice, or 'guards, and welts, and cuts,' or 'a coif, or wrought night-cap?'   And the total failure of the canon just cited proves how inevitably such rules fall into hopeless desuetude after a few years.   Nor would such enumeration be necessary.   One advantage of the deep obscurity of the Ornaments' Rubric has been that it has shown us how possible it is for a Church (except in occasional excitements) to exist without any rule at all on the subject.   Not a single garment is named by name in that rubric, nor in any part of the Prayer Book from beginning to end; [8] and yet on the whole a comely and decent order has been observed in the English Church, only with such change as the silent lapse of time necessarily brings with it.   And it should be observed that in the Irish Church before its recent calamities, in the American Episcopal Church, and in the Established Church of Scotland, not even the shadow of the Ornaments' Rubric exists, nor anything analogous to it.   Custom, and custom alone, has provided the white gown, the black gown, the blue gown, as the case may be.   To this easy yoke, and to this safe guide of custom and common sense, we also might safely commit ourselves.

3. This leads us to another obvious conclusion.   If there be no intrinsic value in these vestments, then, whether

---

[8] The only exception is not in the Prayer Book itself, but in the single office of the Consecration of a Bishop, and in that there is no mention of lawn sleeves or chimere, but only of the 'rochet.'

the law forbids them or enforces them, the same duty is incumbent on all those who regard the substance of religion *Folly o' introducing vestments.* above its forms, namely, that on no account should these garbs, whether legal or illegal, be introduced into churches or parishes where they give offence to the parish or the congregation. The more any clergyman can appreciate the absolute indifference of such things in themselves, the more will he feel himself compelled to withdraw them the moment he finds that they produce the opposite effect to that which he intended them to have. On the necessity of such a restriction, it is a satisfaction to believe that many even of those whose opinions rather incline them to these peculiar usages, would more or less concur. Quarrels produced in parishes by such trivial causes ought to be stifled instantly and at once. The game, however delightful, of maintaining these vestments, is not worth the burning the candle of discord even for a single moment in a single parish. And, on the other hand, as regards those congregations where no offence is given, it seems to be 'straining at a gnat and swallowing a camel,' whilst we freely allow (and no one is disposed to curtail the legal liberty) the preaching and practising of the most extravagant—the most uncharitable—the most senseless doctrines, on whatever side; to stumble at permitting a few congregations here and there to indulge themselves in the pleasure of a few colours and a few shapes to which we know with absolute certainty that no religious significance is intrinsically attached; and of which any significance, that may be imagined to be attached to them by those who use them, can be equally or better expressed by garments of quite another make, and by ceremonies of quite another kind.

If we are really desirous of resisting the malady of reactionary hierarchical sentiment, let us grapple not with these superficial and ambiguous symptoms, but with the disease itself. The refusal to acknowledge State interference with Church affairs, whether on the part of Roman Ultramontanes, Scottish Free Churchmen, or English Liberationists; the

exciting speeches of so-called Liberal candidates to miscalled
Liberal constituents on behalf of what they choose to call
spiritual independence ; the attempts from time to time by
legal prosecution, or angry declamation, to stifle free critical
inquiry in the Church of England ; the refusal to acknowledge
the pastoral character of our Wesleyan or Nonconforming
brethren ; the tendency to encourage a material rather than
a moral and spiritual view of Christian ordinances ; the
reading of the services of the Church inaudibly and unin-
telligibly, in imitation of a Church which employs a dead
language—all these endeavours, conducted with however
conscientious a desire to do good, and however justified by
certain elements in the Church of England, or in human'
nature—are more hostile to the true spirit of the Reformation
than any evanescent fashions of clerical costume, which perish
with the using.   Even to the most extreme Puritan and to the
most extreme Calvinist, we venture to quote, in justification
of an exceptional toleration in these trivial matters, the saying
of the great John Calvin himself, 'They are *tolerabiles ineptiæ*.'

4. Finally, it would be a clear gain to the interests of
practical, moral, spiritual religion, if by granting all feasible
toleration to these innocent archaisms in a few
eccentric places, the majority of Churchmen could
be left free to pursue the improvements which the
Church and nation so urgently need, and which have hitherto
been defeated by the disproportionate and inordinate attention
devoted both by friends and enemies to this insignificant
point.   What is really wanted, both for the good of the Church
and as the best corrective to the superstitious and materialising
tendency which many of us deplore, is not an attempt to
restrain particular external usages, except, as before remarked,
when they give offence to the parishioners ; but, regardless of
any threats, to aim at such improvements as would be desirable,
even if there were not a single Ritualist in existence ; to de-
velop the Protestant elements of the Church, which are
stunted and dwarfed from the fear of offending those who,
whilst they demand for themselves a liberty which liberal

Churchmen have always endeavoured to gain for them, have hitherto too often refused to concede the slightest liberty to others.

The real evils of this tendency, whether in the English or in the Roman Catholic Church, which threatens to swallow up the larger, freer, more reasonable spirit which existed in both Churches fifty years ago, are obvious. The encouragement of a morbid dependence on the priesthood ; a vehement antagonism to the law ; excessive value attached to the technical forms of theology and ritual ; a revival of a scholastic phraseology which has lost its meaning ; a passion for bitter controversy and for exaggeration of differences—all these evils are for the most part beyond the reach of legal or ecclesiastical tribunals, and can only be met, as they can be fully met, first by fearless and dispassionate argument, but secondly and chiefly by the encouragement of a healthier tone in the public mind and clerical opinion, as at once a corrective and a counterpoise. What is needed is not to exterminate, but to act independently of, the party which has so often obstructed improvement by mere clamour and menace. The controversy concerning the lesser points of ceremonial has too much diverted the public attention from the substance to the accidents. The adherents of these vestments count amongst their ranks the wise and the foolish, the serious and the frivolous. Let them, in their own special localities, when they do not impose their own fancies upon unwilling listeners or spectators, by these colours and forms, do their best and their worst. Let them add, if so be, the peacocks' feathers which the Pope borrowed from the Kings of Persia, or the scarlet shoes which he took from the Roman Emperors. Let them freely have, if the law allows it, the liberty of facing to any point of the compass they desire—with Mussulmans to the east, with the Pope to the west, with Hindoos to the north, or with old-fashioned Anglicans to the south. This is no more than is deserved by the zeal of some ; it is no more than may be safely conceded to the scruples of all who can be indulged without vexing the consciences of others. But then let those also who take another view of the main attractions of religion be allowed to enjoy the liberty which, till thirty years ago, was freely permitted.   Let the rules which, if rendered inflexible, cripple the energies of the Church and mar its usefulness be relaxed by some machinery such as was in use in former times, before the modern creation of the almost insuperable obstructions of the majorities of the four Houses of Convocation.   Let each Bishop or Ordinary have the legal power, subject to any checks which Parliament will impose, of sanctioning what is almost universally allowed to pass unchallenged.   Let us endeavour to abate those prolongations and repetitions which have made our services, contrary to the intention of their framers, a byword at home and abroad.   Let us endeavour to secure that there shall be the option of omitting the questionable though interesting document whose most characteristic passages one of the two Convocations has virtually abjured.   Let us permit, openly or tacitly, the modifications in the rubrics of the Baptismal, the Marriage, the Commination, and the Ordination Services, which ought to be an offence to none, and would be an immense relief to many.   Let us seek the means of enabling the congregations of the National Church to hear, not merely, as at present, the lectures, but the sermons of preachers second to none in our own Church, though at present not of it.   Let us be firmly persuaded that error is most easily eradicated by establishing truth, and darkness most permanently displaced by diffusing light; and then whilst the best parts of the High Church party will be preserved to the Church by their own intrinsic excellence, the worst parts will be put down, not by the irritating and often futile process of repression, but by the pacific and far more effectual process of enforcing the opposite truths, of creating in the Church a wholesome atmosphere of manly, generous feeling, in which all that is temporary, acrid, and trivial will fade away, and all that is eternal, reasonable, and majestic will flourish and abound.

# CHAPTER IX.

## THE BASILICA.

WHAT was the original idea which the Christians of the first centuries conceived of a place of worship? What was the model which they chose for themselves when, on emerging from the Catacombs, they looked round upon the existing edifices of the civilised world?

For nearly two hundred years, set places of worship had no existence at all. In the third century, notices of them became more frequent, but still in such ambiguous terms that it is difficult to ascertain how far the building or how far the congregation is the prominent idea in the writer's mind; and it is not, therefore, till the fourth century, when they became so general as to acquire a fixed form and name, that our inquiry properly begins.

Of the public edifices of the heathen world, there were three which lent themselves to the Christian use. One was the circular tomb. This was seen in the various forms of memorial churches which from the Church of the Holy Sepulchre spread throughout the Empire. But this was exceptional. Another was the Temple. Though occasionally adopted by the Eastern Emperors,[1] and in some few instances, as the Pantheon, at Rome itself, it was never incorporated into the institutions of Western Christendom. It was not only that all its associations, both of name and place, jarred with the most cherished notions of Christian purity and holiness, but also that the very construction of the

---

[1] Bingham, viii. 2, 4. The Egyptian temples were many of them so used; as at Athens the Parthenon and the Temple of Theseus.

edifice was wholly incompatible with the new idea of worship, which Christianity had brought into the world. The Temple of Isis at Pompeii (to take the most complete specimen now extant of a heathen temple at the time of the Christian era) at once exhibits the impossibility of amalgamating elements so heterogeneous. It was exactly in accordance with the genius of heathenism, that the priest should minister in the presence of the God, withdrawn from view in the little cell or temple that rose in the centre of the consecrated area; but how should the president of the Christian assembly be concealed from the vast concourse in whose name he acted, and who, as with the voice of many waters, were to reply 'Amen' to his giving of thanks? It was most congenial to the feeling of Pagan worshippers that they should drop in, one by one, or in separate groups, to present their individual prayers or offerings to their chosen divinity; but how was a Christian congregation, which, by its very name of *ecclesia*, recalled the image of those tumultuous crowds which had thronged the Pnyx or Forum, in the days of the Athenian or Roman Commonwealth, to be brought within the narrow limits of the actual edifice which was supposed to be the dwelling of the God? Even the Temple of Jerusalem itself, pure as it was from the recollections which invested the shrines of the heathen deities, yet from its darkness, its narrowness, and the inaccessibility of its innermost cell was obviously inadequate to become the visible home of a religion to which the barriers of Judaism were hardly less uncongenial than those of Paganism itself. A Temple, whether heathen or Jewish, could never be the model of a purely Christian edifice. The very name itself had now, in Christian phraseology, passed into a higher sphere; and however much long use may have habituated us to the application of the word to material buildings, we can well understand how instinctively an earlier age would shrink from any lower meaning than the moral and spiritual sense attached to it in those Apostolical Writings which had taught the world that the true temple of God was in the hearts and consciences of men. And therefore, in the words of Bingham, 'for the first three ages the name is scarce ever' (he might have said never) 'applied to Christian places of worship;' and though instances of it are to be found in the rhetorical language. of the fourth, yet it never obtained a hold on the ordinary language of Christendom. The use of the word in Roman Catholic countries for Protestant churches is probably dictated by the desire to represent the Protestant service as heathen.

What, then, was the ancient heathen structure, whose title has thus acquired a celebrity so far beyond its original intention? It is the especial offspring and symbol of Western civilisation;—Greek in its origin, Roman in its progress, Christian in its ultimate development, the word is co-extensive with the range of the European family. In the earliest form under which we can catch any trace of it, it stands in the dim antiquity of the Homeric age—at the point where the first beginnings of Grecian civilisation melt away into the more primitive forms of Oriental society. It is the gateway of the Royal Palace, in which the ancient Kings, Agamemnon at Mycenæ, David at Jerusalem, Pharaoh at Thebes or Memphis, sat to hear and to judge the complaints of their people; and of which the trace [9] was preserved at Athens in the 'King's Portico' under the Pnyx, where the Archon King performed the last judicial functions of the last shadow of the old Athenian royalty. But it was amongst the Romans that it first assumed that precise form and meaning which have given it so lasting an importance. Judging from the great prominence of the Basilicas as public buildings, and from the more extended application of them in the Imperial times to purposes of general business, the nearest parallel to them in modern cities would doubtless be found in the Town-hall or Exchange. What, in fact, the

*The Basilica.*

*Its form.*

---

[9] It is perhaps doubtful how far the *form* of the word 'Basilica,' though of course itself purely Greek, was ever used with this acceptation in Greece itself. Στοὰ Βασιλέως is the designation of the Athenian portico, and οἶκος or ναὸς Βασιλέως is Eusebius' expression for the Christian Basilica.

rock-hewn semicircle of the Pnyx was at Athens—what the open platform of the Forum had been in the earlier days of Rome itself [1]—that, in the later times of the Commonwealth, was the Basilica—the general place of popular resort and official transactions; but, in accordance with the increased refinement of a more civilised age, protected from the mid-day sun and the occasional storm by walls and roof. There was a long hall divided by two rows of columns into a central avenue, with two side aisles, in one of which the male, in the other the female appellants to justice waited their turn. The middle aisle was occupied by the chance crowd that assembled to hear the proceedings, or for purposes of merchandise. A transverse avenue which crossed the others in the centre, if used at all, was occupied by the advocates and others engaged in the public business. The whole building was closed by a long semicircular recess, in the centre of which sat the prætor or supreme judge, seen high above the heads of all on the elevated [2] 'tribunal,' which was deemed the indispensable symbol of the Roman judgment-seat.

This was the form of the Basilica, as it met the view of the first Christians. Few words are needed to account for its adaptation to the use of a Christian church. Something, no doubt, is to be ascribed, as Dean Mil- man well remarks, to the fact,[3] that ' as these buildings were numerous, and attached to any imperial residence, they might be bestowed at once on the Christians without either interfer- ing with the course of justice, or bringing the religious feelings of the hostile parties into collision.' Still, the instances of

*Its adapta-tion to Chris-tian worship.*

[1] The Tynwald in the Isle of Man is an exact likeness still existing of these early assemblies in the open air.

[2] The 'judgment-hall' or prætorium of the Roman magistrates in the provinces had no further resemblance to the Basilica than in the coincidence of name, which must have arisen from their frequent formation out of the palaces of the former kings of the conquered nations. But so necessary was the elevation of the judge's seat considered to the final delivery of the judgment, that, as has been made familiar to us in one memorable instance (John xix. 13), the absence of the usual tribunal was supplied by a tesse-lated pavement, which the magistrate carried with him, and on which his chair or throne was placed before he could pronounce sentence.

[3] *History of Christianity*, iii. 343.

actual transformation are exceedingly rare—in most cases it must have been impossible, from the erection of the early Christian churches on the graves, real or supposed, of martyrs and apostles, which, according to the almost universal practice of the ancient world, were necessarily without the walls of the city, as the halls of justice, from their connection with everyday life, were necessarily within. It is on more general grounds that we may trace something in the type itself of the Basilica, at least not uncongenial to the early Christian views of worship, independent of any causes of mere accidental convenience. What this was has been anticipated in what has been said of the rejection of the temple. There was now a ' church,' a ' congregation,' an ' assembly,' which could no longer be hemmed within the narrow precincts, or detained in the outer courts of the enclosure—where could it be so naturally placed as in the long aisles which had received the concourse of the Roman populace, and which now became the ' nave ' of the Christian Cathedrals? Whatever distinctions existed in the Christian society, were derived, not as in the Jewi h temple, from any notions of inherent religious differences between different classes of men, but merely, as in the Jewish synagogue, from considerations of order and decency ; and where could these be found more readily than in the separate places still retained by the sexes in the aisles of the Basilica : or the appropriation of the upper end of the building to the clergy and singers? There was a law to be proclaimed, and a verdict to be pronounced, by the highest officers of the new society ; and what more natural than that the Bishop should take his seat on the lofty tribunal of the prætor,[4] and thence

* The Basilica Æmiliana and the Basilica Julia were examples in the Roman Forum of this sort of edifice. But there were others where the judicial character was more strongly impressed on the building. Such were the Basilica Sessoriana, now converted into the Church of Sta. Croce in the Sessorian Palace at Rome ; the Basilica Palatina, still to be traced on the ruins of the Palatine, with its apse and its oblong hall ; the Basilica attached to the palace at Trèves, and since converted into a Protestant church by the late King of Prussia.

rebuke, exhort, or command, with an authority not the less convincing, because it was moral and not legal? There was lastly a bond of communion between all the members of that assembly, to which the occupants of the Temple and the Basilica had been alike strangers—what more fitting than that the empty centre of the ancient judgment-hall, where its several avenues and aisles joined in one, should now receive a new meaning; and that there, neither in the choir nor nave, but in the meeting point of both, should be erected the Altar or Table of that communion which was to belong exclusively neither to the clergy nor to the people, but to bind both together in indissoluble harmony?[5]

There are some general reflections which this transformation suggests. In the first place, it may no doubt have been an accident that the first Christian place of worship should have been taken from an edifice so expressive of the popular life of Greece and Rome,—so exact an antithesis to the seclusion of the Jewish and Pagan Temple. But, if it was an accident, it is strikingly in accordance with all that we know of the strength of the popular element of the early Church,—not merely in its first origin, when even an Apostle

---

[5] The 'atrium' and 'impluvium' of the more private hall seem to have become the models of the outer court and 'cantharus' or fountain of the Basilica. The obvious appropriation of the seats immediately round the altar to the emperor and his attendants, when present, is preserved in the probable derivation of 'chancellor,' from the 'cancelli' or 'rails,' by which that officer sat. In the Eastern Church the screen of the *Iconostasis*, which now divides the nave from the choir, has assumed a solid shape to furnish a stand for the increasing multiplication of sacred pictures. But originally it was a curtain, then a light trellis work. And in the Western Church it has never intruded, until in the fifteenth century, for quite another reason, the screen was introduced to hide the local shrine of the saint, as at St. Albans and Westminster Abbey (if so be) from the eyes of common worshippers. The altar was a wooden structure, as it still is in the Eastern Church. It was gradually changed to stone in the sixth century, from the incorporation of a relic of a saint inside, and the wish to consider it as a tomb (see Chapter XI.). What was therefore once its universal material has since then been absolutely forbidden in the Roman Church. It was also commonly placed in the middle of the apse of the church. The modern practice of its attachment to the eastern wall was absolutely unknown. Its ancient name was 'the Table,' by which it is still always called in the East. (See Chapter III.)

did not pronounce sentence on an offender, or issue a decree
or appoint an officer, without the concurrence of the whole
society; but even in those later times, when Augustine fled from city to city to escape from the elevation which he was destined to receive from the wild enthusiasm
of an African populace; when a layman, a magistrate, an unbaptised catechumen was, on the chance acclamation of an
excited mob, transformed into Ambrose, Archbishop of Milan.
It is precisely this true image of the early Church, the union
of essential religious equality with a growing distinction of
rank and order, that the Basilica was to bring before us in a
visible and tangible shape. It might have been unnatural
if the whole constitution, the whole religion of the three first
centuries, was wrapt up in the institution of Bishops, Priests,
and Deacons; but it could not have been deemed altogether
strange, in an age that still caught the echoes of that contest
which convulsed the early Christian society, between the
last expiring efforts of the popular element of the Church
and the first germ of the rule of the clergy.

Again, the rise of the first edifice of Christian worship,
not out of the Jewish Temple, or even the Jewish Synagogue,
but out of the Roman hall of justice, may be regarded as no inapt illustration of another fact of
early Christian history. We are often reminded
by the polemics of opposite schools of the identity of
early Christian customs and institutions with those of
the older dispensation. Few topics have been more popular
in modern times, whether in praise or blame, than the
Judaic character of the worship, ministry, and teaching
of the three first centuries. But the indisputable share
which the Gentile world has had in the material buildings
of the Christian Church, suggests a doubt whether it
may not have also contributed something to the no less
complex structure of its moral fabric. The influence of
Judaism on the first century, was undoubtedly very great.
On the one hand, the early sects had all more or less something of a Judaising character; on the other hand, even the

Apostles could not have been what they were had they not
been Jews.   But the fall of Jerusalem was in truth the fall
of the Jewish world ; it was a reason for the close of the
Apostolic age—a death-blow to the influence of the Jewish
nationality for a long time to come on the future fortunes
of the world at large.   Something, no doubt, both of its
form and spirit lingered on, in the institutions of that great
society which sprung out of its ruins ; but however much
the mere ceremonial and superficial aspect of the Patristic
age may bear a Jewish physiognomy, it is in the influences
at work in the social fabric of the Roman Empire itself, that
we must seek the true springs of action in the Christian
Church,—so far as they came from any foreign source.   It is
therefore with something more than a mere artistical interest
that we find the Bishop seated on the chair of the Prætor—
the forms of the Cathedral already wrapt up in the halls
of Æmilius and of Trajan.   It is in accordance not only
with the more general influence to which the Christian
society was exposed, from the rhetorical subtleties, the magical superstitions, the idolatrous festivals, and the dissolute
habits of the heathen world at large, but also with the more
especial influence which the purely political spirit of the
Roman State exercised over some of their most peculiar institutions—with the fact that the very names by which the
functions of their officers are described sprung not from the
religious, but from the civil vocabulary of the times, and are
expressions not of spiritual so much as of political power.
‘ Ordo ’ (the origin of our present ‘ orders ’) was the well-
known name of the municipal senates of the empire ; ‘ ordina-
tio ’ (the original of our ‘ ordination ’) was never used by the
Romans except for civil appointments ; the ‘ tribunes of the
people ’ are the likeness which the historian of the ‘ Decline
and Fall,’ recognises in the early Christian Bishops ; the
preponderance of the Gentile spirit of government and the
revival of the spirit of the Roman Senate in the counsels of
Cyprian was the thought which forced itself on the mind of
the last English historian of Rome.   The Church of Rome

developed thus early the idea of authority and subordination. Evils and abuses innumerable no doubt flowed from the excess of this influence on the Christian Church, but in itself it was a true instinct, which no arguments about the contrast of civil and spiritual power were able completely to extinguish.[6] The free spirit of the Roman citizen felt that it could breathe nowhere so freely as in the bosom of the Christian society. The Christian minister felt that no existing office or title to power was so solemn as that of the Roman magistrate; and it was a striking act of homage to the greatness of the empire that by an instinct, however unconscious, the hall of Roman justice should not have been deemed too secular for a place of Christian worship.

Yet once more, we have seen how the very name of Basilica leads our thoughts back to the period of Roman greatness and Grecian refinement, how naturally the several parts of the heathen and the secular edifice adapted themselves to their higher use, how, on the one hand (if we take the Christian service, not in its worse, but in its better aspect), the den of thieves was changed into the house of prayer—the words of heavenly love spoken from the inexorable seat of Roman judgment—the halls of wrangling converted into the abodes of worship;—how, on the other hand, the idea of the public and social life which the Basilica has brought with it from Greece, the idea of an irresistible law and universal dominion which had been impressed upon it by the genius of Rome, first found their complete development under the shadow of that faith which was to preserve them both to the new world of Europe. It is possible to trace, in this transfiguration of the ancient images of Gentile power and civilisation, a sign, however faint, of the true spirit of that faith which here found an outward expression. Had unrestrained scope been given to the tendency which strove to assimilate all Christian worship to the religious ceremonial of Judaism or Paganism, it might have

*The use of art.*

---

* See Renan's *Hibbert Lectures on the Influence of Rome on Christianity and the Catholic Church.*

perpetuated itself by adopting in all cases, as it certainly did
in some, the type, if not of the Roman, at least of the Jewish
temple.   Had the stern indifference to all forms of art prevailed everywhere, and at all times, during the first three
centuries, as it did during the ages of persecution and in the
deserts of the Thebaid, it would probably have swept away
outward localities and forms of worship altogether.

A higher spirit, undoubtedly, than either of these tendencies represent, there has always been in the Christian Church,
whether latent or expressed;—a spirit which would make
religion to consist not in the identification of things with
itself nor yet in a complete repudiation of them—but in its
comprehension and appropriation of them to its own uses;—
which would look upon the world neither as too profane, nor
too insignificant, for the regard of Christians, but rather as
the very sphere in which Christianity is to live and to
triumph.   To what extent such a spirit may have co-existed
with all the counteracting elements which it must have met
in the age of Constantine, we do not pretend to say: but if
the view above given be correct, it is precisely such a spirit
as this which is represented to us in outward form by the
origin of the Christian Basilica.   It is precisely such a monument as best befitted the first public recognition of a religion whose especial claim it was that it embraced not one
nation only, nor one element of human nature only, but all
the nations and all the various elements of the whole world.
The Gothic Cathedral may have had its origin quite independently of its precursors in Italy, and may have been a truer
exponent of the whole range of Christian feeling ; but neither
it, nor any other form of Architecture could have won its way
into the Christian world, unless the rise of the Basilica had
first vindicated the application of Gentile art, whether Roman
or Teutonic, to sacred purposes.   The selection of the Halls
of Justice may have been occasioned by merely temporary and
accidental causes; but the mere fact of the selection of such
sites or such models, unhallowed by ancient tradition, or
primeval awe, was in itself a new phenomenon—was in itself

the sign that a Religion was come into the world, confident
of its own intrinsic power of consecrating whatever it
touched, independently of any outward or external relation
whatever.

A similar tendency may be perceived in the subsequent
adaptation of the successive styles of mediæval and classical
structures to Christian and Protestant worship. The gathering of large masses in the nave or the transepts of cathedrals,
of which only a small portion had been, properly speaking,
devoted to religious uses, is an instance of these edifices
lending themselves to purposes for which they were not
originally intended. But of all such examples, the Basilica
is the earliest and the most striking.

# CHAPTER X,

### THE CLERGY.

It is proposed to state briefly the early constitution of the Christian clergy.[1]

I. It is certain that the officers of the Apostolical, or of any subsequent Church, were not part of the original institution of the Founder of our religion; that of Bishop, Presbyter, and Deacon, of Metropolitan, Patriarch, and Pope, there is not the shadow of a trace in the four Gospels. It is certain that they arose gradually out of the pre-existing institutions either of the Jewish Synagogue, or of the Roman Empire, or of the Greek municipalities, or under the pressure of local emergencies. It is certain that throughout the first century, and for the first years of the second, that is, through the later chapters of the Acts, the Apostolical Epistles, and the writings of Clement and Hermas, Bishop and Presbyter were convertible terms, and that the body of men so-called were the rulers—so far as any permanent rulers existed—of the early Church. It is certain that as the necessities of the time demanded, first at Jerusalem, then in Asia Minor, the elevation of one Presbyter

---

[1] The proofs of what is here stated have been given before in the Essay 'On the Apostolical Office,' in *Sermons and Essays on the Apostolical Age*, and are therefore not repeated here. And it is the less necessary, because they have been in later times elaborated at great length and with the most convincing arguments by Bishop Lightfoot in his 'Essay on the Christian Ministry' appended to his *Commentary on the Epistle to the Philippians*, and by the Rev. Edwin Hatch in his articles on 'Bishop' and 'Presbyter' in the *Dictionary of Christian Antiquities*, as well as in his more recent Bampton Lectures. These may be consulted for any further detail.

above the rest by the almost universal law, which even in republics engenders a monarchical element, the word ' Bishop ' gradually changed its meaning, and by the middle of the second century became restricted to the chief Presbyter of the locality. It is certain that in no instance were the Apostles called ' Bishops ' in any other sense than they were equally called ' Presbyters ' and ' Deacons.' It is certain that in no instance before the beginning of the third century is the title or function of the Pagan or Jewish Priesthood applied to the Christian pastors. From these facts result general conclusions of considerable interest.

1. It is important to observe how with the recognition of this gradual growth and change of the early names and offices

*Identity of Bishop and Presbyter.* of the Christian ministry, the long and fierce controversy between Presbyterianism and Episcopacy, which continued from the sixteenth to the first part of the nineteenth century, has entirely lost its significance. It is as sure that nothing like modern Episcopacy existed before the close of the first century as it is that nothing like modern Presbyterianism existed after the beginning of the second. That which was once the Gordian knot of theologians has at least in this instance been untied, not by the sword of persecution, but by the patient unravelment of scholarship. No existing church can find any pattern or platform of its government in those early times. Churches, like States, have not to go back to a state of barbarism to justify their constitution. It has been the misfortune of Churches, that, unlike States, there has been on all sides equally a disposition either to assume the existence in early days of all the later principles of civilisation, or else to imagine a primitive state of things which never existed at all.

2. These formations or transformations of the Christian ministry were drawn from the contemporary usages of society.

*Origin of the orders.* The Deacons were the most original of the institutions, being invented, as it were, for the special emergency in the Church of Jerusalem. But the Presbyters were the ' sheikhs,' the elders,—those who by seniority had reached the first rank—in the Jewish Synagogue. The Bishops were the same, viewed under another aspect—the 'inspectors,' the 'auditors' of the Grecian churches.[2] These words bear testimony to the fact (as significant of the truly spiritual character of Christianity as it is alien to its magical character) that the various orders of the Christian ministry point to their essentially lay origin and their affinity with the great secular world, of which the elements had been pronounced from the beginning of Christianity to be neither 'common nor unclean.'

3. It is interesting to observe the relics of the primitive condition of the Church, which have survived through all the changes of time.

The Bishop, in the second century, when first he became elevated above his fellow Presbyters, appears for a time to have concentrated in himself all the functions which they had hitherto exercised. If they had hitherto been co-equal Bishops he gradually became almost sole Presbyter. *Vestiges of the primitive usages.* He alone could baptise, consecrate, confirm, ordain, marry, preach, absolve. But this exclusive monopoly has never been fully conceded. In almost every one of these cases the Presbyters have either not altogether lost or have recovered some of their ancient powers. In all Churches the exclusive absorption of the privileges of the Presbyters into the hands of the Bishop has been either resisted or modified by occasional retention of the old usages. Everywhere Presbyters have successfully reasserted the power of consecrating, baptising, marrying, and absolving. Everywhere, except in the English Church, they have, in special cases, claimed the right of confirming. Everywhere they have, with the Bishop, retained a share in the right of ordaining Presbyters. At Alexandria they long retained the right of ordaining Bishops.[3]

We commonly speak of three Orders, and the present elevation of Bishops has fully justified that phrase; but

<hr>

[2] See the authorities quoted in Renan, *St. Paul*, 239.

[3] See *Lectures on the Eastern Church* (Lecture VII.); Bishop Lightfoot (*The Christian Ministry, in Commentary on the Philippians*, pp. 228-236).

according to the strict rules of the Church, derived from those early times, there are but two—Presbyters and Deacons.[4] The Abbots of the Middle Ages represent in the Episcopal Churches the Presbyterian element—independent of the jurisdiction of Bishops, and equal to them in all that concerned outward dignity.

4. Of all the offices in the early Church that of Deacon was subjected to the most extreme changes. Their origin (if, as

The Deacons. is probable, we must identify them more or less with the Seven in the Acts) is the only part of the institution of the Christian ministry of which we have a full description.[5] It was the oldest ecclesiastical function; the most ancient of the Holy Orders. It was grounded on the elevation of the care of the poor to the rank of a religious service. It was the proclamation of the truth that social questions are to take the first place amongst religious instruction. It was the recognition of political economy as part of religious knowledge. The deacons became the first preachers of Christianity. They were the first Evangelists, because they were the first to find their way to the homes of the poor. They were the constructors of the most solid and durable of the institutions of Christianity, namely the institutions of charity and beneficence. Women as well as men were enrolled in the order. They were district visitors, lay-helpers on the largest scale. Nothing shows the divergence between it and the modern Order of Deacons more completely than the divergence of numbers. In the Greek, Roman, and English Churches, and it may be added in the Presbyterian Churches, there are as many Deacons as Presbyters. But in the early Church the Presbyters were the many, the Deacons the few, and their fewness made their office not the smallest but the proudest office and prize in the Church.[6]

---

[4] It would seem that in those centuries the chief pastor of every city was a Bishop, and those who looked after the villages in the surrounding district were called country bishops (χωρεπίσκοποι). Whether they were Presbyters or Bishops in the later sense is a question which from the identity of the two Orders it is impossible to determine with certainty.

[5] Renan, *Les Apôtres*, pp. 120–122.

[6] Jerome, *Epist. ad Evagrium*; Thomasin, *Vetus et Nova Disciplina*, i. ii. 29.

The only institution which retains at once the name and the reality is the Diaconate as it exists in the Dutch Church. The seven Deacons of Rome exist as a shadow in the Cardinal Deacons of the Sacred College of Rome, but only as a shadow. They were the seven chaplains or officers of the Church. Their head was an acknowledged potentate of the first magnitude. He was the *Arch*deacon. Such was Lawrence at Rome, such was Athanasius at Alexandria, such was the Archdeacon of Canterbury in England. If any one were asked who was the first ecclesiastic of Western Christendom, he would naturally and properly say, the Bishop of Rome. But the second is not an archbishop, not a cardinal, but the Archdeacon of Rome. Till the eleventh century this was so absolutely. That office was last filled by Hildebrand, and in the deed of consecration of the Church of Monte Casino, his name succeeds immediately to that of the Pope, and is succeeded by that of the Bishop of Ostia. Since his time the office has been rarely filled, and has been virtually abolished.[7]

5. Before the conversion of the Empire, Bishops and Presbyters alike were chosen by the whole mass of the people[8] in the parish or the diocese (the words at that time were almost interchangeable). The election of Damasus at Rome, of Gregory at Constantinople, of Ambrose at Milan, and of Chrysostom at Constantinople are decisive proofs of this practice. There were, no doubt, attempts in particular instances to modify these popular elections, sometimes by the Bishops, as in Egypt, against the Melitians in the Council of Nicæa, sometimes as at Rome, by the leading clergy of the place, which gave birth to the College of Cardinals, but ultimately in every case by the influence of the sovereign, first of the Emperor, and then of the several princes of Europe.

Appoint-<br>ment.

6. The form of consecration or ordination varied. In the

---

[7] Thomasin, *Vetus et Nova Disciplina*, i. lib. ii. c. 20, s. 3. The Archdeacon of Constantinople ceased about the same time. The first instance of a Presbyter Archdeacon is A.D. 874.

[8] By show of hands ($\chi\epsilon\iota\rho\sigma\tau\sigma\nu\iota\alpha$). Renan's *St. Paul*, p. 238.

Alexandrian and Abyssinian Churches it was and still is, by breathing; in the Eastern Church generally by lifting up *Forms of consecration.* the hands in the ancient oriental attitude of benediction; in the Armenian Church, as also at times in the Alexandrian Church, by the dead hand of the predecessor; in the early Celtic Church, by the transmission of relics or pastoral staff; in the Latin Church by the form of touching the head, which has been adopted from it by all Protestant Churches. No one mode was universal; no written formula of ordination exists. That by which the Presbyters of the Western Church are ordained is not later than the twelfth century, and even that varies widely in the place assigned to it in the Roman and in the English Churches.[9]

7. Of the ordinary ministrations of the early clergy it is difficult to form any conception. One rule, however, is known to have regulated their condition which every Church in Christendom has since rejected except the Abyssinian. It was positively forbidden in the fourth century, evidently in conformity with prevailing usage, for any Bishop, Presbyter, or Deacon to leave the parish or diocese in which he had been originally placed.

The clergy were, as a general rule, married; and though in the Eastern Church this long ceased as regards Bishops, and in the Latin Church altogether, in the Church of the first three centuries it was universal.

The regulations in the Pastoral Epistles, which are under any hypothesis the earliest documents or laws describing the duties of the clergy, dwell very slightly [1] on the office of teaching, do not even mention the sacraments, and are for the most part confined to matters of conduct and sobriety. The teaching functions were added to those of government as the Christian Church grew in intelligence, and have varied with the circumstances of the age. The present Eastern Church, though once abounding in them, is now almost

---

[9] See Chapter VII.

[1] The only expression which bears upon teaching in the catalogue of a

entirely without them ; in the Western Church they have never been altogether absent; in the Protestant churches they have almost absorbed all others.  But in all, unlike the Jewish and Pagan Priesthoods, the intellectual and pastoral attributes have been in theory predominant, and have been the mainstay of the office.

II. From these facts two conclusions follow.

1. In the first beginning of Christianity there was no such institution as the clergy, and it is conceivable that there may be a time when they shall cease to be.  But though the office of the Christian ministry was not one of the original and essential elements of the Christian religion, yet it grew naturally out of the want which was created.  There was a kind of natural necessity for the growth of the clergy in order to meet the increasing needs of the Christian community.  Just as kings, and judges, and soldiers spring up to suit the wants of civil society, so the clergy sprang up to meet the wants of religious society. Even in those religious communities which have endeavoured to dispense with such an order it has reasserted itself in other forms.  The Mussulman religion, properly speaking, admits of no clergy.  But the legal profession has very nearly taken their place.  The Mufti and the Imam are religious quite as much as they are civil authorities.  The English Society of Friends, although they acknowledge no separate Order, yet have always had well-known accredited teachers, who are to them as the Popes and Pastors of their community.

The growth of the clergy.

The intellectual element in the Christian society will always require someone to express it, and this, in some form or another, will probably be the clergy, or, as Coleridge expressed it, the ' Clerisy.'  The mechanical part of the office, which was characteristic of the Priest, did not belong to the office in early Christian times.  The ' elders ' were de-rived from the Jewish synagogue, but it was the excellence of

Bishop's (or Presbyter's) duties in 1 Tim. iii. 2–7, is 'apt to teach' (διδακτικός) in ver. 7, and in Tit. i. ii, the expressions used in i. 9.

Christianity to inspire them with a new life, to make them fill a new place, to make them occupy all the vacant opportunities of good that this world offers.

2. It has been said that the Christian Church or Society existed before the institution of the Christian clergy. In like manner the Christian clergy existed before the institution of Christian Bishops. In the first age there was no such marked distinction as now we find between the different orders of the clergy. It was only by slow degrees that the name of Bishop became appropriated to one chief pastor raised high in rank and station above the mass of the clergy. But here again, it was the demand which created the supply. The demand for distinction and inequality of offices arose from the fact that there is in human nature a distinction and inequality of gifts. If all clergymen were equal in character and power, there would be no place for inequality of rank or station amongst them. It is because, like other men, they are unequally gifted, because there are from time to time amongst them, as amongst others, men who have been endowed with superior natures, that Episcopacy exists and will always exist, in substance if not in form, but often in form also, because the substance of the character claims an outward form in which to embody itself. Doubtless there have been times when the clergy and the Church were able to effect their great objects in the world without the aid of higher officers; just as there have been battles which have been won by the rank and file of soldiers without the aid, or even in spite, of generals. But still the more usual experience of mankind has proved that in all conditions of life there are men who rise above their fellows, and who therefore need corresponding offices in which their more commanding gifts may find a place; and who by the development of those gifts through the higher offices are themselves a standing proof that the offices are necessary. Even in the Apostolic age, before the existence of what we now call Bishops, and when the word Bishop was synonymous with Presbyter or Elder,

Origin of Episcopacy.

there were forward and gifted disciples, like Timotheus and Titus, who took the lead.  Even in Presbyterian Churches we see again and again men who by their superior character and attainments are Bishops in all but in name, and who only need such offices to call out their full energies.  There exist Episcopal Churches, such as those in Greece and Italy, where the Bishops have been so numerous that, as in early times, they have been but Presbyters with another name. But in England, and in former days in Germany, they have always been comparatively few in number, and it is this rarity, this exaltation, which causes that agreement of the office with the natural fitness of things.

III. In what sense can the institution of the Clergy or of Bishops be said to have a divine origin ?  Not in the sense of its having been directly and visibly established by the Founder of Christianity.  Amongst the gifts *Their origin.* which our Lord gave to mankind during His life on earth, the Christian Ministry, as we now possess it, is not one.  He gave us during the years of His earthly manifestation, that which was far greater—which was in fact Christianity— He gave us *Himself*—Himself in His life, in His death, in His mind, in His character, in His immortal life in which He lives for ever—Himself, with the immediate impression of Himself on the characters and the memories of those His friends and disciples who stood immediately around Him, and who carried on the impulse which they derived from personal contact with Him.  But no permanent order of ministers appears in that spiritual kingdom of which he spoke on the hills of Galilee or on the slopes of Olivet.  The Twelve Apostles whom He chose had no successors like themselves.  No second Peter, no second John, no second Paul, stepped into the places of those who had seen the Lord Jesus ; and if their likenesses have been in any measure seen again in later times, it has been at long intervals, few and far between, when great lights have been raised up to rekindle amongst men the expiring flame of truth and goodness by extraordinary gifts of genius or of grace.  The Seventy Disciples that went forth at the Lord's command into the cities of Palestine were soon gathered to their graves, and no order of the same kind or of the same number came in their stead. They went out once, and returned back to their Master, to go out no more. The Church, the Christian Society, existed in those faithful followers, even from the beginning, and will doubtless last to the very end. Wherever in any time or country, two or three are gathered together by a common love and faith, there will be a Christian church. But even for years after the Lord's departure, such a society existed without a separate order of clergy. The whole Christian Brotherhood was full of life, and there was as yet no marked distinction between its different portions. All were alike holy—all were alike consecrated. Therefore it is that the institution of the Christian ministry has never been placed in any ancient Creed amongst the fundamental facts or doctrines of the Gospel; therefore it is that (in the language of the English Church) ordination is not a sacrament, because it has no visible sign or ceremony ordained by Christ Himself.

Yet there is another sense in which the Christian ministry is a gift of our Divine Master. It is brought out in the well-known passage in the Epistle to the Ephesians: 'When He ascended up on high, He led captivity captive, and gave gifts unto men. . . . And He gave some to be apostles, and some to be prophets, and some to be evangelists, and some to be shepherds and teachers.'[2] What is it that is meant by saying that it was only after His withdrawal from us, that He gave these gifts to men, and that amongst these gifts were the various offices, of which two at least (the pastoral and the intellectual) contain the germs of all the future clergy of Christendom? It is this—that not in His earthly life, not in His direct communion with men, not as part of the original manifestation of Christianity, but, (so to speak) as a Divine afterthought, as the result of the complex influences which were showered down upon the earth after its Founder

[2] Eph. iv. 8–11.

had left it, as a part of the vast machinery of Christian civilisation, were the various professions of Christendom formed, and amongst these the great vocation of the Christian ministry.

The various grades of the Christian clergy have sprung up in Christian society in the same ways, and by the same divine, because the same natural necessity, as the various grades of government, law, and science—a necessity only more urgent, more universal, and therefore more divine, in so far as the religious and intellectual wants of mankind are of a more general, of a more simple, and therefore of a more divine kind than their social and physical wants. All of them vary, in each age or country, according to the varieties of age and country—according to the civil constitution, according to the geographical area, according to the climate and custom of east and west, north and south. We find popular election, clerical election, imperial election, ministerial election, ordination by breathing, ordination by sacred relics, ordination by elevation of hands, ordination by imposition of hands, vestments and forms derived from Roman civil life or from a peculiar profession, from this or that school, of this or that fashion—spheres more or less limited, a humble country village, an academic cloister, a vast town population, or a province as large as a kingdom. The enumeration of these varieties is not a condemnation, but a justification of their existence. The Christian clergy has grown with the growth and varied with the variations of Christian society, and the more complex its developments, the more removed from the rudeness and simplicity of the early ages, the more likely they are to be in accordance with truth and reason, which is the mind of Christ.

This, therefore, is the divine and the human side of the Christian ministry. Divine, because it belongs to the inevitable growth of Christian hopes and sympathies, of increasing truth, of enlarging charity. Human, because it arose out of, and is subject to, the vicissitudes of human passions, human ignorance, human infirmities, earthly opportunities.

In so far as it has a permanent and divine character, it has a pledge of immortal existence, so long as Christian society exists with its peculiar wants and aspirations; in so far as it has a human character, it seeks to accommodate itself to the wants of each successive age, and needs the support, and the sympathy, and the favour, of all the other elements of social intercourse by which it is surrounded. It has been at times so degraded that it has become the enemy of all progress. It has been at times in the forefront of civilisation.

# CHAPTER XI.

### THE POPE.

THREE hundred years ago there were three official personages in Europe of supreme historical interest, of whom one is gone, and two survive, though in a reduced and enfeebled form.

The three were the Emperor of the Holy Roman Empire, the Pope of Rome, and the Sultan of Constantinople. They were alike in this, that they combined a direct descent of association from the old classical world, with an important position in the modern world,—a high secular with a high ecclesiastical position,—a strong political influence with a personal authority of an exceptional kind.

The Emperor of the Holy Roman Empire was the greatest sovereign in Europe. He was, in fact, properly speaking, the only sovereign of Europe. Other kings and princes were, in strict parlance, his deputies. He was the fountain of honour whence they derived their titles. He took precedence of them all. He was the representative of the old Roman Empire. In him, the highest intelligences of the time saw the representative of order, the counterpoise of individual tyranny, the majesty at once of Religion and of Law. No other single potentate so completely suggested the idea of Christendom as a united body. No throne in Europe presented in its individual rulers personages of grander character, or at least of grander power, than the Empire could boast in Charlemagne, Frederick Barbarossa, Frederick II., and Charles V. Long before this splendid dignitary passed away, his real power was gone, and Voltaire had truly declared of him that there was in him 'nothing Holy, nothing Roman, and nothing Imperial.' But it was not till our own time, in 1816, when the Holy Roman Empire was changed into the Empire of Austria, that he finally disappeared from the stage of human affairs. The Emperor of Germany, as regards Germany, took the vacant place in 1871, but not as regards Europe.

The two others remain. They in many respects resemble each other and their defunct brother, perhaps in the fragility of their thrones, certainly in the concentrated interest of their historical, political, and religious position. The Sultan perhaps comprises in his own person most of the original characteristics of the institution which he represents. He is at once the representative of the Byzantine Cæsars and the representative of the last of the Caliphs, that is, of the Prophet himself. He is the chief of a mighty empire, and at the same time the head of a powerful and wide-spread religion. Of all the three, he is the one whose person is invested with the most inviolable sanctity. His temporal dominion in Europe has almost vanished. But he still retains ' the Palaces and the Gardens ' of the Bosphorus, and his ecclesiastical authority over his co-religionists remains undisturbed if not undisputed.

It is of the third of this august brotherhood that we propose to speak. The Papacy is now passing through a phase in some degree resembling that of the Holy Roman Empéror in 1806, and that of the Sultan of Constantinople at the present moment. But its peculiarities are too deeply rooted in the past to be entirely shaken by any transitory change.

It is not as an object of attack or defence that this great dignitary is here discussed, but as a mine of deep and curious interest—the most ancient of all the rulers of Europe. He presents many aspects, each one of which might be taken by itself and viewed without prejudice to the others. Some of these are purely historical. Others are political and secular. Others involve questions reaching into difficult problems of religion and theology. They may be briefly enumerated thus :—

The Pope may be considered—I. As the representative of the customs of Christian antiquity; II. As the representative of the ancient Roman Empire; III. As an Italian Bishop and Italian Prince; IV. As 'the Pope,' or chief oracle of Christendom; V. As the head of the ecclesiastical profession; VI. As an element in the future arrangements of Christendom.

I. The Pope is a representative of Christian antiquity. In this respect he is a perfect museum of ecclesiastical curiosities—a mass, if we wish so to regard him, of latent Primitive Protestantism. In him, from the high dignity and tenaciously conservative tendencies of the office, customs endured which everywhere else perished.

*The Pope as the representative of Christian antiquity.*

The public entrance of that great personage into one of the Roman churches, at the time when such processions were allowed by ecclesiastical authority, can never be forgotten. Borne aloft above the surface of the crowd—seen from head to foot—the peacock fans waving behind him—the movement of the hand alone indicating that it is a living person, and not a waxen figure—he completely represented the identification of the person with the institution; he gave the impression that there alone was an office which carried the mind back to the times, as Lord Macaulay says, when tigers and camelopards bounded in the Flavian amphitheatre.

1. Take his ordinary dress. He always appears in a white gown. He is, according to a well-known Roman proverb, 'the White Pope,' in contradistinction to the more formidable 'Black Pope,' the General of the order of the Jesuits, who wears a black robe. This white dress is the white frock of the early Christians,[1] such as we see in the oldest mosaics, before the difference between lay and clerical costume had sprung up; not the 'surplice' of the Church of England, nor the 'white linen robe' of the Jewish priest, but the common classical dress of all ranks in Roman society. To this common white garb the early Christians adhered with more than usual tenacity, partly to indicate their cheerful, fes-

*His dress.*

[1] Gerbet, *Rome Chrétienne*, ii. 44.

tive character, as distinct from mourners, who went in black,
partly to mark their separation from the peculiar black dress
of the philosophical sects with which they were often confounded.  The Pope thus carries on the recollection of an age
when there was no visible distinction between the clergy and
laity ; he shows, at any rate, in his own person, the often
repeated but often forgotten fact, that all ecclesiastical
costumes have originated in the common dress of the time,
and been merely perpetuated in the clergy, or in this case
in the head of the clergy, from their longer adherence to
ancient habits.

2. Take his postures.  At the reception of the Holy Communion, whilst others kneel, his proper attitude is that of
sitting ;  and, although it has been altered of late
years, he still so stands as to give the appearance of
His postures.
sitting.[2]  It is possible that this may have been continued
out of deference to his superior dignity ; but it is generally
believed, and it is very probable, that in that attitude he
preserves the tradition of the primitive posture of the early
Christians, who partook of the Holy Supper in the usual attitude of guests at a meal—recumbent or sitting, as the case
might be.  This has now been exchanged throughout a large
part of Christendom, for a more devotional attitude,—in the
East for standing, in the West for kneeling.  The Pope still
retains in part or in whole the posture of the first Apostles ;
and in this he is followed by the Presbyterians of Scotland
and the Nonconformists of England, who endeavour by this
act to return to that which, in the Pope himself, has never
been entirely abandoned.  It brings before us the ancient
days when the Sacrament was still a supper, when the communicants were still guests, when the altar was still a table.

3. This leads us to another custom retained in the Pope
from the same early time.  The Pope, when he celebrates mass
in his own cathedral of St. John Lateran, celebrates
His altar.
it, not on a structure of marble or stone, such as
elsewhere constitutes the altars of Roman Catholic churches,

<hr>

[2] See note at the end of the chapter.

but on a wooden plank, said to be part of the table on which St. Peter in the house of Pudens consecrated the first communion in Rome. This primitive wooden table—the mark of the original social character of the Lord's Supper—has been preserved throughout the East; and in most Protestant Churches, including the Church of England, it was restored at the Reformation. But it is interesting to find this indisputable proof of its antiquity and catholicity preserved in the very heart of the see of Rome. Some persons have been taught to regard stone altars as identical with Popery; some to regard them as necessary for Christian worship. The Pope, by this usage of the old wooden table, equally contradicts both. The real change from wood to stone was occasioned in the first instance, not by the substitution of the idea of an altar for à table, but by the substitution of a tomb, containing the relics of a martyr, for both altar and table.

4. Again, when the Pope celebrates mass, he stands, not with his back to the people, nor at the north end, nor at the north-west side, of the table, but behind it with his back to the wall, and facing the congregation. This His position. is the exact reverse of the position of the Roman Catholic clergy generally, and of those who would wish especially to imitate them. It much more nearly resembles the position of Presbyterian and Nonconformist ministers at the time of the Holy Communion, when they stand at one side of the table, facing the congregation, who are on the other side. It was the almost necessary consequence of the arrangement of the original basilica, where the altar stood not at the east end, but in the middle of the building, the central point between clergy and laity. It represents, of course, what must have been the position in the original institution as seen in pictures of the Last Supper. It is also the position which prevailed in the Church of England for the first hundred years after the Reformation, and till some years after the Restoration, and is still directly enjoined in the rubrics of the English Prayer Book. The position of a Presbyterian minister at the time of the celebration of the Lord's Supper,

either as he stands in the pulpit, or when descending he takes his place behind the table, with his elders around him, precisely resembles the attitude of an early Christian bishop surrounded by his presbyters.[3]

Here again Protestantism, or if we prefer to call it so, primitive Christianity, appears in the Pope, when it has perished on all sides of him.

5. Another peculiarity of the Pope's celebration of mass gives us a glimpse into a phase of the early Church which is highly instructive. The Gospel and Epistle are read *His language.* both in Greek and in Latin. This is a vestige doubtless of the early condition of the first Roman Church, which, as Dean Milman has well pointed out, was not an Italian but a Greek community—the community to which, as being Greek and Oriental, St. Paul wrote not in Latin but in Greek; the community of which the first teachers, Clement and Hermas, wrote not in Latin but in Greek. It preserves the curious and instructive fact that the chief of Latin Christendom was originally not an 'Italian priest,' but an alien; a Greek in language, an Oriental in race. It gives us an insight into the foreign elements out of which the early Western Churches everywhere were formed. It is in fact a remnant of a state of things not later than the third century. Before that time the sacred language of the Roman Church was Greek. After that time, Greek gave way to Latin, and by the fifth century the Roman clergy were not even able to understand the tongue which to their forefathers in the faith had been sacred and liturgical whilst the language of the 'Vulgate' and the 'Canon of the Mass' were still profane.[4]

6. Again, in the Pope's private chapel, and on all occasions when the Pope himself officiates, there is a total absence *His service.* of instrumental music. This, too, is a continuation of the barbaric simplicity of the early Christian service. The Roman Catholic ritual, as well as that of the Protestant Churches of Holland, Germany, France, Switzerland, and Eng-

<hr>

[3] See Chapter IX.      [4] Rossi, *Roma Sotter*, ii. 237.

land, have joined in defying this venerable precedent. In two branches only of the Church outside the Pope's chapel it still lingers; namely, in the worship of the Eastern churches and in some of the Presbyterian churches of Scotland. At Moscow and at Glasgow still there are places where the sound of an organ would be regarded as a blast from the Seven Hills. But, in fact, the Pope himself is on this point a Greek and a Presbyterian, and in this refusal of the accompaniments of the sublime arts of modern music, is at one with those who have thrown off his allegiance and protests against the practice of those who have accepted it.

7. Again, alone of all great ecclesiastics of his Church, he has no crosier, except a small temporary silver one at ordinations. The simple reason of this is, that being borne *The absence of a crosier.* aloft on the shoulders of his guards, and thus not being obliged to walk like other ecclesiastics, he has no need of a walking-stick. This at once reveals the origin of the formidable crosier—not the symbol of the priesthood against the state—not even the crook of the pastor over his flock, but simply the walking-stick, the staff of the old man, of the presbyter, such as appears in the ancient drama of Greece and Rome, and in the famous riddle of Œdipus. It puts in a vivid form the saying of Pius VII. to a scrupulous Protestant, 'Surely the blessing of an old man will do you no harm.' The crosier was the symbol of old age, and of nothing besides.[5]

These instances might be multiplied: but they are sufficient to show the interest of the subject. They show how we find agreements and differences where we least expect it —how innocent and insignificant are some of the ceremonies

[5] This absence of the crosier has naturally given birth to a brood of false symbolical explanations such as have encompassed all these simple observances. The legend is, that the Pope lost the crosier because St. Peter sent his staff to raise from the dead a disciple at Treves. This disciple afterwards became Bishop of Treves; and the Pope therefore, when he enters the diocese of Treves, is believed on that occasion to carry the crosier. (St. Thomas Aquinas, *Opp.*, vol. xiii. 42.) Another explanation is, that the curve of the crook indicates a restraint of the episcopal power, and that, as the Pope has no restraint, therefore he has no crook. (Ibid.)

to which we attach most importance—how totally different was the primitive state, even of the Roman Church, from that which now prevails both in Roman Catholic and Protestant countries. They are lessons of charity and of wisdom—of caution and of forbearance. In these respects the Pope has acted merely as the shoal which, like the island in his own Tiber, has arrested the straws of former ages, as they floated down the stream of time.

II. These usages belong to him as a Christian pastor, and are the relics of Christian antiquity. But there are others Successor of the Emperors. which reveal him to us in another aspect, and which have drifted down through another channel. No saying of ecclesiastical history is more pregnant than that in which Hobbes declares that ' the Pope is the ghost of the deceased Roman Empire, sitting crowned upon the grave thereof.' This is the true original basis of his dignity and power, and it appears even in the minutest details.

If he were to be regarded only as the successor of St. Peter, his chief original seat would, of course, be in the Basilica of St. Peter, over the Apostle's grave. But this is not the case. St. Peter's Church, in regard to the Pope, is merely a chapel of gigantic proportions attached to the later residence which the Pope adopted under the Vatican Hill. The present magnificent church was erected to be the mausoleum of Julius II., of which one fragment only—the statue of Moses—remains. The Pope's proper See and Cathedral is the Basilica of St. John 'in the Lateran '—that is, in the Lateran palace which was the real and only bequest of Constantine to the Roman Bishop. It had been the palace of the Lateran family. From them it passed to the Imperial dynasty. In it the Empress Fausta, wife of Constantine, usually lived. In it, after Constantine's departure to Constantinople, the Roman Bishop dwelt as a great Roman noble. In it accordingly is the true Pontifical throne, on the platform of which are written the words *Hæc est papalis sedes et pontificalis.* Over its front is inscribed the decree, Papal and Imperial, declaring it to be the mother and mistress of all churches.    In it he takes possession of the See of Rome, and of the government of the Pontifical States.

Although the story of Constantine's abdication to Pope Sylvester is one of the fables of the Papacy, yet it has in it this truth—that the retirement of the Emperors to the East left Rome without a head, and their vacant place was naturally and imperceptibly filled by the chief of the rising community.    To him the splendour and the attributes, which properly belonged to the Emperor, were unconsciously transferred.

Here, as in the case of ecclesiastical usages, we trace it in the small details which have lingered in him when they have perished elsewhere.    The chair of state, the *sella gestatoria*, in which the Pope is borne aloft, is the ancient palanquin of the Roman nobles, and, of course, of the Roman Princes.    The red slippers which he wears are the red shoes, *campagines*, of the Roman Emperor.    The kiss which the faithful imprint on those shoes is the descendant of the kiss first imprinted on the foot of the Emperor Caligula, who introduced it from Persia.    The fans which go behind him are the punkahs of the Eastern Emperors, borrowed from the court of Persia.

The name by which his highest ecclesiastical character is indicated is derived, not from the Jewish High Priest, but from the Roman Emperor.    The Latinised version of the Jewish ' High Priest ' was ' Summus Sacerdos.'    But the Pope is ' Pontifex Maximus,' and the ' Pontifex Maximus ' was a well-known and recognised personage in the eyes of the Roman population, long before they had ever heard of the race of Aaron or of Caiaphas.[6]    He was the high Pagan dignitary who lived in a public residence at the north-east corner of the Palatine, the chief of the college of ' Pontiffs ' or ' Bridge-makers.'    It was his duty to conduct all public sacrifices, to scourge to death anyone who insulted the

---

[6] It is perhaps doubtful how far the word was confined to the Bishops of Rome    But the evidence is in favour of its having been appropriated to them in the first instance.

Vestal Virgins, to preside at the assemblies and games, to be present at the religious ceremony of any solemn marriage, and to arrange the calendar.  His office was combined with many great secular posts, and thus was at last held by the most illustrious of the sons of Rome.  It was by virtue of his pontificate that Julius Cæsar in his pontifical residence enabled Clodius to penetrate into the convent of the Vestals close by.  It is to the pontificate, not to the sovereignty of Julius Cæsar, that we owe the Julian calendar.[7]  From him it descended to the Emperors, his successors, and from them to the Popes.  The two are brought together in the most startling form on the pedestal of the obelisk on the Monte Citorio.  On one side is the original dedication of it by Augustus Cæsar, 'Pontifex Maximus,' to the Sun; on the other, by Pius VI., 'Pontifex Maximus,' to Christ.  When Bishop Dupanloup, in a pamphlet on 'L'Athéisme et le Péril Social,' described the desertion of the Holy Father by the late Emperor of France, it was more appropriate than he thought when he said, 'The Grand Pontiff covers his face with his mantle, and says " *Et tu fili.*"'  It was a Grand Pontiff who so covered his face, and who so exclaimed : but that Pontiff was Julius Cæsar, to whose office the Pope has directly succeeded.

This is more than a mere resemblance of words.  It brings before us the fact that the groundwork of the Pope's power is secular—secular, no doubt, in its grand sense, resting on the prestige of ages, but still a power of this world, and supported always by weapons of this world.

He held, and holds, his rank amongst the bishops of Christendom, as the Bishop of the Imperial City, as the magistrate of that Imperial City when the Emperors left it. So, and for the same reason, Constantinople was the second see ; so, and for the same reason, Cæsarea, as the seat of the

---

[7] For its Pagan origin, see Rossi, ii. 306.  But is it (as he says) only from the Renaissance?  Tertullian applied it ironically in the third century, and it would appear that it was used as a date from the fourth century, instead of the Consulship.  (See Mabillon, and Theiner, *Codex Diplomaticus.*)

Roman Government, not Jerusalem, was the see of the Metropolitan of Palestine.

The secular origin of the primacy of Rome belongs, in fact, to the secular origin of much beside in the early customs of the Church, illustrating and illustrated by them. The first church was a 'basilica,' not a temple, but a Roman court of justice, accommodated to the purposes of Christian worship.[8] The word 'bishop,' *episcopus*, was taken, not from any usage of the Temple or of the Synagogue, but from the officers created in the different subject-towns of Athens ; 'borrowed,' as Hooker says, 'from the Grecians.' The secular origin of the 'holy orders' and 'ordination'[9] have been already indicated. The word and the idea of a '*diocese*' were taken from the existing divisions of the empire. The orientation of churches is from the rites of Etruscan augury. The whole ecclesiastical ceremonialism is, according to some etymologists, the bequest of *Cære*, the sacred city of the Etruscans. The first figures of winged angels are Etruscan. The officiating bishop at ordinations in St. John Lateran washes his hands with *medulla panis* according to the usage of ancient Roman banquets. Of all these Christian usages of secular and Pagan origin, the Pope is the most remarkable example—a constant witness to the earthly origin of his own greatness, but also, which is of more general importance, to the indistinguishable union of things ecclesiastical and things civil, and here, as in the case of the more purely ecclesiastical customs, the investigation of his position shows on the one hand the historical interest, on the other the religious insignificance, of much which now excites such vehement enthusiasm, both of love and of hatred.

III. Following up this aspect of the Pope's position, we arrive at his character as an Italian Bishop and an Italian Prince. Both go together. These belong to the state of things at the beginning of the middle ages, out of which his power was formed. His more general and universal

As 'Italian Prince.'

---

[8] See Chapter IX.

[9] As late as the sixth century Gregory the Great uses 'ordo' for the civil magistrate, and 'clerus' for the clergy. (*Dictionary of Christian Antiquities*, ii. 146–149.)

attributes are derived from other considerations which must be treated apart. But his Italian nationality and his Italian principality are the natural results of a condition of society which has long since perished everywhere else. The Pope's 'temporal power' belongs to that feudal and princely character which was shared by so many great prelates of the middle ages. Almost all the German Archbishops possessed this special kind of sovereignty, and in our own country the Bishops of Durham. The Archbishops of Cologne were Princes and Electors more than they were Archbishops. In the portraits of the last of the dynasty in the palace at Brühl, near Bonn, for one which represents him as an ecclesiastic, there are ten which represent him as a prince or as a soldier. Of all those potentates, the Pope is almost the only one who remains. His principality is now regarded as an anomaly by some, as a miracle by others. But when it first existed, it was one of a large group of similar principalities. When, therefore, the Pope stood defended by his Chassepot rifles, or in his reduced state, still surrounded by his Swiss guards, he must be regarded as the last of the brotherhood of the fighting, turbulent, courtly prelates of the Rhine, of the Prince Bishop of Durham, or the Ducal Bishop of Osnaburgh. His dynasty through its long course has partaken of the usual variations of character which appear in all the other Italian principalities. Its accessions of property have come in like manner; sometimes by the sword, as of Julius II.; sometimes by the donations of the great Countess Matilda; sometimes by the donations of Joanna, the questionable Queen of Naples. Like the other mediæval prelates, the Popes had their hounds, and hunted even down till the time of Pius VI. Mariana, on the road to Ostia, was a famous hunting-seat of Leo X.

If the Pope were essentially what he is sometimes believed to be, the universal Bishop of the universal Church, we should expect to find the accompaniments of his office corresponding to this. But, in fact, it is far otherwise. In most of the conditions of his office, the Italian Bishop and the Italian Prince are the first objects of consideration. That the first prelate of the West should have been, as we have seen, the Bishop of the old Imperial city, was natural enough. But it is somewhat startling to find that the second prelate of the West is not one of the great hierarchy of France, or Germany, or Spain, or England, but the Bishop of the deserted Ostia—because Ostia is the second see in the Roman States. It is he—with the Bishops of Portus and Sabina—who crowns and anoints the Pope. It is he who is the Dean of the Sacred College.

And this runs thoughout. The electors to the office of the Pope, whether in early days or now, were not, and are not, the universal Church, but Romans or Italians.[1] In early days the election was in the hands of the populace of Rome. From the fourth to the eleventh century it was accompanied by the usual arts of bribery, fraud, and occasionally bloodshed. Afterwards it was shared with the civil authorities of the Roman municipality; and so deeply was this, till lately, rooted in the institution, that, on the death of a Pope, the Senator resumed his functions as the supreme governor of the city.[2]

Since the twelfth century the election has been vested in the College of Cardinals. But the College of Cardinals, though restrained by the veto of the three Catholic Powers, is still predominantly Italian; and the result of the election has, since the fourth century, been almost entirely confined to Italian Popes. The one great exception is an exception which proves the rule. During the seventy years when the Popes were at Avignon, they were there as completely French as before and since they have been Italians; and for the same reason—because they were French Princes living in a French city, as now and before they were Italian princes living in an Italian city.

<hr>

[1] See the account in Mr. Cartwright's interesting volume on *Papal Conclaves*, p. 36.

[2] His long train at mass is carried (amongst others) by the Senator of Rome and the Prince 'assisting.'

The feudal sovereignty over Naples was maintained by the giving of a white horse on St. Peter's day by the king of Naples—down till the time of Charles II.; the protest against the annexation of Avignon by France has been abandoned since 1815.

Whatever ingenuity, whatever intrigues, surround the election of a Pope are Italian, and of that atmosphere the whole pontifical dynasty breathes from the time it became a principality till (with the exception of its exile in Provence) the present time.

IV. Then follow the more general attributes of the Pope. He is 'the Pope.' This title was not originally his own. It belonged to a time when all teachers were so called. It is like some of the other usages of which we have spoken, a relic of the innocent infantine simplicity of the primitive Church. Every teacher was then ' *Papa*.' The word was then what it is still in English, the endearing name of ' father.' In the Eastern Church, the custom continues still. Every parish priest, every pastor, is there a ' Pope,' a ' Papa,' and the ordinary mode of address in Russia is ' my father' (' Batinska '). Gradually the name became restricted, either in use or significance. Just as the Bishops gradually rose out of the Presbyters, to form a separate rank, so the name of ' Pope ' was gradually applied specially to Bishops. Cyprian, Bishop of Carthage, in the third century, was constantly entitled ' Most glorious and blessed Pope ; ' and the French bishops, in like manner, were called 'Lord Pope.' There is a gate in the Cathedral of Le Puy, in Auvergne, still called the ' Papal Gate,' not because of the entrance of any Pope of Rome there, but because of an old inscription which records the death of one of the bishops of Le Puy under the name of ' Pope.'[3]

And yet further, if there was any one Bishop in those early times who was peculiarly invested with this title above

As 'the Pope.'

---

[3] The name is first applied to the Bishop of Rome in the letter of a deacon to Pope Marcellus, A.D. 275, but it was not till 400 that they took it formally.

the rest, and known emphatically as ' *the* Pope,' it was not the Bishop of Rome, but the Bishop of Alexandria. From the third century downwards he was ' the Pope ' emphatically beyond all others. Various reasons are assigned for this honour; but, in fact, it naturally fell to him as the head of the most learned church in the world, to whom all the other churches looked for advice and instruction.

In the early centuries, if the Bishop of Rome had the title at all, it was merely like other Bishops. It was in Latin properly only used with the addition ' *My* Pope,'[*] or the like, and this is the earliest known instance of its application to the Roman Pontiff. It was not till the seventh century that it became his peculiar designation, or rather, that dropping off from all the other Western bishops, it remained fixed in him, and it was formally appropriated to its exclusive use in the eleventh. What ' Papa ' was in Greek and Latin, ' Abba ' was in Syriac, and this accordingly was preserved in ' Abbot,' ' Abbé,' as applied to the heads of monastic communities, and to the French clergy, almost as generally as the word ' Papa ' has been in the Eastern Church for the parochial clergy.

It is curious that a word which more than any other recalls the original equality not only of Patriarch with Bishop, of Bishop with Bishop, but of Bishop with Presbyter, should have gradually become the designation of the one pre-eminent distinction, which is the keystone of the largest amount of inequality that prevails in the Christian hierarchy.

It is also to be observed that a word used to designate the head of the Latin Church should have been derived from the Greek and Eastern forms of Christianity.

. What is it which constitutes the essence of this power of the Pope ?

We have already seen that his dignity at Rome is inherited from the Roman Emperors—his territory, from

---

[*] ' Papa suus,' ' Papa meus,' ' Papa noster,' is the only form in which it occurs in the third and fourth centuries, as a term not of office, but of affection, and meaning not a bishop but a teacher. (Mabillon, *Vetera Analecta*, 141.) So the head of the Abyssinian clergy is called *Abouroa*, *i.e.*, ' *our* Father.'

his position as an Italian Prelate. But his power as the Pope is supposed to give him the religious sovereignty of the world.

It is often supposed that he possesses this as successor of St. Peter in the see of Rome. This, however, is an assumption which under any theory that may be held concerning his office, is obviously untenable. That St. Peter died at Rome is probable. But it is certain that he was not the founder of the Church of Rome. The absence of any allusion to such a connection in St. Paul's Epistles is decisive. It is also certain that he was not Bishop of the Church of Rome or of any Church. The office of 'Bishop' in the sense of a single officer presiding over the community (with perhaps the exception of Jerusalem) did not exist in any Church till the close of the first century. The word, as we have seen, was originally identical with the word 'Presbyter.' The alleged succession of the early Roman Bishops is involved in contradictions which can only be explained on the supposition that there was then no fixed Episcopate. There is not only no shadow of an indication in the New Testament that the characteristics of Peter were to belong to official successors, but for the first three centuries there is no indication, or at least no certain indication, that such a belief existed anywhere. It is an imagination with no more foundation in fact than the supposition that the characteristics of St. John descended to the Bishops of Ephesus.

But, further, it is also a curious fact that by the theory of the Roman Church itself, it is not as Bishop of Rome that the Pope is supposed to acquire the religious sovereignty of the world.

It is important to observe by what channel this is conveyed. He becomes Bishop of Rome, as all others become Bishops, by regular consecration. He becomes Sovereign, as all others become Sovereigns, by regular inauguration. But he becomes Pope, with whatever peculiar privileges that involves, by the election of the Cardinals; and for this purpose he need not be a clergyman at all. Those who suppose that he inherits the great powers of his office by the inheritance of an Episcopal succession mistake the case. If other Bishops, as some believe, derive their powers from the Apostles by virtue of an Apostolical succession, not so the Pope. He may, at the time of his election, be a layman, and, if duly elected, he may, as a layman, exercise, not indeed the functions of a Bishop, but the most significant functions which belong to a Pope. The Episcopal consecration, indeed, must succeed as rapidly as is convenient. But the Pope after his mere election is completely in the possession of the headship of the Roman Catholic Church, even though it should so happen that the Episcopal consecration never followed at all.

In point of fact, the early Popes were never chosen from the Bishops, and usually not from the Presbyters, but from the Deacons; and the first who was chosen from the Episcopate was Formosus, Bishop of Portus, in 891. Hildebrand [5] was not ordained priest till after his election. A Pope cannot even exercise the right of a Bishop, unless by dispensation from himself, until he has taken 'possession' of the sovereignty in the Lateran. Three Popes have occupied the chair of St. Peter as laymen: John XIX. or XX.[6] in 1024; Adrian V.[7] in 1276; Martin V. in 1417.[8] Of these, the first reigned for some years, and was ordained or consecrated with the accustomed solemnities. The third was enthroned as a layman, and passed through the grades of deacon, priest, and bishop on successive days. The second reigned only for twenty-nine days, and died without taking holy orders. Yet in that time he had acquired all the plenitude of his supreme authority, and had promulgated decrees modifying the whole system of Papal elections which by his successors were held to be invested with all the sacredness of Pontifical utterances.[9]

---

[5] Bona, i. 189.   [6] Planck, iii. 370.

[7] Adrian V. and Martin V. were 'Cardinal Deacons.' But this is an office which is held by laymen.

[8] Fleury, xxi. 472.

[9] See the facts in Cartwright's *Conclares*, pp. 164, 195. 'Eo ipso sit Pontifex summus totius Ecclesiæ, etsi forte id non exprimant electores.' (Bellarmine, *De Rom. Pont.* ii. 22.)

Since the time of Urban VI., in 1378, the rule has been to restrict the office of Pope to the College of Cardinals. But this has no higher sanction than custom. As late as 1758, votes were given to one who was not a member of the Sacred College ; and the election of a layman even at this day, would be strictly canonical. If the lay element can thus without impropriety intrude itself into the very throne and centre of ecclesiastical authority, and that by the election of a body which is itself not necessarily clerical (for a cardinal is not of necessity in holy orders), and which till at least the last election was subject to lay influences of the most powerful kind (for each of the three chief Catholic sovereigns had a veto on the appointment), it is clear that the language commonly held within the Roman Catholic and even Protestant Churches, both Episcopal and Presbyterian, against lay interference in spiritual matters, meets with a decisive check in an unexpected quarter. If the Pope himself may be a layman, and, as a layman, issue Pontifical decrees of the highest authority, he is a witness against all who are disposed to confine the so-called spiritual powers of the Church to the clerical or Episcopal order.

Here, in this crucial case, the necessity of choosing 'the right man for the right place' overrides all other considerations ; and if it should so happen that the College of Cardinals became convinced that the interests of the world and of the Church were best served by their choosing a philosopher or a philanthropist, a lawyer or a warrior, to the Pontifical chair, there is nothing in the constitution of the Roman see to forbid it. The electors of the chief Pontiff may be laymen, —the sovereign of the Christian world may be a layman. Whether we regard this as a relic of the ancient days of the Church, in which the laity were supreme over the clergy, or as the ideal towards which the Church may be gradually tending, it is equally a proof that there is not, in the nature of things or in the laws of Christendom, any such intrinsic distinction between the clergy and laity as to give to either an exclusive share in matters spiritual or temporal.

Such being the mode by which the Pope, as such, is

chosen, we next proceed to observe what are the functions which, as Pope, he is supposed to exercise.

The word 'Pope' has in common parlance passed with us into a synonym for 'oracle.'  When we say that such a man is 'a Pope in his own circle,' or that 'every man is a Pope to himself,' we mean that he is a person whose word must be taken at once on any subject on which he may choose to speak. There was, as it happens, such an oracle once believed to reside in the Vatican Hill—where now stands the Papal palace—the oracle of the god Faunus; of whom the ancient Latins came to inquire in any difficulty, and received their reply in dreams or by strange voices. Such an oracle the Pope is, by a certain number of his followers, supposed to be. But this has only within the last few years become the doctrine of the Roman Catholic Church, and many of those who maintain it confine the oracular power within very narrow limits, which may be always narrowed further still.   His utterances are to be depended upon only when they relate to matters of faith and morals, and then only when he speaks officially ; and as it will have always to be determined, when it is that he speaks officially, and what matters are to be considered of faith, it is evident that his oracular power may be limited or expanded, exactly according to the will of the recipients.[1] In point of fact the amount of light which the Papal See has communicated to the world is not large, compared with what has been derived from other episcopal sees, or other royal thrones. There have been occupants of the Sees of Constantinople, Alexandria, and Canterbury, who have produced more effect on the mind of Christendom by their utterances than any of the Popes.[2]  Even in the most solemn Papal declarations,

---

[1] A curious trace of the individual character of the Pope being maintained rather than his official character, is that he signs his Bulls not by his official but his personal name, in the barbarous form, *Placet Joannes.*—Wiseman's *Four Popes*, 223.

[2] See Dr. Newman's *Apologia*, p. 407.  'The see of Rome possessed no great mind in the whole period of persecution. Afterwards for a long while it had not a single doctor to show. The great luminary of the western world is St. Augustine ; he, no infallible teacher, has formed the intellect of Europe.

such as annexing South America to Spain, or determining
the canonisation of particular saints, or even in issuing such
a decree as that concerning the Immaculate Conception, the
Popes have acted rather as the mouthpieces of others, or
judges of a tribunal, than on their own individual responsibility. Canonisations, at least in theory, are the result of a
regular trial. The Pope is not supposed to venture to declare
any one a canonised saint until he has been entreated,
'urgently, more urgently, most urgently' (*instanter, instan-
tius, instantissime*), by those who have heard the Devil's as
well as the saint's advocate. The declaration of the recent
dogmas of 1854 and 1870 professed to be the summing up of
a long previous agitation, and the Pope did not issue it till
he had asked the opinions of all the Bishops.

It is the object of these remarks to state facts, not to
discuss doctrines. But the fact is well worth observing,—
first, because it shows how wide and deep is the division in
the Roman Catholic Church on the very question which, more
than any other, distinguishes it from other Churches ; and,
secondly, because it shows how small an amount of certainty or security is added to any one's belief by resting it
on the oracular power of the Pope. On most of the great
questions which agitate men's minds at present, on Biblical
criticism, on the authorship of the Sacred Books, on the
duration of future punishment, he has not pronounced any
opinion at all ; and on others, such as the relations of Church
and State, the condition of the working classes, slavery,
and the like, the opinions he has expressed are either so
ambiguous, or so contradictory, that they are interpreted in
exactly opposite senses by the prelates in Italy and the
prelates in Ireland. Even if it were conceded that such an
oracle exists at Rome, there still is no certainty either as to
its jurisdiction or its meaning. Most of those who have
studied its utterances, however they may respect its venerable
antiquity and honour its occasional wisdom, will carry away
as their chief impression its variations and its failures.

But turning from this much disputed attribute of the

Pope, there is no question in his own communion, there is not
much question out of it, that he is or till very lately was one
of the chief rulers of Christendom. This, rather than his
oracular power, is the characteristic of his office brought out
by Gregory VII. and Innocent III. And this, like so much
which we have noticed, is a relic of a state of things that has
passed away. It is part of the general framework of mediæval Christendom. There were only two potentates of the
first magnitude at that time—the Pope and the Emperor.
The kings were in theory as much subject to one as to the
other. The Pope and the Emperor, though with inextricable
confusion in their mutual relations, were cast as it were in
the same mould. Dante could no more have imagined the
Emperor ceasing than the Pope. Indeed he would have
sooner spared the Pope than the Emperor. He sees no Pope
(except St. Peter) in paradise—no Emperor in hell. When
the Emperor fell in the fall of the Suabian dynasty, the Pope,
instead of gaining by the destruction of his ancient enemy,
was weakened also. They were twin brothers. They were
Siamese twins. The death of the one involves the ultimate
death of the other, at least in the aspect in which they are
correlative. No king, except the German princes, is now
dependent on the Emperor of Germany. No king is now
dependent on the Pope of Rome. The monarchy of Christendom has ceased, for all practical purposes, as certainly
as the monarchy of ancient Rome ceased after the expulsion
of the Tarquins. But when the kings were driven out from
ancient Rome, there was still a king kept up in name to
perform the grand ceremonial offices which no one but a
person having the name of ' king ' or ' Rex ' could discharge.
The ' *Rex sacrificulus* '[3] took precedence of all the other
functionaries, religious or secular, in the old Roman constitution, down to the time of Theodosius. He lived on
the Via Sacra, near the palace of the Pontifex Maximus.
He was the ghost of the deceased Roman kingdom, just

---

[3] He lived on the hill called 'Velia.' Next to him came the Flamen,
who lived in the Flaminian meadows; next the Pontifex Maximus, who
lived by the Temple of Vesta.

as the Pope is the ghost of the deceased Roman Empire.
Such as he was in regard to the external constitution of the
Roman kingdom, such the pope is in regard to the external
constitution of Western Christendom. He takes precedence
still of all the monarchs of Catholic Europe. He always dines
alone, lest a question of precedence should ever arise. The
Papal Nuncio is still the head of the diplomatic body in every
Catholic country. Even Protestant sovereigns, on receiving
a congratulatory address from that body in France or Spain,
must receive it from the lips of the Nuncio. The Pope's rank
is thus an interesting and venerable monument of an extinct
world. His outward magnificence compared with his inward
weakness is one of the most frequently noted marks of his
position in the world.

It is in this capacity that he was seen by Bunyan, in the
cave where lay the giants Pope and Pagan—decrepit, aged,
mumbling. It has been said that Peter has no grey hairs.
This is not the verdict of history. His hairs are very grey ;
he is not what he once was. He exhibits the vicissitudes
of history to an extent almost beyond that of any other
sovereign.

V. This leads us to yet one more attribute of the Pope.
Even those who entirely repudiate his authority, must still
 regard him as the chief ecclesiastic of Christendom.
If there is such a thing as a body of clergy at all,
the Bishop of Rome is certainly the head of the profession.
In him we see the pretensions, the merits, the demerits, of
the clerical office in the most complete, perhaps in the most
exaggerated, form. His oracular power is only what, to a
certain extent, is claimed by the rest of the clergy. It may
not be, perhaps, avowed by any other clergymen, Roman
Catholic or Protestant, often as they may think it or imply it,
that they are infallible, or that they can add, by their own mere
motion, new articles of faith. But wherever such claims exist,
the office of the Pope is an excellent field in which to discuss
the matter. The same reasons which convince us that the
Pope is not infallible may convince us of the same defect in
regard to the less dignified ecclesiastics. The advantages

which the clerical order have conferred on Christendom,
and the disadvantages, are also well seen in the history of the
Popes on a large scale.

Again, the Pope well exemplifies the true nature of the
much confused terms, 'spiritual and temporal power.'  His
spiritual power—that is, his moral and intellectual power
over the minds and consciences of men—is very small.  Even
amongst Roman Catholics, there are very few who really
believe anything the more because the Pope says so ; and the
Popes who have been authors of eminence, are very few and
far between.  Probably few sees, as we have said, in Christendom have really contributed so little through their personal
occupants to the light of the world.  No Pope has ever
exercised the same real amount of spiritual influence as
Augustine, or Aquinas, or Thomas à Kempis, or Luther, or
Erasmus, or Shakespeare, or Loyola, or Hegel, or Ewald.

But his secular power over ecclesiastics is very considerable.
He in many instances controls their temporal positions.  His
tribunals, whatever may be their uncertainty and caprice,
compared to an English court of justice, are still, to the
ecclesiastical world of Roman Catholic Christendom, what
the Supreme Court of Appeal is to the Church of England.

It is against the exercise of this power that Henry II. in
England, and St. Louis [4] in France, and Santa Rosa in
Piedmont, contended.  It is as a protection against it, that
the state in France, Austria, Spain, Italy, Portugal, and
virtually in Prussia, has retained the nomination of the
bishops of those countries in its own hands, and fenced itself
about with concordats and treaties, against the intrusion of
so formidable a rival.  By this protection the Abbot of
Monte Casino, under the present kingdom of Italy, enjoys a
freedom which he with difficulty maintained against the Pope,
and the Archbishop of Paris, almost until he fell a victim
to the fanaticism of the Parisian populace, was upheld by the
Emperor of the French.

VI. It has been the purpose of these remarks to con-

<hr>

[4] See Lanfrey's *Histoire Politique des Papes*, p. 278.

fine them as closely as possible to facts acknowledged by all.

One remaining fact, however, also is certain, that there is no personage in the world whose office provokes such widely different sentiments as that of the Pope. It was said that Pius IX. had two sides to his face—one malignant, the other benevolent. Once, and once only, the malignant side appeared in a photograph, which was immediately suppressed by the police. Whether this is true or not, it is no unapt likeness of the opposite physiognomy which the Papal office presents to the two sides of the Christian world. To the one, he appears as the Vicar of Christ, to the other as Antichrist; to the one as the chief minister and representative of the Holy and the Just, to the other as His chief enemy. Nor is this diversity of aspect divided exactly according to the division of the ancient and modern Churches. There have been members of the Roman Church, like Petrarch, who have seen in the Papal city a likeness of Babylon, as clearly as Luther or Knox. There have been Protestants, like Arnold and Guizot, who have recognised in certain phases of the Papacy a beneficence of action and a loftiness of design, as clearly as Bossuet and De Maistre. Nay even to the same mind, at the same time, the office has alternately presented both aspects, as it did to Dante. And again, the Pope. who, to most Protestants, appears as the representative of all that is retrograde, dogmatic, and superstitious, appears in the eyes of the Eastern Church as the first Rationalist, the first Reformer, the first founder of private judgment and endless schism.

This diversity of sentiment is certainly not the least instructive of the characteristics of the Papal office. Many causes may have contributed towards it, but the main and simple cause is this,—that the Papal office, like many human institutions, is a mixture of much good and much evil; stained with many crimes, adorned with many virtues; with many peculiar temptations, with many precious opportunities; to be judged calmly, dispassionately, charitably, thoughtfully, by all who come across it.   So judged, its past history will become more intelligible and more edifying ; so judging, we may perhaps, arrive, hereafter, at some forecast of what may be its Future in the present and coming movements of the world.

It once chanced that an English traveller, in a long evening spent on the heights of Monte Casino, was conversing with one of the charming inmates of the ancient home of St. Benedict, who was himself, like most of his order in Italy, opposed to the temporal power of the Pope. The Protestant Englishman ventured to ask the liberal-minded Catholic—'How do you forecast the possibility of the accomplishment of your wishes in the face of the stead-fast opposition of the reigning Pontiff and the long traditional policy of the Roman Court?'   He replied, 'I console myself by looking back at the history of the Papacy.   J remember that St. Peter came to Rome a humble fisherman, without power, without learning, with no weapon but simple faith and his life in his hand.   I remember next that when the barbarians came in, and the European monarchies were founded, there came a man as unlike to St. Peter as can possibly be conceived—of boundless ambition, of iron will—Hildebrand, who alone was able to cope with the difficulties of his situation.   Then came the Renaissance, classic arts, pagan literature; and there arose in the midst of them Leo X., as their natural patron, as unlike to Hildebrand as Hildebrand to St. Peter.   Then came the shock of the Reformation—the panic, the alarm, the reaction—the Muses were banished, the classic luxury was abolished, and the very reverse of Leo X. appeared in the austere Puritan, Pius V. And now we have Pius IX. .... And in twenty or a hundred years we may have a new Pope, as unlike to Pius IX. as Pius IX. is unlike to Pius V., as Pius V. was unlike to Leo X., as Leo X. was unlike to Hildebrand, as all were unlike to St. Peter; and on this I rest my hope of the ultimate conciliation of Rome and Italy, of Catholicism and freedom.'

Such, or nearly such, was the consolation administered to

himself by the genial historian of Monte Casino; and such, taken with a wider range, is the consolation which we may minister to ourselves in viewing the changes of an institution which, with all its failings, cannot but command a large share of religious and philanthropic interest. It is always within the bounds of hope, that a single individual, fully equal to the emergency, who should by chance or Providence find himself in that (or any like) exalted seat, might work wonders—wonders which, humanly speaking, could not be worked, even by a man of equal powers, in a situation less commanding. There is a mediæval tale which has even some foundation in fact,[5] that a certain Pope was once accused before a General Council on the charge of heresy. He was condemned to be burned ; but it was found that the sentence could not be legally carried into execution but with the consent of the Pope himself. The assembled Fathers went to the Pope—*venerunt ad Papam*—and presented their humble petition—*et dixerunt, O Papa, judica te cremari*; and the Pope was moved to pity for the inextricable dilemma in which the Fathers were placed. He consented to their prayer. He pronounced judgment on himself—*et dixit, Judico me cremari*; and his sentence was carried into effect—*et crematus est*—and then in reverential gratitude for so heroic an act of self-denial he was canonised—*et postea veneratus pro sancto.* Such, although with a more cheerful issue, might be the solution of the entanglement of the Church by some future Pope. We have but to imagine a man of ordinary courage, common sense, honesty, and discernment—a man who should have the grace to perceive that the highest honour which he could confer on the highest seat in the Christian hierarchy, and the highest service he could render to the Christian religion, would be from that lofty eminence to

---

[5] The tale is founded on the deposition of Gregory V. In the real story the Council was not a General, but a Provincial Council ; the Pope's crime was not heresy, but simony; the sentence pronounced was not death, but deposition.

speak out to the whole world the truth, the whole truth, and nothing but the truth. Such an one, regarding only the facts of history, but in the plenitude of authority which he would have inherited, and 'speaking *ex cathedrâ*, in discharge of his office of pastor and doctor of all Christians,' might solemnly pronounce that he, his predecessors, and his successors, were fallible, personally and officially, and might err, as they have erred again and again, both in faith and morals. By so doing he would not have contradicted the decree of infallibility, more than that decree contradicts the decrees of previous councils and the declarations of previous Popes. By so doing he would incur insult, obloquy, perhaps death. But like the legendary Pope of whom we have spoken, he would have deserved the crown of sanctity, for he would have shown that quality which above all others belongs to saints in the true sense of the word. He would have risen above the temptations of his situation, his order, his office ; he would have relieved the Catholic Church from that which its truest friends feel to be an intolerable incubus, and restored it to light and freedom.

---

## NOTE.

### THE POPE'S POSTURE IN THE COMMUNION.

It is one of the most curious circumstances of the curious practice of the Pope's sitting at the Communion, that amongst Roman Catholics themselves there should be not only the most conflicting evidence as to the fact, but even entire ignorance as to the practice ever having existed. In the leading Roman Catholic journal [6] the statement that such a practice prevailed was asserted to be 'the purest romance;' and though this expression was afterwards courteously withdrawn, yet the fact was still denied, and it appeared that there were even well-instructed Roman Catholics who had never heard of its existence. This obscurity

* *Dublin Review*, 1869.

on the matter may perhaps show that it is regarded as of more importance than would at first sight appear.

1. The Roman Liturgies themselves have no express statement on the subject. They all agree in directing that the Pope retires to his lofty seat—'ad sedem eminentem'—behind the altar, and there remains. Some of them add that he 'stands' waiting for the subdeacon to approach with the sacred elements : but beyond this, with the exceptions hereafter to be noticed, there is no order given.

2. The earliest indication of the Pope's position to which a reference is found is in St. Bonaventura (1221–1274), on Psalm xxi. : 'Papa quando sumit corpus Christi in missâ solemni, sumit omnibus videntibus, nam, *sedens in cathedra*, se convertit ad populum' (Opp. vol. i. pp. 111, 112); and that this was understood to mean that he communicated sitting appears from the marginal note of the edition of Bonaventura published by order of Sixtus V. (1230–1296), 'Papa *quare communicet sedens*.'

Durandus, in his 'Rationale' (iv. § 4, 5, p. 203), and the 'Liber Sacrarum Cærimoniarum' (p. 102), use nearly the same words : 'Ascendens ad sedem eminentem ibi communicat.' This expression, though it would suggest that the Pope was seated, does not of necessity imply it. But the 'Liber Sacrarum Cærimoniarum,' although at Christmas (p. 133) it describes the Pope immediately after his ascension of the chair as 'ibi stans,' when it speaks of Easter (p. 176) expressly mentions the posture of sitting as at least permissible. 'Communione facta, Papa surgit, *si communicando sedebit.*'

Cardinal Bona ('Rer. Lit.' ii. c. 17, 88 ; iii. p. 395)—than whom there is no higher authority—writes : 'Summus Pontifex cum solemniter celebrat *sedens communit* hoc modo.'[7]

Martene (1654–1789), 'De Ant. Eccl. Rit.' i. 4, 10, p. 421, states that 'Romæ summus Pontifex celebrans in suâ *sede consistens* seipsum communicabat. Postea accedebant episcopi et presbyteri ut a pontifice communionem accipiant, episcopi quidem stantes ad sedem pontificis, presbyteri verò ad altare genibus flexis'

The obvious meaning of this passage is that the Pope remains ('consistens')[8] in his place, sitting ; whilst the other clergy, according to their ranks, assume the different postures described,

---

[7] A question has been raised as to the authority on which the Cardinal puts forth his statement. But this does not touch the authority of the Cardinal himself.

[8] The word itself means simply 'keeping his place.'

the bishops standing, the presbyters kneeling.  And this is the view taken of it by Moroni, the chamberlain and intimate friend of the late Pope Gregory XVI., who cites these words as showing 'che in Roma il Papa *communicavasi sedendo nel suo trono*' (Dizionario, vol. xv. p. 126).

It is hardly necessary to confirm these high Roman authorities by the testimony of Protestant Ritualists.  But that it was the received opinion amongst such writers that the Pope sits, appears from the unhesitating assertions to this effect by Bingham, Neale, and Maskell.

3. To these great liturgical authorities on the *theory* of the Papal posture may be added, besides Moroni (whose words just cited may be taken as a testimony to the practice of Gregory XVI.), the following witnesses to the *usage* of modern times.

The Rev. J. E. Eustace, the well-known Roman Catholic traveller through Italy, says : 'When the Pope is seated, the two deacons bring the holy sacrament, which he first reveres humbly on his knees, and then receives in a sitting posture.'  Eustace mentions the practice with some repugnance, and adds—'Benedict XIII. could never be prevailed upon to conform to it, but always remained standing at the altar, according to the usual practice' (Eustace's 'Travels,' ii. 170).

Archbishop Gerbet, who has the credit of having instigated the recent 'Syllabus,' and whose work on 'Rome Chrétienne,' is expressly intended as a guide to the antiquities of Christian Rome, writes as follows :—

' Le Pape descend de l'autel, traverse le sanctuaire et monte au siège pontifical.  *Là, à demi assis*, quoique incliné par respect, *il communie*,' &c.  '*L'attitude du Pape* et cette communion multiple . . . . *retracent la première communion* des Apôtres *assis* à la table du Sauveur.'  ('Rome Chrétienne,' ii. 86, 87.)

The passage is the more interesting as Gerbet's reference to the original attitude shows his belief that it was the retention of the primitive practice.

4. This mass of testimony might be thought sufficient to establish so simple a fact.  But it will be observed that there is a slight wavering in the statement of Martene and of Gerbet ; and this variation is confirmed by the silence or by the express contradiction of other authorities, not indeed so high, but still of considerable weight.

It is stated that in the 'Ordo' of Urban VIII., after the adoration of the sacred elements the Pope immediately rises, 'statim surgit;' and that Crispus, who was sub-deacon to Clement XI., says, 'in cathedrâ *stans* et *veluti erectus* in cruce sanguinem sugit.' These same authorities, with Catalani, also state that *after* the communion 'the Pope takes his mitre and sits down,'·'sumptâ mitrâ sedet,' or 'accipit mitram et sedens,' &c. It is also said to be mentioned as a peculiarity that on Easter Day, 1481, Sixtus IV. was obliged by infirmity to sit down during the communion at High Mass, which, if so be, would imply that it was not the usual posture.

Dr. Bagge (in his book on the Pontifical Mass, 1840) states that 'the Pope does *not receive sitting*, as Eustace and others assert. When the sub-deacon has reached the throne the Pope adores the Sacred Host, the cardinal-deacon then takes the chalice and shows it to the Pope and the people. . . . It is carried from the deacon to the Pope, who, having adored, remains standing.'[9]

5. Between these contradictory statements there is a middle view, which probably contains the solution of the enigma, and is to be found in the statements of two authorities, which for this reason are reserved for the conclusion.

The first is Rocca (1545–1620), who 'was chosen corrector of the press of the Sixtine Bible, and is said to have excelled all others in ecclesiastical knowledge; and who, on account of his perfect acquaintance with rubrics and the Liturgies, was appointed Apostolic Commentator by Pope Clement VIII.'[1]

He writes as follows (in his 'Thesaurus Rituum,' in the 'Commentarium de Sacra S. Pontificis communione,' 20): 'Dicitur autem Summus Pontifex *sedere dum communicat*, vel *quia ipse antiquitus in communicando sedebat*, vel *quia sedentis instar communicabat, sicut praesens in tempus fieri solet*. Summus namque Pontifex ad solium, stans non sedens, ad majorem venerationem repraesentandam, ipsi tamen solio, populo universo spectante, *innixus, et incurvus, quasi sedens communicat*, Christum Dominum cruci affixum, in eaque quodam modo reclinantem repraesentans.'

The other is Pope Benedict XIV. (1740–1758), who thus writes in his treatise 'De Sacrosancto Missæ Sacrificio,' lib. ii. c. 21, § 7: 'Illud autem praetermitti non potest, Romanos quosdam Pontifices in *solemni Missa in solio sedentes, facie ad populum*

---

* These quotations, which I have not been able to verify, are taken from the statements of the writer in the *Dublin Review*, April 1869, pp. 514, 515.

[1] *Dublin Review*, April 1869, p. 516. The same passage extracts from the sentence quoted in the text, 'Summus Pontifex ad solium stans, non sedens,' but omits all that precedes and all that follows.

*conversa, Eucharistiam sumere consuevisse*, ut Christi Passio et Mors exprimeretur, qui propalam passus et mortuus est in conspectu omnium, quotquot nefariæ Crucifixioni adfuere tamen (?) vero Summum Pontificem, cum solemnem celebrat Missam, se aliosque communicare facie quidem ad populum conversa, sed pedibus stantem in solio, corpore tamen inclinato, cum et ipse suscipit, aliisque præbet Eucharistiam. . . . Hinc est quamobrem Pontifex populo, procul et exadverso in faciem eum adspicienti, *videatur sedens communicare*, ut bene observabat post S. Bonaventuram Rocca de solemni communione Summi Pontificis et Casalius de veteribus Sacris Christianorum Ritibus, cap. 81, p. 333, ed. Rom. 1647.'

From these two statements it appears that the Popes in ancient times sat whilst communicating, but that from the close of the sixteenth century they usually stood in a leaning or half-sitting posture.

To these must be added a further statement of Pope Benedict XIV. in a letter addressed in 1757 to the Master of the Pontifical Ceremonies, on the general question of the lawfulness, under certain circumstances, of celebrating Mass in a sitting posture.

The general cases which raise the question are of gout and the like ; but in the course of the discussion the Pope describes some particulars respecting his predecessors bearing on the present subject.

Pius III. was elected to the Pontificate (in 1503) when he was still only a deacon.   He was ordained priest on the 1st of October, and on the 8th of October he himself celebrated Mass as Pope.   On both of these occasions (being troubled by an ulcer in the leg) he sat during the whole ceremony ; a seat was solemnly prepared, in which he was to sit, and the altar arranged in the form of a long table, under which he might stretch his legs (' sedem in quâ sedens extensis cruribus ordinaretur, et mensam longam pro altari ut pedes subtus extendi possent'). It also appears that in the Papal chapel it is considered generally that the Pope has liberty to sit whilst he administers the elements to his court.   It appears, further, that (also without any reference to special cases) the Pope sits during the ceremony of his ordination as sub-deacon, deacon, and presbyter, if he has been elected to the Pontificate before such ordination ; and that the fact of this posture during the Holy Communion was considered by Benedict XIV. to cover the question generally.   It will be sufficient to quote the passage which relates to the ordination of a Pope as priest.   ' In collatione sacerdotii

*sedens Pontifex* manuum impositionem, olei sancti, quod catechumenorum dicitur, unctionem, calicem cum vino et aqua, et patinam
cum hostia, recipit. Quæ omnia luculenter ostendunt haud *inconveniens esse sedere Pontificem in functionibus sacratissimis,*
atque eo *ipso Missam totam a sedente* posse celebrari, *præsertim si
pedibus debilitatis insistere non valeat.*' He concludes with . this
pertinent address on his own behalf to the Master of the Ceremonies :—' Et, siquidem *sedentes* missam celebrare statuimus, tuum
erit preparare mensam altaris cum consecrato lapide,' &c. ' vacuumque subtus altare spatium relinquatur extendendis pedibus idoneum ; confidentes singula dexteritati tuæ singulari perficienda,.
apostolicam tibi benedictionem peramanter impertimur.' [2]

6. The conclusion, therefore, of the whole matter must be this.
In early times, probably down to the reign of Sixtus V. (as indicated in the marginal note on St. Bonaventura), the position of
the Pope was sitting, as a venerable relic of primitive ages.
Gradually, as appears from the words of Eustace, the value of this
tenacious and interesting adherence to the ancient usage was
depreciated from its apparent variation from the general sentiment, as expressed in the standing posture of priests and the
kneeling attitude of the communicants, and it would seem that
before the end of the sixteenth century the custom had been
in part abandoned. But with that remarkable tenacity of ecclesiastical usages, which retains particles of such usages when the larger
part has disappeared, the ancient posture was not wholly given up.
As the wafer and the chalice are but minute fragments of ·the
ancient Supper—as the standing posture of the priests is a remnant
of the standing posture of devotion through the whole Christian
Church—as the standing posture of the English clergyman during
part of the Communion Service is a remnant of the standing posture
of the Catholic clergy through the whole of it— as the sitting
posture of the earlier Popes was a remnant of the sitting or
recumbent posture of the primitive Christian days—so the partial
attitude of the present Popes is a remnant of the sitting posture of
their predecessors. It is a compromise between the ancient historical usage and modern decorum. The Pope's attitude, so we
gather from Rocca and Benedict XIV., and also from Archbishop

<hr>

[2] *Opp.* xvii. 474, 489. It will be observed that the acceptance of the
chalice and paten by the Pope at his ordinations is not of itself the Communion. It must be further noticed that the Pope in thus writing makes
this qualification : ' Dum Romanus Pontifex solemniter celebrat, . . . recipit
sacram Eucharistiam sub speciebus panis et vini stans neque sedens com-

Gerbet, is neither of standing nor of sitting.  He goes to his lofty chair, he stands till the sub deacon comes, he bows himself down in adoration as the Host approaches.  Thus far all are agreed, though it is evident that at a distance any one of those postures might be taken, as it has by some spectators, for the posture at the act of communion.  But in the act of communion, as far as we can gather from the chief authorities, he is in his chair, facing the people, leaning against the back of the chair, so as not to abandon entirely the attitude of sitting—sufficiently erect to give the appearance of standing, with his head and body bent down to express the reverence due to the sacred elements.  This complex attitude would account for the contradictions of eye-witnesses, and the difficulty of making so peculiar a compromise would perhaps cause a variation in the posture of particular Popes, or even of the same Pope on particular occasions.  What to one spectator would seem standing, to another would seem sitting, and to another might seem kneeling.

This endeavour to combine a prescribed attitude either with convenience or with a change of sentiment is not uncommon.  One parallel instance has been often adduced in the case of the Popes themselves.  In the great procession on Corpus Christi Day, when the Pope is carried in a palanquin round the Piazza of St. Peter, it is generally believed that the cushions and furniture of the palanquin are so arranged as to enable him to bear the fatigue of the ceremony by sitting, whilst to the spectators he appears to be kneeling.[3] Another parallel is to be found from another point of view, in one of the few other instances in which the posture of sitting has been retained, or rather adopted, namely in the Presbyterian Church of Scotland.  There the attitude of sitting was rigidly prescribed.  But, if we may trust an account of the Scottish Sacrament, believed to be as accurate as it is poetic, the posture of the devout Presbyterian peasant as nearly as possible corresponds to that which Rocca,

---

municat, prout per errorem scripserunt aliqui, viderique potest tom. ii *Truct. Nostri de Sac. Missæ*, sect. i. c. 20, § 1.'  It is a curious example of what may be called ' the audacity ' which sometimes characterises expressions of Pontifical opinion, that the very passage to which Benedict XIV., in the last year of his life, thus referred to as ' an erroneous statement ' of the Pope's ' sitting at the Communion,' contains his own assertion that ' some of the Roman Pontiffs in solemn mass were accustomed to receive the Eucharist sitting.'  In fact, it is difficult to reconcile the statement in the letter just quoted with the passages which are quoted in the text.

[3] See the minute account of an eye-witness in 1830 in Crabbe Robinson's *Diary*, ii. 469.

Gerbet, and Benedict XIV. give of the Pope's present attitude—
'innixus,' 'incurvus inclinato corpore,' 'à demi assis,' 'une pro-
fonde inclination de corps':—

> ' There they sit  .  .  .  .
>        .  .  .  . In reverence meek
> Many an eye to heaven is lifted,
> Many lips, not heard to speak,
> Mutely moving, on their worship
> From on high a blessing seek.
>
> Hoary-headed elders moving,
> Bear the hallowed wine and bread,
> While devoutly still the people
> Low in prayer bow the head.' *

It is interesting to observe this ancient usage becoming small
by degrees and beautifully less, yet still not entirely extinguished :
reduced from recumbency to sitting, from the sitting of all to the
sitting of a single person, from the sitting of a single person to the
doubtful reminiscence of his sitting, by a posture half-sitting, half-
standing.

The compromise of the Pope's actual posture is a characteristic
specimen of that 'singular dexterity' which Benedict XIV. attributes to his Master of the Ceremonies, and which has so often
marked the proceedings of the Roman court. To have devised a
posture by which, as on the festival of Corpus Christi, the Pope
can at once sit and kneel ; or—as in the cases mentioned by Pope
Benedict XIV.—an arrangement by which the Pope, whilst sitting,
can 'stretch his legs in the vacant space under the altar '; or, as
in the case we have been considering, a position of standing so as
to give the appearance of sitting, and sitting so as to give the
appearance of standing—is a minute example of the subtle genius
of the institution of the Papacy. As the practice itself is a straw,
indicating the movement of primitive antiquity, so the modern
compromise is a straw, indicating the movement of the Roman
Church in later times.

* *Kilmahoe ; and other Poems.*  By J. C. Shairp.

# CHAPTER XII.

### THE LITANY.

THE Litany is one of the most popular parts of the English Prayer Book. It is not one of the most ancient parts, but it is sufficiently ancient to demand an inquiry into its peculiarities, and its peculiarities are sufficiently marked to demand a statement.

I. First, as to its origin. It is one of the parts of the Prayer Book which have their origin in a time neither primitive nor reformed. For four hundred years there were no prayers of this special kind in the Christian Church; nor, again, in the Reformed Church were any prayers like it introduced afresh. It sprang from an age gloomy with disaster and superstition, when heathenism was still struggling with Christianity; when Christianity was disfigured by fierce conflicts within the Church; when the Roman Empire was tottering to its ruin; when the last great luminary of the Church—Augustine—had just passed away, amidst the forebodings of universal destruction. It was occasioned also by a combination of circumstances of the most peculiar character. The general disorder of the time was aggravated by an unusual train of calamities. Besides the ruin of society, attendant on the invasion of the barbarians, there came a succession of droughts, pestilences, and earthquakes, which seemed to keep pace with the throes of the moral world. Of all these horrors, France was the centre. On one of these occasions, when the people had been hoping that, with the Easter festival, some respite would come, a sudden earthquake shook the church at Vienne, on the Rhone.  It was on Easter eve ; the congregation rushed out ; the bishop of the city (Mamertus) was left alone before the altar.  On that terrible night he formed a resolution of inventing a new form, as he hoped, of drawing down the mercy of God.  He determined that in the three days before Ascension day there should be a long procession to the nearest churches in the neighbourhood.  From Vienne the custom spread.  Amongst the vine-clad mountains, the extinct volcanoes of Auvergne, the practice was taken up with renewed fervour.  From town to town it ran through France; it seemed to be a new vent for a hitherto pent-up devotion—a new spell for chasing away the evils of mankind.  Such was the first Litany—a popular supplication, sung or shouted, not within the walls of any consecrated building, but by wild excited multitudes, following each other in long files, through street and field, over hill and valley, as if to bid nature join in the depth of their contrition.  It was, in short, what we should call a revival.[1]

It is only by an effort that we can trace the identity of a modern Litany with those strange and moving scenes.  Our attention may, however, be well called to the contrast, for various reasons.

1. We do well to remember that a good custom does not lose its goodness, because it arose in a bad time, in a corrupt

Its origin.

age, in a barbarous country.  Out of such dark beginnings have sprung some of our best institutions.  In order for a practice or a doctrine to bear good Christian fruit, we need not demand that its first origin

___

[1] Sidonius Apollinaris, i. 7 ; Gregory of Tours (*Hist. Franc.* ii. 6, 34) A.D. 447.  There were some earlier and some later developments of this practice, but this seems the most authentic statement of heir first beginning.  The brief form of ' Kyrie Eleeson ' had existed before.  It first occurs in the heathen worship.  'When we call upon God, we say of him Κύριε ἐλέησον' (Arrian, *Comment. de Epist. Disput.* ii. c. 7).  The Litany for St. Mark's Day was instituted A.D. 590 by Gregory the Great, partly to avert a pestilence, partly as a substitute for a procession which was held by the ancient Romans to propitiate the goddess Robigo, or Mildew.

should be primitive, or Protestant, or civilised ; it is enough that it should be good in itself and productive of good effects.

2. Again, it is well to remember that the goodness of a thing depends not on its outward form, but on its inward spirit. The very word ' Litany,' in its first origin, included long processions, marches to and · fro, cries and screams, which have now disappeared almost everywhere from public devotions, even in the Roman Catholic Church. Those who established it would not have imagined that a Litany without these accompaniments could have any efficacy whatever. We know now that the accompaniments were mere accidents, and that the substance has continued. What has happened in the Litany has occurred again and again with every part of our ecclesiastical system. Always the form and the letter are perishing ; always there will be some who think that the form and the letter are the thing itself ; generally in the Christian Church there is enough vitality to keep the spirit though the form is changed ; generally, we trust, as in the Litany, so elsewhere, there will be found men wise enough and bold enough to retain the good and throw. off the bad in all the various forms of our religious and ecclesiastical life.

3. Again, there is a peculiar charm and interest in knowing the accidental historical origin of this service. To any one who has a heart to feel and an imagination to carry him backwards and forwards along the fields of time, there is a pleasure, an edification in the reflection that the prayers which we use were not composed in the dreamy solitude of the closet or the convent, but were wrung out of the necessities of human sufferers, like ourselves. If, here and there, we catch a note of some expression not wholly suitable to our own age, there is yet something at once grand and comforting in the recollection that we hear in those responses the echoes of the thunders and earthquakes of central France, of the irruption of wild barbarian hordes, of the ruin of the falling empire : that the Litany which we use for our homelier sorrows was, as Hooker says, ' the very

strength and comfort of the Church' in that awful distress of nations. 'The offences of our forefathers,' the 'vengeance on our sins,' the 'lightning and tempest,' the 'plague, pestilence, and famine,' the 'battle, and murder, and sudden death,' the 'prisoners and captives,' the 'desolate and oppressed,' the 'troubles and adversities,' the 'hurt of persecutions,'—all these phrases receive a double force if they recall to us the terrors of that dark, disastrous time, when the old world was hastening to its end, and the new was hardly struggling into existence.

4. Further, it was under a like pressure of calamities that the Litany first became part of our services. It is the earliest portion of the English Prayer Book that appeared in its present English form. It was translated from Latin into English either by Archbishop Cranmer or by King Henry VIII. himself. These are the words with which, on the eve of his expedition to France in 1544, he sent this first instalment of the Prayer Book to Cranmer: 'Calling to our remembrance the miserable state of all Christendom, being at this present time plagued, besides all other troubles, with most cruel wars, hatreds, and disunions, . . . . the help and remedy hereof being far exceeding the power of any man, must be called for of Him who only is able to grant our petitions, and never forsaketh or repelleth any that firmly believe and faithfully call upon Him; unto whom also the examples of Scripture encourage us in all these and others our troubles and perplexities to flee. Being therefore resolved to have continually from henceforth general processions in all cities, towns, and churches or parishes of this our realm, . . . . forasmuch as heretofore the people, partly for lack of good instruction, partly that they understood no part of such prayers and suffrages as were used to be said and sung, have used to come very slackly, we have set forth certain goodly prayers and suffrages in our native English tongue, which we send you herewith.'[2]

Thus it is that whilst the Litany at its first beginning

---

[2] Froude's *History of England*, iv. 482.

expressed the distress of the first great convulsion of Europe in the fall of the Roman empire, the Litany in its present form expressed the cry of distress in that second great convulsion which accompanied the Reformation. It is the first utterance of the English nation in its own native English tongue, calling for divine help, in that extremity of perplexity, when men's hearts were divided between hope and despair for the fear of those things that were coming on the earth.

5. In like manner many a time have those expressions of awe and fear struck some chord in the hearts of individuals, far more deeply than had they been more calmly and deliberately composed at first.

How affecting is that account of Samuel Johnson, whom, in the church of St. Clement Danes, his biographer overheard repeating in a voice, that trembled with emotion, the petition which touched the only sensitive chord in his strong mind, 'In the hour of death and in the day of judgment, good Lord deliver us!' How striking was the use made by a great orator of the words of another clause, when, on the occasion of the omission of the name of an unfortunate princess from the Liturgy, he said that there was at least one passage in the Litany where all might think of her and pray for her—amongst those who were ' desolate and oppressed.'

II. Secondly, it is instructive to notice how in succeeding ages, the particular grievance or want of the time, sometimes well, sometimes ill, has laboured to express itself amongst these petitions.



1. It was natural that, in the reign of Edward VI., when the burdensome yoke of the see of Rome had only just been shaken off, a prayer should have been added—'From the tyranny of the Bishop of Rome, and from all his detestable enormities, good Lord deliver us.' This was perhaps excusable under the circumstances; but it is a matter of rejoicing that, by the wisdom of Elizabeth, this fierce expression should have been struck out.

2. Again, amidst the general unsettlement of civil and

religious society in the time of Henry VIII., and of Charles II., it was no wonder that the petitions should have been crowded with alarms, in the first instance, of 'sedition, privy conspiracy, false doctrine, and heresy,' or 'hardness of heart and contempt of God's commandments;' in the second instance of 'rebellion and schism.'

These expressions dwell too exclusively on the dangers of disorder and anarchy, and too little on the dangers of despotism and arbitrary power. Yet there is one petition, which first came in with the dawn of the Reformation, which no ancient Litany seems to have contained, and yet which attacks the chief sin that called down the displeasure of Christ—the prayer against *hypocrisy*. It is not unimportant to remember that in the prayer against that sin, in its full extent—the sin of acting a part—the sin of disregarding truth—the sin of regarding the outward more than the inward—in that one prayer is summed up the whole spirit of the Reformation.

3. Again, the present Litany stands alone in the prominence which it gives, and the emphasis which it imparts, to the prayer for the sovereign. It was no doubt intended to be the expression of the great principle vindicated in Hooker's 'Ecclesiastical Polity,' that the sovereign, as representative of the law, controls and guides the whole concerns both of Church and State. It was the expression of the wish to secure for the interest of the State no less than for the interest of the clergy, not merely as in the old Litanies, victory abroad, and peace at home, but righteousness and holiness of life, the faith, the fear, and the love of God.

4. Again, as we read some of the petitions we cannot but call to mind the wishes of good men that something might have been added or explained. The prayer against *sudden death*.—Earnestly did the Puritan divines in the time of Charles II. intreat that this might be expanded into what was probably intended, and what in fact existed in the older forms—'From dying suddenly and unprepared.' It was a natural scruple. Many a one has felt that 'sudden death'

would be a blessing and not a curse—and that to those who are prepared, no death can be sudden. The hard, uncompromising rulers of that age refused to listen to the remonstrance; and we, as we utter the prayer in its unaltered form, may justly feel a momentary pang at the thought of the good men on whose consciences they thus needlessly trampled.

Again, let any reflect on the changes meditated by the good men who made the last attempt at revision in 1689:— ' From all rash *censure* and *contention*;' and again, ' from *drunkenness* and *gluttony*,' 'from *sloth* and *misspending of our time*,' 'from *lying and slandering*, from *vain swearing*, cursing and perjury, from *covetousness, oppression*, and all *injustice*, good Lord deliver us;' 'let it please Thee to endue us with the *graces* of *humility* and *meekness*, of *contentedness* and *patience*, of true *justice*, of temperance and purity, of *peaceableness* and *charity*,' 'and have pity upon all that are persecuted for *truth* and *righteousness' sake*.' In these intended additions of Tillotson, Burnet, and Patrick, we see at once the keen sense of the evils, some of them peculiar to that age—of the higher virtues, also peculiar to that age no less.

Again, in our own times it has been recorded of Archbishop Whately, that when he came to the prayer that we might ' be hurt by no persecutions,' he always added internally a prayer, 'that we may not be persecutors.' This was a holy and a noble thought, much needed, well supplied, which perhaps before our age it would hardly have occurred to any ecclesiastic to utter.

In this way the Litany has grown with the growth of Christendom; and may, without any direct change, suggest even more than it says to those who use it rightly.

III. We turn from the occasion and the growth of the Litany to the form in which it is expressed. That form is very peculiar, and its explanation is to be sought in the occasion of its first introduction. The usual mode of *Its form.* addressing our prayers, both in the Scriptures and in the

Prayer Book, is to God, our Father, through Jesus Christ. This is the form of the Lord's Prayer, after which manner we are all taught to pray. This is the form throughout the New Testament, with two exceptions, which shall be noticed presently. This was the general mode of prayer throughout the early ages of the Church. Even those earlier forms of prayer which are most like the Litany are for the first three hundred years of the Church always addressed direct to God the Father.[3] It was the normal condition of the only part of the Liturgy that is of ancient use—that of the Eucharist. In conformity with this is the plan adopted in almost all the collects and prayers in the other parts of the English Prayer Book. Most important is this, both because only by so doing do we fulfil the express commands of Christ and also because it thus keeps before our minds the truth which the Scriptures never allow us to let go, of the Unity of Almighty God. Most fully, too, have the greatest ecclesiastical authorities on this subject recognised both the doctrine and the fact, that prayer ought, as a general rule, to be addressed, and has in the usual form of ancient catholic devotion been always addressed, only to God the Father.

But there are exceptions. No rule, even in these sacred matters, is so rigid as not to admit some variations. The largest number of such variations are in the poetical parts of the service, and are probably connected with the peculiar feeling which led to the use of poetic diction in public worship. But the most remarkable exception is the Litany. It is not perhaps certain that all the petitions are addressed to Christ;[4] but at any rate, a large portion are so addressed. It stands in this respect almost isolated amidst the rest of the Prayer Book. What is the reason—what is the defence for this? Many excellent persons have at times felt a scruple at such a deviation from the precepts of Scrip-

---

[3] See Keble's *Eucharistic Adoration*, p. 114.

[4] 'We beseech Thee to hear us, O Lord,' is in the older Litanies addressed to God (Martene, iii. 52), and so it would seem to be in some of the petitions in the English Litany. But perhaps the most natural interpretation is to regard the whole as addressed to Christ.

ture and from the practice of ancient Christendom.  What
are we to say to explain it?  The explanation may be
found in the original circumstances under which the Litany
was introduced.  When the soul is overwhelmed with
difficulties and distresses, like those which caused the French
Christians in the fifth century to utter their piteous supplications to God, it seems to be placed in a different posture
from that of common life.  The invisible world is brought
much nearer—the language, the feelings, of the heart
become more impassioned, more vehement, more urgent.
The inhabitants, so to speak, of the world of spirits seem
to become present to our spirits; the words of common
intercourse seem unequal to convey the thoughts which are
labouring to express themselves.  As in poetry, so in sorrow,
and for a similar reason, our ordinary forms of speech are
changed.  So it was in the two exceptions which occur in
the New Testament.  When Stephen was in the midst of his
enemies, and no help for him left on earth, then 'the
heavens were opened, and he saw the Son of Man standing
on the right hand of God,' and, thus seeing Him, he addressed
his petition straight to Him—' Lord Jesus, receive my spirit
—Lord lay not this sin to their charge.'  When St. Paul was
deeply oppressed by the thorn in the flesh, then again his
Lord appeared to him (we know not how), and then to Him,
present to the eye whether of the body or the spirit (as on
the road to Damascus), the Apostle addressed the threefold
supplication, 'Let this depart from me,' and the answer, in like
manner, to the ear of the body or spirit, was direct—' My
grace is sufficient for thee.'  So is it in the Litany.  Those who
wrote it, and we who use it, stand for the moment in the
place of Stephen and Paul.  We knock, as it were, more
earnestly at the gates of heaven—we ' thrice beseech the
Lord '—and the veil is for a moment withdrawn, and the
Son of Man is there standing to receive our prayer.  In that
rude time, when the Litany was first introduced, they who
used it would fain have drawn back the veil further still.  It
is in the Litanies of the Middle Ages that we first find the

ınvocations not only of Christ our Saviour, but of those earthly saints who have departed with Him into that other world. These the Protestant Churches have now ceased to address. But the feeling which induced men to call upon them is the same in kind as that which runs through this whole exceptional service: namely, the endeavour, under the pressure of strong emotion and heavy calamity, to bring ourselves more nearly into the presence of the Invisible. Christ and the saints at such times seemed to come out like stars, which in the daylight cannot be seen, but in the darkness of the night are visible. The saints, like falling stars or passing meteors, have again receded into the darkness. Christians by increased reflection have been brought to feel that of them and of their state not enough is known to justify this invocation of their help. But Christ, the Lord and King of the saints, still remains—the Bright and Morning Star, more visible than all the rest, more bright and more cheering, as the darkness of the night becomes deeper, as the cold becomes more and more chill.

We justly acquiesce in the practice which has excluded those lesser mediators. But this one remarkable exception of the Litany in favour of addressing our prayers to the one Great Mediator may be permitted, if we remember that it is an exception, and if we understand the grounds on which it is made. In the rest of the Prayer Book we follow the ancient rule and our Master's own express command, by addressing the Father only. Here in the Litany, when we express our most urgent needs, it may be allowed to us to deviate from that general rule, and invite the aid of Jesus Christ, at once the Son of Man and Son of God.

Such being the case, two important results are involved in this form of the Litany.

1. If, on this solemn occasion, we can thus leave for a moment the prescribed order of devotion, and, with Stephen and Paul, address to Christ the prayers which we usually address to the Father, it implies a unity between the Father and the Son which is sometimes overlooked. Often we

read statements which seem to speak of the Father and the Son as if they were two rival divinities, the one all justice, the other all love; the one bent on destroying guilty sinners, the other striving to appease the Father's wrath; the one judging and forgiving, the other suffering and pleading. Such is the impression we many of us receive from some expressions in Milton's 'Paradise Lost,' and in Protestant and Roman Catholic divines, and from many well-known hymns. It is the reverse of this impression that we receive from the Litany. It is not the wrath of the Father, but the wrath of Christ from which in the Litany we pray to be delivered. It is the goodness and forgiveness, not of the Father, but of Christ, that we entreat for our sins. The mind and purpose of God is made known to us through the mind and purpose of Christ. We feel this truth nowhere more keenly than in the trials and sorrows of life; and we therefore express it nowhere more strongly than in the Litany.

2. Again, the Litany sets before us in its true aspect the meaning of Redemption. What is Redemption? It is, in one word, deliverance. We are in bondage to evil habits, in bondage to fear, in bondage to ignorance, in bondage to superstition, in bondage to sin: what we need is freedom and liberty. That is what we ask for every time we repeat the Litany: 'Good Lord, set us free.' *Libera nos, Domine.*

Deliverance—how, or by what means? By one part of Christ's appearance? by one part of Christianity? by a single doctrine or a single fact? By all—by the whole. Not by His sufferings only—not by His death only—not by His teaching only; but 'by the mystery of His holy incarnation—by His baptism—by His fasting—by His temptation—by His agony and bloody sweat—by His precious death and burial—by His glorious resurrection and ascension, and by the coming of the Holy Ghost.' This wide meaning of the mode of Redemption was a truth sufficiently appreciated in the early ages of the Church; and then it was piece by piece divided and subdivided, till the whole effect was altered and spoiled. Let us go back once more in the Litany to the complex yet simple whole. Let us believe more nearly as we pray.

The particular forms used may be open to objection. We might wish that some of the features had been omitted, or that other features had been added. But there remains the general truth—that it is by the whole life and appearance of Christ we hope to be delivered.

Deliverance from what? From what is it that we ask to be ransomed, redeemed, delivered? This also was well understood in the early Church, though sometimes expressed in strange language. It was, as they then put it, 'deliverance from the power of the devil '—deliverance from that control over the world which was in those days supposed to be possessed by the Evil Spirit. This belief, in form, has passed away. We do not now see demons lurking in every corner. But the substance of the belief remains. We pray in the Litany for deliverance from evil in all its forms; from evil, moral and physical; from the evil in our own hearts; from the evil brought on the world by the misgovernment, and anarchy, and wild passions of mankind; from the evils of sickness and war and tempest; from the trials of tribulation and from the trials of wealth;—from all these it is that we ask for deliverance. Each petition places before us some of the real evils in life which keep us in bondage. In proportion as we get rid of them we share in Christ's redemption. This is the object of the most earnest supplications of the Church; because it is the object of Christianity itself; because it is the purpose for which Christ came into the world; because, if He delivers us not from these, He delivers us from nothing; because, so far as He delivers us from these, He has accomplished the work which He was sent to do. Let us act and think more nearly as we pray.

# CHAPTER XIII.

## THE ROMAN CATACOMBS.

THE belief of the early Christians, that is, of the Christians from the close of the first century to the conversion of the Empire at the beginning of the fourth, is a question which is at once more difficult and more easy to answer than we might have thought beforehand.

It is in one sense extremely difficult.

The popular, the actual belief of a generation or society of men cannot always be ascertained from the contemporary writers, who belong for the most part to another stratum. The belief of the people of England at this moment is something separate from the books, the newspapers, the watchwords of parties. It is in the air. It is in their intimate conversation. We must hear, especially in the case of the simple and unlearned, what they talk of to each other. We must sit by their bedsides; get at what gives them most consolation, what most occupies their last moments. This, whatever it be, is the belief of the people, right or wrong—this, and this only is their real religion. A celebrated Roman Catholic divine of the present day has described, in a few short sentences, what he conceives to be the religious creed of the people of England :—that it consists of a general belief in Providence and in a future life. He is probably right. But it is something quite apart from any formal creeds or confessions or watchwords which exist. Is it possible to ascertain this concerning the early Christians? The books of that period are few and far between, and these books are, for the most part, the works of learned scholars rather than of popular writers. Can we apart from such books discover what was their most ready and constant representation of their dearest hopes here and hereafter? Strange to say, after all this lapse of time it is possible. The answer, at any rate for that large mass of Christians from all parts of the empire that was collected in the capital, is to be found in the Roman Catacombs.

It is not necessary to enter upon the formation of the Catacombs. For a general view it may be sufficient to refer to 'On Pagan and Christian Sepulture,' in the 'Essays' of Dean Milman. For the details of the question it is more than sufficient to refer to the great work of Commendatore De Rossi. It has been amply proved by the investigations of the last two hundred, and especially of the last thirty years, that there were in the neighbourhood of Rome, from the first beginning of the settlement of the Jews in the city, large galleries dug in the rock, which they used for their places of burial. The Christians, following the example of the Jews, did the same on a larger scale. In these galleries they wrote on the graves of their friends the thoughts that were most consoling to themselves, or painted on the walls the figures which gave them most pleasure. By a singular chance these memorials have been preserved to us by the very causes which have destroyed so much beside. The Catacombs were deserted at the time of the invasion of the barbarians, and filled up with ruins and rubbish; and from the sixth to the seventeenth century no one thought it worth while to explore them. The burial of Christian antiquity was as complete as that of Pagan antiquity, and the resurrection of both took place nearly at the same time. The desertion, the overthrow of these ancient galleries has been to the Christian life of that time what the overthrow of Pompeii by the ashes of Vesuvius was to the Pagan life of the period immediately antecedent. The Catacombs are the Pompeii of early Christianity. It is much to the credit of the authorities of the

Roman States that at the time when the excavations began they allowed these monuments to speak for themselves. Many questionable interpretations have been put upon them, but in no respect has there been substantiated any charge of wilful falsification.

We confine ourselves to the simple statement of the testimony which they render to the belief of the second and third centuries. For this reason, we exclude from consideration almost, if not altogether, those subsequent to the age of Constantine. We merely state the facts as they occur; and if the results be pleasing or displeasing to the members of this or that school of modern religious opinion, perhaps it will be a sufficient safeguard that they will be almost equally pleasing or displeasing to the members of all such schools alike.

I. First, what do we learn of the state of feeling indicated in the very structure of the Catacombs beyond what any books could teach us?

The Catacombs are the standing monuments of the Oriental and Jewish character even of Western Christianity. The fact that they are the counterparts of the rock-hewn tombs of Palestine, and yet more closely of the Jewish cemeteries in the neighbourhood of Rome, corresponds to the fact that the early Roman Church was not a Latin but an Eastern community, speaking Greek, and following the usages of Syria. And again, the ease with which the Roman Christians had recourse to these cemeteries is an indication of the impartiality of the Roman law, which extended (as De Rossi has well pointed out) to this despised sect the same protection in respect to burial, even during the times of persecution, that was accorded to the highest in the land. They thus bear witness to the unconscious fostering care of the Imperial Government over the infant Church. They are thus monuments, not so much of the persecution as of the toleration, which the Christians received at the hands of the Roman Empire.

These two circumstances, confirmed as they are from

various quarters, are, as it were, the framework in which the ideas of the Church of the Catacombs are enshrined, and yet they are quite unknown to the common ecclesiastical histories.

3. A similar profound ignorance shrouded the existence of the Catacombs themselves. There are no allusions to the Catacombs in Gibbon, or Mosheim, or Neander; nor, in fact, in any ecclesiastical history, down to the close of the first quarter of this century. Dean Milman's ' History of Christianity' was the earliest exception. Nor again is there any allusion in the Fathers to their most striking characteristics. St. Jerome's narrative of being taken into them as a child is simply a description of the horror they inspired. Prudentius has a passing allusion to the paintings, but nothing that gives a notion of their extent and importance.

II. We now proceed to the beliefs themselves, as presented in the pictures or inscriptions, confining ourselves as much as possible to those which are earliest and most universal. But before entering on these, let us glance for a moment at those which, though belonging to the latest years of this period—the close of the third century—yet still illustrate the general character even of the earlier. The subjects of these paintings are for the most part taken from the Bible, and are as follows : In the New Testament they are the Adoration of the Magi, the Feeding of the Disciples, Zacchæus in the Sycamore, the Healing of the Paralytic, the Raising of Lazarus, the Washing of Pilate's Hands,[1] Peter's Denial, the Seizure of Peter by the Jews. In the Old Testament they are the Creation, the Sacrifice of Isaac, the Stag desiring the Water Brooks, the Striking of the Rock, Jonah and the Whale, Jonah under the Gourd, Daniel in the Lions' Den, the Three Children in the Fire, Susanna and the Elders.

On this selection we will make three general remarks. 1. Whilst it does not coincide with the theology and the art

*The pictures.*

---

[1] Tertullian (*on the Lord's Prayer*, c. 13) censures strongly the practice of washing hands before prayer, and says that on inquiry he found it was in imitation of Pilate's act.

of the modern Western Church, it coincides to a certain degree with the selection that we find in the Eastern Church. The Raising of Lazarus, for example, fell completely out of the range of the Italian painters and out of the scholastic theology of the Middle Ages ; but it may still be traced in the Byzantine traditions as preserved in Russia. In one of the most ancient chapels of the Kremlin there is a representation of the mummy-like form of Lazarus issuing from his tomb, exactly similar to that which appears in the Roman Catacombs. The Three Children, who cease to occupy any important place in the Latin Church, are repeatedly brought forward in the Eastern Church. Three choristers stand in front of the altar at a particular part of the service to represent them, and the only attempt at a mystery or miracle play in the Middle Ages of Russia was the erection of a large wooden platform with the painted appearance of fire underneath, on which three actors stood forth and played by gesture and song the part of the Three Children.

*Continuance in the Eastern, neglect in the Western Church.*

2. Secondly, the mere fact of paintings at all in these early chapels is in direct contradiction to the general condemnation of any painting of sacred subjects in the writers[2] of the first centuries. It is as if the popular sentiment had not only run counter to the written theology, but had been actually ignorant of it.

*Contradiction of theological writers.*

3. Thirdly, the selection of these subjects, whether in the Eastern or in the Western Church, is quite out of proportion to the choice of these same subjects in the books of the time that have come down to us. Few of them are conspicuously present in the writers of the three first, or indeed of the sixteen first centuries ; and of one of them at least, the arrest of Peter by the Jewish soldiers, it is not too much to say that there is no incident recorded in any extant books to which it can with certainty be applied at all.

*Absence of allusion in books of the time.*

---

[2] See the summary of opinions of the Fathers on art in the English translation of Tertullian in the Library of the Fathers. (Notes to the *Apology*, vol. ii. p. 110.)

These points do not illustrate any contradiction to the existing opinions either of Protestant or Catholic Churches in modern times. The subjects to which these paintings relate for the most part do not involve, even by remote implication, any of these disputed opinions. But they indicate a difference deeper than any mere expression of particular doctrines. They show that the current of early Christian thought ran in an altogether different channel, both from the contemporary writers of the early period, and also both from the paintings and the writings of the later period. In the collection of the works of the Fathers of the second and third centuries, it is difficult to find allusion to any one of these topics. Of the paintings of the tenth and eleventh centuries recently discovered in the subterranean church of St. Clement at Rome, not one of all the numerous series is identical with those in the Catacombs.

III. But this peculiarity of the Catacombs thus visible to a certain extent even in the third century, appears still more forcibly when we confine ourselves to the earliest chambers, and to the most important figures which they contain.

There is one such chamber especially, which, according to the Commendatore De Rossi, is the earliest that can be found, reaching back to the beginning of the second century. It is that commonly known as the Catacomb of Sts. Nereus and Achilleus, otherwise of St. Domitilla.

In this chamber there are three general characteristics:—

1. Everything is cheerful and joyous. This, to a certain degree, pervades all the Catacombs. Although some of them *Cheerfulness.* must have been made in times of persecution, yet even in these the nearest approach to such images of distress and suffering is in the figures before noticed—(and these are not found in the earliest stage)—the Three Children in the Fire, Daniel in the Lions' Den, and Jonah naked under the Gourd. But of the mournful emblems which belong to nearly all the later ages of Christianity, almost all are wanting in almost all the Catacombs. There is neither the cross of the fifth or sixth century, nor the crucifix or the crucifixion of

the twelfth or thirteenth, nor the tortures and martyrdoms of the seventeenth, nor the skeletons of the fifteenth, nor the cypresses and death's heads of the eighteenth. There are, instead, wreaths of roses, winged genii, children playing. This is the general ornamentation. It is a variation not noticed in ordinary ecclesiastical history. But it is there. There are two words used in the very earliest account of the very earliest Christian community to which the English language furnishes no exact equivalent; one is their exulting, bounding gladness ($\dot{\alpha}\gamma\alpha\lambda\lambda\dot{\iota}\alpha\sigma\iota s$); the other, their simplicity and smoothness of feeling, as of a plain without stones, of a field without furrows ($\dot{\alpha}\phi\epsilon\lambda\dot{o}\tau\eta s$). These two words from the records of the first century [3] represent to us what appears in the second century in the Roman Catacombs. It may be doubted whether they have ever been equally represented at any subsequent age.

2. Connected with this fact is another. It is astonishing how many of these decorations are taken from heathen sources and copied from heathen paintings. There is Orpheus playing on his harp to the beasts; there is Bacchus as the God of the vintage; there is Psyche, the butterfly of the soul; there is the Jordan as the God of the river. The Classical and the Christian, the Hebrew and the Hellenic, elements had not yet parted. The strict demarcation which the books of the period would imply between the Christian Church and the heathen world had not yet been formed, or was constantly effaced. The Catacombs have more affinity with the chapel of Alexander Severus, which contained Orpheus side by side with Abraham and Christ, than they have with the writings of Tertullian, who spoke of heathen poets only to exult in their future torments, or of Augustine, who regarded this very Orpheus only as a mischievous teacher to be disparaged, not as a type of the union of the two forms of heathen and Christian civilisation. It agrees with the fact that the funeral inscriptions are often addressed *Dis Manibus,* ' to the funeral spirits.'

<hr>

[3] Acts ii. 46

3. We see in the earliest chambers not only the beginning, but in a certain sense the end of early Christian art. By Early Christian art. the time we reach the fourth century the figures are misshapen, rude, and stiff, partaking of that decadence which marks the Arch of Constantine, and which is developed into the forms afterwards called Byzantine. But in the second and third centuries, in the Catacombs of St. Domitilla, of St. Prætextatus, and St. Priscilla, there is in the sweetness of the countenance, the depth of the eyes, the grace and majesty of the forms, an inspiration of a higher source, it may be partly from the contact with the still living art of Greece, it may be from the contact with a purer and higher flame of devotion not yet burnt out in fierce controversy.

There is a figure which occurs constantly in the Catacombs, and which in those earliest of all has a peculiar grace of its own —that of the dead person represented in the peculiar position of prayer, which has now entirely ceased in all Christian churches, but as it may still now and then be seen in Mahometan countries—the attitude of standing with the hands stretched out to receive the gifts which Heaven would pour into them. Such are the figures of the ' Oranti,' as they are technically called, in the Catacombs, men or women, according to the sex of the departed. Such also were the holy hands and upturned eyes of the worshippers in the heathen temples of Greece or Rome. The most perfect representation of this in Christian art is, perhaps, that of the departed Christian in the Catacomb of St. Priscilla. The most perfect representation of this in heathen art is, perhaps, that of the bronze figure of an adoring youth, found in the Rhine, of this same period of the Roman Empire, and now in the Museum at Berlin. An animated description which has been given of this statue in a recent work devoted to Greek art, might, with a few changes of expression, be applied to the painting of the departed Christian in the Catacomb of St. Priscilla. ' His eyes and arms are raised to heaven ; perfect in humanity beneath the lightsome vault of heaven, he stands and prays

—no adoration with veiled eyes and muttering lips— no prostration, with the putting off of sandals on holy ground— no genuflexion, like the bending of a reed waving with the wind,—but such as Iamus in the mid waves of Alpheius might have prayed when he heard the voice of Phœbus calling to him, and promising to him the twofold gift of prophecy.'

Such is the ideal of the worshipping youth of a Pagan temple of that period—such is the transfigured ideal of the worshipping maiden or matron in the Christian Catacomb. Such has not been the ideal of worship in any later age of the Church.

IV. But the question might here be asked, if these sacred decorations are so like what we find in heathen tombs or houses, how do we know that we are in a Christian burial-place at all? What is the sign that we are here in the chamber of a Christian family? What is the test, what is the watchword, by which these early Christians were known from those who were not Christians?

We have already indicated some of the Biblical subjects; we also know well what we should find in the various later churches, whether Greek, Latin, Anglican, Lutheran, or Non-conformist. Some distinctive emblems we should find every-where, either in books, pictures, or statues. But none of these were in the Catacombs even of the third century; and in the Catacombs of the second century not even those which are found in the third and fourth centuries.

1. What, then, is the test or sign of Christian popular belief that in these earliest representations of Christianity is handed down to us as the most cherished, the all-sufficing token of their creed? It is very simple, *The Good Shepherd.* but it contains a great deal. It is a shepherd in the bloom of youth, with a crook or a shepherd's pipe in one hand, and on his shoulder a lamb, which he carefully carries and holds with the other hand. We see at once who it is; we all know without being told. There are two passages in two of the sacred books, which, whatever may be the critical discussion about their

dates, must be inferred from these paintings to have been by that time firmly rooted in the popular belief of the community. One is that from the Third Gospel, which speaks of the shepherd going over the hills of Palestine to seek the sheep that was lost; the other, that from the Fourth Gospel, which says, 'I am the Good Shepherd,' or, as perhaps we might venture to translate it, 'I am the Beautiful Shepherd.' This, in that earliest chamber or church of a Christian family of which we are chiefly speaking, is the one sign of Christian life and of Christian belief. But as it is the only, or almost the only sign of Christian belief in this earliest Catacomb, so it continues (with those other pictures of which we have spoken) always the chief, always the prevailing sign, as long as those burial-places were used. Sometimes it is with one sheep, sometimes with several sheep in various attitudes; some listening to his voice, some turning away. Sometimes it appears in chapels, sometimes on the tombs themselves; sometimes on the tombs of the humblest and poorest; sometimes in the sepulchres of Emperors and Empresses—Galla Placidia and Honorius—but always the chief mark of the Christian life and faith.

On the other hand there is no allusion to the Good Shepherd (with one exception) in the writers of the second century, and very few in the third; hardly any in Athanasius[4] or in Jerome. If we come down much later, there is hardly any in the 'Summa Theologiæ' of Thomas Aquinas, none in the Tridentine Catechism, none in the Thirty-nine Articles, none in the Westminster Confession. The only prominent allusions we find to this figure in the writers of early times are drawn from that same under-current of Christian society to which the Catacombs themselves belong. One is the allu-

---

[4] Origen (*Hom. v. on Jeremiah* iii., 152) has a somewhat detailed reference. His other allusions are of the most perfunctory kind. So also Cyprian (Clem. Alex. *Pæd.* i. 7, 9 ; *Strom.* i. 26), has similar slight references. There is nothing in Irenæus or Justin, and only three passing notices in Tertullian (De Patientiâ, c. 12 ; De Pudicitiâ, c. 9, 13). A more distinct reference is in the Acts of Perpetua and Felicitas.

sion, in an angry complaint of Tertullian,[5] to the chalices used in the Communion, on which the Good Shepherd was a frequent subject; the other is in the once popular book of devotion, the 'Pilgrim's Progress' of the Church of the second century, which was spread far and wide from Italy even to Greece, Egypt, and Abyssinia, namely, the once universal, once canonical, once inspired, now forgotten and disparaged, but always curious book called the 'Shepherd of Hermas.'

This disproportion between the almost total absence of this figure in the works of the learned, and its predominant prevalence where we most surely touch the hearts and thoughts of the first Christians—this gives the answer to the question, —What was the popular Religion of the first Christians? It was, in one word, the Religion of the Good Shepherd. The kindness, the courage, the grace, the love, the beauty, of the Good Shepherd was to them, if we may so say, Prayer Book and Articles, Creed and Canons, all in one. They looked on that figure, and it conveyed to them all that they wanted. As ages passed on, the Good Shepherd faded away from the mind of the Christian world, and other emblems of the Christian faith have taken his place. Instead of the gracious and gentle Pastor, there came the Omnipotent Judge, or the Crucified Sufferer, or the Infant in His Mother's arms, or the Master in His Parting Supper, or the figures of innumerable saints and angels, or the elaborate expositions of the various forms of theological controversy.

These changes may have been inevitable. Christianity is too vast and complex to be confined to the expressions of any single age, or of any single nation, and what was suitable for one age may become unsuited for another. Still, it is useful for us to go back to this its earliest form, and ask what must have been the ideas suggested by it.

(a) It was an instance of that general connection

---

[5] 'As this is a singular instance only of a symbolical representation or emblem, so it is the only instance Petavius pretends to find in all the three first ages.' (Bingham, viii. 8.) So Bingham and Petavius thought. They little knew that the Good Shepherd was the constant Christian emblem.

just now noticed between the new Christian belief and the old Pagan world.  A figure not unlike the Good Shepherd had from time to time appeared in the Grecian wor-ship.  There was the Hermes Kriophorus—Mercury with the ram—as described by Pausanias.  There were also the figures of dancing shepherds in the tombs of the Nasones near Rome.  In one instance in the Christian Catacombs, the Good Shepherd appears surrounded by the Three Graces.[6] In the tomb of Galla Placidia, He might well be the youthful Apollo playing with his pipes to the flocks of Admetus. There had not yet sprung up the fear of taking as the chief symbol of Christianity an idea or a figure which would be equally acknowledged by Pagans.

*Connection with heathen belief.*

(*b*) It represents to us the joyful, cheerful side of Christianity, of which we spoke before.  Look at that beautiful, graceful figure, bounding down as if from his native hills, with the happy sheep nestling on his shoulder, with the pastoral pipes in his hand, blooming in immortal youth.  It is the exact representation of the Italian shepherd as we constantly encounter him on the Sabine hills at this day, holding the stray lamb on his shoulders, with a strong hand grasping the twisted legs as they hang on his breast.  Just such a one appears on a fresco in the so-called house of Livia, on the Palatine.  That is the primitive conception of the Founder of Christianity.  It is the very reverse of that desponding, foreboding, wailing cry that we have often heard in later days, as if His religion were going to die out of the world ; as if He were some dethroned prince, whose cause was to be cherished only by the reactionary, losing, vanquished parties of the world or Church.  The popular conception of Him in the early Church was of the strong, the joyous youth, of eternal growth, of immortal grace.

*The joyous aspect of Christianity.*

(*c*) It represents to us an aspect of the early Christian belief that has not been common in later times, but of which we find occasional traces even in the writings of these earlier centuries, namely, that the first

*The latitude of early Christianity.*

* De Rossi, ii. 358.

object of the Christian community was not to repel, but to include—not to condemn, but to save.　In some of the paintings of the Good Shepherd, this aspect of the subject is emphasised by representing the creature on his shoulder to be not a lamb, but a kid; not a sheep, but a goat.

It is this which provokes the indignant remonstrance of Tertullian in the only passage of the Fathers which contains a distinct reference to the popular representation of the Good Shepherd; and it is on this unchristian protest that Matthew Arnold founds one of his most touching poems.

> *He saves the sheep, the goats he doth not save.*
>
> .　　　.　　　.　　　.　　　.
>
> So spake the fierce Tertullian.　But she sigh'd—
> The infant Church ! of love she felt the tide
> Stream on her from her Lord's yet recent grave
> And then she smil'd; and in the Catacombs
> With eye suffused but heart inspired true,
>
> .　　　.　　　.　　　.　　　.　　　.
>
> She her Good Shepherd's hasty image drew—
> And on his shoulders, not a lamb, a kid.

(*d*) It represents to us the extreme simplicity of this early belief.　It seems as if that key-note was then struck in the popular Christianity of those first ages, which has in its best aspects made it the religion of little children and guileless peasants, and also of childlike philosophers and patriarchal sages.

The simplicity of the early Christianity.

There is nothing here strange, difficult, mysterious.　But there was enough to satisfy the early Christian, to nerve the suffering martyr, to console the mourner.　When Bosio, the first explorer of the Catacombs in the seventeenth century, opened the tomb of which we have been speaking, he was disappointed when he found only the Good Shepherd, and went on to other later chambers and chapels, where there were other more varied pictures, and other more complicated emblems.　He did not know that this one, which he despised for its simplicity, was the most interesting of all, because the earliest of all.

It is possible that others, like Bosio, have gone farther

and fared worse in their dissatisfaction at so simple a representation. It is certain, as has been said, that, till quite modern times,[7] the Good Shepherd, and the ideas which the figure suggested, had become as strange and rare as the doctrines of later times would have seemed strange to the dwellers in the Catacombs.

2. The Good Shepherd, however, is not the only figure which pervades the tomb of Domitilla. There is another which also, in like manner, predominates elsewhere.

It is a vine painted on the roof and on the walls, with its branches spreading and twisting themselves in every direction, loaded with clusters of grapes, and seeming to reach over the whole chamber. And sometimes this figure of the Vine is the only sign of Christian belief. In the tomb of Constantia, the sister of the Emperor Constantine, even the Good Shepherd does not appear ; the only decorations that are carved on her coffin and painted on the walls are children gathering the vintage, plucking the grapes, carrying baskets of grapes on their heads, dancing on the grapes to press out the wine. The period in which the figure of the Vine appears is more restricted than that in which the figure of the Shepherd appears. But taking, again, the tomb of Domitilla as our main example, it is undeniable that if the chief thought of the early Christians was the Good Shepherd, the second was the Vine and the Vintage.

*The vine.*

What is the meaning of this ? There are three ideas which we may suppose to have been represented.

(*a*) The first is that which we have noticed before—the joyous and festive character of the primitive Christian faith. In Eastern countries the vintage is the great holiday of the year. In the Jewish Church there was no festival so gay and so free as the Feast of Tabernacles, when they gathered the fruit of the vineyard, and enjoyed themselves in their green bowers or tabernacles.

*Its joyousness.*

<hr>

[7] It occurs in the pictures of the French Huguenots of the 17th century, preserved in the Protestant Library in the Place Vendôme. See also Rowland Hill's use of it in his *Token of Lore* (*Life of Rowland Hill*, p. 428). In the latter half of this century it has become popular in the Roman Church.

Lord Macaulay once described, with all his force of language and variety of illustration, how natural and beautiful was the origin of the heathen legend, which represented the victorious march of Dionysus, the inventor of the vine, and how everyone must have been entranced at the coming in of their new guest—the arrival of the life-giving grape—scattering joy and merriment wherever he came. Something of this kind seems to have been the sentiment of the early Christian community. No doubt the monastic and the Puritan element existed amongst them in germ, and showed itself in the writings even of the second and third centuries; but it is evident from these paintings that it occupied a very subordinate place in the popular mind of the early Roman Christians.

It may be that the hideous associations which northern drunkenness has imported into these festive emblems have rendered impossible to modern times a symbol which in earlier days and in southern countries was still permissible. It may be that after the disappointments, controversies, persecutions, mistakes, scandals, follies of Christendom for the last seventeen centuries, it is impossible to imagine that buoyant heart, that hopeful spirit, which then was easy and natural. Not the less, however, is it instructive for us to see the joyous gaiety, the innocent Bacchanalia, with which our first fathers started in the dawn of that journey which has since been so often overcast.

(*b*) There was, however, perhaps a deeper thought in this figure. When we see the vine, with its purple clusters spreading itself over the roof of the chamber, it is difficult not to feel that the early Christians had before their minds the recollection of the Parable of 'The Vine and the Branches.' When we remark the juice of the grapes streaming from the feet of those who tread the wine-press—the figures, frequent in the Jewish Scriptures, represented in colossal form over the portal of the Jewish Temple carved still on Jewish sepulchres—it is the same image which culminated to the Christian mind in that sacred apologue.

Its diffusion.

It was the account which they gave to themselves and to others of the benefits of their new religion. What they valued, what they felt, was a new moral influence, a new life stealing through their veins, a new health imparted to their frames, a new courage breathing in their faces, like wine to a weary labourer, like sap in the hundred branches of a spreading tree, like juice in the thousand clusters of a spreading vine.

Where this life was, there was the sign of their religion. By what special channel it came, whether through books or treatises, whether through bishops or presbyters, whether through this doctrine or that, this the paintings in the Catacombs—at least in the earliest Catacombs—do not tell us. All that we see is the Good Shepherd on one side, and the spreading Vine and joyous vintage on the other side. It was an influence as subtle, as persuasive, as difficult to fix into one uniform groove, as what we call the influence of love, or marriage, or law, or civilisation.

(c) The figure of the Vine, as seen in the Catacombs, suggests perhaps one other idea—the idea of what was then meant by Christian unity. The branches of the vine are infinite; no other plant throws out so many ramifications which twist and clasp and turn and hang and creep and rise and fall in so many festoons and roots and clusters and branches, over trees and houses; sometimes high, sometimes low, sometimes graceful, sometimes deformed, sometimes straight, sometimes crooked. But in all there is the same life-giving juice, the same delicious fragrance. That is the figure of the Vine as we see it in the tomb of St. Domitilla. It is a likeness—whether intended or not—of the variety and unity of Christian goodness.

Its variety.

V. There is one other subject on which we should naturally expect in these Catacombs to learn some tidings of the belief of the early Christians, and that is concerning the future life and the departed. This we gather partly from their paintings, but chiefly from their epitaphs.

The epitaphs.

In these representations there are three such characteristics, agreeing with what we have already noticed.

1. First, there is the same simplicity.  If for a moment we look at the paintings of this subject, in what form are the souls of the dead presented to us?  Almost always in the form of little birds; sometimes with <sup>Their simplicity.</sup> bright, gay plumage—peacocks, pheasants, and the like; more often as doves.  There was here, no doubt, the childlike thought, that the soul of man is like a bird of passage, which nestles here in the outward frame of flesh for a time, and then flies away beyond the sea to some brighter, warmer home.  There was the thought that the Christian soul ought to be like 'the birds of the air,' according to the Gospel phrase, without anxiety or solicitude.  There was the thought also that each Christian soul is, like the dove, a messenger of peace, is part of the heavenly brood which flies upwards towards that spirit of which it is the emanation and the likeness.

And when we come to the epitaphs of the ancient dead we find still the same simple feeling.  There is no long description; till the third century, not even the date; no formal profession of belief; no catalogue either of merits or demerits; but, generally speaking, one short word to tell of the tender sentiment of natural affection : ' My most sweet child ; ' ' My most sweet wife ; ' ' My most dear husband ; ' ' My innocent dove ; ' 'My well-deserving father or mother ; ' ' Innocent little lamb ; ' ' Such and such an one lived together, without any complaint or quarrel, without taking or giving offence.'

Amongst all the epitaphs and monuments of Westminster Abbey, there is one, and one only, which reminds us of the Catacombs.  It is that of a little Yorkshire girl, who lies in the cloisters, and who died in the midst of the troubles which preceded the Revolution of 1688.  There are just the dates, and the name of her brother, whom the parents had lost a short time before, and who is buried in St. Helen's Church, in York : and all that they say of her or of the crisis of the age is, ' *Jane Lister, dear child.*'  That is exactly like the Catacombs; that is the perpetual sympathy of human nature.

In these words the whole Christian world, from the nineteenth century to the first, 'is kin.'

And if, in the outpouring of this natural affection, the survivors from time to time refuse to lose sight of the dead in the other world, it is still to be remarked that the communion with them rests on this family bond, and on none other. There is a touching devotional poem of modern date, which seems more than any other to recall the peculiar feeling of the early Catacombs in this respect. It is that of the Russian poet Chamiakoff, on visiting the nursery of his dead children :—

> Time was when I loved at still midnight to come,
> My children, to see you asleep in your room ;
> Dear children, at that same still midnight do ye,
> As I once prayed for you, now in turn pray for me.[8]

2. But besides these expressions of natural affection, there are two expressions of religious devotion which constantly occur. The first is repeated almost in every epitaph
The idea of rest.
—'*In peace.*' It is the phrase which the early Christians took from the Jews. In the Jewish Catacombs it is found in the Hebrew word—'*Shalom.*' As the expressions just quoted indicate the link between the belief of the early Christians and the natural feelings of the human heart, so does this indicate the link between their belief and that of ancient Judaism. But its earnest reiteration gives a special force to it. It conveys their assurance that whatever else was the other world, it was at least a world of rest. The wars, the jealousies, the jars, the contentions, the misapprehensions, the disputes of the Roman Empire and of the Christian Church, would there at last be finished. 'Sleep' —'repose'—is the word—indefinite, but sufficient—for the condition of their departed friends. The burial places of the world henceforth became what they were first called in the Catacombs—or at least first[9] called on an extensive scale—'cemeteries,' that is, 'sleeping-places.'

---

[8] I have ventured to borrow the translation of the Rev. William Palmer.

[9] Mommsen says that the words κοιμητήριον, *accubitorium*, are not exclusively Christian. But for practical purposes they are so.

3. There is one other phrase which occurs frequently after the mention of 'peace,' and that is, '*Live in God,*' or 'thou shalt live in God,' or 'mayest thou live in God,' or 'thou livest in God.' This is the yet farther The idea of immortality. step from simple innocence, from Oriental resignation. That is the early Christians' expression of the ground of their belief in immortality. We might perhaps have expected some more precise allusion to the sacred name by which they were especially called, or to some of those Gospel stories of which we do, at least in the third century, find representations in their pictures. But in these epitaphs it is not so. They were content in the written expression of their belief to repose their hopes in the highest name of all.

These simple words—'*Vive in Deo*' and '*Vivas in Deo*' —sometimes it is '*Vive in Bono*'—describe what to them was the object and the ground of their existence for the first three centuries. They last appear in the year 330, and after that appear no more again till quite modern times, in express imitation of them, as for example in the beautiful epitaph on the late lamented Duke John of Torlonia, in the Church of St. John Lateran. As a general rule, nowhere now, either in Roman Catholic or Protestant churches, do we ever see these once universal expressions of the ancient hope. They have been superseded by more definite, more detailed, more positive statements. Perhaps if they were now used they would be thought Deistic, or Theistic, or Pantheistic, or Atheistic. But when we reflect upon them, they run very deep down into the heart both of philosophy and of Christianity. They express the hope that, because the Supreme Good lives for ever, all that is good and true will live for ever also. They express the hope that because the Universal Father lives for ever, we can safely trust into His loving hands the souls of those whom we have loved, and whom He, we cannot help believing, has loved also.

Perhaps the more we think of this ancient style of epitaph, the more we shall find that it is not the less true because it is now never written; not the less consoling because it is so ancient; not the less comprehensive because it is so simple, so short, and so childlike.

VI. Let us briefly sum up what has been said on these representations of the early Christian belief.

1. They differ widely in proportion, in selection, and in character, from the representations of belief which we find in the contemporaneous Christian authors, and thus give us a striking example of the divergence which often exists between the actual living, popular belief, and that which we find in books. They differ also in the same respects, though even more widely, from the forms adopted, not only by ourselves, but by the whole of Christendom, for nearly fifteen hundred years. They show, what it is never without interest to observe, the immense divergence in outward expression of belief between those ages and our own. The forms which we use were unused by them, and the forms which they used for the most part are unused by us.

2. The substance of the faith which these forms expressed is such as, when it is put before us, we at once recognise to be true.

It might sometimes be worth while to ask whether what are called attacks or defences of our religion are directed in the slightest degree for or against the ideas which, as we have seen, constitute the chief materials of the faith and life · of the early Christians. In a well-known work of Strauss, entitled 'The Old and New Belief,' there is an elaborate attack on what the writer calls 'the Old Belief.' Of the various articles of that 'old belief' which he enumerates, hardly one appears conspicuously in the Catacombs. Of the special forms of belief which appear in the Catacombs, hardly one is mentioned in the catalogue of doctrines so vehemently assailed in that work. The belief of the Catacombs, as a general rule, is not that which is either defended by modern theologians [1] or attacked by modern sceptics.

[1] In the Lateran Museum are two or three compartments of epitaphs classed under the head of 'illustrations of *dogmas*.' But there is only one

3. When we reflect that these same ideas which formed
the all-sufficing creed of the early Church, are not openly
disputed by any Church or sect in Christendom, it may be
worth while to ask whether, after all, there is anything very
absurd in supposing that all Christians have something in
common with each other. The pictures of the Good Shepherd
and of the Vine, the devotional language of the epitaphs—
whether we call them sectarian or unsectarian, denomina-
tional or undenominational—have not been watchwords of
parties; no public meetings have been held for defending or
abolishing them, no persecutions or prosecutions have been
set on foot to put them down or to set them up. And yet
it is certain that, by the early Christians, they were not
thought vague, fleeting, unsubstantial, colourless, but were
the food of their daily lives, their hope under the severest
trials, the dogma of dogmas, if we choose so to call them,
the creed of their creed, because the very life of their life.

doubtful example of any passage relating to a dogma controverted by any
Christian Church.

# CHAPTER XIV.

## THE CREED OF THE EARLY CHRISTIANS.

The formula into which the early Christian belief shaped itself has since grown up into the various creeds which have been adopted by the Christian Church. The two most widely known are that of Chalcedon, commonly called the Nicene Creed, and that of the Roman Church, commonly called the Apostles'. The first is that which pervaded the Eastern Church. Its original form was that drawn up at Nicæa on the basis of the creed of Cæsarea produced by Eusebius. Large additions were made to it to introduce the dogmatical questions discussed in the Nicene Council. It concluded with anathemas on all who pronounced the Son to be of a different Hypostasis from the Father. Another Creed much resembling this, but with extensive additions at the close, and with an omission of the anathemas, was said to have been made at the Constantinopolitan Council, but was first proclaimed at the Council of Chalcedon.[1] It underwent a yet further change in the West from the adoption of the clause which states that the Holy Ghost proceeds from the Son, as well as from the Father. The Creed of the Roman Church came to be called the 'Apostles' Creed,' from the fable that the twelve Apostles had each of them contributed a clause. It was successively enlarged. First was added the ' Remission of Sins,' next ' the Life Eternal.' Then came[2] the ' Resur-

---

[1] See Chapter XVI.

[2] This clause unquestionably conveys the belief, so emphatically contradicted by St. Paul (1 Cor. xv. 35, 36, 50), of the Resurrection of the

rection of the Flesh.'   Lastly was incorporated the 'Descent [3] into Hell,' and the 'Communion of the Saints.'   It is observable that the Creed, whether in its Eastern or its Western form, leaves out of view altogether such questions as the necessity of Episcopal succession, the origin and use of the Sacraments, the honour due to the Virgin Mary, the doctrine of Substitution, the doctrine of Predestination, the doctrine of Justification, the doctrine of the Pope's authority. These may be important and valuable, but they are not in any sense part of the authorised creed of the early Christians. The doctrine of Baptism appears in the Constantinopolitan Creed, but merely in the form of a protest against its repetition.   The doctrine of Justification might possibly be connected with 'the Forgiveness of Sins,' but no theory is expressed on the subject.   Again, most of the successive clauses were added for purposes peculiar to that age, and run, for the most part, into accidental questions which had arisen in the Church.   The Conception, the Descent into Hell, the Communion of Saints, the Resurrection of the Flesh, are found only in the Western, not in the original Nicene Creed.   The controversial expressions respecting the Hypostasis and the Essence of the Divinity are found only in the Eastern, not in the Western Creed.

But there is one point which the two Creeds both have in common.   It is the framework on which they are formed. That framework is the simple expression of faith used in the Baptism of the early Christians.   It is taken from the First Gospel,[4] and it consists of 'the name of the Father, the Son, and the Holy Ghost.'

corporeal frame.  It has been softened in the modern rendering into the 'Resurrection of the Body,' which, although still open to misconception, is capable of the spiritual sense of the Apostle.  But in the Baptismal Service the original clause is presented in its peculiarly offensive form.

[3] This was perhaps originally a synonym for 'He was buried,' as it occurs in those versions of the Creed where the burial is omitted.  But it soon came to be used as the expression for that vast system—partly of fantastic superstition, partly of valuable truth—involved in the deliverance of the early Patriarchs by the entrance of the Saviour into the world of shades.

[4] It is not certain that in early times this formula was in use.  The

I. It is proposed to ask, in the first instance, the Biblical meaning of the words. In the hymn *Quicunque vult*, as in Dean Swift's celebrated 'Sermon on the Trinity,' there is no light whatever thrown on their signification. They are used like algebraic symbols, which would be equally appropriate if they were inverted, or if other words were substituted for them. They give no answer to the question what in the minds of the early Christians they represented.

1. What, then, is meant in the Bible—what in the experience of thoughtful men—by the name of *The Father*? In one word it expresses to us the whole faith of what we call *Natural* Religion. We see it in all religions. 'Not only is the omnipresence of something which passes comprehension, that most distinct belief which is common to all religions, which becomes the more distinct in proportion as things develope, and which remains after their discordant elements have been cancelled; but it is that belief which the most unsparing criticism leaves unquestionable, or rather makes ever clearer. It has nothing to fear from the most inexorable logic; but, on the contrary, is a belief which the most inexorable logic shows to be more profoundly true than any religion supposes.'[5] As mankind increases in civilisation, there is an increasing perception of order, design, and good-will towards the living creatures which animate it. Often, it is true, we cannot trace any such design; but whenever we can, the impression left upon us is the sense of a Single, Wise, Beneficent Mind. And in our own hearts and consciences we feel an instinct corresponding to this—a voice, a faculty, that seems to refer us to a Higher Power than ourselves, and to point to some Invisible Sovereign Will, like to that which we see impressed on the

first profession of belief was only in the name of the Lord Jesus (Acts ii. 38, viii. 12, 16, x. 48, xix. 5). In later times, Cyprian (Ep. lxiii.), the Council of Frejus, and Pope Nicholas the First acknowledge the validity of this form. Still it soon superseded the profession of belief in Jesus Christ, and in the second century had become universal. (See *Dictionary of Christian Antiquities*, i. 162.)

[5] Herbert Spencer, *First Principles*, p. 15.

natural world.   And, further, the more we think of the Supreme, the more we try to imagine what His feelings are towards us—the more our idea of Him becomes fixed in the one simple, all-embracing word that He is the *Father*.   The word itself has been given to us by Christ.   It is the peculiar revelation of the Divine nature made by Christ Himself.   Whereas it is used three times in the Old Testament, it is used two hundred times in the New.   But it was the confirmation of what was called by Tertullian the testimony of the naturally Christian soul—*testimonium animæ naturaliter Christianæ*.   The Greek expression of ' the Father of Gods and men ' is an approach towards it.   There may be much in the dealings of the Supreme and Eternal that we do not understand; as there is much in the dealings of an earthly father that his earthly children cannot understand. Yet still to be assured that there is One above us whose praise is above any human praise—who sees us as we really are—who has our welfare at heart in all the various dispensations which befall us—whose wide-embracing justice and long-suffering and endurance we all may strive to obtain— this is the foundation with which everything in all subsequent religion must be made to agree.   ' One thing alone is certain : the Fatherly smile which every now and then gleams through Nature, bearing witness that an Eye looks down upon us, that a Heart follows us.'[6]   To strive to be perfect as our Father is perfect is the greatest effort which the human soul can place before itself.   To repose upon this perfection is the greatest support which in sorrow and weakness it can have in making those efforts.   This is the expression of Natural Religion.   This is the revelation of God the Father.

2. What is meant by the name of the Son ?

It has often happened that the conception of Natural Religion becomes faint and dim.   ' The being of a God is as certain to me as the certainty of my own existence.   Yet when I look out of myself into the world of men, I see a

* Renan's *Hibbert Lectures for* 1880, p. 202.

sight which fills me with unspeakable distress. The world of men seems simply to give the lie to that great truth of which my whole being is so full. If I looked into a mirror and did not see my face, I should experience the same sort of difficulty that actually comes upon me when I look into this living busy world and see no reflection of its Creator.'[7] How is this difficulty to be met? How shall we regain in the world of men the idea which the world of Nature has suggested to us? How shall the dim remembrance of our Universal Father be so brought home to us as that we shall not forget it or lose it? This is the object of the Second Sacred Name by which God is revealed to us. As in the name of the Father we have *Natural* Religion—the Faith of the Natural Conscience—so in the name of the Son we have *Historical* Religion, or the Faith of the Christian Church. As 'the Father' represents to us God in Nature, God in the heavenly or ideal world—so the name of 'the Son' represents to us God in History, God in the character of man, God, above all, in the Person of Jesus Christ. We know how even in earthly relationships, an absent father, a departed father, is brought before our recollections in the appearance of a living, present son, especially in a son who by the distinguishing features of his mind or of his person is a real likeness of his father. We know also how in the case of those whom we have never seen at all there is still a means of communication with them through reading their letters, their works, their words. So it is in this second great disclosure of the Being of God. If sometimes we find that Nature gives us an uncertain sound of the dealings of God with his creatures, if we find a difficulty in imagining what is the exact character that God most approves, we may be reassured, strengthened, fixed, by hearing or reading of Jesus Christ. The Mahometan rightly objects to the introduction of the paternal and filial relations into the idea of God, when they are interpreted in the gross and literal sense. But in the moral and spiritual sense it is true that the

<hr>

[7] Dr. Newman, *Apologia*, p. 241.

kindness, tenderness, and wisdom we find in Jesus Christ is
the reflection of the same kindness, tenderness, and wisdom
that we recognise in the governance of the universe.  His
life is the Word, the speech that comes to us out of that
eternal silence which surrounds the Unseen Divinity.  He
is the Second Conscience, the external Conscience, reflecting, as it were, and steadying the conscience within each of
us.  And wheresoever in history the same likeness is, or
has been, in any degree reproduced in human character,
there and in that proportion is the same effect produced.
There and in that proportion is the Word which speaks
through every word of human wisdom, and the Light which
lightens with its own radiance every human act of righteousness and of goodness.  In the Homeric representations of
Divinity and of Humanity, what most strikes us is that,
whereas the human characters are, in their measure, winning,
attractive, heroic, the divine characters are capricious, cruel,
revengeful, sensual.  Such an inversion of the true standard
is rectified by the identification of the Divine nature with
the character of Christ.  If in Christ the highest human
virtues are exalted to their highest pitch, this teaches us that,
according to the Christian view, in the Divine nature these
same virtues are still to be found.  If cruelty, caprice, revenge, are out of place in Christ, they are equally out of
place in God.  To believe in the name of Christ, in the
name of the Son, is to believe that God is above all
other qualities a Moral Being—a Being not merely of
power and wisdom, but of tender compassion, of boundless
charity, of discriminating tenderness.  To believe in the
name of Christ is to believe that no other approach to
God exists except through those same qualities of justice,
truth, and love which make up the mind of Christ.  ‘ Ye
believe in God, believe also in me,’ is given as His own
farewell address.  Ye believe in the Father, ye believe in
Religion generally; believe also in the Son, the Christ.
For this is the form in which the Divine Nature has been
made most palpably known to the world, in flesh and blood,

in facts and words, in life and death.  This is the claim that Christianity and Christendom have upon us, with all their infinite varieties of institutions, ordinances, arts, laws, liberties, charities—that they spring forth directly or indirectly from the highest earthly manifestation of Our Unseen Eternal Father.

The amplifications in the Eastern and Western Creeds have, it is true, but a very slight bearing on the nature of the Divine Revelation in Jesus Christ.  They do not touch at all (except in the expression ' Light of Light ') on the moral, which is the only important, aspect of the doctrine.  They entirely (as was observed many years ago by Bishop Thirlwall) ' miss the point.'  Bishop Pearson, in his elaborate dissertation on this article of the Creed, is wholly silent on this subject.  These expositions do not tell us whether the Being of whom they speak was good or wicked, mild or fierce, truthful or untruthful.  The Eastern Creed by its introduction of the expressions ' for us,' ' for our salvation,' to a certain extent conveys the idea that the good of man was the purpose for which He lived and suffered.  But the Western Creed does not contain even these expressions.  The Fifteenth of the XXXIX. Articles, and by implication a single phrase in the Seventeenth, are the only ones which express any belief in the moral excellence of Christ.  The Second, Third, Fourth, Fifth, Thirty-first, which speak on the general subject of His person are silent on this aspect.  The clause which related to the moral side of the Saviour's character, ' Who lived amongst men,' had been in the Palestine Creed, but was struck out of the Eastern Creed at the council of Nicæa.  But nevertheless the original form of the belief in ' the only Son ' remains intact and acknowledged by all.  It contains nothing contrary to His moral perfections; and it may admit them all.  We take the story of the Gospels as it has appeared to Voltaire, Rousseau, Goethe.  We take it in those parts which contain least matter for doubts and difficulties.  We speak of ' the method ' and ' the secret ' of Jesus as they have been presented to us in the most modern works. 'The origin of Christianity forms the most heroic episode of the history of humanity. . . . Never was the religious consciousness more eminently creative; never did it lay down with more absolute authority the law of the future.'[8] It is important to notice that the testimonies to the greatness of this historical revelation are not confined to the ordinary writers on the subject, but are even more powerfully expressed in those who are above the slightest suspicion of any theological bias.

It is not the Bishop of Gloucester and Bristol, it is Matthew Arnold, who affirms,—

Try all the ways to righteousness you can think of, and you will find that no way brings you to it except the way of Jesus, but that this way does bring you to it.

It is not Bishop Lightfoot, it is the author of 'Supernatural Religion,' who asserts,—

The teaching of Jesus carried morality to the sublimest point attained, or even attainable by humanity. The influence of His spiritual religion has been rendered doubly great by the unparalleled purity and elevation of His own character. Surpassing in His sublime simplicity and earnestness the moral grandeur of Châkya-Mouni, and putting to the blush the sometimes sullied, though generally admirable, teaching of Socrates and Plato, and the whole round of Greek philosophers, He presented the rare spectacle of a life, so far as we can estimate it, uniformly noble and consistent with His own lofty principles, so that the 'imitation of Christ,' has become almost the final word in the preaching of His religion, and must continue to be one of the most powerful elements of its permanence.

It is not Lord Shaftesbury, it is the author of 'Ecce Homo,' who says,—

The story of His life will always remain the one record in which the moral perfection of man stands revealed in its root and unity, the hidden spring made palpably manifest by which the whole machine is moved. And as, in the will of God, this unique

<hr>

[8] Renan's *Hibbert Lectures for* 1880, p. 8.

man was elected to a unique sorrow, and holds as undisputed a sovereignty in suffering as in self-devotion, all lesser examples and lives will for ever hold a subordinate place, and serve chiefly to reflect light on the central and original example.

It is no Bampton lecturer, it is John Stuart Mill, who says,—

It is the God incarnate, more than the God of the Jews or of Nature, who, being idealised, has taken so great and salutary a hold on the modern mind. And whatever else may be taken away from us by rational criticism, Christ is still left,—a unique figure, not more unlike all His precursors than all His followers, even those who had the direct benefit of His teaching.

It is not Lacordaire, it is Renan, who affirms,—

In Jesus was condensed all that is good and elevated in our nature. . . . God is in Him. He feels Himself with God, and He draws from His own heart what He tells of His Father. He lives in the bosom of God by the intercommunion of every moment.[9]

Those few years in which that Life was lived on earth gathered up all the historical expressions of religion before and after into one supreme focus. The ' Word made flesh ' was the union of religion and morality, was the declaration that in the highest sense the Image of Man was made after the Image of God. ' Æterna sapientia sese in omnibus rebus, maximè in humanâ mente, omnium maximè in Christo Jesu manifestavit.'[1] In the gallery through which, in Goethe's ' Wilhelm Meister,' the student is led to understand the origin and meaning of religion, he is taught to see in the child which looks upwards the reverence for that which is above us—that is, the worship of the Father. ' This religion we denominate the Ethnic; it is the religion of the nations, and the first happy deliverance from a de-

---

[9] This series of extracts is quoted from an admirable sermon by Mr. Muir, preached before the Synod of Lothian and Tweeddale November 5, 1879.

[1] Spinoza, Ep. xxi. vol. iii. p. 195.

grading fear.' He is taught to see in the child which looks downwards the reverence for that which is beneath us. 'This we name the Christian. What a task it was . . . to recognise humility and poverty, mockery and despising, disgrace and wretchedness and suffering—to recognise these things as divine.' This is the value of what we call *Historical* Religion. This is the eternal, never-dying truth of the sacred name of the Son.

3. But there is yet a third manifestation of God. *Natural* religion may become vague and abstract. *Historical* religion may become, as it often has become, perverted, distorted, exhausted, formalised: its external proofs may become dubious, its inner meaning may be almost lost. There have been oftentimes Christians who were not like Christ—a Christianity which was not the religion of Christ. But there is yet another aspect of the Divine Nature. Besides the reverence for that which is above us, and the reverence for that which is beneath us, there is also the reverence for that which is within us. There is yet (if we may venture to vary Goethe's parable) another form of Religion, and that is *Spiritual* Religion. As the name of the Father represents to us God in Nature, as the name of the Son represents to us God in History, so the name of the Holy Ghost represents to us God in our own hearts and spirits and consciences. This is the still, small voice—stillest and smallest, yet loudest and strongest of all—which, even more than the wonders of nature or the wonders of history, brings us into the nearest harmony with Him who is a Spirit—who, when His closest communion with man is described, can only be described as the Spirit pleading with, and dwelling in, our spirit. When Theodore Parker took up a stone to throw at a tortoise in a pond, he felt himself restrained by something within him. He went home and asked his mother what that something was. She told him that this something was what was commonly called conscience, but she preferred to call it the voice of God within him. This, he said, was the turning-point in his life, and this was his mode of accepting

the truth of the Divinity of the Eternal Spirit that speaks to our spirits.  When Arnold entered with all the ardour of a great and generous nature into the beauty of the natural world, he added: 'If we feel thrilling through us the sense of this natural beauty, what ought to be our sense of moral beauty,—of humbleness, and truth, and self-devotion, and love?  Much more beautiful, because more truly made after God's image, are the forms and colours of kind and wise and holy thoughts and words and actions—more truly beautiful is one hour of an aged peasant's patient cheerfulness and faith than the most glorious scene which this earth can show. For this moral beauty is actually, so to speak, God Himself, and not merely His work.  His living and conscious servants are—it is permitted us to say so—the temples of which the light is God Himself.'

What is here said of the greatness of the revelation of God in the moral and spiritual sphere over His revelation in the physical world, is true in a measure of its greatness over His revelation in any outward form or fact, or ordinance or word. To enter fully into the significance of what is sometimes called the Dispensation of the Holy Spirit, we must grasp the full conception of what in the Bible is meant by that sacred word, used in varying yet homogeneous senses, and all equally intended by the Sacred Name of which we are speaking.  It means the Inspiring Breath,[2] without which all mere forms and facts are dead, and by which all intellectual and moral energy lives.  It means[3] the inward spirit as op- posed to the outward letter.  It means the freedom of the spirit, which blows like the air of heaven where it listeth, and which, wherever it prevails, gives liberty.[4]  It means the power and energy of the spirit, which rises above the[5] weakness and weariness of the flesh—which, in the great movements of Providence,[6] like a mighty rushing wind,

<hr>

[2] Gen. i. 2, vi. 3; Exod. xxxv. 31; Judges xi. 29, xiii. 25, xiv. 6, 19, xv. 14; Isa. lxi. 1; Ezek. i. 12, iii. 12, xxxvii. 14; Luke iv. 18; John i. 33.
[3] Psalm li. 10, 11, 12; 2 Cor. iii. 6.    [4] John iii. 8; 2 Cor. iii. 17.
[5] Matt. xxvi. 41.    [6] Acts ii. 4, 17.

gives life and vigour to the human soul and to the human race.

> One accent of the Holy Ghost
> The heedless world has never lost.

To believe in a Presence [7] within us pleading with our prayers, groaning with our groans, aspiring with our aspirations —to believe in the Divine supremacy of conscience—to believe that the spirit is above the letter—to believe that the substance is above the form [8]—to believe that the meaning is more important than the words—to believe that truth is greater than authority or fashion or imagination,[9] and will at last prevail—to believe that goodness and justice and love are the bonds of perfectness,[1] without which whosoever liveth is counted dead though he live, and which bind together those who are divided in all other things whatsoever—this, according to the Biblical uses of the word, is involved in the expression: 'I believe in the Holy Ghost.' In this sense, there is a close connection between the later additions of the Creeds and the original article on which they depend. The Universal Church, the Forgiveness of Sins, are direct results of the influence of the Divine Spirit on the heart of man. The hope of 'the Resurrection of the Dead and of the Life of the World to Come,' as expressed in the Eastern Creed, are the best expressions of its vitality. The Communion of Saints in the Western Creed is a beautiful expression of its pervasive force. Even the untoward expression, 'the Resurrection of the flesh,' may be taken as an awkward indication of the same aspiration for the triumph of mind over matter.

II. Such is the significance of these three Sacred Names as we consider them apart. Let us now consider what is to be learned from their being thus made the summary of Religion.

1. First it may be observed that there is this in common between the Biblical and the scholastic representations of

---

[7] Rom. viii. 16, 26; Eph. ii. 18.
[9] Gal. v. 22; Eph. v. 9.
[8] John iv. 25.
[1] John xiv. 17, 26; xv. 26; xvi. 13.

the doctrine of the Trinity. They express to us the comprehensiveness and diversity of the Divine Essence. We might perhaps have thought that as God is One, so there could be only one mode of conceiving Him, one mode of approaching Him. But the Bible, when taken from first to last and in all its parts, tells us, that there is yet a greater, wider view. The nature of God is vaster and more complex than can be embraced in any single formula. As in His dealings with men generally, it has been truly said that

> God fulfils Himself in many ways,
> Lest one good custom should corrupt the world,

so out of these many ways and many names we learn from the Bible that there are especially these three great revelations, these three ways in which He can be approached. None of them is to be set aside. It is true that the threefold name of which we are speaking is never in the Bible brought forward in the form of an unintelligible mystery. It is certain that the only place [2] where it is put before us as an arithmetical enigma is now known to be spurious. Yet it is still the fact that the indefinite description of the Power that governs all things is a wholesome rebuke to that readiness to dispose of the whole question of the Divine nature, as if God were a man, a person like ourselves. The hymn of Reginald Heber, which is one of the few in which the feeling of the poet and the scholar is interwoven with the strains of simple devotion—

> Holy, holy, holy, Lord God Almighty—

refuses to lend itself to any anthropomorphic speculations, and takes refuge in abstractions as much withdrawn from the ordinary figures of human speech and metaphor, as if it had been composed by Kant or Hegel. To acknowledge this triple form of revelation, to acknowledge this complex aspect of the Deity, as it runs through the multiform ex-

[2] 1 John v. 7.

pressions of the Bible—saves, as it were, the awe, the reverence due to the Almighty Ruler of the Universe, tends to preserve the balance of truth from any partial or polemical bias, presents to us not a meagre, fragmentary view of only one part of the Divine Mind, but a wide, catholic summary of the whole, so far as nature, history, and experience permit. If we cease to think of the Universal Father, we become narrow and exclusive. If we cease to think of the Founder of Christianity and of the grandeur of Christendom, we lose our hold on the great historic events which have swayed the hopes and affections of man in the highest moments of human progress. If we cease to think of the Spirit, we lose the inmost meaning of Creed and Prayer, of Church and Bible, of human character, and of vital religion. In that apologue of Goethe before quoted, when the inquiring student asks his guides who have shown him the three forms of reverence, 'To which of these religions do you adhere?' 'To all the three,' they reply, 'for in their union they produce the true religion, which has been adopted, though unconsciously, by a great part of the world.' 'How then, and where?' exclaimed the inquirer. 'In the Creed,' replied they. 'For the first article is ethnic, and belongs to all nations. The second is Christian, and belongs to those struggling with affliction, glorified in affliction. The third teaches us an inspired communion of saints. And should not the three Divine Persons[3] justly be considered as in the highest sense One?'

2. And yet on the other hand, when we pursue each of these sacred words into its own recesses, we may be thankful that we are thus allowed at times to look upon each as though each for the moment were the whole and entire name of which we are in search. There are in the sanctuaries of the old churches of the East on Mount Athos sacred pictures intended to represent the doctrine of the Trinity, in

---

[3] Goethe probably used this expression as the one that came nearest to hand. To make it correct, it must be taken, not in the modern sense of individual beings, but in the ancient sense of 'Hypostasis,' or 'ground-work'

which, as the spectator stands at one side, he sees only the figure of Our Saviour on the Cross, as he stands on the other side he sees only the Heavenly Dove, as he stands in the front he sees only the Ancient of Days, the Eternal Father. So it is with the representations of this truth in the Bible, and, we may add, in the experiences of religious life.

Sometimes, as in the Old Testament, especially in the Psalms, we are alone with God, we trust in Him, we are His and He is ours. The feeling that He is our Father, and that we are His children, is all-sufficing. We need not be afraid so to think of Him. Whatever other disclosures He has made of Himself are but the filling up of this vast outline. Whatever other belief we have or have not, we cling to this. By this faith lived many in Jewish times, who obtained a good report, even when they had not received the promise. By this faith have lived many a devout sage and hero of the ancient world, whom He assuredly will not reject. So long as we have a hope that this Supreme Existence watches over the human race—so long as this great Ideal remains before us, the material world has not absorbed our whole being, has not obscured the whole horizon.

Sometimes, again, as in the Gospels or in particular moments of life, we see no revelation of God except in the world of history. There are those to whom science is dumb, to whom nature is dark, but who find in the life of Jesus Christ all that they need. He is to them the all in all, the True, the Holy, the express image of the Highest. We need not fear to trust Him. The danger hitherto has been not that we can venerate Him too much, or that we can think of Him too much. The error of Christendom has far more usually been that it has not thought of him half enough— that it has put aside the mind of Christ, and taken in place thereof the mind of Augustine, Aquinas, Calvin, great in their way,—but not the mind of Him of whom we read in Matthew, Mark, Luke, and John. Or if we should combine with the thought of Him the thought of others foremost in

the religious history of mankind, we have His own command
to do so, so far as they are the likenesses of Himself, or so
far as they convey to us any sense of the unseen world, or
any lofty conception of human character. With the early
Christian writers, we may believe that the Word, the Wisdom of God which appeared in its perfection in Jesus of
Nazareth, had appeared in a measure in the examples of
virtue and wisdom which had been seen before His coming.
On the same principle we may apply this to those who have
appeared since. He has Himself told us that in His true
followers He is with mankind to the end of the world. In
the holy life, in the courageous act, in the just law, is the
Real Presence of Christ. Where these are, in proportion as
they recall to us His divine excellence, there, far more than
in any consecrated form or symbol, is the true worship due
from a Christian to his Master.

Sometimes, again, as in the Epistles, or in our own solitary communing with ourselves, all outward manifestations
of the Father and of the Son, of outward nature and of Christian communion, seem to be withdrawn, and the eye of our
mind is fixed on the Spirit alone. Our light then seems to come
not from without but from within, not from external evidence
but from inward conviction. That itself is a divine revelation. For the Spirit is as truly a manifestation of God as is
the Son or the Father. The teaching of our own heart and
conscience is enough. If we follow the promptings of truth
and purity, of justice and humility, sooner or later we shall
come back to the same Original Source. The witness of the
Spirit of all goodness is the same as the witness of the life
of Jesus, the same as the witness of the works of God our
Creator.

3. This distinction, which applies to particular wants
of the life of each man, may be especially traced in the
successive stages of the spiritual growth of individuals and
of the human race itself. There is a beautiful poem of a
gifted German poet of this century, in which he describes
his wanderings in the Hartz Mountains, and as he rests in

the house of a mountain peasant, a little child, the daughter
of the house, sits at his feet, and looks up in his troubled
countenance, and asks, 'Dost thou believe in the Father,
the Son, and the Holy Ghost?'   He makes answer in words
which must be read in the original to see their full force.
He says: 'When I sate as a boy on my mother's knees, and
learned from her to pray, I believed on God the Father, who
reigns aloft so great and good, who created the beautiful
earth and the beautiful men and women that are upon it,
who to sun and moon and stars foretold their appointed
course.   And when I grew a little older and bigger, then
I understood more and more, then I took in new truth
with my reason and my understanding, and I believed on
the Son—the well-beloved Son, who in his love revealed
to us what love is, and who for his reward, as always
happens, was crucified by the senseless world.   And now
that I am grown up, and that I have read many books
and travelled in many lands, my heart swells, and with
all my heart I believe in the Holy Ghost, the Spirit of
God.   It is this Spirit which works the greatest of miracles,
and shall work greater miracles than we have yet seen.   It
is this Spirit which breaks down all the strongholds of oppression and sets the bondsmen free.   It is this Spirit which
heals old death-wounds and throws into the old law new
life.   Through this Spirit it is that all men become a race
of nobles, equal in the sight of God.   Through this Spirit
are dispersed the black clouds and dark cobwebs that be-
wilder our hearts and brains.'

> A thousand knights in armour clad
>   Hath the Holy Ghost ordained,
> All His work and will to do,
>   By His living force sustained.
> Bright their swords, their banners bright;
> Who would not be ranked a knight,
>   Foremost in that sacred host?
> O, whate'er our race or creed,
> May we be such knights indeed,
>   Soldiers of the Holy Ghost.

III. The name of the Father, the Son, and the Holy
Ghost will never cease to be the chief expression of Christian
belief, and it has been endeavoured to show what is the true
meaning of them. The words probably from the earliest
time fell short of this high signification. Even in the Bible
they needed all the light which experience could throw upon
them to suggest the full extent of the meaning of which they
are capable. But it is believed that on the whole they contain
or suggest thoughts of this kind, and that in this development of their meaning, more than in the scholastic systems
built upon them or beside them, lies their true vitality.

*Apparet domus intus, et atria longa patescunt.*

The true interest of the collocation of these three words in
the Baptismal formula instead of any others that might have
found a place there, is not that the Christians of the second
or third century attached to them their full depth of meaning, but that they are too deeply embedded in the Biblical
records to have been effaced in those ages by any heterogeneous speculation, and that, when we come to ask their
meaning, they yield a response which the course of time has .
rather strengthened than enfeebled. However trite and commonplace appear to us the truths involved in them, they were
far from obvious to those early centuries, which worked upon
them for the most part in senses quite unlike the profound
religious revelations which are becoming to us so familiar.
And then there still remains the universal and the deeper
truth within. In Christianity nothing is of real concern
except that which makes us wiser and better; everything
which does make us wiser and better is the very thing which
Christianity intends. Therefore even in these three most
sacred words there is yet, besides all the other meanings
which we have found in them, the deepest and most sacred
meaning of all—that which corresponds to them in the life
of man. Many a one has repeated this Sacred Name, and
yet never fulfilled in himself the truths which it conveys.
Some have been unable to repeat it, and yet have grasped

the substance which alone gives to it spiritual value. What
John Bunyan said on his death-bed concerning prayer is
equally true of all religious forms: ' Let thy heart be without words rather than thy words without heart.' Wherever
we are taught to know and understand the real nature of the
world in which our lot is cast, there is a testimony, however
humble, to the name of the Father; wherever we are taught
to know and admire the highest and best of human excellence, there is a testimony to the name of the Son ; wherever
we learn the universal appreciation of such excellence, there
is a testimony to the name of the Holy Ghost.

# CHAPTER XV.

### THE LORD'S PRAYER.

No one doubts that the Lord's Prayer entered into all the Liturgical observances of the Early Church. No one questions its fundamental value.

1. First, let us observe the importance of having such a form at all as the Lord's Prayer left to us by the Founder of our faith. It was said once by a Scottish statesman, 'Give to anyone you like the making of a nation's laws—give me the making of their ballads and songs, and that will tell us the mind of the nation.' So it might be said, ' Give to anyone you like the making of a Church's creed—or a Church's decrees or rubrics—give me the making of its prayers, and that will tell us the mind of the Church or religious community.' We have in this Prayer the one public universal prayer of Christendom. It contains the purest wishes, the highest hopes, the tenderest aspirations which our Master put into the mouths of His followers. It is the rule of our worship, the guide of our inmost thoughts. This prayer on the whole has been accepted by all the Churches of the world. In the English Liturgy it is repeated in every single service—too often for purposes of edification. The reason evidently is because it was thought that no service could be complete without it. This is the excuse for what otherwise would seem to be a vain repetition. Again, it is used so frequently in the Roman Catholic Church that its two first words have almost passed into a name for a prayer generally—*Pater Noster*,—which is the Latin of ' Our Father.' It has been translated into almost all languages. It is used, at least in modern times, in all the Presbyterian

Churches of Scotland, and in most of the English Nonconformist Churches. However great may be the scruples which any community may entertain against set forms, there is hardly any which will refuse to use this prayer. The Society of Friends is probably the only exception. Whatever may be the case with other formularies or catechisms, this at least is not a distinctive formulary; it is common to the whole of Christendom—nay, as we shall see, it is common to the whole of mankind. Luther calls it ' the Prayer of Prayers.'  Baxter says, ' The Lord's Prayer, with the Creed and Ten Commandments, the older I grew, furnished me with a most plentiful and acceptable matter for all my meditations.'  Archbishop Leighton, the only man who was almost successful in joining together the Churches of England and Scotland, was, we are told, especially partial to the Lord's Prayer, and said of it, ' O, the spirit of this prayer would make rare Christians.'  Bossuet, the most celebrated of French divines, and Channing, the most celebrated of American divines, both repeated it on their death beds.  Channing said, ' This is the perfection of the Christian religion.'  Bossuet said, ' Let us read and reread incessantly the Lord's Prayer.  It is the true prayer of Christians, and the most perfect, for it contains all.'  On the day of his execution it was repeated by Count Egmont, leader of the insurrection in the Netherlands.  On the day of his mortal illness it summed up the devotions of the Emperor Nicholas of Russia.  Even those who knew nothing about it have acknowledged its excellence.  A French countess read this prayer to her unbelieving husband in a dangerous illness.  ' Say that again,' he said, ' it is a beautiful prayer. Who made it ? '

2. Again, in the Early Church it was the only set form of Liturgy.  It was, so to speak, the whole Liturgy; it was the only set form of prayer then used in the celebration of the Holy Communion.  Whatever other prayers were used were offered up according to the capacity and choice of the minister.[1]  But there was one prayer fixed and universal,

---

[1] See Chapter III.

and that was the Lord's Prayer. The Clementine Liturgy alone omits it. From that unique position it has been gradually pushed aside by more modern prayers. But the recollection of its ancient pre-eminent dignity is still retained in the older liturgies by its following immediately after the consecration prayer; and in the modern English Liturgy, although it has been yet further removed, yet its high importance in the service is indicated by its being used twice—once at the commencement and immediately after the administration. Whenever we so hear it read we are reminded of its original grandeur as the root of all liturgical eucharistic services everywhere. It is an indication partly of the immense change which has taken place in all liturgies: it shows how far even the most ancient that exist have departed from their original form. But it reminds us also what is the substance of the whole Communion service; what is the spirit by which and in which alone the blessings of that service can be received.

3. And now let us look at its outward shape. What do we learn from this? We may infer from the occurrence of any form at all in the teaching of Christ that set forms of prayer are not in themselves wrong. He, when He was asked by His disciples, 'Teach us to pray,' did not say, as He might have done, 'Never use any form of words—wait till the Spirit moves you—take no thought how you shall speak, for it shall be given you in the same hour what you should speak—"out of the abundance of your heart your mouth shall speak."' There are times when He did so speak. But at any rate on two occasions He is reported to have given a fixed form of words. But as He gave a fixed form, so neither did He bind His disciples to every word of it always and exclusively. He did not say, 'In these words pray ye,' but on one occasion, 'After this manner pray ye.' And as if to bring out still more distinctly that even in this most sacred of all prayers it is the spirit and not the letter that is of any avail, there are two separate forms of it given in the Gospels according to St. Matthew and St. Luke, which, though the same in substance, differ much in detail. 'Give

us this day our daily bread' it is in St. Matthew; 'Give us day by day our daily bread' it is in St. Luke. 'Forgive us our debts as we forgive our debtors' it is in St. Matthew; 'Forgive us our sins; for we also forgive every one that is indebted to us' it is in St. Luke. And yet, besides, it may be observed that there is a still further variation in the Lord's Prayer as we read it in the English Liturgy from the form in which we read it in the Authorised Version of the Bible—'Forgive us our trespasses as we forgive them that trespass against us,' is a petition that is the same in sense but different in words from what it is either in St. Matthew or St. Luke. And again, what we call the doxology at the end, 'For thine is the kingdom, and the power, and the glory,' is not found at all in St. Luke, nor in the oldest manuscripts of St. Matthew, and is never used at all in the oldest Churches of Europe. The Roman Catholic Church absolutely rejects it. The Greek reads it but not as part of the Lord's Prayer. Pope, the Roman Catholic poet, imagined that it was written by Luther. In the best MSS. of St. Luke are omitted 'Our;' 'which art in heaven;' 'Thy will be done in earth as it is in heaven;' and 'Deliver us from the evil.' All these variations show the difference between the spirit and the substance, between the form and the letter. The Lord's Prayer is often repeated merely by rote, and has often been used superstitiously as a charm. These slight variations are the best proofs that this formal repetition is not the use for which it was intended. In order to pray as Jesus Christ taught us to pray we must pray with the understanding as well as with the spirit— with the spirit and heart as well as with the lips. Prayer in its inferior form becomes merely mechanical; but in its most perfect form it requires the exercise of the reason and understanding. This distinction is the salt which saves all prayers and all religions whatever from corruption.

4. There is yet a further lesson to be learned from the general form and substance of the Lord's Prayer. Whence did it come? What, so to speak, was the quarry out of which it was hewn? It might have been entirely fresh and new. It might

have been brought out for the first time by ' Him who spake as never man spake.' And in a certain sense this was so. As a whole it is entirely new. It is, taking it from first to last, what it is truly called, ' the Lord's Prayer '—the Prayer of our Lord, and of no one else. But if we take each clause and word by itself, it has often been observed by scholars that they are in part taken from the writings of the Jewish Rabbis. It was an exaggeration of Wetstein when he said, ' Tota hæc oratio ex formulis Hebræorum concinnata est.' But certainly in the first two petitions there are strong resemblances. ' Every scribe,' said our Lord, ' bringeth forth out of his treasury things new and old.' And that is exactly what He did Himself in this famous prayer. Something like at least to those familiar petitions exists in some hole or corner of Jewish liturgies. It was reserved for the Divine Master to draw them forth from darkness into light, and speak out on the housetop what was formerly whispered in the scholar's closet—to string together in one continuous garland the pearls of great price that had been scattered here and there, disjointed and divided. We learn from this the value of selection, of discrimination, of study, in the choice of our materials of knowledge, whether divine or human, and especially of our devotion. We are not to think that a saying, or truth, or prayer is less divine because it is found outside the Bible. We are not to think that anything good in itself is less good because it comes from a rabbinical or heathen source.

5. Observe its brevity. It is indeed a comment upon the saying, ' God is in heaven, and thou upon earth ; therefore let thy words be few.' No doubt very often we pray in forms much longer than this ; but the shortness of the Lord's Prayer is compatible with its being the most excellent of all prayers, and with compressing our devotion into the briefest compass. In fact the occasion on which it is introduced lays the chief stress on its shortness. It was first taught in express contrast to the long repetitions of the heathen religions. ' They think that they shall be heard for

their much speaking. Be not ye therefore like unto them, for your Father knoweth what things ye have need of before ye ask Him. After this manner therefore pray ye.' Every-one, however difficult he may find it to make long prayers, however pressing his business may be, morning, noon, and night, may have time for this very short prayer. How long does it take? One minute. How many sentences does it contain? Seven. The youngest as well as the oldest—the busiest as well as the idlest—the most sceptical as well as the most devout—can at least in the day once or twice, if not in the early morning or the late evening, use this short prayer. There is nothing in it to offend. They who scruple or who throw aside the Prayer Book, or the Directory, or the Catechism, or the Creed, at least may say the Lord's Prayer. They cannot be the worse for it. They may be the better.

6. And now let us look upon the substance of the sentences as they follow one another. We have said that a nation's religious life may be judged by its chief prayers. For example, the Mohammedan religion may fairly claim to be represented by the one prayer that every Mussulman offers to God morning and evening. It is in the first chapter of the Koran, and it is this—

> Praise be to God, Master of the Universe,
> The Merciful, the Compassionate,
> Lord of the day of Judgment.
> To Thee we give our worship,
> From Thee we have our help.
> Guide us in the right way,
> In the way of those whom Thou hast loaded with Thy
>     blessing,
> Not in the way of those who have encountered Thy
>     wrath, or who have gone astray.

Let us not despise that prayer—so humble, so simple, so true. Let us rather be thankful that from so many devout hearts throughout the Eastern world there ascends so pure an offering to the Most High God. Yet surely we may say in no proud or Pharisaic spirit that, compared even with this exalted prayer of the Arabian Prophet, there is a richness, a fulness, a height of hope, a depth of humility, a breadth of meaning in the prayer of the Lord Jesus which we find nowhere else, which stamps it with a divinity all its own.

'Our Father which art in Heaven.' Our Father, not *my* Father. He is the God not of one man, or one church, or one nation, or one race only—but of all who can raise their thoughts towards Him. Father. That is the most human, most personal, most loving thought which we can frame in speaking of the Supreme Being. And yet He is in Heaven. That is the most remote, the most spiritual, the most impersonal thought which we can frame concerning Him. Heaven is a word which expresses the ideal, the unseen world, and there infinitely raised above us all is the Father whom we adore. 'Hallowed be Thy name.' That is the hope that all levity, that all profaneness may be banished from the worship of God; not only that our worship may be simple, solemn, and reverent, but that our thoughts concerning Him may be consecrated and set apart from all the low, debasing, superstitious, selfish ends to which His name has so often been turned. 'O Liberty,' it was once said, 'how many are the crimes that have been committed in thy name!' 'O Religion,' so we may also say when we repeat this clause of the Lord's Prayer, 'how many are the crimes that have been committed in thy name!' May that holy name be hallowed by the acts and words of those who profess it! 'Thy kingdom come.' This is the highest hope of humanity: that the rule of supreme truth, and mercy, and justice, and beauty, may penetrate every province of thought, and action, and law, and art. It has been said there are some places on earth where we have to think what is the one single prayer which we should utter if we were sure of its being fulfilled. This would be, 'Thy kingdom come.' 'Thy will be done.' That is the expression of our entire resignation to whatever shall year by year and day by day befall us. Resignation which shall calm our passions, and control our murmurs, and curtail our griefs, and kindle our cheerfulness. It is, as Bishop Butler has said, the whole of religion. Islam derives its name from it. 'IN EARTH AS IT IS IN HEAVEN.' These are words which lift our souls up from the world in which we struggle with manifold imperfections to the ideal heavenly world, where all is perfect. Party strife—crooked ends—ignominious flatteries—are they necessary? Let us hope that a time may come when they will be unnecessary. 'GIVE US THIS DAY OUR DAILY BREAD.' Here we turn from heaven back to earth, and ask for our needful food, our enjoyment, our sustenance from day to day. It is the one petition for our earthly wants. We know not what a day may bring forth. Give us only, give us at least what we need, of sustenance both for body and soul. 'Enough is enough'—ask not for more.[2] 'Enough for our faith, enough for our maintenance when the sun dawns and before the sun sets.' 'FORGIVE US OUR TRESPASSES AS WE FORGIVE THEM THAT TRESPASS AGAINST US.' Who is there that has not need to forgive some one—who is there that has not the need of something to be forgiven? The founder of Georgia said to the founder of Methodism, 'I never forgive any one.' John Wesley answered, 'Sir, I trust you never sin.' 'LEAD US NOT INTO TEMPTATION.' The temptations which beset us. How much of sin comes from the outward incidents and companionships round us! How much of innocence from that good Providence which wards off the corrupting, defiling, debasing influences that fill the earth! Save us, we may well ask, from the circumstances of our age, our country, our church, our profession, our character; save us from those circumstances which draw forth our natural infirmities—save us from these, break their force. And this is best accomplished by the last petition, 'DELIVER US FROM EVIL'; that is, deliver us from the evil,[3] whatsoever it is, that lurks even

---

[2] See Bishop Lightfoot's treatise on the word ἐπιούσιος.

[3] ἀπὸ τοῦ πονηροῦ, 'the evil,' not 'the Evil One.' So it must be translated in Matt. v. 37, 39, as well as in Matt. vi. 13, and in John xvii. 15, where ἐκ appears to fix the meaning.

in the best of good things.  From the idleness that grows out of youth and fulness of bread—from the party spirit that grows out of our political enthusiasm or our nobler ambition —from the fanatical narrowness which goes hand in hand with our religious earnestness—from the harshness which clings to our love of truth—from the indifference which results from our wide toleration—from the indecision which intrudes itself into our careful discrimination—from the folly of the good, and from the selfishness of the wise, Good Lord deliver us.  'FOR THINE IS THE KINGDOM, AND THE POWER, AND THE GLORY, FOR EVER AND EVER, AMEN.'  So Christendom has added its ratification to the words of Christ.  It is the thankfulness which we all feel for the majesty and thought and beauty which our heavenly Father has shown to us in the paths of nature or in the greatness of man.

We have thus briefly traversed these petitions.  When our Lord's disciples came and asked for a form of prayer, not as John's disciples had received from their master, they thought, no doubt, that He would give them something peculiar to themselves—something that no one else could use.  They little knew what the peculiarity, the singularity of their Master's Prayer would be —that it was one that might be used by every church, by every sect, by every nation, by every member of the human family.  It is possible that some may be inclined to complain of this extreme comprehensiveness and indefiniteness, and to say there is something here which falls short of the promise in St. John's Gospel.  'If ye shall ask anything in My name I will do it.'  But the answer is that here, as before, this prayer is a striking example of the greatness of the spirit above the letter.  In the letter it does not begin or end in the actual name of Jesus Christ.  That familiar termination which to our ears has become almost the necessary ending to every prayer, and which is used in every church, whether Unitarian or Trinitarian, is not here.  We do not close our Lord's Prayer with the words 'through Jesus Christ our Lord.'  We do not invoke the holy name of Jesus either at the beginning or end.  But not the less is it in the fullest sense a prayer in the name of Christ.  In the name of Christ, that is (taking these words in·their Biblical sense), 'in the spirit of Christ,' 'according to the nature and the will of Christ,' copied from the lips of Christ, adopted as His one formulary of faith at His express commandment. In this true meaning of the words the Lord's Prayer is more the Prayer of our Lord, is more entirely filled with the name and spirit of Christ, than if the name of the Lord Jesus Christ were repeated a hundred times over.  In Pope's 'Universal Prayer' there is much which is condemned by religious persons, and we do not undertake to defend the taste or the sentiment of it in every part.  But assuredly that which is its chief characteristic, its universality, is exactly in spirit that which belongs to the prayer of Christ. It is expressed in those well-known words—

> Father of all ! in every age,
>   In every clime ador'd,
> By saint, by savage, and by sage,
>   Jehovah, Jove, or Lord.

It is this very characteristic of the prayer which makes it to be in His name.  It is this very universality which overflows with Himself, and which makes the prayer of the · philosopher to be a paraphrase of His Prayer.  He is in every syllable of this sacred formula, as He is not equally in any other formula.  He is in the whole of it, and in all its parts. Of these, the most sacred of all the words that He has given us, it ·is true what He said of all His words—they are not mere words, they are spirit and they are life.

# CHAPTER XVI.

## THE COUNCIL AND CREED OF CONSTANTINOPLE.

IT may be interesting in connection with the history of the early Creeds to add an account of the circumstances under which they came into existence. Of the Apostles' Creed we have already spoken.[1] The Nicene Creed was the result of the Council of Nicæa, and this, though in a form totally different from that which now bears the name, is the original Creed of the Empire, and its formation has been described in the 'Lectures on the Eastern Church.'[2] The Athanasian Creed is of much later date, and has also been the subject of a separate treatise.[3] There remains therefore only the Creed commonly called the Creed of Constantinople, which is now adopted by the Churches of Rome and England, and the Lutheran Churches, and through the whole of the Eastern Church, with the exception of the Coptic, Nestorian, and Armenian branches. In order to do this, it will be necessary to describe the Council, with which its composition is traditionally connected, the more so as the assembly has never yet been adequately portrayed. After this description it will be our object to examine into the nature and pretensions of the Creed which is usually supposed to have sprung out of it.

The city of Constantinople had been [4] almost ever since the

---

[1] Lecture XIV.     [2] *Lectures on the Eastern Church*, Lecture iv.

[3] *The Athanasian Creed*, with a Preface.

[4] The usual authorities which describe the Council are the ecclesiastical historians of the following century—Socrates, Sozomen, Theodoret. But far more important than these are the letters, orations, and autobiographical poems of Gregory Nazianzen, who was not only a contemporary

Council of Nicæa in the hands of the great party which was called by the name of the heresiarch Arius, and which embraced all the princes of the Imperial House from Constantine the Great to Valens (with the exception of the 'apostate' Julian), as well as the Gothic tribes on the frontier.  But the 'orthodox' or so-called 'Catholic' party, to which the name of Athanasius still gave life, struggled on; and when the rude Spanish soldier Theodosius restored peace to the Empire, his known opinions in favour of the orthodox doctrine gave a hope of returning strength to the cause which had vanquished at Nicæa.  Under these circumstances, the little community which professed the Athanasian belief at Constantinople determined on the step of calling to their assistance one of the leaders of those opinions from the adjacent province of Asia Minor.  Basil would have been the natural choice; but his age and infirmities rendered this impossible.  Accordingly, they fixed

Gregory Nazianzen. on Gregory, commonly called 'of Nazianzus.'  Unlike the school in the English Church which, in the time of the Nonjurors, and afterwards, sanctions the intrusion of new bishops into places already pre-occupied by lawful prelates, the orthodox community at Constantinople showed a laudable moderation.  Gregory was already a bishop, but a bishop without a diocese.  Appointed to the see of Sasima, he had never undertaken its duties, but contented himself with helping his aged father in the bishopric of his birthplace Nazianzus.  Accordingly he was ready to the hands of the minority of the Church of Byzantium, without any direct infringement of the rights and titles of Demophilus, the lawful bishop of Constantinople.

He came from his rustic retreat reluctantly.  He was prematurely old and infirm.  His bald head streaked with a few white hairs, and his bent figure, were not calculated to

but an eyewitness of most of what he describes.  We must add from modern times the learned Tillemont, the exact Hefele, and the elaborate and for the most part impartial narrative of the Duc de Broglie, all of them belonging to the more moderate school of the Roman Church.

command attention. He was retiring, susceptible, and, in his manners, simple to a fault. It is this contrast with the position which was forced upon him that gives the main interest to the curious cycle of events of which he thus became the centre.

Constantinople was crowded with the heads of the different ecclesiastical parties, awaiting the arrival of the new Emperor. There were the Arian bishops in possession of the Imperial sees. There were the semi-Arians, who by very slight concessions on both sides might be easily included in the orthodox community. There were the liberal Catholics, who were eager to grant such concessions. There were the Puritan Catholics, who rigidly spurned all compromise. With these divisions there was a vast society, hardly less civilised, less frivolous, less complex, than that of our great capitals now, entering into those abstract theological questions as keenly as our metropolitan circles into the political or ecclesiastical disputes which form the materials of conversation at the dinner-tables of London or in the saloons of Paris. Everywhere in that new capital of the world—at the races of the Hippodrome, at the theatres, at feasts, in debauches,[5] the most sacred names were bandied to and fro in eager disputation. Every corner, every alley of the city, the streets, the markets, the drapers' shops, the tables of moneychangers and of victuallers, were crowded with these 'offhand dogmatisers.'[6] If a trader was asked the cost of such an article, he answered by philosophising on generated and ungenerated being. If a stranger inquired the price of bread, he was told 'the Son is subordinate to the Father.' If a traveller asked whether his bath was ready, he was told 'the Son arose out of nothing.'

The shyness as well as the piety of Gregory led him to confine his appearance in public to the pulpit. So completely had the orthodox party been depressed, that they

---

[5] Gregory Naz. *Or.* 22–27.

[6] αὐτοσχέδιοι δογματισταί. Gregory Nyssa, *De Deitate Filii*, vol. ii. p. 898.

had no church to offer him for his ministrations. They went back for the moment to the custom which, beginning at or before the first conversion of the Empire, was in fact the origin of all the early Christian churches. Every great Roman house had attached to it a hall, which was used by its owner for purposes of justice or of public assemblies, and bore (at least in Rome) the name of ' basilica.' [7]   Such a hall was employed by Gregory on this occasion 'in the house where he had taken up his quarters. An extempore altar was raised, and in accordance with the ancient Eastern practice of separating the sexes, a gallery was erected for the women, such as on a gigantic scale still exists in the Church of St. Sophia ; showing at once the importance of the female element in these Byzantine congregations, and also the prominence given to an element in ecclesiastical architecture which is regarded by modern ecclesiologists as utterly incongruous. To this extemporised chapel he gave the name of the *Anastasia*, or Church of the Resurrection or Revival ; in [8] allusion to the resurrection, as he hoped, of the orthodox party in the Church, much as Nonconformists gave to their places of worship the names, not of the ancient saints, but of such events, or symbols, as seemed to indicate their solitary position in a corrupt world or church—*Ebenezer*, ' the stone of help ; ' *Bethesda*, ' the house of help.' The building was soon crowded ; the crush at the entrance was often terrific ; the rails of the chancel were broken down ; the congregation frequently burst out into loud applause. It required a more than mortal not to be touched and elated by these signs of the effect produced by his oratory. As the aged Wilberforce used long after his retirement from public life to recall the results of his eloquence in the House of Commons—' Oh ! those cheers,

---

[7] See Chapter IX.

[8] It furnishes a curious example of the growth of a legend from a name. Socrates records the miracle of a woman falling from the gallery without injury to life, as the origin of the title. As we know the real meaning of the name, it is obvious that the reverse is the true account of the matter. A Novatian chapel had borne the same name for the same reason.

those delightful cheers!' so Gregory, years afterwards, used to be visited in his solitary dreams by visions of his beloved *Anastasia*; the church brilliantly illuminated; himself, after the manner of the ancient bishops, aloft on his throne at the eastern end, the presbyters round him, and the deacons in their white robes below; the crowd thronging the church, every eye fixed on him; the congregation sometimes wrapt in profound silence, sometimes breaking out into loud shouts of approbation.

But these bright days were destined to have a sad morrow. The sermons, which consisted usually of abstract disquisitions on the disputed doctrines, but sometimes of counsels towards moderation, veiled under a eulogy of the great Athanasius,[9] provoked the jealousy or hostility of the opposite party, or perhaps of the more zealous members of his own. On one occasion a body of drunken artisans broke into the church, accompanied by an army of beggars, of furious nuns,[1] and, the usual accompaniment of riots at that time, ferocious monks. A violent conflict ensued—some of the priests and neophytes were wounded. The police hesitated to interfere—ostensibly on the ground that it was impossible to decide which were the assailed and which the assailants. Gregory, with a questionable prudence, had surrounded himself with a body of orthodox fanatics, with whom he had but little sympathy, and whose hostility to the moderation of the venerable Basil might have well roused his suspicion. They slept in his house, they assisted him in preparing his sermons, they formed a guard about him in these tumults. One of them was no less a person than the youthful Jerome, then on his way from the farther East, whose fierce and acrid temper rendered him a staunch but perilous friend, and who lost no occasion of expressing his admiration of Gregory—his 'beloved master,' 'to whom there

---

[9] This is the date of the oration on Athanasius, according to M. de Broglie.

[1] M. de Broglie says 'des femmes débauchées.' But it is clear from Gregory's account (*Or.* xxiii. 5, xxxv. 3; *Ep.* 77; *Carm. de Vitâ Suâ*, 660, 670), that they were the nuns or consecrated virgins.

was no equal in the Western Church.'[2]   There was another
who rendered a yet more dubious assistance.  Maximus or

Maximus.

Heron was one of the class of those wild Egyptians
who played some years later so disgraceful a part in
the train of Cyril of Alexandria.   He had once been a philosopher of the Cynical sect, and, although ordained, still wore
their curious costume.   In all these disturbances his figure
was conspicuous.   He wielded a long staff in his hands.   A
tangled mass of curls—half of their natural black, half
painted yellow—fell over his shoulders.[3]   A dirty shirt
enveloped his half-naked limbs, which he occasionally drew
aside to show the scars of wounds which he professed to
have received in some persecution.   At every word of
Gregory he uttered shouts of delight, at every allusion to
the heretics he uttered yells of execration.   The most
sinister rumours, however, were circulated against his
private character.   Even the marks on his back were
whispered to be the effects of a severe castigation with which
he had been visited for some discreditable transaction.   But
Gregory was infatuated, as is sometimes the case with the
most sagacious and the most incorruptible of men, by the
charms of assiduous flattery, and by the advantage of having
near him an ally who stopped at nothing in defence of a
cause which he thought right.   Such is the secret of the
ridiculous eulogy which Gregory pronounced on Maximus in
his presence, in a sermon which still remains as a monument of the weakness into which party-spirit can betray
even a thoughtful and pious man.   His dear 'Heron was
a true model of the union of philosophy and religion'[4]
—a 'friend from an unexpected quarter'—a 'dog'—

[2] Many questions passed between them on Biblical criticism and on
ecclesiastical policy. (Jerome *Contra Rufin.* i. 13; *De Viris Illustribus,*
c. 117.)

[3] De Vit. 754, 766.

[4] Gregory Naz., *Or.* xxv. 1, 2. It is from his companion St. Jerome
that we are able to substantiate the identity of Maximus with the Heron
of this strange discourse. 'The names were changed,' says Jerome, 'in
order to save the credit of Gregory from having alternately praised and
blamed the same man.' (*De Viris Illustribus,* c. 117.)

alluding to the title of his philosophical sect of the Cynics
or 'Dogs'—'a dog indeed in the best sense : a watch-dog,
who guards the house from robbers'—finally, it was not too
much to say, 'his successor in the promised see of Constantinople.' This last hint was not thrown away on 'the Dog.'
There was no time to be lost. The Emperor was on his
way to Constantinople. Whoever was the orthodox cham-
pion in possession of the see, would probably be able to keep
it. Maximus communicated his designs to his Egyptian
fellow-countrymen amongst the bishops. They, as the
orthodox of the orthodox, entered at once into his plan,
which received the sanction of Peter, successor of
Athanasius in the see of Alexandria. Alexandria at that
time was, saving the dignity of the new capital of Constantinople, the chief city of the Eastern world. Its ecclesiastical primacy in the East had hitherto been undisputed.
The Bishop of Alexandria was at this time the only 'Pope'
or 'Father' of the Church. He had long enjoyed the
title. It is a probable conjecture [5] that in this stroke
of elevating an Egyptian of the Egyptians to the see of
Constantinople there was a deliberate intention of grasping
the primacy of the Imperial Church. All was prepared. A
large sum of money, placed at the disposal of Maximus by a
Thasian presbyter who had been to the Golden Horn to buy
marble, was employed in securing the services of a number
of Alexandrian sailors. Gregory was confined to his house
by illness. With this mixed multitude to represent the
congregation, the Egyptian bishops solemnly consecrated
Maximus at the dead of night. The elevation to this high
dignity was rendered still more marked by the metamor-
phosis in his outward appearance. 'They took "the dog,"'
says Gregory, in whose eyes the Cynic now assumed a very
different aspect, 'and shaved him ; the long locks in which
his strength resided were shorn off by these ecclesiastical
Dalilahs.' But Maximus had overreached himself. This
was too startling a contrast. When he appeared in the

[5] Milman's *History of Christianity under the Empire*, vol. iii. p. 115.

morning, cropt, and well-dressed ·as a bishop, an inextinguishable roar of laughter resounded through the city. Gregory felt that he was included in the general ridicule. He determined on leaving Constantinople. Then a reaction took place. The mob veered round. They insisted on forcing Gregory at once into the contested see. They dragged him in their arms to the episcopal chair. He struggled to escape. He stiffened his legs, so as to refuse to sit. The perspiration streamed from his face. They pushed and forced him down. The women wept, the children screamed. At last he consented, and then was left to repose. He endeavoured to recover his equanimity by retiring for a time to a villa on the shores of the Sea of Marmora, there to wander, as he tells us, at sunset—unconscious of the glory which at that hour lights up that wonderful prospect with a glow of magical splendour, but not insensible to the melancholy sentiment inspired by the rolling waves of the tideless sea along the bays of that winding shore.

There were two other claimants for the vacant see—each waiting with the utmost expectation the only hand which could seat them securely in their places, the hand of Theodosius. At Thessalonica the Emperor met Maximus, who, seeing that he was coldly received, took refuge at Alexandria, under the shelter of the prelate who was at that time the eastern oracle of the ecclesiastical world. Theodosius in this difficulty appealed to the western oracle at Rome. The Bishop of Rome was glad of the opportunity of striking a blow at once at the independence and the superior civilisation of the East. Damasus, who had a sufficient tincture of letters to write the verses that may still be read in the Roman catacombs, fired off an answer which by the same blow killed one and wounded the other rival. Maximus was to be rejected, not on account of his scandalous vices, but because he still wore the garb of a philosopher. 'No Christian can wear the clothes of a pagan philosopher.' And then, with a covert attack on Gregory himself, he added,

'Philosophy, friend of the world's wisdom, is the enemy of faith, the poison of hope, the war against charity.' The advice thus proffered was followed up by a recommendation to the Emperor to summon a General Council for the settlement of the disputed succession.

This accordingly was the origin of the Council of Constantinople. Theodosius meanwhile took the matter of the See of Constantinople into his own hands. To the actual Bishop, the Arian Demophilus, he proposed the orthodox confession or resignation; Demophilus honourably resisted the temptation. 'Since you fly from peace,' said the Emperor, 'I will make you fly from your place.' So summary was the deposition of a prelate in those days, when the breath, not of a prelate but of an Emperor, was sufficient to depose the greatest bishops in Christendom. To Gregory he turned with a no less imperious expression of his will: 'Constantinople demands you, and God makes me his instrument to give you this church.' The election was still nominally in the hands of the people, but the mandate of the Emperor was more powerful than any *congé d'élire*. It was on the 26th of November—one of those dreary days on which the winds from the Black Sea envelop the bright city of Constantinople with a shroud of clouds dark as night, which Gregory's enemies interpreted into a sinister presage of his ill-omened elevation. The Emperor rode in state to the church where the ceremony was to take place. The immense multitude of the Arian population who were to lose their bishop, and perhaps themselves to be banished with him—old men, women, and children, threw themselves in vain before his horse's feet. The Spanish soldier rode on immovable, as if he were on his way to the field of battle. It was, says Gregory himself, the likeness of a city taken by storm. By the Emperor's side was the pale, stooping, trembling candidate for the see, hardly knowing where he was till he found himself safe within the church, behind the rails of the chancel, where he sat side by side with the magnificent Emperor, who in his imperial purple was raised there aloft as the chief person in the place. It was the 'Church of the Apostles,' that earliest mausoleum of Christian sovereigns, the first germ of St. Denys, the Escurial, and Westminster Abbey, where Constantine and his successors lay entombed, and where in after days was to rise a yet more splendid .edifice, the mosque which the Mussulman conqueror Mahomet II. built in like manner for himself and his dynasty. There was still a hesitation, or seeming hesitation, as to which way the popular feeling would turn. Suddenly, by one of those abrupt transitions common in Eastern skies, a ray of sunlight burst through the wintry clouds, and flashing from sword to sword along the ranks of soldiers, and from gem to gem on the rich dresses of priest and courtier, finally enveloped the bald white head of Gregory himself as with a halo of glory. The omen was at once accepted. A shout like thunder rose from the vast congregation, 'Long live our Bishop Gregory!' In the high galleries rang the shrill cries of the women in response. With a few faint protestations, Gregory consented to mount the Episcopal chair, and the long dispute was terminated.

Within six weeks after this event, took place one of those double-sided movements which, without revealing any actual

Funeral of Athanaric. duplicity in the actors, disclose the hollowness of their pretensions and opinions. On the same day that a rigid decree condemned and banished the Arians of the empire from the walls of every city,[6] there arrived in Constantinople the chief of the whole Arian world, Athanaric the Goth, seeking shelter in the court of his conqueror from a domestic revolution. He was received with as much honour as if he had been the most orthodox of mankind, and then a few days after his arrival he wasted away and died. His funeral, heretic as he was, was conducted with a magnificence which

---

[6] Demophilus the Arian bishop, on the promulgation of this edict, very naturally quoted the evangelical precept, 'If they persecute you in one city, flee to another.' 'Not so,' says Socrates the ecclesiastical historian. 'The text means that you must leave the city of the world and go to the city of the heavenly Jerusalem.'

excited the wonder and admiration of the Goths even far away
beyond the Danube.

Meanwhile the day for the opening of the Council drew
on.  Even Gregory did not consider his elevation secured
till he had received its confirmation.  The month of May
had come—the season when the navigation of the Mediter-
ranean was open, and when the Bishops could safely embark
from their distant dioceses.  It was the first General
Council that had assembled in the Imperial city.  When its
predecessors met at Nicæa, this was because Constantinople
was not yet founded.  But now there was no locality at once
so central, and so august, as the great Christian capital.
Called as the Council was emphatically ' by the commandment and will' of the Emperor, it could meet nowhere but
under the shadow of the Imperial throne.  Although
less distinguished by the character and fame of its          Its members.
members than that earlier synod, and although still  more
exclusively confined to the Eastern Church, it was not without some brilliant ornaments.  There were the friends of
Basil, well versed in his moderate counsels.  Chief amongst
them was his brother Gregory of Nyssa, reckoned by the 5th
and 7th General Councils amongst the highest authorities of
the Church.[7]  He had lately returned from his journey to
Syria, on a mission of peace-making—filled with indignation
against the follies and scandals of the pilgrimages.  He
brought with him his elaborate work against the recent
heretics, which in spare moments he read aloud to his friend
the new Bishop of Constantinople and to their joint
admirer, the youthful Jerome.[8]  There was Cyril of
Jerusalem, now in his advancing years, with whom Gregory
had there become acquainted, and who himself had originally
belonged to the semi-Arian section of the Church.  There
was Melitius, the just and gentle Bishop of Antioch, so
much revered in his own city that his portrait was found
everywhere, on rings, on goblets, in the saloons of palaces,
in the private chambers of great ladies.  It might be con-

7 Tillemont, ix. 601.                    8 Jerome, *De Vir. Ill.* c. 128.

jectured that one of these likenesses had wandered far West, from an incident which occurred on the first visit of the Bishops to the Emperor. The reception which he gave to Melitius was of the most flattering kind; he flew up to him, singled him from the rest, pressed him to his bosom, and kissed his eyes, lips, breast, head, and hand. He had, he said, in a vision on the eve of his election to the empire, seen a venerable person approach who wrapped him in his imperial mantle, and placed the diadem on his head. This personage he now recognised in the Bishop of Antioch. Such a welcome of itself designated Melitius to be President of the Council. In fact, in the absence of the Bishops of Rome and Alexandria, the Bishop of Antioch occupied the chief place. And the *mellifluous* character of *Melitius* (to use the pun of Gregory) well adapted him for the office.

The first work which the Council had to undertake was the decision of the contest for the see of Constantinople. The absence of Maximus, and of the Egyptian bishops, who were detained at Alexandria around the deathbed of their chief, rendered Gregory's triumph easy. But it is characteristic of his moderation, and of that of Melitius, that when there was a proposal of proceeding against the bishops who had taken part in the nomination of Maximus, it was abandoned on the grounds—too often lost sight of in the heat of controversy—that, as they were detained in Alexandria, it would be unjust to condemn them in their absence without hearing their defence.

This auspicious beginning of a generosity unusual on such occasions was suddenly cut short by the death of Melitius. The grief felt on the event was testified by the magnificence of his obsequies. The body was wrapped in a silken shroud, worked by one of the noble ladies of Constantinople. It was carried in procession to the imperial mausoleum in the Church of the Apostles; all the bishops assisted, with their clergy, singing psalms in the different dialects—probably the Greek dialects—of Asia Minor and Syria. Funeral orations were pronounced, amongst others,

by Gregory of Nyssa. The sacred remains were then sent
home to Antioch; and it marks the difference between
ancient and modern usage, that an express order from the
Emperor was required to enable the funeral procession, as a
special favour, even to enter the walls of the various cities
through which it passed.

The first question to be discussed by the Council, thus
deprived of its head, and placed, as a matter of course, under
the presidency of Gregory Nazianzen, now the recognised
bishop of the Imperial city, was occasioned by the very
calamity which they were now deploring. Ostensibly called
together to decide certain grave theological questions then
pending, their main interest was centred, as usually happens
in popular assemblies, whether secular or ecclesiastical, on a
question purely personal.

The Church of Antioch had been lately divided by two
contending factions. Melitius, who had thus been carried to
his grave with all the honours of a saint, was the Contentions
lawful, but, in the eyes of an extreme party at at Antioch.
Antioch, not the orthodox, bishop of that see. He had in
his youth, it was said, been infected by the subtle errors of
Arius; and, in his later years, he had joined Basil in the noble
attempts of that distinguished divine to moderate the rage of
controversy, and to accept, without further test or questioning,
all who were willing to adopt the creed of Nicæa, which down
to that time had expressed no precise definition of the complicated opinions that were now arising on the nature of the
Third Hypostasis of the Trinity.[9] This moderation was a
grave offence in the judgment of the partisans of extreme
orthodoxy. They refused to communicate with Melitius: and
they received from Sardinia, from the hands of the stern
fanatic Lucifer of Cagliari, a bishop of the name of Paulinus,
who became the head of a dissenting community within the
Church of Antioch, priding itself on its superior orthodoxy
and refusing to acknowledge the legitimate bishop, and maintained chiefly in its position not by any support from the

---

[9] Gregory, *Or.* xliii. 19.

national churches of the East, but from the more eager [1]
zealots of the Western Empire, who fanned the flames
of discord. 'This ridiculous and causeless schism'[2] had
engaged the attention of Melitius before he left his diocese.
The case had been referred to the imperial councillors, who
had decided in Melitius's favour; and he then proposed to
Paulinus, as a middle course, that the government of the
Church should remain in *statu quo* till the death of either,
in which case the other should succeed to the vacant see.
To this, after some hesitation, Paulinus acceded; and all the
chief clergy at Antioch swore to observe the compact.

On the death of Melitius, the very case provided for had
occurred : and Gregory immediately proposed to the Council
that the convention should be carried out. He appealed to
the oaths by which it was supported; he reminded them
that 'if two angels were candidates for the disputed see, the
quarrel was not worth the scandal it occasioned.' With a
disinterestedness the more remarkable because he had been
fiercely attacked by Paulinus for his moderate counsels in
former times, he entreated them to abide by the agreement,
and hinted at the danger of rousing the passions of the
western bishops, who were in favour of their nominee
Paulinus. Never did Gregory plead with more eloquence
or in behalf of a juster cause. But he pleaded in vain.
Even before Melitius's death, the contending factions in
this Antiochene quarrel had flown at each other's throats,
canvassing right and left everyone that came across them,
with cheers and counter-cheers.[3] The question had passed
from the region of justice and of faith into a mere party
struggle. Now that the time for a pacific settlement had
arrived, the Melitians would not hear of submitting to the
odious Paulinus. Nor could they be conciliated by the
appeal of Gregory. His influence had been shaken by his
weakness in the affair of Maximus; and, besides, his allusion
to the fear of the West roused all the slumbering passions of

---

[1] De Broglie, vol. i. pp. 121-123.    [2] *Ibid.* p. 424.
[3] Gregory, *De Vit.* 1555.

the jealous East.  He has himself described the effect of his speech :—' A yell, rather than a cry, broke from the assembled episcopate.'  ' They threw dust in his face ; they buzzed about him like a swarm of wasps; they cawed against him like an army of crows.'  The young were most ardent, but they were hounded on by the old.  An argument against the West, which seemed to the youthful partisans of the East irresistible, was that Christianity must follow the course of the sun, not from west to east, but from east to west; and the Eastern bishops supported this view, ' showing their tusks,' says Gregory, ' as if they had been wild boars.' [4] From the midst of this tumult, he appealed to Modarius, an Imperial officer, a Goth, to allay the ecclesiastical clamour. [5] He pointed out to him that these episcopal gatherings, so far from putting an end to the evil, merely added confusion to confusion.  It would seem that this appeal was also in vain. Theodosius, whether from scruple or policy, was determined to leave the bishops to themselves.  The precedent set by Constantine at Nicæa had passed into a law.  That sagacious ruler, when he received the mutual complaints and accusations of the bishops of the First General Council against each other, put them all into the fire without reading them; and in accordance with this contemptuous but charitable act, an imperial decree was passed on the occasion of the Second Council, [6] prohibiting bishops to appear against each other in courts of law.  Theodosius, however, though unwilling to interfere directly, determined to exercise an indirect influence on the largest scale.  He summoned from across the border the only western bishops who were available—those of Macedonia, which, according to the division then established, belonged to the Western Empire.  Their appearance might have turned the scale in behalf of Gregory's counsels, but at the same moment that they entered Constantinople, there arrived in the Golden Horn an equal accession to the

----

[4] *De Vit.* 1305.                              [5] *Ep.* 136.
[6] *Cod. Theod.* XI. t. **xxxix.** 1. 9.  As explained, with every appearance of reason, by M. de Broglie (vol. i. p. 434), after Godefroi.

opposite faction from Egypt.  The Egyptian bishops were with their new 'Pope,' and boiling over with indignation against Gregory for his rejection of their old favourite Maximus.  The Macedonian bishops also proved more unmanageable than Theodosius had anticipated.  They brought with them, as Gregory expresses it, the 'rough breath of the North-Wester.'  Their uncompromising austerity, and the subtle controversial spirit of the eastern prelates, found a common ground in attacking the unfortunate Gregory.  There was one joint in his ecclesiastical harness which presented an opening for the darts of the rigid precisians of the time.  The Council of Nicæa had peremptorily forbidden, on

Deprivation pain of deprivation from orders, any translation—
of Gregory. not only from see to see, but from parish to parish.[7]

From that hour to this, in every church of Christendom, human ambition and obvious convenience have been too strong for the decree even of so venerable a body as the First Œcumenical Council.  But, general as the violation of the decree was, it was only when personal interests could be served by reviving it, that attention was called to the practice.  Gregory had been Bishop of Sasima before he was elevated to the see of Constantinople.  This was enough ; and although the fact had been perfectly known at the time when his election to the see was confirmed by this very Council ; although there was no reason for proceeding against him, rather than against any of the many bishops and presbyters who had equally broken the decree of Nicæa ; although there was no occasion for reviving the question in his case at this particular moment ; yet the leading members of the Council had the meanness to condemn in him what they forgave in those with whom they had no quarrel ; to take advantage of his temporary unpopularity to press against him a measure which justice would have required to be pressed against numberless others.  To Gregory personally the retirement from his bishopric was no great sacrifice.  The episcopate had always been a

<hr>

[7] See Chapter IX.

burden to him; he 'neighed like an imprisoned horse for his green pastures[8] of study and leisure.' He determined at once to 'make himself the Jonah of the tempest.' Yet when it came to the point, even he could not believe that the Council would have the base ingratitude to accept a resignation so nobly and promptly offered. But generosity towards a fallen foe is a difficult virtue. A few, in disgust at their associates, followed Gregory as he left the Council. The rest remained, and rejoiced in the departure of an honest and therefore a troublesome chief. 'I have not time or disposition,' says Gregory, 'to unravel their intrigues, so I will be silent.' He then visited the Emperor, hoping, perhaps in spite of himself, to obtain a reversal of his own sentence. But Theodosius, though far more deeply affected than the Synod, adhered to the resolution of leaving the bishops to settle their own affairs; and after a pathetic and eloquent farewell, delivered in the Church of the Apostles; after a glowing description—true even after the vicissitudes of thirteen hundred years—of the great opportunities of Constantinople, 'the eye of the world, the knot which links together East and West; the centre in which all extremes combine,'—Gregory quitted that glorious city for ever, and hastened to bury his old age and his cares in the solitude of his ancestral home at Nazianzus. He might, perhaps, have acted a more dignified part had he buried in oblivion all remembrance of the causes of his retirement. But history has ratified the truth of the invectives which his vanity or his righteous indignation extorted from him. The pent-up flow of his emotion, as he says, could not be restrained,[9] and the result is an elaborate picture of the bishops of that time, doubtless of those whom he had known at the Council, and who had cast him out from their ranks as 'an evil and unholy man.' This extraordinary description would be justly considered a libel on any modern ecclesiastical assembly, and is thus instructive, as showing the impression produced on a contemporary and a canonised saint by an

<hr>

[8] *De Vit.* 1860–70.        [9] *Ad Episc.* (vol. ii. pp. 824, 829).

institution and an age, to which later times have looked back with such unquestioning reverence.[1] 'They are actors on a gigantic scale.' 'They walk on stilts.' 'They grin through borrowed masks.' They seem to him as though they had come in answer to the summons of a herald who had convoked to the Council all the gluttons, villains, liars, false-swearers of the Empire. They are 'chameleons that change their colour with every stone over which they pass.' They are 'illiterate, low-born, filled with all the pride of upstarts fresh from the tables of false accountants,' 'peasants from the plough,' or from the spade, 'unwashed blacksmiths,' 'deserters from the army and navy, still stinking from the holds of the ships,' or with the brand of the whip or the iron on their bodies. The refined Gregory was doubtless acutely sensitive to the coarseness of vulgarity and 'the ignorance which never knows when to be silent.' But he is aware of the objection that the Apostles might be said also to have been unlearned men. 'Yes,' he replies, as if anticipating the argument of the apostolical or papal succession, 'but it must be a real Apostle; give me one such, and I will reverence him however illiterate.'[2] 'But these,' he returns to the charge, 'are timeservers, waiting not on God but on the rise and flow of the tides, or the straw in the wind'— 'angry lions to the small, fawning spaniels to the great'— 'flatterers of ladies'—'snuffing up the smell of good dinners' —'ever at the gates not of the wise but of the powerful'[3]— 'unable to speak themselves, but having sufficient sense to stop the tongues of those who can'—'made worse by their elevation'—'affecting manners not their own'—'the long beard, the downcast look, the head bowed, the subdued

---

[1] M. de Broglie has evaded some of these dark colours by transferring them to the Arian bishops; much in the same way as the mutual recriminations of the Bishops of Nicæa have been disposed of by wrongly referring them to the heretics. But there can be no question that Gregory is speaking of those who dismissed him from his office (see *De Episc.* 150, *Ad Episc.* 110), and therefore of the Council collectively.

[2] *Ad Episc.* pp. 200–230.

[3] *De Episc.* pp. 330–350, 635.

voice '—' the slow walk '—' the got-up devotee ' [4]—' the wisdom anywhere but in the mind.'

If such is a faithful character of the prelates at the Council, it needed not any special provocation to justify the well-known protests of Gregory, which, in fact, are even tame and flat after these sustained invectives. 'Councils, congresses, we greet afar off, from which (to use very moderate terms) we have suffered many evils.' 'I will not sit in one of those Councils of geese and cranes.' 'I fly from every meeting of bishops, for I never saw a good end of any such,[5] nor a termination, but rather an addition of evils.'

The Council was thus left without a head, and Constantinople without a bishop. Accordingly one of the chief objects for which the Synod had been called together was by its own folly frustrated. Whilst the Council hesitated, others took the matter into their own hands. The solution was one which forcibly illustrates the ecclesiastical usages of those times, as unlike to those of our time as it is possible to conceive.

There was a magistrate at Constantinople named Nectarius, remarkable for his dignified manners. He was a native of Tarsus, and, being on the point of returning home, called on his countryman Diodorus, Bishop of Tarsus, then at the Council, to ask whether he could take any letters for him. Diodorus, perhaps not without the partiality of a fellow-citizen, was so much struck by his venerable white locks and his splendid priestly appearance, that he determined, if possible, to have him raised to the vacant bishopric. He accordingly communicated his name to the Bishop of Antioch, who at first laughed at the notion as preposterous, but at last consented, partly as a favour, partly in jest, to add his name at the end of the list to be submitted to the Emperor.[6]

Meantime the claims of Nectarius appear to have been whispered about in the groups of loiterers who may always

Election of Nectarius.

---

[4] Πιστὸς ἐσκευασμένος, *Ibid.* 150.
[5] *Ibid.* vol. ii. p. 106, 110; *De Vit.* 855.
[6] Sozomen, vii. c. 8.

be seen in an Eastern city, and thus to have reached the Court. The Emperor the moment he saw the list, put his finger on Nectarius's name, ran over the other candidates, then came back to Nectarius, and declared him bishop, to the general amazement of the Council, who, nevertheless, at once acquiesced in the decision.

Not only, however, was Nectarius a layman and a magistrate, but he was unbaptised, and not only unbaptised, but he had purposely delayed his baptism, according to the bad practice of that age, in order to reserve for the last moment the cancelling of the sins of a somewhat frivolous youth and manhood. But this discovery was made too late, and the Emperor adhered to his decision with an obstinacy so surprising that it was afterwards supposed by Nectarius's admirers that he must have had a special inspiration. In the opinion of some this strange episcopate turned out extremely well. But this is not the natural inference from the facts that we know concerning it.[7] Its beginning certainly was not creditable. Nectarius learned his episcopal duties as fast as he could from one of his Cilician friends, Cyriacus, Bishop of Adana, whom, by the advice of Diodorus, he retained with him for some time.[8] He also surrounded himself with a circle of his own countrymen, and amongst others was anxious to ordain as his chaplain and deacon, Martyrius, a physician, who had been formerly one of his boon companions, but who now declined Nectarius's proposal on the characteristic ground, that he, having been baptised long before, had lost the chance of clearing himself which Nectarius, by his postponement of the sacred rite, had so prudently reserved.

Such was the new head of the Council and of the clergy of Constantinople to be introduced into his office by an accumulation, in the course of a few days, of the ceremonies of baptism, ordination, and consecration, each of which at that

---

[7] The bad character of Nectarius's episcopate is fairly brought out by Tillemont, vol. ix. p. 488.

[8] Sozomen, vii. 9.

time implied weeks if not years of preparation. The scandal of Nectarius's elevation caused so much talk as to revive once more the hopes of Maximus the Dog, who seduced no less a person than Ambrose [9] and the other bishops of the West to take up his cause. But Nectarius held his own, supported, as he was, by Emperor and Council, and also by a kindly note from his deposed rival, 'cast away by the ungrateful city like a flake of foam or a fragment of sea-weed' on the Bosphorus.

Meanwhile, under these auspices, the Council hastened to wind up its affairs, and to approach the decision of the theological questions for which the Bishops had mainly been summoned. By this time they were so thoroughly demoralised and discredited by their internal quarrels, that the thirty-six heretical prelates who were present took courage to offer a determined front, and, to the surprise alike of Emperor and Council, fixed a day for their departure, and left Constantinople, protesting against any further attempts on the part of the assembly. But the majority which remained, however reduced in numbers and authority by this secession, were relieved to feel themselves at liberty to conclude their task without any further discussion.

From the most authentic accounts it would appear that they confined themselves to issuing a series of decrees or canons. Of these the first strongly condemned in a mass the various heresies of the time. The second, third, and fourth endeavoured to determine the jurisdictions and precedencies of the different Bishops of the Empire, annulling the election of Maximus, and giving to the see of Constantinople a rank second only to that of Rome, on the express ground that Constantinople was a second Rome. This order is important as embodying the fact that the several dignitaries of Christendom took their position not according to the sacred or apostolic recollections of their sees, but according *Canons of Constantinople.*

---

[9] Tillemont, vol. ix. pp. 501, 502. It was on this occasion that Maximus came out with an orthodox book in order to procure the favour of the Emperor.

ing to the civil rank of the cities where they resided. The exaltation of Constantinople was assuredly owing not to any apostolic dignity, but to its being the capital of Constantine, and the bishop of old Rome, in like manner, assuredly occupied the first place, not because he was the successor of Peter, but the bishop of the capital of the world.[1]

It was[2] the 9th of July, and the summer heats impended, which, though tolerable at Constantinople, would render the return of the bishops to their several homes increasingly difficult. Theodosius, now that their work was over, felt that his was to begin, broke silence, and affirmed by an imperial decree the condemnation of the heresies which they had issued, and the rank of the bishops which they had established. Their proceedings were closed by a splendid funeral ceremony, in which the remains of Paul, the first bishop of the imperial city, were transferred in state from Ancyra to a church[3] in Constantinople built for his rival and successor Macedonius. Paul had been present at the Council of Nicæa as a child of twelve years old, in attendance on Alexander, Bishop of Byzantium, and this incident of his posthumous honours thus seems to link together the first two assemblies of the Christian Church.

It has been thought necessary to give this description of a Council, because it illustrates so many feelings of the time. The Creed of Constantinople. We now come to the question of what is commonly called the Creed of Constantinople. In the common traditions[4] of ecclesiastical history, the third part of the Nicene Creed is said to have been added by the Fathers of

---

[1] The 4th, 5th, 6th, and 7th Canons commonly ascribed to this Council are shown by Hefele (*Concilien-Geschichte*, ii. pp. 13, 14, 18–27) to be of a later date. See also Professor Hort's *Dissertations*, pp. 95–100.

[2] Hefele. (*Concilien-Geschichte*, ii. p. 12.)

[3] The fame of the funeral was so great that a belief sprang up among the people, and especially among the ladies of Constantinople, that St. Paul the Apostle was buried in the church. (Sozomen, vii. c. 9.) It is a good instance of the growth of a legend from the confusion of an obscure with a celebrated name. Many such doubtless have arisen.

[4] 'Added by the Fathers of the first Council of Constantinople.' (Catechism of the Council of Trent, Article VIII.) Long after the Council a

the Council of Constantinople to resist a new heresy concerning the Third Hypostasis in the Trinity, and the Nicene Creed thus enlarged is designated as ' the Creed of Constantinople.' But this designation, though not quite as erroneous as that which speaks of the ' Apostles' Creed,' and of ' Athanasius's Creed,' or which describes this altered confession as ' the Nicene Creed,' is very nearly as destitute of foundation. There is no trace in the records of the Council of any such formal enunciation of any new creed ; on the contrary they appeal to the existing Nicene Creed as adequate for all theological purposes. Such too is the language of Gregory Nazianzen a few years after the meeting of the Council.[5]

Then follows the period of eighty years, which are filled by the two Councils of Ephesus and that of Chalcedon. They are given in great detail by Fleury, Tillemont, Milman, and Amédée Thierry. They are described with such liveliness in the contemporary historians and acts as to leave little to be desired. The shorthand writers report to us not only every speech, but every cry of approval or disapproval, and every movement by which the assembly was swayed to and fro. At times their reports were taken with difficulty, the violence of the chief actors being such that the notes of the reporters were effaced as soon as written, and that their fingers were broken in the attempt to prevent them from writing. But they remain a wonderful, perhaps a unique, monument of the point to which stenography had reached in the fourth century.

The dispute which occasioned the Councils of Ephesus was the refusal of Nestorius,[6] Archbishop of Constantinople, to describe the Virgin Mary by a Greek expression to which the Western languages furnish no exact equivalent. It suffices

chapel was shown in Constantinople, under the name of ' Concord,' where the creed was said to have been drawn up. (Tillemont, ix. p. 495, where the whole matter is well discussed.)

[5] See Hefele. (*Concilien-Geschichte*, ii. p. 11.)

[6] I have given the titles of the Roman, Constantinopolitan, and Alexandrian sees as they were at the time. ' Pope ' and ' Patriarch ' were later.

to state that in no Protestant church could the expression be used without grave offence. Never was there a time when Pascal's humorous description of theological terms was more applicable: ' The difference between us is so subtle that we can hardly perceive it ourselves ; any one else would find it difficult to understand. Happy,' he exclaims in righteous indignation, ' are the nations who never heard of the word. Happy are they who preceded its birth.' [7] Had Nestorius been Cyril, or Cyril Nestorius, the two parties would have changed accordingly.[8] The expression over which the battle was fought was never admitted into any Creed of the Church. Neither at Ephesus nor Chalcedon was there on this ground any addition to what already existed.

We must not suppose that the Councils acted from spontaneous conviction. A determined mob from Constantinople—from Syria—from Egypt—pressed upon them from without. It was like the tyranny which the Clubs exercised over the Convention in the time of the French Revolution. The monks were for the most part laymen, but laymen charged with all the passions of clergy. The religious orders of the West have never been used for such purposes, nor, it must be added, subjected to such treatment. We are told at the beginning of the conflict that Nestorius himself was the aggressor. The monks, who were the first to catch any scent of heresy, were in the first instance stripped and lashed with loaded whips—laid on the ground and beaten as they lay. But these passions and penalties were not confined to one party. Cyril brought with him from Alexandria the savage guard of his palace, the Parabolani, or ' Death-defiers,' whose original function was to bury the dead,

<hr>

[7] *Provincial Letters* I. and III. For an instructive discussion of the intricacies, contradictions, and obscurities of the theological terms used in these controversies, see Cardinal Newman's *History of the Arians*, Appendix, 432–444.

[8] How the same expressions become orthodox and heterodox in turn is seen from the *Homoousion* (see *Lectures on Eastern Church*, Lecture iv. p. 137), and from the adoption by Nestorius and the denial by Cyril of words officially incorporated with the Creed: ' Incarnate of the Holy Ghost and of the Virgin Mary.' (Professor Hort's *Dissertations*, 112.)

but whose duty it now became to protect the Archbishop against all enemies; the sailors, whose rough life laid them open to anyone who hired them; the sturdy porters and beggars, and the bathing-men from the public baths.  These men sate at the doors of the Council, and the streets ran red with the blood which they shed without scruple.  Barsumas, the fierce monk with his band of anchorites as fierce as himself, came thither with his reputation ready made for knocking heretics on the head with the huge maces which he and his companions wielded with terrible force on any-one who opposed them.  The whole was crowned at the critical moment by the entrance of a body of soldiers with drawn swords and charged lances, or with chains to carry off the refractory members to prison.  Some hid themselves under the benches; some were compelled to sign the de-crees in blank.  Flavian, Archbishop of Constantinople, lay watching for the moment of escape, when Dioscorus, the Archbishop of Alexandria, perceiving him, struck him in the face with his fist; the two deacons, one of them afterwards himself Archbishop of Alexandria, seized him round the waist and dashed him to the ground.  Dioscorus kicked the dying man on the sides and chest.  The monks of Barsumas struck him with their clubs as he lay on the ground.  Bar-sumas himself cried out in the Syrian language, ' Kill him, kill him.'  He expired from this savage treatment in the course of a few days.

Such were the scenes of disorder, reaching their height in the Council, afterwards called the Robber Council at Ephesus,[9] but of which the indications spread through the whole period.  Dioscorus's violence differed from that of Cyril in degree only, not in kind.  The same crowd of ruffians were in all these assemblies, and the fate which threatened the hesitating bishops was similar.

Another influence, more gentle and more orderly but equally potent, was that of the Imperial Court.  Theodosius

---

[9] The decrees of the Council were directed to be revised at Chalcedon, but the Imperial Government declined to condemn the Council itself.

II. and his wife Eudocia—Marcian, the honest soldier, and his wife Pulcheria—were never absent from the thoughts of the leaders of the assemblies. To persuade, cajole, circumvent the Imperial emissaries was the incessant effort of either side. It was not by accident that the decision of each of these assemblies coincided with the opinions of the high personages then reigning in the court. The wavering mind of Theodosius II. was the point to be won at the Council of Ephesus. Chrysaphius, the great courtier, was the chief supporter of the Robber Council. Marcian and Pulcheria received the tumultuous acclamations of the Council of Chalcedon. 'To Marcian the new Constantine—to Pulcheria the new Helena.' The personal motives of each of these high dignitaries entered deeply into the controversy. Theodosius was the enemy of anyone who brought him into trouble. Chrysaphius was the enemy of Archbishop Flavian, who had refused him the accustomed fees at Easter. Pulcheria was influenced by jealousy of her sister-in-law Eudocia, and her hatred of Chrysaphius. The letters of the Emperors were reckoned as 'sacred.' The Councils were convoked entirely at their summons.

Another baser element in these considerations was the gross bribery practised by Cyril. Together with this acted the influences, not unusual in such controversies—the desertion of the unpopular cause by half-hearted friends; Nestorius abandoned by those who had looked up to him as their oracle—Dioscorus left alone in the Council of Chalcedon by those who had followed him through all his violences in the Robber Council. There was also that which always produces an effect on a mixed assembly—the horror expressed by weak-minded disciples, who profess to be and are really shocked by some rash expression on the part of their master, and speak with bated breath and tears in their eyes—such as Acacius of Mitylene and Theodotus of Ancyra; or again some argumentative dialectician who wishes to push all arguments to their extremities, such as Eusebius of Dorylœum, the old advocate who never would leave the simple Eutyches to himself.

There were also the rivalries of the great sees: Alexandria, twice over, in the person of Cyril and in the person of Dioscorus, irritated by the preponderance of Constantinople and of Antioch—Rome, at the Robber Council, irritated in the person of its legates, who vainly endeavoured to get a hearing for their master's letter. There was the opening for every kind of private rancour—discontented deacons, ambitious priests, denouncing their bishops when the occasion offered, before the commissioners sent down by the Imperial Government. There was the pardonable weakness of the bishops, afraid of their constituencies, afraid of their congregations, afraid of their clergy. There were aged prelates prostrate on the floor, with their faces on the ground, crying, 'Have mercy upon us; have pity upon us.' 'They will kill us at home.' 'Have pity on our grey hairs.' There were also the bishops of Asia, alarmed for their popularity if they sacrificed the privileges of the see of Ephesus. 'Have pity upon us; they will murder our children; have pity on our children; have pity on us.' It is a scene which reminds us of the most pitiable scenes in the elections of some of our modern representative assemblies.

A curious circumstance must be noticed as guiding the decisions of both assemblies. The claim of Ephesus was suggested on the ground of its accessibility by land and sea, and its ample supply of provisions in the wide plain of the Cayster. But there was a further cause not mentioned, not perhaps occurring to those who summoned the Council, but which materially contributed to its final result. Ephesus was the burial-place, according to tradition, of the Virgin Mother, who with John the Evangelist had taken refuge there in the close of the first century. The church in which the assembly was to be held was the only one in the world as yet dedicated to the Virgin Mary. In the mind of the Ephesian populace she had taken the place of the sacred image of Diana which had so excited them four centuries earlier. The passions of the people, as described in the nineteenth chapter of the Acts, might seem to have been recalled in some of the scenes of the Council. All these circumstances contributed to the success of the anti-Nestorian cause; and, although the honour of the Virgin was not the primary cause of the agitation of the question, the triumph of Cyril's party in Ephesus was celebrated as such.

The reasons for the selection of Chalcedon were still more remarkable. It was the nearest approach to Constantinople without being in the city itself. Chalcedon was Scutari. It was that splendid promontory dear to Englishmen, dear to all who have ever from its height contemplated that glorious view. Even in that age the beauty of the situation attracted the admiration of spectators. But it was yet more than this. The church in which the Council was to be held was that which contained the remains [1] of the virgin martyr St. Euphemia. She was the oracle, the miracle-worker, of the neighbourhood. The Archbishop of Constantinople on great emergencies entered the shrine, and (like the Bishop of Petra on like occasions with the sacred fire at Jerusalem) inserted a sponge into the tomb, which he drew out filled with the martyr's blood, which was then distributed, as a cure for all evils, to all parts of the Empire. It was in this same tomb that at the close of the Council the magistrates and bishops placed the disputed documents which contained the faith of the assembly; and tradition added that the dead woman raised in her hand the roll which contained the true doctrine,[2] and that the roll which contained the heretical doctrine lay dishonoured at her feet.

The whole proceedings of the Council of Ephesus have been summarised by an eminent personage [3] who knew what he was saying, and said what he meant.

'Even those Councils which were œcumenical have nothing to boast of in regard to the Fathers, taken individually,

---



[1] They were afterwards transferred to Saint Sophia, and subsequently to the Abbey of Saint Euphemia in Calabria.

[2] I have seen pictures at Athos representing this tradition.

[3] Cardinal Newman's *Historical Sketches*, pp. 335–337, 350, 351.

which compose them.  They appear as the antagonist host
in a battle, not as the shepherds of their people. . . .

'  " What is the good of a Council," Cyril would say, " when
the controversy is already settled without one ? " in something
like the frame of mind of the great Duke of Wellington years ago, when he spoke in such depre-
ciatory terms of a " county meeting." . . . How the
Emperor fixed the meeting of the Council for Pentecost, June 7 ; how Nestorius made his appearance with a
bodyguard of two imperial cohorts; how Cyril brought up
his fifty Egyptian bishops, staunch and eager, not forgetting
to add to them the stout seamen of his transports; how
Memnon had a following of forty bishops, and reinforced
them with a like body of sturdy peasants from his farms;
how the assembled Fathers were scared and bewildered
by these preparations for battle, and, wishing it all over,
waited with impatience a whole fortnight . for the Syrian
bishops while Cyril preached in the churches against Nestorius; how in the course of this fortnight some of their
number fell sick and died ; how the Syrians, on the other hand,
had been thrown out by the distance of their sees from Antioch (their place of rendezvous), from the length of the land
journey thence to Ephesus, by the wet weather and the bad
roads, by the loss of their horses, and by the fatigue of their
forced marches; how they were thought by Cyril's party to
be unpunctual on purpose, but by themselves to be most unfortunate in their tardiness, because they wished to shelter
Nestorius; how, when they were now a few days' journey
from Ephesus, they sent on hither an express to herald their
approach, but how Cyril would not wait beyond the fortnight,
though neither the Western bishops nor even the Pope's
legates had yet arrived ; how on June 22 he opened the
Council in spite of a protest from 61 out of 150 bishops there
assembled ; how within one summer's day he cited, condemned, deposed, and degraded Nestorius, and passed his
twelve theses of doctrine called " Anathematisms," which the
Pope apparently had never seen, and which the Syrian

Cardinal<br>Newman's<br>description<br>of the Coun-<br>cil of Ephe-<br>sus.

bishops, then on their way to Ephesus, had repudiated the year before as Apollinarian; and how, as if reckless of this imputation, he suffered to stand among the formal testimonies to guide the bishops in their decision gathered from the Fathers, and still extant, an extract from a writing of Timotheus, the Apollinarian, if not of Apollinarius himself, ascribing this heretical document to Pope Julius, the friend of Athanasius; how in the business of the Council he showed himself confidential with Eutyches, afterwards the author of that very Monophysite heresy of which Apollinarius was the forerunner; how on the fifth day after these proceedings the Syrian bishops arrived, and at once, with the protection of an armed force, and without the due forms of ecclesiastic law, held a separate Council of forty-three bishops, Theodoret being one of them, and anathematised Cyril and Memnon and their followers; and how the Council terminated in a discussion, which continued for nearly two years after it, till at length Cyril, John, and Theodoret, and the others on either side, made up the quarrel by mutual explanations—all this is matter of history.'

Such is the summary of one not likely to overcharge the picture of the misdeeds of the Council of Ephesus. We will add the literal report of some of the scenes that took place at the Council of Chalcedon. It is from the Acts of the Council.[4]

'The illustrious Judges and the honourable Senate ordered that the most reverend Bishop Theodoret should enter, that he may be a partaker of the Council, because the holy Archbishop Leo had restored the bishopric to him; and the most sacred and pious Emperor has determined that he is to be present at the Holy Council. And on the entrance of Theodoret, the most reverend bishops of Egypt, Illyricum, and Palestine called out: "Have mercy upon us! The faith is destroyed. The Canons cast him out. Cast out the teacher of Nestorius." The most religious bishops of the East and those of Pontus, Asia, and Thrace

Report of the Council of Chalcedon.

---

[4] Hardouin, ii. 74.

shouted out: "We had to sign a blank paper; we were scourged, and so we signed. Cast out the Manichæans; cast out the enemies of Flavian; cast out the enemies of the Faith." Dioscorus, the most religious Bishop of Alexandria, said: "Why is Cyril cast out? He it is who is anathematised by Theodoret." The Eastern and Pontic and Asian and Thracian most religious bishops shouted out: "Cast out Dioscorus the murderer. Who does not know the deeds of Dioscorus?" The Egyptian and the Illyrian and the Palestinian most religious bishops shouted out: "Long years to the Empress!" The Eastern and the most religious bishops with them shouted out: "Cast out the murderers!" The Egyptians and the most religious bishops with them shouted out: "The Empress has cast out Nestorius. Long years to the Orthodox Empress! The Council will not receive Theodoret." Theodoret, the most religious bishop, came up into the midst and said: "I have offered petitions to the most godlike, most religious and Christ-loving masters of the world, and I have related the disasters which have befallen me, and I claim that they shall be read." The most illustrious Judges and the most honourable Senate said: "Theodoret, the most religious bishop, having received his proper place from the most holy Archbishop of the renowned Rome, has occupied now the place of an accuser. Wherefore suffer that there be not confusion at the hearing, and that the things which have had a beginning may be finished, for prejudice from the appearance of the most religious Theodoret will occur to no one, reserving afterwards every argument for you and for him if you desire to make one on one side or the other; especially if without writing there appears to be a testimony to his orthodoxy from the most religious Bishop of Antioch, the Great City." And after Theodoret, the most religious bishop, had sat down in the midst, the Eastern and the most religious bishops who were with them shouted out: "He is worthy! He is worthy! The Egyptians and the most religious bishops who were with them shouted out: "Do not call him a bishop! He is not a bishop! Cast out the fighter against God! Cast out the Jew!" The Easterns and the most religious bishops who were with them shouted out : " The Orthodox for the Council ! Cast out the rebels! Cast out the murderers !" The Egyptians and the most religious bishops who were with them shouted out : " Cast out the fighter against God! Cast out the insulter against Christ! Long years to the Empress! Long years to the Emperor! Long years to the Orthodox Emperor! Theodoret has anathematised Cyril." The Easterns and the most religious bishops who were with them shouted out : " Cast out the murderer Dioscorus !" The Egyptians and the most religious bishops with them shouted out : " Long years to the Senate! He has not the right of speech. He is expelled from the whole Synod !" Basil, the most religious Bishop of Trajanopolis, in the province of Rhodope, rose up and said : " Theodoret has been condemned by us." The Egyptians and the most religious bishops with them shouted out : " Theodoret has accused Cyril. We cast out Cyril if we receive Theodoret. The Canons cast out Theodoret. God has turned away from him." The most illustrious Judges and the most honourable Senate said : " These vulgar cries are not worthy of bishops, nor will they assist either side. Suffer, therefore, the reading of all the documents." The Egyptians and the most religious bishops with them shouted out : " Cast out one man, and we will all hear. We shout out in the Cause of Religion. We say these things for the sake of the Orthodox Faith." The most illustrious Judges and the honourable Senate said : " Rather aquiesce, in God's name, that the hearing of the documents should take place, and concede that all shall be read in proper order." And at last they were silent. And Constantine, the most holy Secretary and Magistrate of the Divine Synod, read these documents.'

One more painful scene must be given—the insistance that Theodoret should pronounce a curse on his ancient friend. ' The most reverend bishops all stood before the rails of the most holy altar and shouted : " Theodoret must now anathematise Nestorius." Theodoret, the most reverend bishop, passed into the midst and said : " I gave my petition to the most divine and religious Emperor, and I gave the documents to the most reverend bishops occupying the place of the most sacred Archbishop Leo ; and, if you think fit, they shall be sent to you, and you will know what I think." The most reverend bishops shouted : " We want nothing to be read—only anathematise Nestorius." Theodoret, the most reverend bishop, said : " I was brought up by the orthodox, I was taught by the orthodox, I have preached orthodoxy, and not only Nestorius and Eutyches, but any man who thinks not rightly, I avoid and count him an alien." The most reverend bishops shouted out : " Speak plainly ; anathema to Nestorius and his doctrine—anathema to Nestorius and to those who befriend him !"' Theodoret, the most reverend bishop, said : 'Of truth I do not speak, except that the Creed is pleasing to God. I came to satisfy you, not because I think of my country, not because I desire honour, but because I have been falsely accused, and I anathematise every impenitent heretic. I anathematise Nestorius and Eutyches, and every one who says that there are two Sons.' Whilst he was speaking, the most reverend bishops shouted out : ' Speak plainly ; anathematise Nestorius and those who think with him.' Theodoret, the most reverend bishop, said ɩ ' Unless I set forth at length my faith I cannot speak. I believe——' And whilst he spoke the most reverend bishops shouted : ' He is a heretic ! he is a Nestorian ! Thou art the heretic ! Anathema to Nestorius and to any one who does not say that the Holy Virgin Mary is the Parent of God, and who divides the only begotten Son into two Sons.' Theodoret, the most reverend bishop, said : ' Anathema to Nestorius and to whoever denies that the Holy Virgin Mary is the Parent of God, and who divides the only begotten Son into two Sons.' I have subscribed the definition of faith and the epistle of the most holy Archbishop Leo. And after all this he said, ' Farewell.' [5]

[5] Hardouin, ii. 448.

It is the conduct of the 3rd and 4th Councils in their collective capacity which more than justifies the objections of Gregory Nazianzen to the 2nd Council. It is this which represents the official voice of the clergy of the Church in that age. If there is any clear manifestation of common sense and charity it is in the conduct of the Imperial Commissioners, who controlled and guided the Council of Chalcedon. The faithfulness of the reporters lets us see step by step Theodoret's agonising reluctance openly to disavow his friend, and at last his indignant ' Farewell.'

But there is discernible at times the indication of a better feeling through this furious party spirit. John of Antioch with 'the Eastern bishops,'—Flavian him- *Moderate tendencies.* self at the earlier period,—resolutely continued to insist on the duty of conciliatory measures. The Arch- bishop of Rome, also, especially after the experience of the Robber Council, recommended a halt in the vehement pur- suit after heresy, and to be content with letting things alone. Above all there is the one man, Theodoret, whose position, with many drawbacks, may in some respects be compared to the isolated position of Lord Falkland. He had the courage to defend his former friend Nestorius—to declare that he had never been properly deposed, and that his suc- cessor would be an usurper. He submitted at the last, and brought his ancient friend Alexander of Hierapolis to submit also, but only for the sake of peace. He rejoiced with an exceeding joy on hearing of the repose of the Christian world on the death of the turbulent Cyril—' The East and Egypt are henceforth united; envy is dead, and heresy is buried with her.' [6] He was still attacked with ignoble animosity by Dioscorus. But on the whole, and with a formal submis- sion on his part, he was accepted. The admiration in which he was held is to a certain degree an anticipation of the

---

[6] The genuineness of this letter has been doubted, but chiefly because of its attack on Cyril. It was quoted against Theodoret at the fifth General Council. See the question argued on both sides in Hefele, iii. p. 851.

judgment of the English historian—'Who would not meet the judgment of the Divine Redeemer loaded with the errors of Nestorius rather than with the barbarities of Cyril?'[7] It may also be a comment on the saying of the contemporary Isidore, 'Sympathy such as Theodoret's may not see clearly, but antipathy such as Cyril's does not see at all.'[8]

It was in accordance with this more moderate feeling that we may believe the decree to have been issued which has made the Council of Ephesus memorable.

In the sixth session, in a spirit which endeavoured to control the ardour of controversy, it was ordered that no one should set forth or put together or compose any creed other[9] than that defined at Nicæa on pain of deposition if clergy, of excommunication if laity. *Decree of Ephesus against a new Creed.* The original form of the Creed of Nicæa, which this decree is intended to guard, must here be given :—

We believe in one God, the Father Almighty, Maker of all things both visible and invisible; and in one Lord Jesus Christ, the Son of God, begotten from the Father, only begotten, that is to say, from the substance of the Father; God of God, Light of Light, true God of true God; begotten not made; of one substance with the Father; by Whom all things were made, both things in heaven and things on the earth; Who for us men and for our salvation came down, and was made flesh; was made man, suffered, and rose again on the third day; ascended into the heavens; cometh to judge the quick and the dead; and in the Holy Spirit. But those who say there was a time when He was not, and before being begotten He was not, and that He came out of what was not existing, or that He is of another person (ὑποστάσεως) or essence (οὐσία), or is created, or is variable, or is changeable,—all these the Catholic and Apostolic Church anathematises.

With this decision the Council of Ephesus believed that

---

[7] Milman's *Latin Christianity*, i. 145.

[8] Quoted in Cardinal Newman's *Historical Sketches*, ii. 356.   The whole letter is worth reading.

[9] It has been argued that ἑτέραν means of 'a discordant creed,' and is distinguished from ἄλλην, 'another.'   This is completely disproved by Professor Swainson, *Nicene and Apostles' Creeds Compared*, p. 166, who shows that the two words were used promiscuously.

it had for ever excluded the possibility of any new confession
of faith, and had placed the Creed of Nicæa on an impreg-
nable basis. The motive is obvious: to protect what had
already been done in the first General Council, and to guard
against the multiplication of creeds, of which that age had
already had sufficient experience. It is curious that in both
particulars this decree entirely failed. The creed of Nicæa,
as thus set forth, has now been discontinued throughout the
whole Church of the West, and, with the exception of the
Monophysite, Nestorian, and perhaps the Armenian Churches,[1]
throughout the whole Church of the East. Its anathemas
are no longer recited, although in the time of its first promulgation they were regarded as of the utmost importance; [2]
and in other respects, as · shall be noticed presently, its
contents have undergone serious modifications. The Creeds
which it was intended to prevent have been multiplied
beyond imagination in the numberless Creeds of the fifth
century, the Athanasian Creed of the ninth, the confessions
of Trent, Augsburg, Geneva, and London of the sixteenth
century.

It is by no means clear by what process the change was
effected, but we can faintly trace it through the discussions
Creed of<br>Constanti-<br>nople. of the time. The first step, as usual in these
innovations, was the most momentous. Previous to
the Council of Constantinople, which, as we have already seen,
adopted no creed of its own, there was a creed existing in the
writings of Epiphanius,[3] which agreed in many respects with
the creed now commonly, but erroneously, known as the
Creed of Constantinople. Besides this, there is a considerable resemblance between the present form of that creed, and
what is preserved to us as the Creed of Jerusalem [4] in the
writings of Cyril, the bishop of that city. There is, further,
a late tradition that the form of the creed now professing to

<hr>

[1] See Swainson's *Nicene and Apostles' Creed Compared*, p. 143.
[2] See *Lectures on Eastern Church*, Lect. IV.
[3] Epiphanius, *Anchoratus* (pp. 77-83), A.D. 374.
[4] See Hort's *Dissertation*, p. 74, in which it is argued with much learning
that the Creed was on the basis of the Creed of Jerusalem.

be that of Constantinople was drawn up by Gregory of Nyssa, who was present, as we have seen, in that assembly. But it was in the Council of Chalcedon, for the first time, that we have the startling announcement made by Aetius, Archdeacon of Constantinople, that he was going to read what had been determined upon by the 150 bishops congregated in Constantinople. It is conjectured that, from one or other of the three sources indicated, from the writings of Epiphanius, or of Cyril of Jerusalem, or of Gregory of Nyssa, this creed may have been the subject of some conversation in the Council of Constantinople, and that this was made the ground or the pretext of its being represented by Aetius as the creed of that Council itself. The accuracy of Aetius, as of the other members of the Council, is not above suspicion.[5] The creed was as follows :—

We believe in one God, the Father Almighty, Maker of heaven and earth, and of all things visible and invisible ; and in one Lord Jesus Christ, the Son of God, the only begotten, Who was begotten from the Father before all worlds, Light of Light, true God of true God ; begotten, not made ; of one substance with the Father, by Whom all things exist ; Who for us men and for our salvation came down and was made flesh of the Holy Ghost and of Mary the Virgin, and was made man, and was crucified for us under Pontius Pilate, and suffered and was buried, and rose again the third day according to the Scriptures, and ascended into the heavens, and sitteth on the right hand of the Father, and cometh again with glory to judge the quick and the dead ; of whose kingdom there shall be no end ; and in the Spirit, which is holy, which is sovereign and lifegiving, which proceedeth from the Father ; Which with the Father and the Son is worshipped and glorified ; Which spake by the prophets ; in one holy Catholic and Apostolic Church ; we acknowledge one Baptism for the remission of sins ; we look for the resurrection of the dead, and the life of the world to come.

This creed, although twice formally recited at the Council of Chalcedon, yet was not allowed to take the exclusive

---

[5] Swainson's *Nicene and Apostles' Creeds*, pp. 94-96; Tillemont, ix. p. 421, xiv. p. 442; Hort's *Dissertation*, pp. 74-76.

place given by the Council of Ephesus to the Creed of Nicæa. The decree of Ephesus was still sufficiently powerful to restrain the Chalcedonian Fathers from introducing this creed, so-called of Constantinople, into the place of the one authorised Confession of Faith. But as time rolled on this provision was doubly set aside. The Creed of Nicæa, as we have seen, is now read in no European Church; and the creed, professedly of Constantinople, really the production of some unknown Church or Father, gradually superseded it. The Emperor Justin, in the year 568, first ordered that it should be recited in the public services of the Church; and from that moment it has assumed its present position.

It is difficult to trace precisely the motives by which this great change was effected. It would appear, however, to have been the result of that lull in ecclesiastical controversy which succeeded to the terrible scenes of the Ephesian and Chalcedonian Councils.[6] Some of the additions to the Nicene Creed might have seemed to have incurred the censure of the Ephesian Council not only in the letter but in the spirit. The clause, ' He was begotten of the Holy Ghost and of Mary the Virgin,'[7] did not exist in the Creed of Nicæa, and was in fact vehemently contested in the Council of Ephesus, as having been brought forward by Nestorius and as expressive of his view. The clauses also relating to the Divine Spirit were not contained in the original Creed of Nicæa, and were perhaps added in order to meet the Macedonian heretics. The omission or transposition of the words, ' God of God,' ' the Only begotten,' ' that is to say, from the substance of the Father,' are, to say the least, unwarranted interferences with a document where every word and every position of every word are deemed of importance. But the Creed of Chalcedon (or Constantinople), however doubtful its origin, may still be regarded as, on the whole, an improvement on that memorable document which it supplanted, although under the penalty of deprivation of their orders to

<hr>

[6] Hort's *Dissertations*, pp. 110–136.
[7] Ibid. p. 112.

all the clergy and bishops who use it, and of excommunication to the laity who adopt it. The acquiescence (if so be) of the original Council of Constantinople in a private document which came before them, sanctioned by the authority of Cyril of Jerusalem, and of Gregory of Nyssa, would be in conformity with the abstinence from further dogmatism into which they were driven almost inevitably by a weariness of the whole transaction in which they were involved. With this also would· agree the more moderate counsels which we have already noticed, belonging to what may be called the central party at Ephesus and Chalcedon, and the deference at last paid to Theodoret. The total omission of the Nicene anathemas was a distinct step in this direction. The condemnation of any one who expressed that the Son was of a different 'person' (or 'hypostasis') from the Father, might well become startling to those who were becoming familiar with the later formula, which at last issued in the directly contrary proposition by pronouncing a like anathema on any one who maintained that He was of the same 'hypostasis.'

It was one of the constant charges against Basil and Gregory that they were unwilling to define precisely and polemically the doctrine of the Divine Spirit. Those who read the exposition of this doctrine as set forth in the Greek [a] of these clauses will be surprised to see how wonderfully the harshnesses and roughnesses that appear in the English or Latin translation disappear in the subtle, yet simple, language of the original. What may have been the feelings of the followers of Macedonius we know not ; but we may be certain that no sect now existing, whether belonging to the so-called orthodox or the so-called heretical churches, could find any difficulty in accepting, in their original form, the abstract and general phrases, in which the Biblical doctrine

[a] Τὸ πνεῦμα, τὸ κύριον, τὸ ζωοποιοῦν, τὸ ἐκ τοῦ Πατρὸς ἐκπορευόμενον, τὸ σὺν Πατρὶ καὶ Υἱῷ συμπροσκυνούμενον συνδοξαζόμενον, τὸ λαλῆσαν διὰ τῶν Προφητῶν· compared with 'the Lord and Giver of Life. who proceedeth from the Father and the Son,' &c.   (See Hort, pp. 82, 85, 86.)

of the impersonality and neutrality of the Sacred Influence is set forth.

Again, the limitation of the holy inspiration (the ' Holy Spirit spoke by the prophets ') is a remarkable instance at once of insight into the true nature of the Biblical writings, and also of the moderation of the highest minds of that age, compared with the fanciful and extravagant theories that have sometimes prevailed in modern times on that subject. The other parts of the Bible, the other writings of the great and good, are no doubt the offspring of the Divine Mind, but it is in the prophetical writings that the essence of Christian morality and doctrine is brought out.

Yet once more, the definition of Baptism (' I believe in one Baptism for the remission of sins '), which has been sometimes quoted as if decisive of the whole question then at issue on the intricate question of the mystical or moral effect of Baptism, is couched in terms so studiously general as to include not only Christian Baptism, but the Baptism of John, from which, in the language of technical theology, no transcendental operations could be expected. Only by the most violent anachronisms and distortions of language can the scholastic doctrines of the sudden transformation of baptised infants be imported into words which embrace the doctrine of Baptism in the largest formula which the comprehensive language of Scripture has furnished.[9]

Again, the questionable phrase, ' the Resurrection of the Flesh ' in the Apostles' Creed is here represented by the Biblical expression, ' Resurrection of the Dead.'

Lastly, it is to be observed that Nicephorus ascribes all these changes to Gregory of Nyssa, whose great name, if he in any way took them up, would, more than any other single cause, have led to their popular acceptance, not only from his own learning and genius, but from the fame of his brother Basil, and from the influence—at any rate at the beginning of the Council—of his friend. The tradition that these words were derived from Gregory of Nyssa,

* See Chapter I.

whether borne out by historical evidence or not, has never been disputed on dogmatical grounds, is important as showing that the orthodox Eastern Church was not ashamed of receiving its most solemn declaration of Christian faith from one who, had he lived in our times, would have been pronounced by some as a dangerous heretic. There can be no doubt in the mind of any one [1] who has examined his writings—and it is freely admitted, indeed urged, by theologians without the slightest suspicion of latitudinarianism—that Gregory of Nyssa held the opinion shared with him by Origen, and although less distinctly by Gregory of Nazianzus, that there was a hope for the final restoration of the wicked in the other world. And whether or not he actually drew up the concluding clauses of the so-called Creed of Constantinople, there is no doubt that Gregory of Nyssa was present at the Council of Constantinople—that he, if any one, must have impressed his own sense upon them—and that to him, and through him to the Council, the clause which speaks of the ‘life in the world to come’ must have included the hope that the Divine justice and mercy are not controlled by the powers of evil, that sin is not eternal, and that in that ‘world to come,’ punishment will be corrective and not final, and will be ordered by a Love and Justice, the height and depth of which is beyond the narrow thoughts of man to conceive.

[1] See especially *Catech. Orat.* ch. xxvi. De iis qui prematurè abripiuntur, ch. xv. De Anima et Resurrectione (on Phil. ii. 10 ; 1 Cor. xv. 28). The contrary has been maintained by a recent writer, Vincenzo, in four volumes, on the writings of Gregory of Nyssa. But this is done, not as in former times (Tillemont, vol. ix. p. 602), by denying the genuineness of the passages cited in favour of the milder view, but by quoting passages from other parts of his works, containing apparently contradictory sentiments. This might be done equally in the case of Origen, of Archbishop Tillotson, and of Bishop Newton, and to any one who knows the writings of that age proves absolutely nothing.

# CHAPTER XVII.

## THE TEN COMMANDMENTS.

THE Ten Commandments were always in the Christian Church united with the Lord's Prayer and the Creed (whether longer or shorter) as a Christian Institution. In earlier Catholic times, they were used as a framework of moral precepts; in Protestant times they were written conspicuously in the churches. In either case, there are important principles involved in the prominence thus given to them, which demand consideration. In order to do this, we must trace the facts to their Jewish origin.

I. Let us first examine what were the Ten Command- ments in their outward form and appearance when *Outward form.* they were last seen by mortal eyes as the ark was placed in Solomon's Temple.

1. They were written on two tables or blocks of stone or rock. The mountains of Sinai are of red and white granite. *Israelite arrange- ments.* On two blocks of this granite rock—the most last- ing and almost the oldest kind of rock that is to be found in the world, as if to remind us that these Laws were to be the beginning and the end of all things—were the Ten Commandments, the Ten Words, written. They were written, not, as we now write them, only on one side of each of the two tables, but on both sides, so as to give the idea of absolute completeness and solidity. Each block of stone was covered behind and before with the sacred letters. Again, they were not arranged as we now arrange them. In the Fourth, for example, the reason for keeping holy

the seventh day is, in Exodus, because 'God rested on the seventh day from the work of creation'; in Deuteronomy it is to remind them that 'they were once strangers in the land of Egypt.' Probably, therefore, these reasons were not actually written on the stone, but were given afterwards, at two different times, by way of explanation; so that the first four Commandments, as they were written on the tables, were shorter than they are now. Here, as everywhere in the Bible, there may be many reasons for doing what is right. It is the doing of the thing, and not the particular occasion or reason, which makes it right. Another slight difference was that the Commandments probably were divided into two equal portions, so that the Fifth Commandment, instead of being, as it is with us, at the top of the second table, was at the bottom of the first. The duty of honouring our parents is so like the duty of honouring God, that it was put amongst the same class of duties. The duty to both, as in the Roman word ' pietas,' was comprised under the same category, and so it is here understood by Josephus, Philo, and apparently by St. Paul.[1]

These differences between the original and the present arrangement should be noted, because it is interesting to have before us as nearly as we can the exact likeness of those old Commandments, and because it is useful to remember how even these most sacred and ancient words have undergone some change in their outward form since they were first given, and yet still are equally true and equally venerable. Religion does not consist in counting the syllables of the Bible, but in doing what it tells us.

2. When the Christian Church sprang out of the Jewish Church, it did not part with those venerable relics of the earlier time, but they were still used to teach Chris-  tian children their duty, as Jewish children had been taught before. But there were different arrangements introduced in different parts of the world. The Talmudic and

---

[1] Ewald's *History of the People of Israel*, vol. i. pp. 581–592, English translation.

z

the modern Jewish tradition, taking the Ten Commandments strictly as Ten Words or Sentences (Decalogue), makes the First to be the opening announcement: 'I am the Lord thy God, which brought thee out of the land of Egypt,' and the Second is made up of what in our arrangement would be the First and Second combined. The Samaritan division, preserved in the roll on Mount Gerizim, puts the First and Second together, as the First, and then adds [2] at the end an Eleventh, according to our arrangement, not found in the Hebrew Pentateuch, which will be noticed as we proceed.

When the Christians adopted the Commandments there were two main differences of arrangement. There was the division of Augustine and Bede. This follows the Jewish and Samaritan arrangement of combining in one the First and Second Commandments of our arrangement. But inasmuch as it has no Eleventh Commandment, like the Samaritan, nor any 'First Word,' like the Jewish, it makes out the number ten by dividing the last Commandment into two, following here the arrangement of the clauses in the Hebrew of Deuteronomy, and in the LXX. both of Deuteronomy and Exodus, so as to make the Ninth Commandment—'Thou shalt not covet thy neighbour's wife,' and the Tenth, 'Thou shalt not covet thy neighbour's house,' &c. This is followed by the Roman Catholic Church and the Lutheran Church. The division followed by Origen and Jerome is the same as that followed in England and Scotland. It is common to all the Eastern Churches, and all the Reformed Protestant Churches. Here, again, the various arrangements give us a useful lesson, as showing us how the different parts of our doctrine and duty may not be quite put together in the same way, and yet be still the same. And also it may remind us how the very same arrangements, even in outward things, may be made by persons of the most opposite way of thinking; it is a warning not to judge any one by the mere outward sign or badge that they wear. No one could be more unlike to the Roman Catholic Church

---

[2] See Prof. Plumptre, in *Dictionary of the Bible*, vol. iii. pp. 1465–1466.

than the Reformer Luther, and yet the same peculiar arrangement of the Ten Commandments was used by him and by them. No one could be more unlike to the Eastern Church than John Knox, or Calvin, or Cranmer, and yet their arrangement of the Ten Commandments is the same.

II. What are we to learn from the place which the Ten Commandments occupied in the old dispensation ?

We learn what is the true foundation of all religion. The Ten Commandments are simple rules ; most of them can be understood by a child. But still they are the very *Importance of the Commandments.* heart and essence of the old Jewish religion. They occupy a very small part of the Books of Moses. The Ten Commandments, and not the precepts about sacrifices, and passovers, and boundaries, and priests, are the words which are said to have been delivered in thunder and lightning at Mount Sinai. These, and not any ceremonial ordinances, were laid up in the Most Holy Place, as the most precious heritage of the nation. ' There was nothing in the ark save the two tables of stone, which Moses put there at Horeb.'

*Do your duty.* This is what they tell us. *Do your duty to God and your duty to man.* Whatever we may believe, or feel, or think, the main thing is that we are to do what is right, not to do what is wrong. Therefore it is that in the Church of England and in the Reformed Churches of the Continent they are still read in the most sacred parts of the service, as if to show us that, go as far as we can in Christian light and knowledge, make as much as we will of Christian doctrine or of Christian worship, still we must never lose hold of the ancient everlasting lines of duty.

III. But it may be said, Were not those Ten Commandments given to the Jews of old ? Do they not refer to the land of Egypt and the land of Palestine. We love *Spirit of the Commandments.* and serve God, and love and serve our brethren, not because it is written in the Ten Commandments, but because it is written on the tables of our hearts by the Divine Spirit on our spirits and consciences. But herein lies the very meaning of their having become a Christian Institution.

In the Sermon on the Mount Jesus Christ took two or three of these Commandments, and explained them Himself to the people. He took the Sixth Commandment, and showed that for us it is not enough to remember, ' Thou shalt not kill,' but that the Commandment went much deeper, and forbade all angry thoughts and words. This was intended to apply to all the other Commandments. It is not in their letter, but in their spirit, that they concern us ; and this, no doubt, is what is meant by the prayer which in the Church of England follows after each of them, and at the end of all of them, ' Incline our *hearts* to keep this law,' 'Write all these Thy laws in our *hearts*, we beseech Thee.'

1. Let us take them one by one in this way. The First Commandment is no longer ours in the letter, for it begins by saying, 'I am the Lord thy God, *who brought thee out of the land of Egypt.*' He did not bring us up out of the land of Egypt, and so completely has this ceased to apply to us, that in the Commandments as publicly read, the Church of England has boldly struck out these words altogether. But the spirit of the Commandment still remains ; for we all need to be reminded that there is but one Supreme Mind, whose praise and blame are, above all, worth having, seeking, or deserving.

*The First Commandment.*

2. The Second Commandment is no longer ours in the letter, for the sculptures and paintings which we see at every turn are what its letter forbade, and what the Jews, therefore, never made. Every statue, every picture, not only in every church, but in every street or room, is a breach of the letter of the Second Commandment. No Jew would have ventured under the Mosaic dispensation to have them. When Solomon made the golden lions and oxen in the Temple, it was regarded by his countrymen as unlawful. The Mahomedan world still observes the Second Commandment literally. The ungainly figures of the lions in the court of the Alhambra, contrasted with the

*The Second Commandment.*

exquisite carving of arabesques and texts on the walls, is an exception that amply proves the rule. The Christian world has entirely set it aside. But in spirit it is still important. It teaches us that we must not make God after our likeness, or after any likeness short of absolute moral perfection. Any fancies, any doctrines, any practices which lead us to think that God is capricious or unjust or untruthful, or that He cares for any outward thing compared with holiness, mercy, and goodness—that is the breach of the Second Commandment in spirit. It was said truly of an attempt to introduce ceremonial forms of the Christian religion, 'It is so many ways of breaking the Second Commandment.' Every attempt to purify and exalt our ideas of God is the keeping of the Second Commandment in spirit, even although we live amidst pictures and statues and sculptures of things in heaven and things in earth and things under the earth.

3. The Third Commandment. Here the original meaning of the Commandment is more elevated and more spiritual than that which is commonly given to it. Many see *The Third Commandment.* in it only a prohibition of profane swearing or false swearing. It means this—but it means much more. It means that we are not to appeal to God's name for any unworthy purpose. It is a protest against all those sins which have claimed the sanction of God or of religion. The words are literally 'Thou shalt not bring the Holy Name to anything that is vain, that is, to anything that is unholy, hollow, empty.' The plea and pretext of God's name will not avail as an excuse for cruelty or hypocrisy or untruthfulness or undutifulness. The Eternal will not hold him guiltless who taketh His name in vain—that is, who brings it to an unjust or unrighteous cause. All the wicked persecutions carried on, all the wicked wars waged, all the pious frauds perpetrated in the name of the Holy God, are breaches of the Third Commandment, both in its letter and in its spirit.

4. The Fourth Commandment. Here, as in the Second

Commandment, there is a wide divergence between the letter
The Fourth Command-ment. and the spirit. In its letter it is obeyed by no Christian society whatever, except the Abyssinian Church
in Africa, and the small sect of the Seventh-Day Baptists in
England. They still keep a day of rest on the Saturday, the
seventh day of the week. But in every other country the
seventh day is observed only by the Jews, and not by
the Christians. And again, only by the Jews, and not by
Christians anywhere, are the Mosaic laws kept which forbade
the lighting of a single fire, which forbade the walking beyond a single mile, which forbade the employment of a single
animal, which visited as a capital offence the slightest employment on the seventh day. And again, the reasons given
in the two versions of the Fourth Commandment are passed
away. We cannot be called, as in Deuteronomy, to remember that we were strangers in the land of Egypt, for many of
us were never in Egypt at all. We cannot be called, as in
Exodus, to remember that the earth was made in six days, for
we most of us know that it took, not six days, but millions of
ages, to bring the earth from its void and formless state to its
present condition. The letter of the Fourth Commandment
has long ceased. The very name of ‘the Lord’s Day’ and of
‘the first day of the week’ is a protest against it. The very
name of Sabbath is condemned by St. Paul.[3] The Catechism
of the Church of England speaks of the duty of serving God all
the days of our life, and not of serving Him on one day alone.
But the principle which lay at the bottom of the Fourth
Commandment has not passed away. Just as the prohibition
of statues in the Second Commandment is now best carried
out by the avoidance of superstitious, unworthy, degrading
ideas of the nature of God, so the principle of the observance
of the Sabbath in the Fourth Commandment is aimed against
worldly, hard, exacting ideas of the work of man. The principle of the Fourth Commandment enjoins the sacred duty
of rest—for there is an element of rest in the Divine Nature
itself. It enjoins also the sacred duty of kindness to our

<hr>

[3] Col. ii. 16.

servants and to the inferior animals—'for remember that thou wast a servant in the land of Egypt.'  How this rest is to be carried out, within what limits it is to be confined, what amount of innocent recreation is to be allowed, how far the Continental nations have erred on the one side or the Scottish nation on the other side, in their mode of observance, whether the observance of the English Sunday is exactly what it ought to be, or in what respects it might be improved —these are questions which this is not the place to discuss. It is enough to say that amidst all the variations in the mode of observing the Sunday, it is still possible, and it is still our duty to bear in mind the principle of the ancient Law.  'I was *in the Spirit* on the Lord's Day': that is what we should all strive to attain—to be raised at least for one day in the week above the grinding toil of our daily work—above the debasing influence of frivolous amusements —above the jangling of business and controversy—raised into the high and holy atmosphere breathed by pure and peaceful lives, bright and beautiful thoughts, elevating and invigorating worship.  Although the day has been changed from the seventh day to the first day everywhere—nay, even had it been further changed, as Calvin intended, from Sunday to Thursday—even had it yet been further changed, as Tyndale, the foremost of the English Reformers, proposed, from the seventh day to the tenth day—yet still there would survive the solemn obligation founded, not on the Law of Moses, but on the Law of God in Nature, the obligation of rest and of worship as long as human nature remains what it is, as long as the things which are temporal are seen, and the things which are eternal are unseen.[4]

5. The Fifth Commandment.  Here, again, the letter has ceased to have any meaning for us.  'That thy days may be long in the land which the Lord thy God giveth *The Fifth Commandment.* thee.'  We have no claim on the inheritance of the land of Canaan.  No amount of filial reverence will secure for us the possession of the goodly heights of Lebanon, or the

[4] See Prof. Tyndall's admirable Address on the Sabbath at Glasgow.

forests of Gilead or the rushing waters of Jordan. But the ordinance of affection and honour to parents has not diminished, but grown with the years which have passed since the command was first issued. The love of son to mother, the honour of children to parents, is far stronger now than in the days of Moses.

It is often discussed in these days whether this or that principle of religion is natural or supernatural. How often is this distinction entirely without meaning! The Fifth Commandment—sacred to the dearest, deepest, purest, noblest aspirations of the heart—is natural because it is supernatural, is supernatural because it is natural. It is truly regarded as the symbol, as the sanction of the whole framework of civil and religious society. Our obedience to law, our love of country, is not a bond of mere expediency or accident. It is not a worldly, unspiritual ordinance, to be rejected because it crosses some religious fancies or interferes with some theological allegory. It is binding on the Christian conscience, because it is part of the natural religion of the human race and of the best instincts of Christendom.

6. The Sixth Commandment. The crime of murder is what it chiefly condemns, and no sentimental feelings of modern times have ever been able to bring the murderer down from that bad pre-eminence as the worst and most appalling of human offenders. It is the consummation of selfishness. It is the disregard of the most precious of God's earthly gifts—the gift of life. But the scope of the Commandment extends much further. In the Christian sense he is a breaker of the Sixth Commandment who promotes quarrels and jealousies in families, who indulges in fierce, contemptuous words, who fans the passions of class against class, of church against church, of nation against nation. In the horrors of war it is not the innocent soldier killing his adversary in battle, but the partisans on whatever side, the ambitious in whatever nation, the reckless journalists and declaimers of whatever opinions, by which angry passions are fostered, that are the true responsible authors of the

horrors which follow in the train of armies and in the fields of carnage.  In the violence of civil and intestine discord, it is not only human life that is at stake, but that which makes human life precious.  ' As well kill a good man as a good book,' was the saying of Milton, and so we may add in thinking of those who care neither to preserve nor to improve the inheritance which God has given us, ' As well kill a good man as a good institution.'

7. The Seventh Commandment.  Of this it is enough to say that here also we know well in our consciences that it is not only the shameless villain who invades the sanc- The Seventh Command-ment. tity of another's home and happiness that falls under the condemnation of that dreadful word which the Seventh Commandment uses.  It is the reader and writer of filthy books; it is the young man or the young woman who allows his or her purity and dignity to be soiled and stained by loose talk and loose company.  If the sacredness of the marriage bond be the glory of our English homes, no eccentricities of genius, no exceptional misfortunes—however much we may excuse or pity those who have gone astray—can justify us in making light of that which disregarded in one case is endangered in all, which, if lost in a few cases, is the ruin of hundreds.  It is not the loss of Christianity, but of civilisation; not the advance to freedom, but the relapse into barbarism.

8. The Eighth Commandment.  ' Thou shalt not steal.' That lowest, meanest crime of the thief and the robber is not all that the Eighth Commandment condemns.  It The Eighth Command-ment. is the taking of money which is not our due, and which we are forbidden to receive; it is the squandering of money which is not our own, on the racecourse or at the gambling table; it is the taking advantage of a flaw or an accident in a will which gives us property which was not intended for us, and to which others have a better claim than we.  He is the true observer of the Eighth Commandment not only who keeps his hands from picking and stealing, but he who renders just restitution, he who, like the great Indian soldier, Outram, the Bayard of modern times, would

not claim any advantage from a war which he had victoriously conducted, because he thought the war itself was wrong; he who is scrupulously honest, even to the last farthing of his accounts, with master or servant, with employer or employed; he who respects the rights of others, not only of the rich against the poor, not only of the poor against the rich, but of all classes against each other. These, and these only, are the Christian keepers of the Eighth Commandment.

9. The Ninth Commandment. ' Thou shalt not bear false witness.' False witness, deliberate perjury, is the crown and consummation of the liar's progress. But what a world of iniquity is covered by that one word, *Lie*. Careless, damaging statements, thrown hither and thither in conversation; reckless exaggeration and romancing, only to make stories more pungent; hasty records of character, left to be published after we are dead; heedless disregard of the supreme duty and value of truth in all things—these are what we should bear in mind when we are told that we are not to bear false witness against our neighbour. A lady who had been in the habit of spreading slanderous reports once confessed her fault to St. Philip Neri, and asked how she should cure it. He said, ' Go to the nearest market-place, buy a chicken just killed, pluck its feathers all the way as you return, and come back to me.' She was much surprised, and when she saw her adviser again, he said, ' Now go back, and bring me back all the feathers you have scattered.' ' But that is impossible,' she said; ' I cast away the feathers carelessly; the wind, carried them away. How can I recover them ? ' ' That,' he said, ' is exactly like your words of slander. They have been carried about in every direction; you cannot recall them. Go, and slander no more.'

10. The Tenth Commandment. The form of the Commandment speaks only of the possessions of a rude and pastoral people—the wife of a neighbouring chief, the male and female slaves, the Syrian ox, the Egyptian ass. But the principle strikes at the very highest heights of civilisation and at the very innermost secrets of the

heart. Greed, selfishness, ambition, egotism, self-importance, money-getting, rash speculation, desire of the poor to pull down the rich, desire of the rich to exact more than their due from the poor, eagerness to destroy the most useful and sacred institutions in order to gratify a social revenge, or to gain a lost place, or to make a figure in the world—these are amongst the wide-reaching evils which are included in that ancient but most expressive word ' covetousness.' ' I had not known sin,' says the Apostle Paul, ' but for the law which says, *Thou shalt not covet*.'  So we may all say. No one can know the exceeding sinfulness of sin who does not know the guilt of selfishness; no one can know the exceeding beauty of holiness who has not seen or felt the glory of unselfishness.

IV. These are the Ten Commandments—the summary of the morality of Judaism, the basis of the morality of Christian Churches.   We have heard it said of such and such an one with open, genuine countenance, that he looked as if he had the Ten Commandments written on his face.   It was remarked by an honest, pious Roman Catholic of the last generation, on whom a devout but feeble enthusiast was pressing the use of this and that small practice of devotion, ' My devotions are much better than those.   They are the devotions of the Ten Commandments of God.'

In the Reformed American Church and in the Reformed Churches of France, and intended by the last Reformers of the English Liturgy in 1689, though they failed to carry the point, after the Ten Commandments are read in church comes this memorable addition, which we ought all to supply in memory, even although it is not publicly used :—' Hear also what our Lord Jesus Christ saith.'   This is what is taken as the ground of the explanation of the Commandments in all Christian Catechisms of our duty to God.   Everything in what we call the first table is an enlargement of that one simple command, ' Thou shalt love the Lord thy God.' Everything in the second table of our duty to our neighbour is an enlargement of the command—' Thou shalt love thy neighbour as thyself.' The two together are the whole of religion. Each of itself calls our attention to what is the first and chief duty of each of the two tables. God, the Supreme Goodness, and the Supreme Truth, is to be served with no half service ; it must be a service that goes through our whole lives. We must place Him above everything else. He is all in all to us. Truth, justice, purity are in Him made the supreme object of our devotion and affection. 'Let no man,' says Lord Bacon, 'upon a weak conceit of sobriety or an ill-applied moderation, think or maintain that a man can search too far or be too well studied in the Book of God's Word or in the Book of God's Works.' Man is to be served also with a love like that which we give to ourselves. Selfishness is here made the root of all evil ; unselfishness the root of all goodness. Toleration of every difference of race or creed is summed up in the expression 'thy neighbour.'

It was a saying of Abraham Lincoln, 'When any church will inscribe over its altar as its sole qualification for membership the Saviour's condensed statement of the substance of both Law and Gospel in those two great Commandments, that church will I join with all my heart and with all my soul.' There may be an exaggeration in the expression, but the thing intended is true. If any Church existed which in reality and in spirit put forth those two Commandments as the sum and substance of its belief, as that to which all else tended, and for the sake of which all was done, it would indeed take the first place amongst the Churches of the world, because it would be the Church that most fully had expressed the mind and intention of the Founder of Christendom.[5]

V. There was an addition which the English divines of the time of William III. wished to make to the recital of the Ten Commandments in church. It was baffled by the obstinate prejudice of the inferior clergy. But its intention was singularly fine. It was that, on the three

*The Eight Beatitudes.*

---

[5] The subject is treated at length in 'The Two Great Commandments,' in *Addresses at St. Andrews*, pp. 155–187.

great festivals, instead of the Ten Commandments of Mount Sinai should be read the Eight Beatitudes of the Mountain of Galilee, in order to remind us that beyond and above the Law of Duty, there is the happiness of that inward spirit which is at once the spring and the result of all duty—the happiness, the blessedness which belongs to the humble, the sincere, the unselfish, the eager aspirant after goodness, the generous, the pure, the courageous. That happiness is the highest end and aim of all religion.

VI. There is one addition yet to be made, which has never been suggested by authority.

We sometimes hear in conversation of an Eleventh Commandment invented by the world, in cynical contempt of the old Commandments, or in pursuit of some selfish or wicked end. Of such an Eleventh Commandment, whether in jest or earnest, we need not here speak. It is enough to be reminded of it, and pass it by. But there is also what may be called the Eleventh Commandment of Churches and sects. In the oldest and most venerable of all ecclesiastical divisions—the ancient Samaritan community, who have for centuries, without increase or diminution, gathered round Mount Gerizim as the only place where men ought to worship—there is, as noticed above, to be read upon the aged parchment-scroll of the Pentateuch this commandment, added to the other Ten, ‘Thou shalt build an altar on Mount Gerizim, and there only shalt thou worship.’[6] Faithfully have they followed that command; excommunicating, and excommunicated by, all other religious societies, they cling to that Eleventh Commandment as equal, if not superior, to all the rest. This is the true likeness of what all Churches and sects, unless purified by a higher spirit, are tempted to add. ‘Thou shalt do something

The Eleventh Commandment.
of the Samaritans;

---

[6] The Eleventh (or in the Samaritan division, the Tenth) Commandment of the Samaritans is here somewhat abridged. It consists of Deut. xxvii. 2–7, xi. 30, interpolated in Exod. xx., with the alteration of Ebal into Gerizim. I venture to quote the substance of two passages from *Lectures on the Church of Scotland*, pp. 3, 4, 6–8. There is a striking story of Archbishop Usher in connection with it (see ibid., pp. 4–6).

for this particular community, which none else may share. Thou shalt do this over and above, and more than thy plain duties to God and man. Thou shalt build thine altar on Mount Gerizim, for here alone our fathers have said that God is to be worshipped. Thou shalt maintain the exclusive sacredness of this or that place, this or that word, this or that doctrine, this or that party, this or that institution, this or that mode of doing good. Thou shalt worship God thus and thus only.' This is the Eleventh Commandment according to sects

of sects;

and parties and partisans. For this we are often told to contend more than for all the other Ten together. For an Eleventh Commandment like to this, half the energies of Christendom have been spent, and spent in vain. For some command like this men have fought and struggled and shed their own blood and the blood of others, as though it were a command engraven on the tables of the everlasting law; and yet, again and again and again, it has been found in after ages that such a command was an addition as venerable, perhaps, and as full of interest, but as superfluous, as misleading, as disproportionate, as that Eleventh Samaritan commandment—'Thou shalt build an altar on Mount Gerizim, and there only shalt thou worship.'

But there is a divine Eleventh Commandment—' A new

of the Gospel.

commandment I give unto you, that ye love one another; As I have loved you, that ye also should love one another.'

It is contained in the parting discourse of St. John's Gospel, and it is introduced there as a surprise to the Apostles. ' What? Are not the Ten Commandments enough? Must we always be pressing forward to something new? What is this that He saith, " A new commandment? " We cannot tell what He saith.' Nevertheless it corresponds to a genuine want of the human heart.

Beyond the Ten Commandments there is yet a craving for something even beyond duty, even beyond reverence. There is a need which can only be satisfied by a new, by an Eleventh Commandment, which shall be at once old and new—which shall open a new field of thought and exertion for each generation of men; which shall give a fresh, undying impulse to its older sisters—the youngest child (so to speak) of the patriarchal family. The true new commandment which Jesus Christ gave was, in its very form and fashion, peculiarly characteristic of the Christian Religion.

The novelty of the commandment lay in two points. First, it was new, because of the paramount, predominant place which it gave to the force of the human affections, the enthusiasm for the good of others, which was,—instead of ceremonial, or mere obedience, or correctness of belief,—henceforth to become the appointed channel of religious fervour. And secondly it was new, because it was founded on the appearance of a new character, a new manifestation of the character of Man, a new manifestation of the character of God. Even if the Four Gospels had been lost, we should see, from the urgency with which the Apostles press this new grace of Love or Charity upon us, that some diviner vision of excellence had crossed their minds. The very word which they used to express it was new, for the thing was new, the example was new, and the consequences therefore were new also.

It may be said that the solid blocks or tables on which the Ten Commandments were written were of the granite rock of Sinai, as if to teach us that all the great laws of duty to God and duty to man were like that oldest primeval foundation of the world—more solid, more enduring than all the other strata; cutting across all the secondary and artificial distinctions of mankind; heaving itself up, now here, now there; throwing up here the fantastic crag, the towering peak, there the long range which unites or divides the races of mankind. That is the universal, everlasting character of Duty. But as that granite rock itself has been fused and wrought together by a central fire, without which it could not have existed at all, so also the Christian law of Duty, in order to perform fully its work in the world, must have been warmed at the heart and fed at the source by a central fire of its own—and that central fire is Love—the gracious, kindly, generous, admiring, tender movements of the human affections ; and that central fire itself is kept alive by the consciousness that there has been in the world a Love beyond all human love, a devouring fire of Divine enthusiasm on behalf of our race, which is the Love of Christ.  It is not contrary to the Ten Commandments.  It is not outside of them, it is within them ; it is at their core ; it is wrapped up in them, as the particles of the central heat of the globe were encased within the granite tables in the Ark of the Temple.  'What was it that made him undertake the support of the Abolition of the Slave-trade ?' was asked of an eminent statesman respecting the conduct of another.  'It was his love of the human race.'

This was what the Apostle Paul meant by saying, 'Love is the fulfilling of the Law.'  This is what St. Peter meant by saying, 'Above all things, have fervent,' enthusiastic 'Love.'  This is what St. John meant when, in his extreme old age, he was carried into the market-place of Ephesus, and, according to the ancient tradition, repeated over and over again to his disciples the words which he had heard from his Master, 'Little children, love one another.'  They were vexed by hearing this commandment, this Eleventh Commandment, repeated so often.  They asked for something more precise, more definite, more dogmatic ; but the aged Apostle, we are told, had but one answer :—'This is the sum and substance of the Gospel ; if you do this, I have nothing else to teach you.'  He did not mean that ceremonies, doctrines, ordinances were of no importance ; but that they were altogether of secondary importance.  He meant that they were on the outside of religion, whereas this commandment belonged to its innermost substance ; that, if this commandment were carried out, all that was good in all the rest would follow ; that, if this commandment were neglected, all that was good in all the rest would fade away, and all that was evil, and one-sided, and exaggerated, would prevail and pervert even the good.  He meant and his Master meant that, as the ages rolled on, other truths may be folded up and laid aside; but that this would always need to be enforced and developed.

Love one another in spite of differences, in spite of faults, in spite of the excesses of one or the defects of another. Love one another, and make the best of one another, as He loved us, who, for the sake of saving what was good in the human soul, forgot, forgave, put out of sight what was bad—who saw and loved what was good even in the publican Zaccheus, even in the penitent Magdalen, even in the expiring malefactor, even in the heretical Samaritan, even in the Pharisee Nicodemus, even in the heathen soldier, even in the outcast Canaanite. Make the most of what there is good in institutions, in opinions, in communities, in individuals. It is very easy to do the reverse, to make the worst of what there is of evil, absurd, and erroneous. By so doing we shall have no difficulty in making estrangements more wide, and hatreds and strifes more abundant, and errors more extreme. It is very easy to fix our attention only on the weak points of those around us, to magnify them, to irritate them, to aggravate them; and, by so doing, we can make the burden of life unendurable, and can destroy our own and others' happiness and usefulness wherever we go. But this was not the new love wherewith we are to love one another. That love is universal, because in its spirit we overcome evil simply by doing good. We drive out error simply by telling the truth. We strive to look on both sides of the shield of truth. We strive to speak the truth in love, that is, without exaggeration or misrepresentation; concealing nothing, compromising nothing, but with the effort to understand each other, to discover the truth which lies at the bottom of the error; with the determination cordially to love whatever is lovable even in those in whom we cordially detest whatever is detestable. And, in proportion as we endeavour to do this, there may be a hope that men will see that there are, after all, some true disciples of Christ left in the world, 'because they have love one to another.'

A A

# INDEX.

www.ingramcontent.com/pod-product-compliance
Lightning Source LLC
Chambersburg PA
CBHW051218120726
47905CB00004B/1175